WHO ON EARTH WAS JESUS?

The Modern Quest
for the Jesus of History

First published by O Books, 2008
O Books is an imprint of John Hunt Publishing
Ltd., The Bothy, Deershot Lodge, Park Lane,
Ropley, Hants, SO24 0BE, UK
office1@o-books.net
www.o-books.net

Distribution in:

UK and Europe
Orca Book Services
orders@orcabookservices.co.uk
Tel: 01202 665432 Fax: 01202 666219 Int. code
(44)

USA and Canada
NBN
custserv@nbnbooks.com
Tel: 1 800 462 6420 Fax: 1 800 338 4550

Australia and New Zealand
Brumby Books
sales@brumbybooks.com.au
Tel: 61 3 9761 5535 Fax: 61 3 9761 7095

Far East (offices in Singapore, Thailand, Hong
Kong, Taiwan)
Pansing Distribution Pte Ltd
kemal@pansing.com
Tel: 65 6319 9939 Fax: 65 6462 5761

South Africa
Alternative Books
altbook@peterhyde.co.za
Tel: 021 555 4027 Fax: 021 447 1430

Text copyright David Boulton 2008

Design: Stuart Davies

ISBN: 978 1 84694 018 7

A CIP catalogue record for this book is available
from the British Library.

Printed in the US by Maple Vail

O Books operates a distinctive and ethical publishing philosophy in
all areas of its business, from its global network of authors to
production and worldwide distribution.

No trees were cut down to print this particular book. The paper is
100% recycled, with 50% of that being post-consumer. It's processed
chlorine-free, and has no fibre from ancient or endangered forests.

This production method on this print run saved approximately
thirteen trees, 4,000 gallons of water, 600 pounds of solid waste,
990 pounds of greenhouse gases and 8 million BTU of energy. On its
publication a tree was planted in a new forest that O Books is
sponsoring at The Village www.thefourgates.com

WHO ON EARTH WAS JESUS?

The Modern Quest
for the Jesus of History

DAVID BOULTON

BOOKS

Winchester, UK
Washington, USA

ALSO BY DAVID BOULTON

History and Current Affairs:

Jazz in Britain (1958)

Voices from the Crowd (ed.) (1964)

Objection Overruled (1968)

The UVF 1966-73: an Anatomy of Loyalist Rebellion (1974)

The Making of Tania Hearst (1975)

The Lockheed Papers (1978, UK)

The Grease Machine (1978, USA)

Adam Sedgwick's Dent (ed.) (1984)

Hope on, Hope Ever! (ed.) (1988)

The Third Age of Broadcasting (1991)

Theology, Humanism and Quakerism:

Early Friends in Dent:

    The English Revolution in a Dales Community (1986)

A Reasonable Faith (1996)

The Faith of a Quaker Humanist (1997)

In Fox's Footsteps (1998)

Gerrard Winstanley and the Republic of Heaven (1999)

Will the Real Jesus Please Stand Up (2000)

Real Like the Daisies or Real Like I Love You?:

    Essays in Radical Quakerism (2002)

Militant Seedbeds of Early Quakerism (2005, USA)

The Trouble with God:

    Religious Humanism and the Republic of Heaven (2002)

The Trouble with God:

    Building the Republic of Heaven (rev. 2005)

Godless for God's Sake (ed.) (2006)

ABOUT THIS BOOK...

'The best and most thorough account of the breadth and variety of historical Jesus scholarship. Boulton's writing is lively, his perceptions informed, and his judgments fair. Highly recommended'.
- **MARCUS BORG**, former Chair, Society of Biblical Literature, Historical Jesus Section, and author of *Meeting Jesus Again for the First Time*, the world's single best-selling book by a contemporary Jesus scholar.

'Everyone ought to read it, especially those with no sympathy for religion and its crazier adherants... David Boulton is an investigative journalist and this book is an enormous achievement, with its vivid descriptions of what scholars have uncovered... It's all here, and it's as up-to-date as you are likely to get.'
- **RICHARD HOLLOWAY**, former Bishop of Edinburgh.

'A unique treasure! A fair, objective and exhaustive summary of historical Jesus discoveries... scholarly, yet lucidly written for non-academic readers... A masterly achievement, with a challenging conclusion.'
- **LLOYD GEERING**, CBE, former Principal of Theological Hall, Knox College, Dunedin, NZ, and author of *Tomorrow's God*.

'*We begin the process of becoming critical readers of the Bible the first time we are dissatisfied with being told what the text means and decide to see for ourselves... We may listen to and read many opinions - the more the better - but ultimately it is up to us. We must give the text our own careful scrutiny to see what it means... It seems one simply cannot hold serious scholarly opinions at second hand.*'- Robert M Price, founding editor, *Journal of Higher Criticism* and author of *The Incredible Shrinking Son of Man*, in *The Fourth R*, Nov-Dec 2007

'*You scholars and Pharisees occupy the chair of Moses. This means you're supposed to observe and follow everything they tell you. But don't do what they do; after all, they're all talk and no action... You scholars and Pharisees, you impostors! Damn you!*'
Jesus, Matthew 23: 2-3, 13 ("Scholars' Version")

CONTENTS

FOREWORD

by Richard Holloway

In one of the great theological texts of the 20th century, *The Quest of the Historical Jesus*, published in 1906, Albert Schweitzer said scholars who were intent on finding the real Jesus, the Jesus of history, were like people peering into a deep well and seeing their own reflections. It sounds dismissive, and was probably intended to be, but it is worth thinking about, nevertheless. Whether we like it or not, and whether or not we have a religion ourselves, what people see when they look down the well of history can have profound consequences for us all.

One of the most dramatic and disconcerting aspects of recent history has been the return of religion. Those of us brought up on the sociology of the 1960s were preparing - sadly or eagerly - for the final eclipse of religion in the West. The secularization thesis claimed that history was moving inexorably towards the final collapse of religion. Like many prophecies before and since, the reality has turned out to be very different. Religion is back, religion with a grudge, religion with something ugly on its mind. It reminds me of that bit in *The Shining* when Jack Nicholson finally cracks and takes an axe to the door behind which his wife and child are sheltering, grinning maniacally and shouting: 'Here's Johnny!' Well, if that's the kind of figure you see looking back at you when you look down the well of history at your religious founder, then we are all in trouble.

David Boulton's brilliant and timely book is well aware of that dangerous possibility, which is why everyone ought to read it, especially those with no sympathy for religion and its crazier adherents. His book operates on two levels. Boulton is an investigative journalist by trade, and here he sets out to find out what historians have discovered when they have gone searching for the man scholars describe as the Jesus of History before he became the Christ of Faith. On this level alone the book is an enormous achievement. He tries to maintain a professional objectivity throughout his researches, while wryly acknowledging that that's not really humanly possible. So what you get is a vivid description of what scholars have said in the past, and what living scholars are saying today, about the figure at the bottom of that 2000 years deep well. Apart from the excitement of the story of the scholarly quest itself, the book will be a useful resource for people who want a one-volume guide to a multi-volume industry. It's all here, and it's as up-to-date as you are likely to get in what is a fast-moving business.

But there is a deeper level to this book, a level that brings me back to that reflection gazing back at me from the well of history. If, as Schweitzer hinted, we are never going to get at the absolutely incontro-vertibly real Jesus, but only at refined versions of ourselves when we look for him, then what we ourselves believe and long for is going to be important. The theological category that is key to the interpretation of Jesus is his approach to what theologians call 'apocalyptic': that strand of religious tradition that relates to the End Times, the coming of God into history to establish justice and peace. Did Jesus subvert and humanize that turbulent tradition, thereby making it possible for us still to draw on his dream of a righteous human community? Or did he belong to the crazy end of the apocalyptic hope, which eagerly looks forward to the day when God will arrive on earth to exalt his true believers and damn the rest of us to eternal torment? Does the Jesus you see down the well of history come in peace, or with an axe in his hand? As the passionate conclusion to this fine book demonstrates, this is a question that's important to us all.

Richard Holloway, former Bishop of Edinburgh and Primus of the Scottish Episcopal Church, chairs the Joint Board of the Scottish Arts Council and Scottish Screen. His latest book is 'How to Read the Bible'.

AUTHOR'S PREFACE

Jesus saved fallen women, and one he saved for himself was Mary from Magdala. They made babies together, thereby founding the French royal family. He was crucified but escaped, crucified but survived, crucified but resuscitated, not crucified at all... He died of old age in France... India... Egypt...America. He was gay, and it was through gay sex that his followers were initiated into the kingdom of heaven. He was the product of a magic-mushroom-eating cult. He was really a woman named Mildred...

The churches have suppressed the Amazing Truth for two millennia, substituting a bizarre story that Jesus was fathered by God, walked on water, brought the dead back to life, died, descended into hell, and rose again to live and reign in heaven, where he maintains one-to-one communication with his followers on earth...

If John Lennon could claim that the Beatles were bigger than Jesus, inventive writers and pseudo-scholars were soon on hand to prove him wrong and demonstrate that at the name of Jesus the tills in the great chain of bookstores can still be made to ring out a joyful sound. All it takes is a generous dose of conspiracy theory, a tabloid distaste for inconvenient evidence, Dan Brown's genius for blurring fact and fiction and Lord Archer's combination of chutzpah and snake-oil salesmanship to extract big advances from co-conspiratorial publishers and big bucks from a gullible reading public.

Of the making of Jesus books, then, there is no end. And in this welter of sensationalism, this cacophony of corrupt claims and cynical salesmanship, where does the general reader turn for knowledgeable guidance on what could be fact and what is likely to be fiction in the old, old story?

Where do we go if we want to ask, intelligently: Who on Earth *was* Jesus?

Where else but to the body of scholarship dedicated to the tough task of filtering history from mystery, evidence from conjecture, and critical from wishful thinking? So where to find them? How to trust them?

To begin with, we must distinguish the serious scholar from the charlatan. The serious scholar will have taken the trouble to equip himself or herself with the tools of the historian's trade: a good working knowledge of the languages, cultures, literary genres, oral traditions, power politics, religious controversies and social mores of first-century Galilee in particular and the Greco-Roman world in general. Second, the serious scholar will respect the evidence and follow where it leads, even (or especially) when it leads where he doesn't want to go. We must not expect even the most scholarly scholar to be free of presumptions, opinions, prejudices, personal ambition or the cultural baggage we all lug around with us. Scholars and charlatans alike are only human (and according to Matthew 23:13-33 in the Jesus Seminar's "Scholars' Version", Jesus didn't have too high an opinion of them: "You scholars and Pharisees, you impostors! Damn you...You spawn of Satan! How are you going to escape Hell's judgment?").

What we must demand of our guides is evidence of intellectual integrity, respect for truth, and due humility in face of the complexity of the quest on which they have embarked. Where do we find these virtues? There are whole armies of specialists in this field. Some spend their entire working lives in the academy, the fruit of their researches hidden in the pages of specialist journals invisible to the general reader. Others have broken free from the academic closet to achieve fame, even fortune, as best-selling authors: Crossan, Borg, Vermes, Wright, and others we shall meet in these pages. What Jesus have they been looking for? What Jesus have they found?

Readers embarking on this magical mystery tour of historical investigation will soon encounter an awkward fact. *Historians do not always agree. Decades of painstaking historical Jesus research have not produced a scholarly consensus on who this man Jesus was.* What I aim to do with this book is provide a rough guide to the main schools of historical Jesus scholarship a century after the publication of Albert Schweitzer's pioneering *Quest of the Historical Jesus*. Schweitzer summarized the conclusions of nineteenth century scholars who knew nothing of the Nag Hammadi codices and Dead Sea scrolls lying undisturbed under the lone and level sands of Egypt. I give the best account I can of the work of modern historians and Jesus detectives whose expanded database of evidence and sharper technological toolkit has revolutionized the contemporary quest and, for those with eyes to see and ears to hear, transformed our understanding of an Iron Age visionary who unwittingly shaped the religious, social and cultural history of the next two thousand years.

Acknowledgments

Some whose work I discuss are unknown to me personally, some I have met in the flesh as well as on the page, some are personal friends. I am grateful to all of them, and take this opportunity to apologize for any omissions, misunderstandings or distortions which may have crept into my cruelly foreshortened and inevitably inadequate summaries of their life's work. I hope that what I have written will encourage readers to turn to the originals as acknowledged in the text and listed in the bibliography.

I have benefited from the kindly encouragement of Geza Vermes, John Dominic Crossan, Marcus Borg, Robert J Miller and Roy W Hoover, and the practical support and fellowship of Charlene Matejovsky and the scholars of the Jesus Seminar. Also, my Quaker colleagues and my Humanist comrades have contributed in ways they probably wouldn't recognize. But if this book is to have a dedicatee it must be one who has far greater memorials to his name. It was Bob Funk who set me on the trail of a demystified, demythologized Jesus. His response when I told him I was embarking on this project was "Put me down for the first one off the press!" His death in 2006 deprives me of that pleasure, but not of this opportunity to record my loving appreciation of this scholar among scholars who made it his mission to rescue a wholly human Jesus from the clutches of the superstitious, the credulous, the humorless, the unscrupulous and the dangerously fanatical. The Jesus of the Jesus Seminar Funk founded is not the only historical Jesus on offer, and for many not the most persuasive; but few among his critics would dispute his place of honor alongside David Friedrich Strauss, Albert Schweitzer and the great icons of rational, critical Jesus scholarship. I was touched by his enthusiastic support and honored by his friendship.

Notes and sources

These will be found at the end of each chapter, and full bibliographical details follow at the end of the book. Biblical quotations are generally from the Authorized (King James) Version, except where it is clearly more appropriate or accurate to cite a modern version, or the version used by the scholars we happen to be focusing on in a particular passage.

I have bowed to my publisher's gentle insistence that I favor American spelling, except in direct quotation from English English. I ask for the forgiveness of British and Commonwealth readers, and for the understanding of Americans when they come across the inevitable slip, since old habits die hard.

David Boulton
Dent, Cumbria,
November 2007

PART 1
SOURCES

1

WHY SEARCH FOR THE

HISTORICAL JESUS?

Does it really matter who Jesus was? Does it even make any difference whether he existed or not? Even if we think it might matter and might make a difference, is it possible after two thousand years to recover something, anything, of the authentic historical Jesus (if he existed) or the origins of the Jesus myth (if he didn't)?

What, in any case, do we mean by an "authentic" Jesus? Why should we suppose that an early-first-century Jesus, if we can find him, is any more "authentic" than the Jesus of developed tradition? (Is Shakespeare's literary hero a less "authentic" Hamlet than the flesh-and-blood Amlet of ancient history?). What reliable documentation do we have? What reliable archaeological, anthropological, or other evidence? And if there is evidence, can we trust the experts to interpret it without letting their own prejudices, core beliefs, cultural conditioning and human power-plays determine their conclusions? Can we trust ourselves? Do we suppose we are objective seekers after truth, untainted by the prejudices and cultural biases which we readily ascribe to the experts? Who do we recognize as experts anyway? And how do we, the inexperts, decide between them when they disagree among themselves, as of course they do?

I have begun with a quiver of questions, all of which follow from the big question which forms the title of this book: Who on Earth was Jesus? The "on Earth" bit is deliberate. We are not concerned here with a magical Jesus "above the bright blue sky". The Jesus story developed in extraor-dinary ways once a Jesus movement began to spread in Jewish and gentile communities around the Mediterranean in what came to be called the first century Anno Domini, and continued to develop in ways the earliest members of the movement could never have imagined as a dominant version of it became the ideology of the Roman empire and "Christendom". But this book is not about the Jesus of church and state, the Jesus shaped by the needs and imaginations of later generations. Its primary focus is not the church's "Christ of faith" but Jesus BC: Jesus before Christianity. Jesus as earthly prophet, not Jesus as celestial policeman.

To put it another way, this book is not about *Jesus Christ* at all, though we shall necessarily be asking the experts what they think first-century Jewish and non-Jewish members of the Jesus movement meant by "Christ". Retired Bishop John Selby Spong has commented sardonically that some people seem to think Jesus' family name was Jesus Christ, as if his parents were Joseph and Mary Christ and brothers James and Judas were James and Judas Christ! But "Christ", of course, is a title or description, not a surname. We shall be examining the search for the man behind the title, the man who preceded the title, whatever that title may mean or have meant: the human Jesus of history rather than the spirit-Jesus of theology. And the experts we consult will be historians rather than theologians - acknowledging as we must that good historians are aware that they peer at the past through lenses colored by cultural experience, which includes theology, and that sensible theologians are not necessarily strangers to historical and rational methodologies. I am not concerned to knock speculative theology and theologians, but my aim is to bring into focus the evidence-based data unearthed by historical enquiry.

I bring to this no specialist expertise in either first-century Mediterranean history or academic theology. I have spent much of my working life as an investigative journalist in print and broadcasting, which means first asking questions, then finding out where to go and who to go to for answers, then trying to make sense of what comes out of the process, and that is what I'll be doing in this personal quest for the Jesus of history. I acknowledge it as a personal quest because the who, what and why of Jesus has nagged away at me ever since my childhood upbringing in an evangelical Christian home, where he was treated as one of the family, always a benevolent if unseen friend, guide and comforter rather than an oppressive lord and master. When I grew up and moved on from the naive faith of my childhood, Jesus the son of man wouldn't leave me alone. Who was this historical person whose reported teachings and actions had shaped what we have been pleased to call western civilization? (But don't let's forget Gandhi's answer when he was asked what he thought of western civilization: "I think it would be a good idea!"). I do not call myself a follower of Jesus: that would be both a presumption and, given the difference between his world and mine, an impossibility. But he has followed me, and I am curious to know who on Earth he was.

If Jesus was God in human form (which has to be a theological, not an historical judgment) his supreme importance is self-evident, since to know "what Jesus really said" would be to know God's truth. If he was a human teacher, his lasting influence on western culture, his role in shaping our roots, must surely command our historical curiosity. And if he was not a man but a myth, or if the Jesus of even the earliest texts is already so completely mythologized as to wholly obscure his historical identity, what does that tell us about religion, culture, story, power? Who on Earth was this Jesus?

I am a writer by trade. In a long string of books, articles and television films I have investigated a host of subjects including the treatment of conscientious objectors in the First World War, the financial scams of multinational companies and the influence of protestant fundamentalism on the development of "loyalist" private armies in Ulster. In such subjects I have never had to stray far from my own familiar culture, relying on a mass of documentation in my own familiar English language. Even when enquiring into the origins and early development of the Quaker movement, which required me to get to grips with the unfamiliar world of seventeenth-century piety and politics, I had the advantage of being able to read the letters, pamphlets, journals and records of the time, sometimes in their originals. But it is a very different matter when it comes to investigating the facts that might shape a Jesus biography, or formulating a developed theory of who or what Jesus was. I have no command of ancient Greek, Hebrew, Aramaic or Coptic. The religious culture of first-century Galilee and Judea is as far removed from the secular culture of my twentyfirst-century world as Abraham Lincoln was from Abraham of Ur.

So I must necessarily turn to the relatively small band of scholars whose special expertise is the languages of first-century Palestine and the social, political and religious context in which Jesus and his story are set. That, then, is what this book is for: not to offer yet another lay-person's view of Jesus, since we have such books without number, some pious, some polemical, some illuminating, some ingeniously inventive or speculative, some sensational, some shamelessly commercial and some plain silly. Instead, I hope to offer the reader a fair account of where some of the best of Jesus scholarship stands in the first decade of the twentyfirst century.

I shall try to make clear what is broadly agreed by scholars from different perspectives and what remains controversial or contentious. It will not be my job to mediate between them: only a scholar among scholars could attempt that - and it would be a thankless task! This does not mean that the reader will be denied the occasional offer of a personal opinion, but it does serve as a warning not to give my opinion more weight than it deserves as the view of a lay enquirer. It is the opinions and findings of the Jesus historians that will occupy front and center stage.

The road map

I have organized this enquiry into three parts. The first deals with *Sources*, biblical and extra-biblical, Christian, Jewish and secular: the raw material which scholars must sift, analyze, test and evaluate in reaching for an evidence-based assessment of the man behind the texts. I preface this with an account of the scholarship of the past, which laid the foundations for today's quest. This usually means no more than a brisk trot through the "old quest", courtesy of Albert Schweitzer, but we shall take in avenues of early scholarship of which Schweitzer was unaware.

In the second part we turn from sources to *Interpretations*, looking at what current scholarship is making of all the available data. In the American Jesus Seminar and the work of its most prominent members - Marcus Borg, John Dominic Crossan, Robert Funk - we find much of the scholarship of Schweitzer overturned to reveal a Jesus who preached a kingdom among us *now* rather than an apocalyptic kingdom to come in the *future*. This view is contested by a rival school including Geza Vermes and E P Sanders. From them we turn to the *radically skeptical* schools of Burton Mack, George Wells and scholars like Robert Eisenman and Alvar Ellegard who have challenged mainstream reconstructions of Jesus, and to the *conservatively skeptical* scholars - N T Wright, James Dunn and Joseph Ratzinger - who may be said to represent the post-postmodern fight-back against critical scholarship divorced from faith.

In part three, *Consequences*, we seek out areas of broad agreement, separating them out from some of the key issues that remain unresolved and subject to continuing scholarly debate. Finally, we ask what all this means for a contemporary understanding of who on Earth Jesus was.

Along the way we allow ourselves to be side-tracked into a number of digressions - *"The invention of the narrative gospel"*, *"Pious forgeries"*, *"Did Jesus have a love life?"*, *"Jesus' language and literacy skills"*, *"Jesus, the prostitute's fee and the High Priest's privy"*, and many more such cameos.

Seeking a pure Jesus and finding a congenial one

But two words of caution as we begin. Much of the impetus and motivation driving the quest for the "actual words" spoken by the historical Jesus has been the faith that, if we can ever discover them or agree what they were, we shall at last have an "original", a "pure" Christianity: God's own truth. (See Cameo *The quest for purity and truth* at the end of this chapter). This can lead to a view that anything considered an early editorial elaboration or interpretation of Jesus' own words must in some way contaminate, distort or weaken his message, producing a "less authentic" Christianity, so that Paul's theology, or John's, or that of the second, third or fourth-century church, is viewed not simply as a *development* of Jesus' recorded teachings, more a *distortion*. But there are other possibilities. If, for instance, we were to accept the view of those scholars who have decided that Jesus was a Jewish holy man preaching exclusively to those he believed to be God's chosen people, his own race, might we not consider that Paul's more universalist or internationalist interpretation of Jesus' message gives us an improved, more liberal Christianity than the original xenophobic version?

So we need to be wary of falling into the assumption that, by scraping away what scholars may argue are the accretions of later Christian commentators till we uncover Jesus' "actual words", we necessarily arrive at better religion, better ethics, better teaching, just because it seems that Jesus himself said it. The later "accretions" may turn out to be more *authentic for us*, if less *authentic historically* - as with my Hamlet-Amlet parallel above. A simpler way of putting this is to say that, even if we are persuaded that this or that group of scholars really has found what the historical Jesus actually said, it doesn't necessarily follow that these scholars have unearthed a set of intrinsic truths beyond possibility of re-interpretation and critical reassessment. If Jesus was only human, he may have got it wrong. Indeed, to be human is to be a product of one's culture, age, and state of knowledge. To be human is to be fallible.

And the second caution. The late Robert Funk, in setting up the Jesus Seminar, famously warned his fellow scholars to beware of finding (or creating) an entirely congenial Jesus! We too must take care not to make the same mistake, gleefully appropriating scholarship that appears to support our prejudices and rejecting views simply because they challenge or affront our preconceptions. If the Jesus we find is the Jesus we wanted to find, the odds are that we have misused the quest to create a Jesus in our own image. And a Jesus in our own image is unlikely to bear much likeness to Jesus of Galilee two thousand years ago.

Cameo: The quest for purity and truth

"The outstanding characteristic of our age appears to be a desire to reach back to the greatest attainable purity, to the basic truth free of jargon. Affecting the whole of our outlook, it has necessarily included the domain of our religious thought and behaviour, and with it, in the Western world, the whole subject of Judaeo-Christian culture and spirituality. A search is being made for the original meaning of issues with which we have become almost too familiar and which with the passing of the centuries have tended to become choked with inessentials, and it has led not only to a renewed preoccupation with the primitive but fully developed expression of these issues in the Scriptures, but also to a desire for knowledge and understanding of their prehistory." - **Geza Vermes, "The Complete Dead Sea Scrolls in English", p 24**

2

THE LONG SEARCH:

QUESTING OLD AND NEW

As mentioned in the previous chapter, summaries of what is sometimes called "the Old Quest" often consist of little more than a precis of Albert Schweitzer's survey. Schweitzer's work did indeed aim to cover and criticize a century or more of Jesus scholarship, but it was hardly comprehensive. As we shall see, there was a wider range of enquiry both within and beyond Germany, and within and beyond the boundaries of church and academy, than Schweitzer appeared to recognize. We need to acquaint ourselves with this early work before focusing on what was built on its foundations.

1. Gospel harmonies

The production of literary "lives of Jesus" had begun even before the end of the first century. By the middle of the second, clerical scholars were at war over which of the many rival gospels portrayed an authentic Jesus and which were dubious or heretical. Biblical criticism proper may be said to have begun with Tatian, a scholar in the mid-second century who studied the differences and contradictions apparent in the four gospels that would eventually be included in the New Testament canon. Tatian produced a "harmonized gospel" called the *Diatessaron* ("four-in-one"), which claimed to resolve the anomalies. How he managed this feat (did Jesus desecrate the temple at the beginning of his ministry, as per John, or at the end, as per Mark, Matthew and Luke? - or did he do it twice?) we can only guess, since no text of the *Diatessaron* has survived and it is known only from references by other writers before its suppression in the fifth century.

Once such gospel harmonies - Tatian's was followed by others - had been declared heretical in the interest of asserting and protecting the authority of the canonical books, such scholarly criticism, if that is what it was, faded for a thousand years as the church's focus on the supernatural Christ of faith elbowed aside the scholars' quest for the human Jesus of history.

2. A kosher Jesus

When, in the late Middle Ages, scholars again began to show an interest in ancient texts which might throw light on puzzling gospel passages, they turned to rabbinic Jewish writings of the second and later centuries to give the earliest Christian literature an historical and literary context. In Spain particularly, Catholic scholars were assisted by educated Jewish converts (voluntary or enforced), the *converso*, whose knowledge of Hebrew helped make sense of what had always been obscure in Greek and Latin translations. Faithful Jewish scholars, meanwhile, researched their own history from the perspective of their own tradition. Geza Vermes emphasizes that the text-wars which followed, in which Christian and Jewish scholars crossed literary swords, were "neither detached, objective, nor for that matter edifying"[1]. But they paved the way for what he calls "a quasi-'scientific' use of post-biblical Judaica in New Testament interpretation", and this development may be traced not only in medieval Spain but also in seventeenth-century England.

Christopher Cartwright (1602-58), a Yorkshire clergyman and Cambridge graduate, and John Lightfoot (1603-75), Master of St Catherine's, Cambridge, produced respectively *Mellificium Hebraicum* (London,1660) and *Horae Hebraicae et Talmudicae* (Leipzig, 1658-74), interpreting Jesus' sayings and other New Testament passages in the light of contemporary Jewish literature. Lightfoot explained in a preface to his section on Matthew that "without the slightest doubt... the best and most genuine method to unravel the [meaning of] the obscure passages of the New Testament (of which there are many) is through research into the significance of the phrases and sayings in question according to the ordinary dialect and way of thinking of that [Jewish] nation". As Vermes comments, "These words, written in Latin three hundred years ago, sound extraordinarily modern and would be largely approved today"[2].

3. A Jesus within

Cartwright and Lightfoot produced their work in the white heat of the English revolution when, mid-century, monarchy and established church were in turn abolished, re-established and reformed. The radical religious, political and social ferment of the times provoked a shock-wave of biblical criticism which was as likely to find popular expression in the alehouse as erudite profession in the university. Ranters and Quakers denied the infallibility of the scriptures and insisted that a "Christ within", known "experimentally", was more authentic than "one crucified at Jerusalem 1600 years ago". For Samuel Fisher, a Presbyterian minister turned Baptist turned Quaker, the Bible was "a huge heap of uncertainties", not the Word of God as the puritan establishment insisted, but "a bulk of heterogeneous writings compiled together by men" who had "crowd[ed] them into a canon or standard for the trial of spirits, doctrines, truths - and by them alone"[3]. It was no more divinely inspired than the Apocrypha - or even the Koran.

Christopher Hill, one of the most perceptive historians of this period, comments that Fisher's writings constitute "a remarkable work of popular Biblical criticism, based on real scholarship". They "mark the end of an epoch, the epoch of protestant Bibliolatry... It is the end of the authority of the Book; but by no means a return to the authority of tradition. It is simply the end of authority... Fisher deserves greater recognition as a precursor of the English enlightenment than he has yet received"[4].

4. A rationalized Jesus

The great intellectual shift known as the Enlightenment, with its emphasis on reason, natural law and evidence-based enquiry put what had traditionally been regarded as "revealed scripture" under new scrutiny. In 1703 a Unitarian minister, Thomas Emlyn, was prosecuted in Ireland for his *Humble Inquiry into the Scripture Account of Jesus Christ*, which questioned Jesus' divinity. In England, another Enlightenment-influenced Unitarian, Thomas Woolston, was brought to trial for his *Discourses on the Miracles of our Saviour*, which proposed natural rather than supernatural explanations. He was detained until his death in 1733[5]. But it is the work of an otherwise obscure German professor of oriental languages at the University of Hamburg, Samuel Reimarus (1694-1768), that is now regarded (thanks to Schweitzer) as beginning the modern quest for the historical Jesus.

Reimarus aimed to strip away Christian "inventions" to reveal a credible historical narrative. His Jesus was a wholly human Jewish prophet who had preached that God was about to liberate the Jews from Roman rule by establishing a new earthly kingdom in which he, Jesus, would reign as king. For this political challenge he was arrested, tried and executed. At his death, he bitterly charged God with having forsaken him. But his followers refused to accept that their mission had failed. With deliberate intent to deceive, they stole Jesus' body and made up the story that he had risen from the dead. This was designed to keep alive the hope of revolt leading to a new Jewish kingdom, with a promise that Jesus would return at any moment to claim his throne.

For the Enlightened rationalist Reimarus, since miracles were impossible they had to be inventions or exaggerations, intended to give credence to Jesus as a divinely empowered wonder-worker. As it became clear that hopes of a new kingdom were delusory, Reimarus argued, a new story was put about: that Jesus had died willingly as a sacrificial lamb, and that those who claimed the sacrifice and joined the church would become citizens of a heavenly kingdom not of this world. In Reimarus's view, the church had rescued a deluded prophet of doom from the obscurity he deserved and triumphantly created a supernatural Christ of faith from the God-forsaken Jesus of history.

While this somewhat crude deception theory failed to win lasting support among scholars, it is nevertheless recognized that Reimarus pioneered a new ground-rule for critical New Testament interpretation, one which has since become normative. As he himself put it, "I find great cause to separate completely what the apostles say in their own writings from that which Jesus himself actually said and taught". Consequently, "It is not to be assumed that Jesus intended or strove for anything in his teaching other than what may be taken from his own words"[6].

Reimarus published nothing of this in his lifetime, no doubt fearing (with good cause) that the wrath of a religious establishment might well cost him his university position and respectable reputation. He circulated his manuscript *Apologia or Defence of the Rational Worshippers of God* to a few close friends, and even when selected portions were published as *Fragments* between 1774 and 1778, shortly after his death, the identity of the author was not revealed. As I have indicated, Reimarus remains best-known from the careful summary of his work by Schweitzer who, while disavowing its deception theory, recognized its scholarship and hailed its publication as "one of the greatest events in the history of criticism".

Arguably more important for future biblical scholarship was the work of Reimarus's contemporary Johann Griesbach, the first scholar to set the Greek texts of the first three gospels side by side for readers to compare and contrast. His book, published in the 1770s, was called *Synopsis Evangeliorum Matthaei, Marci et Lucae*, from which the term "synoptic gospels" originated.

Biblical criticism was also beginning to put down roots in white Anglo-Saxon protestant America. Thomas Jefferson risked his illustrious political career by undertaking his own study of what Jesus had "really said", as distinct from what the gospel writers had said he'd said. America's founding father was probably the first Jesus scholar to compile his own proposed list of authentic Jesus sayings, which became known as the Jefferson Bible. It consisted of a harmonized gospel in seventeen short chapters, beginning with a non-miraculous birth and ending abruptly in

Jesus's burial. Miracles, exorcisms and supernatural events were all excluded.

This scandalized Jefferson's opponents in the 1801 presidential election (a Christian-fundamentalist component in such elections is nothing new), who claimed that if he were elected he would bring down the wrath of God by substituting his new Bible for the old throughout America. Jefferson nevertheless fought off his critics and won a famous electoral victory. But despite his power and popularity it was the old Bible that survived and prospered, while Jefferson's dropped into obscurity. The scaremongering, nevertheless, was probably a factor in ensuring that the complete Jefferson Bible, entitled *The Life and Morals of Jesus of Nazareth, Extracted Textually from the Gospels in Greek, Latin, French and English*, was not published until 1904, some 78 years after his death.

Writers like the unitarians Emlyn, Woolston and Jefferson and the Lutheran Griesbach were motivated by post-Reformation protestant conviction that true Christian religion, free of Catholic corruption and primitive superstition, could be recovered by stripping away anything and everything that could not be attributed directly to Jesus himself. Reimarus had a more secular agenda, as had Heinrich Paulus, a professor of theology at the University of Heidelberg. His *Das Leben Jesu*, published in two volumes in 1828 and, like the work of Reimarus, known to English readers primarily through Schweitzer's summary, writes off recorded accounts of Jesus' miracles as the regrettable misunderstandings of observers lacking a modern, educated appreciation of the laws of nature.

According to Paulus, Jesus may have *seemed* to walk on water when paddling at the shore. He may have *seemed* to quell the storm when the weather just happened to improve as he awoke. He may have *seemed* to heal by supernatural means when any apparent improvement in health was clearly due to psychological manipulation. (Coleridge had recently coined the word "psychosomatic", from Greek words meaning mind and body, to describe mind-over-matter healing). As a modern commentator remarks, "Paulus' book evoked a good deal of opposition at the time of its appearance, but its ideas continued (and still continue) to resurface, especially in writings of those who do not otherwise know what to do with the miracles" (other than scrub them from the record, as Jefferson had done)[7].

5. A humanist Jesus

In the 1830s, however, there appeared two books which moved Jesus scholarship forward from the reductionist rationalism of Reimarus, Paulus and Jefferson. The first to appear in English was *An Inquiry Concerning the Origins of Christianity* by a radical Unitarian layman, Charles Hennell. Published in Britain in 1838, with a second edition in 1841, the *Inquiry* sought once again to separate out the historical facts of Jesus' life from the "later accretions" produced by myth, fantasy and wishful-thinking. Hennell worked his way through the four biblical gospels in turn, arguing that each demonstrated a different authorial viewpoint which determined both selection and interpretation of Jesus' recorded sayings and doings. This understanding of a different authorial viewpoint for each gospel is now received wisdom. It was a new insight in Hennell's day.

Each major story was studied by Hennell with a view to teasing out the points at which objectivity gave way to invention, history to mythology. The miracles in particular were interpreted as parables, what later scholars would term "true fictions", illustrations of what Jesus was saying rather than records of what he was doing. Hennell concluded that there was insufficient evidence to support the view that Jesus was divinely born, worked miracles, rose again or ascended into heaven. He was "a noble-minded reformer and sage" - the first use of the term "sage" in this context, subsequently a key concept for the Jesus Seminar - "martyred by crafty priests and brutal soldiers". Still recognizably a child of Enlightenment thinking, this Jesus was more complex and nuanced than the deluded doomster of Reimarus and Paulus and the wholly de-contextualised preacher-teacher of Jefferson and the progressive

Unitarians.

But Hennell's pioneering work was overshadowed by a much more influential book marking the new thinking of the 1830s. This was *The Life of Jesus Critically Examined* by David Friedrich Strauss (1808-1874), a young Lutheran professor at the University of Zurich. Strauss's huge fourteen-hundred-page two-volume work first appeared in German in 1835-6, three years ahead of Hennell's English publication. The methodology and argument of the two works is similar, leading some to suppose that Hennell could have read Strauss while preparing his own book. Like Hennell, Strauss worked his way through each gospel in turn, noting the similarities of the first three and the contrasting nature of John, which led him to suggest what Jesus scholars have since almost unanimously accepted: that John is likely to be much less valuable than the synoptics for recovering the historical Jesus. (Strauss, however, accepted the then-prevalent assumption that Matthew and Luke preceded Mark, which was thought to have drawn its material from them: a view which textual critics would shortly and decisively overturn)

Unlike Paulus and the rationalizers, and more emphatically than Hennell, Strauss regarded most of the gospel stories not as "inventions" of the early church or "misunderstandings" of credulous Jesus-followers but as myths developed on the pattern of older religious writings, particularly the Jewish scriptures of the Old Testament. The Jesus stories were indeed historical in a sense, but history interpreted through myth, not history as objective factual record of "what really happened". Jesus was not *in fact* miraculously born of a virgin, but the virgin-birth story illustrated his followers' perception of him as unique. No real live dove fluttered down from the skies and no audible voice boomed out from the clouds when the beloved Son, well-pleasing to his Father, was baptized, but the story was told to emphasize the point that this man Jesus had God's full approval. "Myth" was used by Strauss not as a way of suggesting the story was false, but as an assertion of its poetic or psychological truth. With this insight Strauss transformed biblical scholarship -

for good or ill, according to liberal or conservative preference, but for ever.

Most controversial of all, however, was Strauss's christology: his view of what was meant by the claim that Jesus was divine. Strauss was a pupil of the Lutheran philosopher-theologian G W F Hegel who had argued in his ground-breaking book *The Phenomenology of Spirit* (1807) that God existed only as humanity's historically and culturally developed consciousness of "the mysterious other", the divine. Strauss argued that the idea of the divine could not be realized in one man but must be understood as dispersed throughout humanity. For the orthodox, Hegel, Strauss and Ludwig Feuerbach (who developed the idea further in *The Essence of Christianity*, 1841) were simply atheists, where their predecessors from Reimarus to Paulus had at least been Deists or Unitarians. Today they are best understood as pioneers of modern Christian humanism.

There was another characteristic of Strauss' monumental work which pointed to the future. Much of the earlier Jesus scholarship had suggested by implication that enlightened enquiry had undone the mistakes of the past, solved the old mysteries, and bequeathed to present and future generations a rational Jesus and a rational Christianity. The job was done! Strauss, on the other hand, recognized that the job had scarcely started. Grasping the size of the task which would face them, he called for more objective historical research to be undertaken by scholars unencumbered by prior conceptions, historical or theological. Unceremoniously fired from his university post, he nevertheless spent the rest of his life researching, revising and laying the foundations of modern Jesus scholarship.

As it happened, Hennell and Strauss were linked by the then unknown figure of Mary Ann Evans, a friend of Hennell's sister Caroline who introduced her to Hennell shortly after the *Inquiry* was published. Already in transition from a pious evangelicalism to the Hennell circle's humanistic Unitarianism, Mary Ann was soon commissioned by Hennell's friends and fellow-liberals to make an English translation of Strauss' *Life of Jesus*

Critically Examined, which appeared in three volumes in 1846. Having translated perhaps the most important piece of Jesus scholarship of the nineteenth century, Mary Ann went on to prove her own genius by producing some of the finest and most enduring novels in the English language - *Middlemarch, Adam Bede* and *The Mill on the Floss* - under the pseudonym George Eliot. (For good measure, she also translated Feuerbach's *Essence* and Spinoza's *Ethics*)

6. Dumps in the sands

Strauss's call for more research proved timely. Only three years after publication of his *Life*, a chance find in the remote monastery of St Catherine in the Sinai Peninsula opened up a vast new field of enquiry. A German scholar, Konstantin von Tischendorf (1815-1874), visited the monastery in 1844 and discovered 43 leaves of parchment containing the oldest-known version of part of the New Testament in Greek. On a follow-up visit in 1859 he persuaded the monks to show him the remaining leaves which made up the entire codex containing the New Testament and other books, dating to early in the fourth century. He dubbed it *Codex Sinaiticus*.

What made Tischendorf's find of exceptional importance was that in some passages its readings differed significantly from the versions that scholars had been used to working with, as became apparent when he issued his own critical edition of the Greek New Testament in instalments between 1869 and 1872. More dramatically than ever before, scholars and theologians were puzzling over variant texts and acquiring better tools for dating them. For theologians and the man and woman in the pew this posed a disturbing question: which version had the authority of authentic scripture? For biblical historians the question was: which version, if any, was an authentic replication of a lost original, or most accurately expressed the views of the faith communities that created the gospels in the first place?

Textual criticism, as the experts call it, was not an entirely new discipline. A century earlier, the German Lutheran pastor Johann Albrecht Bengel (1687-1752), disconcerted by the variant readings of the Greek New Testament known to specialist scholars even before the new discoveries of the nineteenth century, had developed a set of objective critical principles for categorising variants into groups or "families" by determining which version can be explained as derived from another. A guiding principle was that, where a choice had to be made between a difficult and an easy reading, the difficult was more likely to pre-date the easy one, and therefore more likely to reflect a lost original. In 1743 Bengel produced his own Greek New Testament, substituting his preferred variants for the received versions of church tradition, but placing at the foot of each page the variations he had discarded. Every variant was separately discussed in an appendix, and his new methodology of textual criticism was explained in a concluding essay. It remains a vital part of the modern scholar's toolkit.

Tischendorf's discovery of *Codex Sinaiticus* opened up a whole new chapter of textual criticism, and confusion was further confounded when yet another fourth-century codex, to be known as *Codex Vaticanus*, was found beneath a mound of dust in the Vatican vaults and published contemporaneously with *Codex Sinaiticus* in 1868-72. Now the hunt was on for more and earlier gospel fragments. "Discoveries of new manuscripts became a flood towards the close of the nineteenth century: thousands of papyri were retrieved from dumps in the sands of Egypt at such exotic places as Oxyrhynchus"[8]. Each new discovery demanded renewed critical assessment and set in motion a new wave of research. This continued throughout the twentieth century, first with Chester Beatty's 1930 purchase from Egyptian dealers of a batch of third-century papyri, a century older than *Sinaiticus* and *Vaticanus*; then the Nag Hammadi texts discovered in 1945; and finally the Dead Sea Scrolls which began to appear in 1947. In calling for more research, David Friedrich Strauss could hardly have realized what an avalanche of new materials would become available for future Jesus sleuths.

Another traveller to Syria, Sinaia and Palestine was Joseph-Ernest Renan, who had abandoned training for the French priesthood to study Semitic languages. Although neither the *Sinaiticus* nor *Vaticanus* codices had yet been published, much of the new material was available to an assiduous scholar and Renan made some use of it in his best-selling *Life of Jesus*, published in Paris in 1863. Renan proposed that the gospel accounts were based on legends rather than history or myth (legends being pseudo-historical stories lacking both the factual basis of good history and the poetic truth of good mythology) and that an authentic biography of Jesus must necessarily rely more on literary imagination than the recovery of hard evidence. His *Life* exemplified this approach and was thereby condemned by both historians and churchmen (who, true to form, had him removed from his university post) - but not by the French public, whose eagerness to read about a Jesus purged of clerical accretions ensured that the book went through eight printings in its first twelve weeks and earned it a place in Schweitzer's magisterial survey.

7. The end of the 'Old Quest'

Two more turn-of-the-century Jesus detectives figured strongly in Albert Schweitzer's *Quest*. One was William Wrede, whose contribution was to produce a distinctive school of skeptical scholarship which we shall be looking at in chapter 11. But in shaping Schweitzer's own conclusions, the more important was Johannes Weiss, whose *Jesus' Proclamation of the Kingdom of God* was published in 1892. Weiss was an early pioneer of what became known as *form criticism*, in which each biblical story or event is studied in relation to its supposed origin in oral tradition. Where *textual criticism* focused on differences in the various versions of the same text, *form criticism* concentrated on the process by which a story had come to take the form in which it appeared in the gospels. To get at the truth of a story, historical or theological, it was necessary to understand its context in a particular time, place and culture. So, for instance, the only way to make sense of Jesus' words about the "kingdom of heaven" was to situate them in a context of contemporary kingdom expectations.

Weiss first, and Schweitzer in his wake, identified the essence of Jesus' teaching as his *eschatological* warnings. The word *eschatology* means the study of last things, the end-time. For Schweitzer, drawing heavily on Weiss, critical study of the form of Jesus' many references to the coming kingdom convinced him that these sayings best preserved an early, authentic oral tradition of what Jesus had really said. Whatever the church had later turned him into, the historical Jesus was a prophet seized with the conviction that the end of the world was imminent and that God was about to intervene by sending a supernatural "Son of Man" (not initially identified by Jesus as himself) to establish a new world order. Early in his ministry he had sent his disciples out to preach this message, telling them "Ye shall not have gone over the cities of Israel till the Son of Man be come" (Matt.10:23). The disciples duly went through the towns and cities, and they returned, but the Son of Man had *not* come. Jesus had apparently been proved wrong. Jesus then became convinced that he himself must be the "Son of Man". His suffering and death, deliberately orchestrated, would inaugurate the promised kingdom. So he went to Jerusalem to seek his own death. In Schweitzer's oft-quoted words, he

"...lays hold of the wheel of the world to set it moving on that last revolution which is to bring all history to a close. It refuses to turn, and He throws Himself upon it. Then it does turn: and crushes Him. Instead of bringing in the eschatological conditions, He has destroyed them. The wheel rolls onward, and the mangled body of the one immeasurably great Man, who was strong enough to think of Himself as the spiritual ruler of mankind and to bend history to His purpose, is hanging upon it still. That is His victory and His reign"[9].

But for all its rhetorical grandeur this *apocalyptic* view of the end-time could only mean that Jesus was doubly deluded, first in supposing the end of the world was nigh, and then in his crazed conviction that an act of self-sacrifice on his part would force God's tardy hand in bringing in the kingdom. In what sense, then, was he "the one immeasurably great Man", since he proved no less misguided in his expectations than all the harbingers of doom before and after him who have stood on street corners and mountain tops to cry the Day of the Lord? What claim did this failed prophet have to be seen as "the spiritual ruler of mankind", destined to "bend history to his purpose"? The Jesus of history had blown it. His sacrifice was courageous and wholly altruistic, but this was the courage and altruism of a fanatical preacher tainted with religious mania.

A Jesus who had got things so badly wrong had no relevance for the modern age. Schweitzer himself recognized this. "The historical Jesus", he wrote, "will be to our time a stranger and an enigma": the quest for a real, relevant Jesus was over. An organist and musicologist as well as a theologian, Albert Schweitzer spent the rest of his long life dividing his time between humanitarian work in Africa and playing the organ music of the more easily accessible historical Johann Sebastian Bach.

There was another sense in which Schweitzer seemed to have brought the Jesus quest to a close. His survey of questers from Reimarus to Wrede and Weiss convinced him that, however well-intentioned and however committed to scholarly objectivity, historians invariably ended up with a Jesus they happened to find congenial, a Jesus made in their own image, or the image of their own times. Mark Allan Powell sums it up well: "For the non-Christian, the historical Jesus rather conveniently turned out to be a fraud. For the Christian, the historical Jesus seemed in every case to end up believing things that the author believed and valuing whatever the author valued. The scholars, Schweitzer claimed, had modernized Jesus, dressing him in clothes of their own design. Their interest, whether conscious or not, was in discovering a figure who would be relevant for their time, and this interest prevented them from seeing Jesus as a figure in his own time, as a figure of the past, a figure in *history*."[10]

Having recognized that this was what the questers tended to do,

Schweitzer simply turned this upside down. His Jesus *was* past history, a Galilean Jew immersed in end-of-the-world fantasies. This made him romantic but irrelevant in a world which had seen his fantasies come to nothing. Even his ethical teaching had little relevance to the modern world. It might be possible to summon up love for your enemies if you believed you were living in the "last days" and by so doing you could hope to survive the end-time and enter the new kingdom, but this "interim ethic" was irrelevant nineteen hundred years later when kingdom-come had *not* come and showed no sign of coming, however many times its coming, "on earth, as it is in heaven", was urged in pious mumbles in pulpits and pews. If you wanted a relevant Jesus you could pick and mix from the gospel stories and find the Jesus of your choice. But if you were looking for the historical Jesus you had to take him as you found him: and Schweitzer found him heroic but crazy, romantic but wrong.

It might be said that Schweitzer himself failed to avoid his own trap. Living and writing at the turn of a century marked by faith in the inevitability of human progress and a confidence that everything or very nearly everything that could be discovered had been discovered, Schweitzer produced a Jesus to end all Jesuses, after a quest to end all quests. And for many a long year in the twentieth century it seemed that he may have been right. The search for an authentic Jesus of history stopped dead in its tracks, itself seemingly consigned to history, and it was another half century before a new generation of sleuths found a way out of the blind alley where the old quest had been dumped.

8. Between quests

The historical Jesus having been pronounced either irrecoverable or irrelevant, historians now vacated the field, leaving it as they had found it in the possession of the theologians. Rudolf Bultmann (1884-1976) is usually cited as prime mover in the theological project of ditching the Jesus of history and restoring as the central preoccupation of theologians and church-goers Jesus as the Christ of faith. Christian theology, he taught, was derived not from speculative notions of what Jesus may or may not have said and done but from the *stories and traditions* (whether historical, mythical, legendary or literary was beside the point) inspired by his life and work - and, more importantly, his death and resurrection. For Bultmann, Christianity began at Easter: the point at which the object of faith is no longer a natural Jewish teacher but a supernatural, death-defying cosmic Christ.

The point of the end-time sayings, said Bultmann, was not exactly what Jesus had said, or even exactly what he had meant. Rather, the point was that "In every moment slumbers the possibility of its being the escha-tological moment: you must awaken it": an exhortation to live *as if* the kingdom of heaven were at hand, whether or not you think Jesus actually prophesied a literal doomsday, imminent or in the distant future. There was no once-and-for-all meaning in the Bible stories. Meanings had to be remade for our own times. For Bultmann and his many followers it mattered not a jot whether Jesus really had told a particular story or his later followers had put it into his mouth, or just made it up. It was the task of the Christian, the modern disciple of Jesus, to live by the stories which constituted the tradition, reinterpreting and remythologizing them for the present rather than trying to pin them back into a lost past. In this, Bultmann anticipated postmodernism's emphasis on text as the "property" of the reader no less than the writer. But as John Bowker comments wryly, "Since Bultmann, like many of his skeptical successors, held few serious conversations with historians, the lack of rigorous histo-riography underlying his work is obvious"[11].

9. Back on the trail

The inter-war years of the twentieth century were dominated by the anti- or non-historical theologies of Bultmann, Karl Barth and the multitide of believers at pulpit and pew level for whom finding faith was more important than finding facts. But three factors brought the apparently discredited historical Jesus back into the frame in the 1940s.

First, the second world war, and particularly the holocaust, raised questions which were no less acute for history than for theology. The Nazi leadership, not universally admired for the sophistication of its religious opinions but anxious to secure the support of the German churches, had spread the view that Jesus was a sound anti-Semite. In their reading of history (which ignored the inconvenient fact that Jesus was himself a Jew) the Jesus who had denounced the Pharisees, cleaned up the temple and died at the hands of the Jewish mob helped validate the Nazi project of Jewish extermination. Inevitably, many theologians felt the need to combat the Nazis' crass and crude version of the historical Jesus with a better-authenticated model. It was one thing for Schweitzer's quest to have ended with a deluded fanatic, but quite another for the Third Reich to declare that the historical Jesus was a proto-Nazi whose cross symbol was merely an early version of the swastika. The need to proclaim a non-Nazi Jesus led them straight back on the trail of a more authentic Jesus of history.

The second factor leading to a revival of the quest was the two sensational finds of whole libraries of ancient papyri in "dumps in the sand" of Egypt and Palestine - the Nag Hammadi library of largely gnostic Christian writings unearthed by Mohammed Ali (not the dancing-like-a-butterfly, stinging-like-a-bee pugilist) in 1945 and the Dead Sea Scrolls found in 1947. Both inspired new historical research on religious and social life in first-century BCE[12] Palestine and the Mediterranean, and into the origins and early development of the Christian church, bringing Jesus himself down to earth from the clouds where inter-war theology had left him floating free of historical moorings.

The third factor was an ironic turn within Bultmann's own circle of pupils and followers. Bultmann maintained that a theology of the New Testament, a theology of the risen Christ, was not *dependent* on the message of an historical Jesus. But he conceded that the existence of an historical Jesus and his teachings constituted a *presupposition* for Christian theology, and that post-Easter christology was therefore implicit in the message of the pre-Easter Jesus. This could only mean that the link between pre-Easter Jesus and post-Easter Christ was, after all, a matter for *historical* investigation. In 1953 Ernst Käsemann, a former pupil of Bultmann, pushed wide open the door which Bultmann had been content to leave provocatively ajar. Käsemann gave what proved to be an influential lecture at Bultmann's own university, Marburg, entitled "The Problem of the Historical Jesus", arguing that Christian theology could be made to support anything - including the holocaust and a Nazi Jesus - unless it was thoroughly grounded in historical reality. A revived quest had been made possible, he argued, by the newly-discovered texts, new research techniques, and advances in disciplines such as archaeology and ancient languages. Jesus the man, Jesus of Galilee, was back in business.

Exactly fifty years after first publication of Schweitzer's *Quest*, Gunther Bornkamm published *Jesus of Nazareth*, first in German in 1956 and four years later in English. In both German - and English-speaking countries it quickly became a standard text in universities and seminaries. Apart from reconnecting history and theology as Käsemann had urged, Bornkamm took issue with the Schweitzerian view that Jesus believed and taught that an imminent divine intervention would usher in the kingdom of heaven. Jesus' kingdom, suggested Bornkamm, was more subtle than that. Jesus had used the "kingdom of heaven" and "kingdom of God" to symbolise both *a present and a future* experience of the presence of God. The kingdom was here and now, in the fellowship of the poor and the outcast, *and* it was a new world within the old, already under construction by those who lived in the light of Jesus' teachings. This neatly removed from Jesus the stigma of failed prophet, but it proved harder to shift the legacy of Schweitzer's insistence that a genuinely historical Jesus would be irrelevant and a relevant Jesus almost certainly unhistorical. As we shall see throughout this book, the issue of whether the end-time sayings originated with Jesus or his followers, and the related issue of what on earth they meant anyway, continued and continue to divide Jesus detectives.

While Bornkamm, accepting the synoptic gospels as reliable sources, asserted the historical accuracy of certain basic facts about Jesus (that he was a Jew from Nazareth, spoke Aramaic, was baptized by John, challenged the religious authorities, overturned the temple tables and was executed as a threat to the religious and social order), he did not attempt a saying-by-saying, parable-by-parable analysis to determine which were the authentic words of Jesus and which had been inserted, invented, altered or otherwise introduced by later editors and gospel writers. This more forensic approach was reintroduced by an American scholar, Norman Perrin, in a series of books published between 1963 and 1976, culminating in *Jesus and the Language of the Kingdom.*

Making bold use of the method known as *redaction criticism*, which attempts to date, interpret and authenticate the words attributed to Jesus by the theological context in which the gospel editors (redactors) place them, Perrin produced a list of "authentic" Jesus sayings some years before the Jesus Seminar, John Dominic Crossan and Geza Vermes each attempted the same exercise on rather more ambitious scales. Commenting on Perrin's pioneering attempt at a credible list, Mark Allan Powell writes that he "helped to define many of the criteria for historical judgments" that came to the fore in the scholarship that followed. "His own preference was to err on the side of caution: 'the nature of the synoptic tradition is such that the burden of proof will be upon the claim to authenticity'. This philosophy came to be expressed through the popular motto 'When in doubt, leave it out', meaning that nothing will be affirmed as authentic unless it is absolutely certain. Thus, Perrin was able to claim that while a great deal more of the New Testament gospel material about Jesus' teaching is *possibly* authentic, the strictest canons of historical research allow us to affirm only selected items as an 'irreducible minimum'"[13].

The revival of interest in the historical Jesus, who he really was and what he really said and did, sparked off by post-war discoveries and by growing academic dissatisfaction with Bultmann's historically ungrounded theologizing, picked up pace in the 1980s and was in full steam by the 90s. Its center had shifted from Germany to the United States, where the quest was fuelled by a perceived need to offer the liberal churches a more credible Jesus than the disembodied supernaturalized Christ of the growing fundamentalist churches and the meek-and-mild Friend-above-the-bright-blue-skies they proffered to little children of all ages. Another factor in the explosion of investigative Jesus scholarship was the availability of new information technology which made the work of specialists in the most obscure academies instantly available to other investigators across the world. The same world-wide web that enabled an unprecedented spread of coarse pornographic imagery also made possible an exponential expansion of historical Jesus detective work.

Which brings us to the present. But before we turn to contemporary schools of Jesus scholarship in Part II we must set out the range of sources available to them. We cannot hope to understand their work and their debates without some knowledge of the texts which make up their raw material. Over the next few chapters we shall lay them out, book-by-book, text-by-text.

Notes to Chapter 2

[See Bibliography on page 408 for full details of works cited]

1 Vermes, *Jesus Jewish Context*, 54

2 as above, 68-9

3 Samuel Fisher, *The Rustics Alarm to the Rabbies*, 1660

4 Hill, 208-15

5 Nicolas Walter, *Blasphemy Ancient and Modern*, 33-4. Walter cites several similar prosecutions during the18th century.

6 Reimarus, ed. C H Talbert, *Fragments*, 64, Fortress Press, Philadelphia, 1971, p 64

7 Powell, 21

8 Funk, *Five Gospels*, 8

9 Schweitzer, 370

10 Powell, 22

11 Bowker, *Oxford Dictionary*, 180

12 Except when directly quoting writers who use the traditional BC and AD dating system I have followed most modern scholars in using the religiously and culturally neutral BCE (Before Common Era) and CE (Common Era).

13 Powell, 27

3

THE GAP

Historians work from sources, mostly written texts. Such documents have to be evaluated. Who wrote them? When? Why? For whom? Are they contemporary first-hand eye-witness reports or were they written some time after the events they describe? Just how reliable are they?

Jesus historians face a problem right at the start. There is *no contemporary documentation whatever on the life of Jesus.* By "contemporary" I mean the first three decades of the first century, beginning shortly before the death of Herod the Great (4 BCE) and ending during the prefectship of Pontius Pilate (26-36 CE), probably around 30 CE. If, in this specific time period and in the specific location of what is still sometimes called the Holy Land, a man named Jesus lived and taught as Christian tradition has asserted for two thousand years, nobody thought to mention it at the time in their books, poems, letters or state records. Or if they did, these writings lie as yet undiscovered, perhaps in a Dead Sea cave, in a long-buried vault under war-ravaged Jerusalem, or in the carbonized libraries of Herculaneum.

We should not be surprised by this silence. Jesus may have lived according to the tradition into his early thirties but the period of his ministry was very short: barely one year according to Matthew, Mark and Luke, possibly three according to John. Almost the whole of that short time was apparently spent in the northern province of Galilee, far removed from the hub of Jewish political and religious life in Jerusalem, not to mention the distant center of the empire, Rome. He would have been seen by the authorities as just another travelling holy man and miracle-worker, one more potential trouble-maker, a little local difficulty in one of the empire's less distinguished backwaters. There were no newspapers to record such matters or comment on them. The overwhelming majority of those who may have witnessed Jesus in action were illiterate and would not make notes about what they had seen and heard. Even if his followers did make extravagant claims for him - that he was to be "king of the Jews", their messianic liberator - such upstarts were ten a mite, and were routinely crucified. It was nothing to write home about, certainly nothing worth adding to the bureaucrats' pile of state records.

Some forty years passed after the death of Jesus before the appearance of Mark, the first surviving narrative gospel, and another ten or twenty before Matthew and Luke produced their more expansive accounts. Jesus didn't begin to filter into recorded history till a widespread movement, fanning out across the Roman empire and attracting a literate, urban following, particularly among Greek-speaking Hellenistic Jews and "God-fearers" (gentiles sympathetic to Jewish monotheism), put his name into the written records on which our knowledge of him must be based. This process began, not with the gospels as we know them but with the writing and circulation of Paul's letters, and with the first collections of remembered stories and sayings which the gospel writers eventually incorporated into their narratives. But until these developments began in the 50s, memories of the historical Jesus were preserved and transmitted orally for twenty years. Jesus historians have to negotiate this information gap.

Chinese whispers: the oral tradition

There is a story that, some twenty years after the death of Abraham Lincoln in 1865, admirers of the great man set out to record oral memories of what he had said and done. They talked to relatives, neighbors, servants and other close associates, carefully noting every-thing they were told. But when they came to put the oral archive together to make a coherent portrait they discovered that there were so many contradictions and discrepancies, particularly in the recollection of Lincoln's exact words, that it was impossible to produce a reliable account. The project was abandoned.

The problem is not new. The Greek historian Thucydides, writing in the fifth century BCE, described how he tackled the task of reporting the speeches made by various leaders in the Peloponnesian war:

"It has been difficult to recall precisely the words they actually spoke. This is the case whether they were speeches I myself heard or whether they were words reported to me from other sources. As a consequence, the various speakers were made to say what was appropriate, as it seemed to me, to the subject, although I attempted to stick as close as possible in every case to the general scope of the speech"[1].

Every reporter knows the problem, and most solve it as Thucydides did. Some years ago I scripted *Invasion*, a dramatized reconstruction for television of the arguments that had gone on behind closed doors in the Kremlin in 1968 when the Soviet leaders abducted the entire Czechoslovak Communist party leadership in an attempt to persuade them to reverse their reform program and acquiesce in the Soviet invasion of their country. Not being a member of either the Soviet Praesidium or the Czechoslovak party leadership, I wasn't there myself. I relied on the detailed recollections of one Czech party secretary who was present throughout, supplemented by the memories of another. I was obsessively anxious to get it right, to be "authentic". But faced with discrepancies due either to lapses of memory or to the natural tendency of my informants to re-structure memories to suit their own purposes or put themselves center-stage, I necessarily found myself doing as Thucydides had done two and a half millennia earlier. I made my speakers "say what was appropriate, as it seemed to me, to the subject, although I attempted to stick as close as possible in every case to the general scope of the speech".

The value of oral tradition, particularly in the absence of written records, is now well recognized by historians, and oral history has become a discipline in its own right. Its practitioners are well aware of the limitations of memory and have developed their own guidelines for evaluating what they are told. They know that memory best retains sayings and anecdotes that are short, striking and provocative, rather than long speeches. Oft-repeated sayings, stories and jokes are also more easily and reliably remembered than one-offs. The gist (Thucydides' "general scope") of a story or political speech or sermon is better-retained than any of the actual words spoken, though striking slogans and jokes with memorable punch-lines stick in the memory. Robert Funk, describing how the Jesus Seminar studied what was known about the transmission of oral tradition in order to formulate its own rules of oral evidence, noted that "one experiment has shown that most people forget the *exact wording* of a particular statement after only sixteen syllables intervene between the original statement and the request to recall that wording. But the same experiment has proved that most people are quite good at recalling the gist of what was heard or read"[2].

Most people also retain in the memory only what they want to retain, and interpret what they remember, or what they think they remember, in line with their own views or prejudices. This is especially true when opinions rather than facts are being recollected and passed on. Recollection of political or religious discourse is rarely neutral and dispassionate! When the recollection is invoked specifically to advance or reinforce a particular point of view, it is most likely to be colored or distorted. This is clearly important when it comes to evaluating the oral transmission of the words of Jesus. Those who passed on the stories were not dispassionate or neutral observers. They remembered in order to make a point, and what they remembered was what helped them make that point, whether it was that Jesus meant his message exclusively for Jews or that he intended it for the whole world. Rival polemics produced rival "memories" and rival tendencies or factions within the Jesus movement as it spread around the Mediterranean basin.

Moreover, even assuming a general intention among members of the early Jesus movement to remember a parable or aphorism accurately, the oral historian cannot ignore the "Chinese whispers" effect: every repetition and re-telling is liable to produce a change, however slight[3]. We must not imagine that the gospels were written by trained researchers who went out into the field to interview actual eye- or ear-witnesses. The Jesus stories were collected years after they were told and had been filtered through many memory banks before they were fixed on paper. It was less a case of "Well, I was there and I can tell you exactly what Jesus said...", more likely a case of "This is what our community of Jesus followers believe he said, because we know someone who says he was there at the time, or we heard it from our mothers and fathers or the next-door neighbor, and we've discussed it endlessly ever since, and this is what we reckon he meant..." To which imaginary conversation we might add something like: "And anyway, our religious understanding, based on what the scriptures say and what God has told us through our leaders, is that this really is how it was...". As Robert Funk puts it,

"We can imagine Jesus speaking the same aphorism or parable on different occasions. We can further imagine that his followers would find themselves repeating these same sayings in contexts of their own, not in Jesus' precise words, but in their own words as they recalled the essence of what he had said. Various leaders in the Jesus movement would then have started to develop their own independent streams of tradition, and these streams would eventually culminate in written gospels like Thomas and the ones we find in the New Testament."[4].

From their study of what is known of the transmission of oral tradition, the Jesus Seminar formulated four "rules of oral evidence":

• The oral memory best retains sayings and anecdotes that are short, provocative, memorable - and oft-repeated.
• The most frequently recorded words of Jesus in the surviving gospels take the forms of aphorisms and parables.

- The earliest layer of the gospel tradition is made up of single aphorisms and parables that circulated by word of mouth prior to the written gospels.
- Jesus' disciples remembered the core or gist of his sayings and parables, not his precise words, except in rare cases[5].

To add to all this we need to reiterate that Jesus spoke in one language, a local dialect of Aramaic, and the written record of what he said was made in another, Greek[6]. Chinese whispers circulating around a room in a single language usually emerge with significant changes. Chinese whispers transmitted in a single language through two or more decades are even more likely to emerge corrupted. How much more so, then, when the whispers originate in one language, rural and oral, and end up twenty years later in a quite different one, global and literary? By then it will surely be something of a miracle if they still convey the authentic gist and spirit, let alone the precise meaning and intonation, of the original.

When we read that Jesus said "Blessed are the peacemakers, for they shall be called the children of God", we need to remember that we are reading a sixteenth century *English* rendering of what was considered by the translators to be the best version available of centuries-old *Greek* texts, which themselves relied on someone's reported *memory* of what had been spoken twenty or more years earlier in an *Aramaic* dialect.

Jesus reconstructed, or Jesus remembered?

This particular understanding of how the oral tradition worked is contested by some scholars. James Dunn argues that most historical Jesus questers have been barking up the wrong tree, seeking an elusive "Jesus reconstructed" instead of an authentic "Jesus remembered". Dunn's critique stems from a radically different approach to the oral tradition and the problem of the gap. We shall come back to this argument when we focus on the Jesus Seminar and its critics in chapter 7.

In the face of such apparently intractable problems, a number of scholars in the field have written off the "quest for the historical Jesus" as hardly less fanciful than the quest for the Holy Grail. Some of these skeptics have concluded that the legendary or mythological accretions have so totally obscured and extinguished any historical original that we are left with nothing but the Jesus *story*, rather than *history*. Radicals and "neo-liberals" have tended to conclude that nothing in the *story* is guaranteed to be *historically* reliable, while the quests of "neo-conservatives" like Dunn and N T Wright end up where they started, with an historical Jesus identical to their church's Jesus of faith, a Jesus who was and remains God incarnate.

But liberals and conservatives, secular historians and theologians alike, have no option but to rely on what remains of the written sources. They are all we have. Over the remaining chapters of Part I we shall lay out these sources before we move on in Part II to see what different schools of historical Jesus scholarship make of them.

Notes to Chapter 3

1 Funk, *5 Gospels*, 27

2 as above, 28. It is sometimes argued that this "minimalist" account of how oral memory works ignores evidence that in pre-literate societies vast quantities of literature - the scriptures, epic poems, ancestral legends - were committed wholesale to memory and transmitted faithfully without recourse to written text. But there is no evidence that this applied to speeches and sermons by teachers and preachers.

3 "Chinese whispers" is a children's game where a message is whispered into the ear of the person next to you, who passes it on to his neighbor in similar fashion until it has been round the whole group. The final version is then compared with the original message. The game points up the way mis-hearings, well-intentioned improvements or plain misrepresentations can corrupt the original in process of transmission.

4 Funk, *5 Gospels*, 29

5 as above, 28

6 Aramaic was a local language, Greek and Latin the universal languages of the Roman empire. By the first century, even the ancient Hebrew scriptures were known to most Jews only in the Greek version as translated (according to tradition) by seventy scholars (hence *Septuagint*). Paul's letters, the gospels and all surviving Christian literature of the period were written for a cosmopolitan Greek-reading and Greek-speaking public.

4

GOSPEL TRUTH

After some twenty years of Chinese whispers or memorized litanies, Jesus made his quiet entry into written history. The earliest known references to him are in Paul's letters, written in the 50s. For reasons to be discussed later, these tell us little about Jesus the man, as distinct from Paul's vision of the "risen Christ", and record little of his teaching. They were followed more than twenty years later by Mark, the first of the series of four narrative gospels in the New Testament. Scholars disagree on precisely when the other gospels were written in the form in which we know them, but we may deduce that Matthew probably composed his version in the 80s, Luke in the late 80s or 90s, and John at around the turn of the first century. Some scholars propose early dates (60s onwards) for the gospel of Thomas and other gospel fragments which never made the biblical canon, but this remains highly controversial. By the end of the first century Jesus has also begun to figure, briefly and enigmatically, in secular literature. Taken together, then, these are the written records, the documentary sources, that reveal (or hide) the historical Jesus, all of them written many years after his death. How do scholars evaluate them?

Historians operate on the *general principle* that the earlier the record of an event or saying, the better chance there is of its accuracy and reliability. (This can be no more than a general principle, as there are sometimes good reasons for preferring a report that is distanced from the events recorded). On this basis, then, we shall look at the main sources in as close to chronological order as we can get, and see what our scholars make of them.

1. Paul's letters

An outline of Paul's biography can be stitched together from what is said of him in Luke's Acts of the Apostles, a late-first-century account of the early Christian church. Two problems must be borne in mind. First, we need to remember that Luke's account, both in his gospel and in Acts, was written from a particular theological and political perspective (as were the writings of his contemporaries). The author was not primarily concerned with historical objectivity. His aim was to produce an account of the development of the early church that accorded with the suppositions, mythologies, theology and religious politics of his particular community, and reconciling it all with the conflicting narratives emerging in other Jesus communities. This produced a picture of Paul that met the Luke community's needs, rather than a disinterested, historically accurate biography. Secondly, Acts has to be read in conjunction with Paul's own attested writings, which offer sparse but occasionally conflicting biographical detail.

From these sources we derive our picture of Paul, first known as Saul, a Jewish native of Tarsus in Cilicia who claimed Roman citizenship, was brought up as a Pharisee (a Jewish sect distinguished from the more numerous and more conservative Sadducees by rigorous observance of Jewish religious law and by belief in an after-life). By his own account Paul was a fierce opponent of the early Jesus movement, but while on his way to Damascus in Syria to suppress a new Jesus community he had what he believed to be a direct encounter with the spirit of the crucified Jesus which transformed him into as zealous a supporter of the movement as he had been a persecutor - and a supporter, moreover, who would transform its mission.

The Damascus road u-turn is dated by some scholars to the early 30s, and by most to no later than the early 40s. Paul immediately assumed a controversial leadership role as a roving missionary, setting up new Jesus groups and working tirelesssly to mold them to his own particular vision, much influenced, it seems, by contact with or knowledge of some of the Mediterranean mystery cults. He seems to have been restlessly searching for a new religious paradigm which would take into account both Jewish tradition and the insights of the popular mystery cults which flourished in the Hellenized empire (the Greco-Roman world) and attracted independent Jewish thinkers, particularly in the dispersed ("diaspora") communities remote from Jerusalem. His Damascus road experience, whatever it was, seems to have been his *eurika* moment of enlightenment when it struck him that the Jesus movement he was so vigorously perse-cuting had the potential to subsume Jewish and gentile traditions and become the nucleus of a reformed Judaism which could develop into a new universal religion.

Paul's uneasy relationship with the leadership of the Jesus movement in Jerusalem is acknowledged and recorded in Acts (where it is never-theless diplomatically played down). While the embryonic church was still no more than an ill-defined set of disparate Jewish communities on their way to becoming a new Jewish sect, there was powerful resistance to his vision of the movement as embracing gentiles as well as Jews. According to the Acts narrative it seems that, for a time, a pragmatic compromise was reached whereby the Jerusalem leadership ran a Jewish Jesus community based in the city while Paul was licensed to build a largely autonomous movement including both Hellenized Jews and gentiles which had its centers outside Judea and Galilee. Paul's single most important innovation was his insistence that pagan converts did not have to become Jews in order to become Christians. Fully grown pagan men, after all, were unlikely to warm to the prospect of undergoing a ceremony in which the foreskin of a fully-grown penis would be sliced away as the price of church membership. After the fall of Jerusalem and destruction of the temple in 70 CE, which fatally weakened the Jewish Jesus community, Paul's universalism became the dominant tendency within a rapidly diversifying Jesus movement. That also meant that Paul's more mystical heaven-centered theology, where Jesus was increasingly understood as the incarnation of God, began to triumph over the more earth-centered, even Palestine-centered outlook of those who had known and attached themselves to a Galilean holy man whom Paul had never met, except "in the spirit".

Scholars date the first of Paul's letters, 1 Thessalonians, to around late 50 or 51 CE[1]. It was written from Athens to a group of "followers of us and the Lord" (1 Thess.1:6), both gentiles and Jews, which he himself had established or helped establish in the Greek city of Thessalonica, probably in the middle or late 40s. Its opening words are a salutation in the name of "God our Father and the Lord Jesus Christ". *This is the first time that Jesus' name is mentioned in any historical document which has come down to us.* It tells us something about Paul's view of Jesus - that he was to be understood as "Lord" and "Christ". But the modern reader will peruse it in vain for any human detail about the man whose name appears between these two honorary titles. Nor is there a single illuminating word here about Jesus' teachings.

For Paul in 1 Thessalonians Jesus is a spirit in heaven, to be mentioned in the same breath as "God our Father" and the Holy Ghost (1: 1, 5-6), and be venerated as Lord. He is the son of "the living and true God" (1: 9-10). That he had once lived on earth Paul recognizes by a reference to "the Jews" who, he says, "both killed the Lord Jesus and their own prophets" (2: 14-15), but the only mention of Jesus' *teachings* is by way of Paul's own "commandments we gave you by the Lord Jesus" (4: 2) - that is, Paul's own teachings as communicated to him by Jesus from heaven. Paul lists abstention from non-marital sex, lust, and fraudulent practice - all commonplaces of conventional morality, Jewish and gentile - but invests them with his own authority as one who speaks on behalf of the son of "the living and true God".

He expects and requires his readers and listeners (since the letter is intended to be read aloud "unto all the holy brethren", 5: 27) to understand that he, Paul, is speaking with the authority of Jesus, whom he links with the God both Jews and Greeks have always worshipped in their different ways. But he does not consider it necessary to cite the man Jesus directly. The Thessalonian Jesus-community already know that they are "taught of God to love one another", but Paul invokes his own authority rather than any remembered words of Jesus to command that they do so "more and more" (4: 9-10). Paul does not say "Jesus said..." but "I command", reinforcing his own teaching as revelations or messages from a Jesus-spirit who has spoken to and conferred authority on him from heaven.

This tells us plainly that, by the time Jesus is first written about, some twenty years before the first gospel, his humanity is less important *to this author and his community* than his divine status, and his life less important than his death.

Only rarely does Paul make explicit reference to sayings of Jesus-on-earth. In 1 Corinthians 2:9 he writes: "As it is written, Eye hath not seen, nor ear heard, neither have entered into the heart of man, the things that God hath prepared for them that love him". Paul does not say where this is written, and no direct source has been found. But in the gospel of Thomas 17 Jesus says (Jesus Seminar's "Scholars Version") "I will give you what no eye has seen, what no ear has heard, what no hand has touched, and what has not arisen in the human heart". Could Paul be quoting a version of this Jesus saying from the source also used by the author of Thomas? In Acts 20:35 Luke has Paul remind the elders of Miletus of "the word of the Lord Jesus, who himself said, 'It is more blessed to give than to receive'". But this saying too has not been found in any other source. It may be that both the eye-ear and the giving-receiving saying were in general currency, and it suited Paul's missionary purpose to invest the first with the authority of holy writ and the second with the authority of "the Lord Jesus". It is all grist to the scholar's mill.

This first letter to the Thessalonians, the very earliest surviving Christian document, gives us a glimpse of how much the Jesus movement, or at least Paul's faction of it, appears to have changed in the twenty or so years since Jesus' death - unless we are to read it as showing how Paul was fashioning a new religion from a heady mix of Jewish, gentile and Jesus-movement ideas. In particular, perhaps, it gives us a revealing clue as to how a movement of hope had been created out of the despair and humiliation of the crucifixion. Paul preached that the Jesus who had been killed and had ascended to heaven was about to return to rescue believers from divine judgment. An important reason for writing his letter was that his lieutenant Timothy, having just returned from a recent visit to the Thessalonians, had reported to Paul that the church there was getting restless about the delay in Jesus' return, which the community had been led to expect any day, at any time. There was anxiety that some members had died before their moment of glory. Others were not feeling so well themselves. Would they miss out?

Paul assured them that they would not. Just as Jesus had risen again, he writes, so too would the "dead in Christ" - those believers who had died while waiting. He paints a joyful picture. At any moment "the Lord himself shall descend from heaven with a shout, with the voice of the archangel, and with the trump of God". Then "the dead in Christ shall rise first". Next, "we which are alive and remain shall be caught up together with them in the clouds to meet the Lord in the air: and so shall we ever be with the Lord" (4: 13-18). They were to "comfort one another with these words", and untold numbers, patiently waiting, have done so ever since. This is perhaps the earliest evidence of an apocalyptic mind-set within one section - Paul's - of the emerging Christian church. But had the historical Jesus shared that mind-set?

Combing through the later letters (one to the Galations written from Ephesus around 52-53; the first epistle to the Corinthians, also written from Ephesus in the winter of 53-54; one to the Philippians from Ephesus or Rome; and one to the Romans written from Corinth around 55-56)[2], the pattern is similar. Some scholars think Paul may be drawing directly on Jesus traditions known to him by oral transmission and possibly from Q (a lost but reconstructable source used by Matthew and Luke which we shall focus on in the next chapter) when he tells Roman believers to "bless them which persecute you" and "recompense to no man evil for evil" (Rom. 12: 14, 17, possibly after Q's "love your enemies and pray for your persecutors", as preserved in Lk.6: 27-36 and Matt.5: 44). Others point out that this was received piety, as Jesus himself appears to have acknowledged, according to Q-in-Matthew 7:12, where he summarizes this aspect of his message as "...all things whatsoever ye would that men should do to you, do ye even so to them", emphasizing that "this is the law and the prophets". Whatever he did or did not know of the earthly Jesus, Paul the Pharisee (he claimed to have been a student of the Pharisee leader Gamaliel) certainly knew his law and his prophets. And as a cultured, widely-traveled Roman citizen, he may well have been aware that the "golden rule" had its counterparts not only in Jewish but in Greek and Egyptian sources. (It is also attested in Chinese, Indian and Persian traditions). The point is that Paul did not necessarily get it from Jesus of Galilee (as distinct from Jesus in Heaven), nor does he claim to have done so.

Twice Paul does invoke the authority of "the Lord" directly, once in 1 Corinthians 7: 10 where he seems to know of Jesus's prohibition of divorce (recorded later in Mark 10: 2-9, but perhaps available to Paul in the oral tradition), and again in 1 Corinthians 9: 14 where he interprets Jesus' "the workman is worthy of his meat" (Matt.10: 10) as a command by the Lord that those who preach the gospel should get their living by the gospel. But again, these may be interpreted as examples of Paul putting his own commands, which were hardly unorthodox, on the tongue of "Christ", believing as he clearly did that he, Paul, was the heavenly Christ's chosen mouthpiece.

Paul's references to the betrayal of Jesus that had led to his trial and execution, to his resurrection and his expected second coming, demonstrate his familiarity with an already established Jesus-movement tradition, the passion story, which was evidently circulating orally and would not be written up in the biblical gospels until a generation later. But if we only had Paul's letters to go by we would know virtually nothing of Jesus' distinctive sayings and teachings. Scholars remain divided on whether this is because Paul (a) was ignorant of them, (b) knew of them but considered them of little importance compared with Jesus' cosmic message of salvation, or (c) failed to quote them in his letters because the sayings were so widely circulated and so familiar within the Jesus communities he was addressing that it was unnecessary to repeat common knowledge. For whatever reason, most historical Jesus scholars have concluded that the treasure-house of Paul's letters tells us much about the early development of what would later become the dominant form of Christianity, but remarkably little about Jesus himself.

2. The non-Pauline letters

The same is true of New Testament letters not written by Paul. James and 1 Peter, for instance, contain teachings which parallel those of the sermon on the mount, but they are not specifically ascribed to Jesus. As distinguished New Testament scholars Gerd Theissen and Annette Merz comment, "Anonymous traditions are occasionally taken up in the New Testament writings which otherwise have been handed down as sayings in the mouth of Jesus. There can be no methodologically guaranteed way of discovering whether they were known to their several authors as sayings of the Lord"[3]. Almost all scholars, incidentally, have abandoned the theory that the epistle of James was written by James the brother of Jesus (Mk.6:3) who is believed to have been martyred in 62 CE, though John Bowker holds that his authorship at "a date as early as 40 CE... is not impossible"[4]. Even if most scholars changed their minds and came to accept this possibility, however, it would add nothing to our knowledge of the teachings of Jesus, unless it were also assumed that James in the 40s or 50s was teaching exactly what Jesus had taught in the late 20s. The ascription of 1 Peter to Peter the apostle is also doubted, and 2 Peter is considered by virtually all scholars as another second-century "pious forgery" (about which, see chapter 6). These have their place in the history of the early church, but they offer no reliable evidence on the content of Jesus' teaching.

3. The biblical gospels

When we come to the gospels it is useful to bear in mind Geza Vermes's dry comment that "gospel truth" is "only the evangelists' picture"[5]. Nevertheless, although the four biblical gospels give us theologically framed accounts from much later in the century, they are vital as potential sources of historical information. Indeed, without them we would know virtually nothing of the Galilean Jesus. We shall look at each of them in chronological order, bearing in mind that they all draw on earlier source material. Of this earlier material, suffice it to say here that if scholars can identify parts of the gospels as earlier - perhaps much earlier - than the date of composition of the book in which the material is embedded, they will have moved us closer to Jesus' own time and arguably closer to historical authenticity. The nature of this "embedded" material will be discussed in the next chapter. Here we propose to review scholarly assessments of the biblical gospels in the form in which we now know them.

What circumstances caused these gospels to be written? According to church tradition, Paul was put to death under Nero, whose reign ended in 68 CE. In 70 CE a Jewish revolt against the Romans was put down, Jerusalem was sacked and the temple - symbol and soul of the Jewish religion - was destroyed. The leadership of the Jesus movement within Judaism had already been weakened by the murder in 62 CE of its leader, James, claimed by some communities as Jesus' brother, and the martyrdom in Rome of Peter. It is likely that the balance of power within a rapidly diversifying Jesus movement had already shifted from the Jesus-for-Jews-alone view, spread by its earliest itinerant leaders in Palestine and Syria, to the universalist emphasis of Paul and his communities in Asia Minor and the Aegean. The death of James and the fall of Jerusalem clearly accelerated this process of gradual detachment from Judaism as thoroughly Hellenized gentile converts in cities far removed from Judea began to dominate the Jesus movement.

The cataclysmic events of 70 CE produced a new generation of leaders, one of whose tasks was to heal the many rifts in the early church, not the least of which was that between those who emphasized Jesus' humanity and those who had come to see him as a divine being. Recognising that the generation which had known the human Jesus was passing away, and perhaps conscious that something seemed to have gone wrong with Paul's confident prediction of an early second coming, they thought it timely to gather oral traditions and such written accounts as were then in circulation to construct an authorized version of the Jesus story - not only what he was said to have said but also what he was said to have done. In so doing, the authors or compilers of narrative gospels were drawing on two precedents. One was the work of the eighth century BCE Jewish scribes who had pulled together strands of saga, poetry, history, wisdom-literature, mythology and legend to forge a coherent story of their own origins and a sense of their own emerging Jewish identity. The other was a distinctive Greek literary tradition of heroic proto-biography. The first to marry these two traditions was the author of Mark's gospel. (See Cameo, *The Invention of the Narrative Gospel,* page 50).

Mark

Most modern scholars date Mark's main text to the early or mid-70s, inferring this from both its literary style and from an assumption that its emphasis on Jesus as a prophet of the destruction of the temple must have been written after the destruction actually happened in 70 CE. Its author or editor is unknown: the tradition that it was written by the John Mark mentioned in Acts as one of Paul's companions dates from the second century and originated with Papias, bishop of Hierapolis in Asia Minor in the 120s, who is quoted by later church fathers as teaching that Mark was "the interpreter of Peter", who set down "carefully, but not in order" Peter's memories of Jesus' words and actions[6]. But scholars no longer consider this or any other of Papias's speculations to be historically grounded, and when they refer to Mark they mean either the unknown author/editor or the text of the gospel itself.

Cameo: The invention of the narrative gospel

We are now so familiar with the narrative gospels in the Bible that it rarely occurs to us to ask where this kind of writing came from. Did the author or compiler of Mark invent the form, rather as Defoe is said to have invented the novel and Petrarch the sonnet? Or was there already a literary form at hand, which he simply borrowed?

Whatever genre the narrative gospel belongs to, scholars are virtually unanimous in their view that it has little connection with that of modern biography. The authors of Mark, Matthew, Luke and John were not objective historians who reconstructed events by researching in libraries and interviewing surviving friends and relations of Jesus. Biographers and biographies did not exist as the genres and disciplines we know today. The gospel writers were primarily preachers. They had "good news" to proclaim, and the narrative gospel was the literary framework within which they proclaimed it.

*The word "gospel" is a translation of the Latin word "evangelium", which in turn is derived from Greek. According to Helmut Koester in **Ancient Christian Gospels**, it was first used by Aristophanes (c450 - c388 BCE) to mean "bringing good news", such as victory in battle. As a noun, in classical Greek usage it came to mean the **reward** for bringing good news, or a **thank-offering** for it. By imperial Roman times it was often used to mean news itself: the content of news, whether good, bad or indifferent. Koester sees the term as elevated to a new dignity in imperial inscriptions such as that from Priene (9 BCE) to "the god" and "savior" Augustus, whose birth was "the beginning of his good messages [or gospels]".*

Within Hebrew tradition, the word appears in the Septuagint

*(Greek) version of the Jewish scriptures or "Old Testament", where it can mean any kind of news or message, until Isaiah, where it takes on the particular meaning of the good news of the beginning of the rule of Yahweh, the "proclamation to the poor". Taken up by the early Jesus movement, the noun was used as a synonym of "the message" or "the preaching", and the verb meant "to bring the message" or "to preach". Koester counts 48 usages in Paul's genuine letters (which of course precede the narrative gospels). Since the message that was preached was, to the early Christian community, indeed "good news", the word was re-invested with its older Greek sense of positive or joyful content, and those who preached the good news, the **evangelium**, were called **evangelists**, or gospel-makers. For Christians, there was no good news other than the good news proclaimed by Jesus: the gospel.*

But it is by no means clear that the writers of the four biblical books we now call gospels thought of their work as a new kind of literary genre to which they attached the name. Mark's opening sentence introduces "The beginning of the gospel of Jesus Christ...", but "the gospel" here is the message, not the book. Luke refers to his own and other similar books as "accounts" or "narratives", not as gospels. Neither Matthew nor John uses the term as a literary description: the titles "Gospel according to..." were all added later.

So while we can analyze the changing meanings of the word "gospel", this does not tell us where the genre of a narrative gospel came from. Scholars have pointed out that, while the gospel-writers were clearly influenced by literary forms developed over centuries of Jewish writing, there was nothing like a gospel narrative in the Hebrew scriptures. The lives of Moses, Samuel and David were well represented in the literature, but no-one had thought to pull their stories into a narrative proto-biography. The form of a narrative gospel, as distinct from the word "gospel" meaning message, was unknown in Jewish tradition. The gospel writers must have taken it from somewhere else, unless Mark invented the form from scratch.

Since first-century Christianity had its roots in both Judaism and the overarching Hellenistic culture (that is, the culture of the Greco-Roman empire), it is not surprising to discover that the form of the four narrative gospels appears to be patterned on a genre of "life" stories or proto-biographies already fully developed within Greek literature. Since Herodotus in the fifth century BCE, Greek story-tellers had put together improving and inspirational tales about their "heroes". A hero was generally someone who had died a noble death, as martyr to a cause. But the Greeks believed that those who died nobly had been destined to do so by Fate. They had literally been born to die their noble death. Moreover, Fate had often signaled the noble end by preliminary signs and wonders, such as a miraculous birth, a supernatural infancy event, and the occasional miracle in adulthood. So the Hellenistic life-narrative of, say, an heroic king or warrior tended to consist of the following components:

1. Origins, often supernatural.

2. Youth - one or more infancy stories, prefiguring the wisdom or nobility that was to come.

3. Adulthood - great deeds, often miraculous.

4. Martyrdom or heroic death, leading to cult status thereafter.

After the death of Socrates, who was neither a king nor a

warrior but no less a hero, a fifth component came to be added between 2 and 3, or 3 and 4: a summary of the great man's teachings.

Lane C McGaughy offers an example:

"The brief biography of Theagenes, as recorded in Pausanias' **Description of Greece**, illustrates well the structure and function of the various parts of a hellenistic biography; (1) Theagenes was conceived as the result of a union between the immortal Heracles (disguised as his father Timosthenes) and his human mother [a sign that he was fated for future greatness]; (2) at age nine Theagenes lugs home a bronze statue (presumably weighing hundreds of pounds) from the town square [a signal that he will become the world's greatest athlete]; (3) a summary of his heroic achievements as an adult: sure enough, he won 1,400 crowns (= gold medals) at various Olympiads and other games and thus fulfilled his preordained destiny; (4) the establishment of a cult to the divinized Theagenes after his death" **("Infancy Narratives and Hellenistic Lives" in Forum, NS 2/1, Spring 1999).**

McGaughy argues that Matthew, Mark, Luke and John used the Hellenistic formula "to provide the framework for the independent units of Jesus tradition that they received from various oral and written sources". Mark omits a miraculous birth story, and John loftily presents his hero as existing before his human birth, but Matthew and Luke follow the template closely. The four gospels are highly original in theological content, but their literary form is clearly derived from well-established Greek-gentile literary conventions.

As with the other gospels, it was written in Greek. Some scholars, notably John Bowker, have found Mark's Greek "crude" and his theological overview "rough"[7]. Philip Sellew of the Jesus Seminar puts the point a little differently, considering it "written in a lively and direct story-teller's style. The Greek prose employed is the informal language of ordinary men and women who made up the common eastern Mediterranean culture in the first century. Instead of the polished literary style of an accomplished artistic writer, in this gospel we find an immediacy and simplicity of description". Nevertheless Sellew accepts that there is "a certain harshness and awkwardness in expression; repetition of favored words and constructions; a sketchiness in character-ization" - features which have led many scholars to believe that "Mark's story is still close somehow, both stylistically and historically, to the oral preaching environment"[8]. Traditionally thought to have been composed in Rome, some scholars now argue for Greek-speaking Syria[9]. Wherever it was written it is unlikely to have been Jerusalem or Judea. By the time of its composition the Jesus movement was already multi-centered, and each center was well advanced in developing its own distinctive traditions and interpretations. Mark may have been written from within a Christian community which particularly venerated John Mark as its patron sage and therefore ascribed its gospel to him - or it could as well be the work of another man named Mark - or even a man not named Mark. Like the other biblical gospels, it carries no by-line, the ascription "according to Mark" being added later to distinguish it from other gospels.

But however close its style to "the oral preaching environment", most if not all was written some forty years after the supposed events which it purports to describe, and the Greek text probably did not reach its final form until well into the second century. For this reason some scholars, such as most of those associated with the Jesus Seminar, are cautious about treating it as a prime source for clues to the authentic words and deeds of Jesus, preferring to place more reliance on the earlier material they find embedded in Matthew and Luke. Others, like Burton Mack, consider Mark (and the later gospels) so mythologized as to be incapable of revealing any reliable information about the man Jesus.

Ranged against the cautious and the skeptical are those scholars who argue for Mark's essential reliability. Theissen and Merz suggest that its originator is not so much an author as "a collector, in so far as he demonstrably takes up written and oral material from the tradition which varies in both form and theology". They detect within the gospel:

• a consecutive *passion narrative* which probably already existed in written form...;
• oral or written (collections of) *miracle stories*;
• apocalyptic traditions, especially the '*Synoptic apocalypse*' Mark 13, which had probably already been fixed in writing;
• *disputations and didactic sayings* for which sometimes a written basis is conjectured; in addition a further tradition of sayings, e.g. the probably already traditional collection of parables and metaphors in Mark 4."[10]

To these proposed "layers", written by different hands at different times, some possibly as early as the 50s, some scholars would add an independently produced parables collection. Theissen and Merz conclude that "some of the material from the tradition presented in Mark goes back a very long way and represents an important source for the reconstruction of the teaching and the life of Jesus"[11]. This sounds promising, until we learn that there is no scholarly consensus on what may reliably be considered early enough to assign to Jesus himself.

In any case, the Jesus Seminar historians tend to be cautious about the ability of scholars to "isolate other sorts of pre-Marcan sources, such as a postulated series of miracle stories, or cycles of controversy dialogues, or collections of mysterious sayings coupled with explanations"[12]. Even Theissen and Merz, after proposing Mark's reliance on a range of earlier sources, consider that because the gospel's "form is determined by the author's theological premises" it is "historically worthless" as a source for a Jesus biography[13]. In this they follow an innovative study of the gospel by Karl Ludwig Schmidt, published in 1919, which argued that its narrative framework was simply a literary device imposed on the material by Mark's editor, who collected each little self-contained story (or "pericope") from oral or the earliest written sources and then made up the narrative links between them in order to suggest a coherent life-story. As the American scholar Burton Mack puts it, Schmidt's bombshell created "havoc":

"[It] effectively brought to an end the old quest for the historical Jesus with its desire for a biography and its unexamined assumption that the basic plot of the narrative gospels was essentially historical record. With the finding that Mark was responsible for the gospel plot, all that was left from the time before Mark were fragments of memory traditions, bits and pieces of oral lore, and perhaps a few collections of parables and stories that someone, for reasons as yet unknown, had hung together by theme"[14].

Mack, then, considers Mark almost entirely fictional. But less radical scholars such as E P Sanders and N T Wright have continued to assert the gospel's essential reliability. There is general agreement, however, that the version of Mark which made it into the canon - the Mark in our Bible - is not a "first edition". Additions to the original (if there was an "original", as distinct from an organically developing text) were clearly made before Mark achieved its canonical form, particularly the series of "supplements" which together impose a "happy ending" (16: 9-20).

More controversially, some scholars[15] have argued that canonical-Mark is not simply an original with later editorial additions but a second-century censored version of an original but now lost "Secret Mark" written in the 70s. This theory derives from the reported discovery in 1958 of part of a previously unknown letter of Clement of Alexandria (c.150-215), according to which the author of Mark revised his original to include "whatever would be appropriate for those who are advancing with respect to gnosis (secret knowledge)" in order to "initiate the hearers into the shrine of the truth which is hidden by seven veils".

On this theory, then, by the late second-century there were at least two distinct versions of Mark in circulation, a "public Mark" for general church consumption and a "secret Mark" for a narrow circle of initiates. But which came first? Did gnostic Christians in the second century add gnostic passages to public-Mark in order to create Secret Mark, or did anti-gnostic Christians remove what they regarded as gnostic-sounding passages from Secret Mark to create a safe public-Mark? And which bears better witness to the acts and sayings of the historical Jesus? The mystery of Secret Mark is explored (or exploded) in the Cameo *Sex, Lies and Fraud in Secret Mark* on page 58.

Mark-as-we-know-it is much the shortest of the biblical gospels. It has no birth or childhood stories and begins with Jesus' baptism by John and his emergence as an independent teacher and exorcist. Philip Sellew engagingly summarizes it as follows:

"Through a rapid tumble of arresting scenes we watch Jesus emerge on the public stage, newly baptized and victorious over Satan, masterful yet oddly mysterious (chap.1). A reluctant champion of the diseased and demon-possessed, Jesus does spiritual battle against the 'unclean spirits' arrayed against him and his cause, 'God's imperial rule' [along with "God's domain", the Jesus Seminar's preferred translation of "the kingdom of God"]. Larger and larger crowds of onlookers are soon drawn to Jesus' doings, crowds who form a chorus that is always curious, often sympathetic, but also frequently rather menacing in aspect (chaps. 2-3). What attracts these crowds is Jesus' quick success as faith healer and exorcist extraordinaire; soon Jesus turns to confront the crowds with strange yet telling speech (4: 1-34). As Jesus and his small band of disciples move through the little towns, barren countryside, and stormy lake that make up the gospel's controlling landscape, the sense of

Cameo: Sex, lies and fraud in Secret Mark

*In 1973 Morton Smith, professor of ancient history at Columbia University, published two books making a sensational claim (**Clement of Alexandria and a Secret Gospel of Mark**, and **The Secret Gospel**).*

Smith described how, fifteen years earlier in 1953, he had been working in the library of the fifth-century monastery of Mar Saba, near Jerusalem, when he came across a copy of a previously unknown letter of Clement of Alexandria (c.150-215). In this letter Clement wrote that the author of Mark had revised his gospel to include "whatever would be appropriate for those who are advancing with respect to gnosis (secret knowledge)" in order to "initiate the hearers into the shrine of the truth which is hidden by seven veils".

*Scholars were intrigued. John Dominic Crossan and Helmut Koester were among the first to hail the discovery of the letter and its quotations from "Secret Mark". As Koester commented in **The Complete Gospels** (p 410), it "led many to conclude that canonical Mark is not the direct descendent of that early version of Mark used by Matthew and Luke, but rather of the Secret Gospel of Mark. In other words, what moderns have come to know as the Gospel of Mark is in fact a version of Secret Mark from which some, but not all, of the esoteric passages have been removed. If this is true, then the Secret Gospel of Mark will have provided us with some rather striking new information about the early transmission history of the Gospel of Mark".*

One reason why the existence of a Secret Mark was embraced enthusiastically is that it seemed to solve a problem that had long puzzled New Testament scholars. Secret Mark as quoted in the

Clementine letter has a significant story which is missing from Mark as we now know it. This story tells of Jesus raising a young man from the dead after visiting the man's tomb and rolling away the stone. The story is placed between canonical-Mark's 10.34 and 10.35, where some scholars had long perceived a strange lack of continuity, suggesting that something is missing. The young man is dressed "only in a linen cloth draped over his naked body". Once raised, the young man is initiated into the "mystery of God's domain".

Scholars saw that this story appeared to make sense of a curious passage in canonical-Mark 14:51-52 which had long baffled commentators. After the disciples fled at Jesus' arrest, "there followed him a certain young man, having a linen cloth cast about his naked body; and the young man laid hold on him". Canonical Mark tells us nothing more about this mysterious young man who was evidently more courageous and faithful than the disciples, unless we are supposed to understand that he is the same "young man" who is found by the women sitting in Jesus' empty tomb and telling them "He is risen" (16: 4-8). But the Secret Mark story of an identically-described young man whom Jesus raises from the dead after rolling away the stone from his tomb appeared to put these disjointed references in a new light. The identity of the youth and the point of the story becomes clear: as Jesus had rolled away the young man's tomb-stone, the young man had done the same for Jesus. The initiate's resurrection by Jesus foreshadows or prefigures that of Jesus himself, as if the youth were saying "See, he is risen - as he raised me!"

But even as scholars debated the relevance of all this to the quest for the historical Jesus, suspicion began to grow that Morton Smith's discovery might not be what it seemed. Particular attention was focused on a passage about this mysterious youth. "The young man looked at him intently and loved him; and he began pleading with him that he might be with him... And when it was evening the young man came to him, wearing a linen cloth over his naked body. He stayed with him that night, for Jesus was teaching him the mystery of the Kingdom of God."

Morton Smith interpreted this as meaning that Jesus and the young man had sex together to seal their spiritual unity. After all, the youth was naked except for a linen cloth. He spent the night with Jesus, being initiated into the mysteries of the kingdom, which, Smith argued, freed him from "the laws ordained for and in the lower world", adding that freedom from the law "may have resulted in completion of the spiritual union by physical union". For good measure Smith suggests that "manipulation, too, was probably involved; the stories of Jesus' miracles give a very large place to the use of his hands".

These clear imputations of homo-erotic activity predictably enraged many orthodox Christians, and some of Smith's fellow scholars began to smell a rat. Among the first doubters was his old Harvard Divinity School professor Arthur Darby Nock who confessed to an instinct that the Clement letter was not genuine. Smith had photographed three pages of the copy he had seen at Mar Saba, and the writing was widely accepted as an eighteenth-century hand. Was it, then, an eighteenth-century forgery? Others were prepared to accept the authenticity of the letter but wondered whether, known or unbeknown to Clement, the text of Secret Mark itself was genuine or a second-century forgery. Much discussed in private was the suspicion that Smith himself was the forger, and after Smith's death the accusation was made explicit by his own former student and research assistant Jacob Neusner, who called it "the forgery of the century". Another commentator, Donald Harman Akenson, suggested in 2000 that Smith's claim to have discovered the Clement letter and its Secret Mark quotations was "a nice ironic gay joke at the expense of... self-important scholars".

*This did not put an end to the controversy. Some scholars, self-important or not, continued to argue for a Secret Mark, even if they distanced themselves from Smith's interpretation that, for the "spiritually advanced" in Mark's community, unity with Jesus and initiation into the mystery of the kingdom involved mutual masturbation or sodomy. Only forensic examination of the manuscript could resolve the issue - but it was soon apparent that this was not an option. Writing up the controversy in 2003, Bart D Ehrman reported that the librarian of the Greek Patriarchate in Jerusalem, into whose custody the manuscript had been placed, had cut the Clement letter from the book into which it had supposedly been copied, and claimed that he no longer knew where the pages were. Ehrman concludes: "Did the librarian hide the pages, to keep scholars from rifling through the monks' treasured possessions looking for lost Gospels? Did he burn the pages simply to get them off his hands? Where are they now? Do they still exist?... What is certain is that no-one has carefully examined the book itself, and it may be that no-one ever will". (Ehrman, **Lost Christianities**, pp 70-84, whose entertaining account of the whole business I have followed here).*

What the controversy emphasizes is the problems and pitfalls serious scholars face in evaluating copies of copies of copies of lost originals, especially in a field where forgeries ancient and modern are abundant. Is Smith's Secret Mark genuine? Could it be a very early text telling us something we are told nowhere else

> *about Jesus and his teachings? Or is it a late addition, showing us how Jesus' teachings came to be distorted a century and a half after his death? Or is it an ancient invention, or an eighteenth century forgery, or an elaborate joke at the expense of scholars who take themselves too seriously? Or is it the sad and irresponsible product of a scholar indulging a particular form of homo-erotic fantasy? Or could it still turn out to be a genuine gospel, once considered holy scripture by a Christian community, but now discarded because of a mischievous or scandalous interpretation?*
>
> *My guess is that Smith forged the letter and thereby invented Secret Mark. But as Bart Ehrman suggests, we'll probably never know for sure.*

inevitable confrontation and foreboding grows stronger and stronger. Opposition to his practices and his disciples' habits comes from social and religious leaders, both those in Galilee and others summoned from Jerusalem (e.g., 3: 19-22; 7: 1-21). Eventually Jesus himself will lead his group to the capital city for the final confrontation that leads to his arrest and death"[16].

A dominant theme in Mark is the essentially mysterious nature of Jesus and his mission. Not only are his closest disciples mystified as to his real identity, but Jesus himself seems intent on keeping them in the dark. When he does reveal his grim mission - to be punished, to die and to rise from the dead - he commands the disciples to keep it to themselves. This secrecy is peculiar to Mark, and some scholars think it makes little sense unless understood as a survival of a genuine Secret Mark, with its gnostic insistence that full understanding of the mysteries was always to be reserved to an initiated few. William Wrede, on the other hand, proposed that Mark's picture of Jesus as one who wanted to keep his divine identity secret until his death and resurrection is best understood as a late-first-century understanding projected back into Jesus' lifetime. Mark's problem, Wrede suggested, was that many of his readers had known Jesus personally and would say "That's not the Jesus I remember! He never claimed to be the Son of God!" - to which Mark would respond, "You were obviously not in on the secret, which could only be revealed after his death!" This century-old interpretation, which we shall return to in Chapter 11, has been revived by several scholars, notably Gerd Theissen[17].

Scholars seeking the holy grail of a strictly historical biography of Jesus rather than a life-story tainted by later theologizing have tended to conclude, with such very different interpreters as the Jesus Seminar, Vermes, Theissen and Merz, that the value of Mark as history is limited. Where there has been far less agreement - indeed, a scholarly stand-off - is in the interpretation of Jesus' proclamation that "the kingdom of God is at hand": his very first words, in Mark's account (1: 15). The question of whether Jesus himself preached an "apocalyptic" message or whether apocalyptic words were put into his mouth by his followers after his death remains perhaps the most contentious of all the controversies dividing modern scholars, and we shall find ourselves visiting it a number of times before turning to it in our end-chapter on the end-time in Part III.

How far and how quickly copies of early versions of Mark's narrative circulated among the widely dispersed Jesus movement in the 70s and 80s is impossible to say. We know little about how "books" were "published" in those days[18]. Nor may we assume that it was the only gospel in circulation. Some scholars believe an early version of the gospel of Thomas had preceded Mark, as had other written sayings-collections, and other gospels of which we now know little or nothing may already have been circulated, as many more were in the following century. It is possible that Mark is simply one of several, distinguished from others by the accident of its survival. "Accident", on the other hand, may be a misjudgment. Mark survived, perhaps, because its developed Christology best served the changing needs and understandings of the dominant factions of the

Jesus movement, and was so firmly established by the time Matthew and Luke arrived on the publishing scene that it could not be dislodged.

Matthew

Matthew was long assumed to be the first gospel written, simply because it had traditionally been placed first in the New Testament. Even when modern scholars began to look at the gospels critically, with a pioneer study by Johann Griesbach in 1776 that drew attention to the very different nature of Matthew, Mark and Luke on one hand and John on the other, the priority of Matthew was assumed. Griesbach actually proposed that Mark was the last of the three synoptics, composed as a shortened and harmonized version of Matthew and Luke - a kind of *Readers' Digest* edition. But since the 1830s the overwhelming majority of scholars have agreed that Matthew came after Mark, and current opinion dates it in its present form after 80 CE and before 100 CE, most likely in the 80s.

Like Mark, it was anonymous, and its attribution to Matthew the tax-collector is again a speculation of the inventive bishop Papias who is quoted by later church fathers as claiming that "Matthew organized the sayings in the Hebrew language, but everyone has translated them as best he could". No scholar now believes in a Hebrew original for this Greek gospel, and the attribution to "Matthew" is used to designate either the unknown author/editor or the text itself. Theissen and Merz suggest that it originated in the Greek Syrian churches, because it is the first gospel to use the Greek word *ecclesia* meaning congregation or church, it refers to Judea as "beyond the Jordan" (4: 24), and it tells of Jesus' message reverberating "throughout Syria"[19]. (Note, incidentally, how much of the early material is now thought by modern scholars to have originated in Syria, suggesting that this may have been where the Jesus movement was strongest around the end of the first century, due in part to mass migration in the wake of the persecution of all forms of Judaism that followed the failure of the Jewish revolt against Rome of 66-74 CE)

Matthew seems to have been produced to meet a new situation in the

Jesus movement, or that part of the movement grouped around a "Matthean community"[20], which made necessary a radical revision and amplification of Mark. A decade or so after the destruction of the temple and the fall of Jerusalem which shattered the entire Jewish religious structure, including both Christian and non-Christian parties, the Matthean community, explains Bernard Brandon Scott,

"...is engaged in intense debate with rabbinic Judaism that is itself creating new institutions to replace the destroyed temple. Both groups are trying to define themselves... Prior to the temple's destruction there were many different competing interpretations of what it meant to be an Israelite. But the destruction of Jerusalem set in motion for Judaism and Christianity a long process of consolidation and self-definition that reached its first definitive form around the beginning of the third century. In Judaism this process received a powerful impetus with the triumph of Pharisaism and rabbinic Judaism. In Christianity this process eventuated in what was to become the orthodoxy reflected in the early creeds and institutions. The Matthean group, recently expelled from the synagogue (5: 11), is contesting with the synagogue over who is the true Israel. The Christians and Jesus stand in the line of John the Baptist and the prophets. For this reason the summary of Jesus' message is the same as that of John the Baptist (3: 2; 4: 17), and John, the last of the prophets, baptizes Jesus. The Pharisees erected the tombs of the prophets (23: 29) and they persecute the Christians who follow the prophets (5: 12). The line of true Israel is, then, the prophets, John the Baptist, Jesus, and the Matthean community."

Brandon Scott continues:

"This forging of a self-definition over and against emerging rabbinic Judaism is important to remember in reading Matthew's gospel. The debate is not between Judaism and Christianity, nor between Jew and Gentile, but between two parties within Judaism. Both groups are withdrawing and consolidating into antagonistic camps. The rejection of the Pharisees in Matthew implies neither the rejection of Judaism nor the Law. Even though the Pharisees sit in the chair of Moses (23: 2), yet the standard epithet for them is 'phonies' or 'impostors'. Both Jesus and John the Baptist address them as 'spawn of Satan' (3:7; 12:34; 23:33) and John prophesies that their end is near. As 'phonies' they practice their religion in public (6:1-2); they cleanse the outside of the cup, but inside they are 'full of greed and dissipation' (23:25). As for the Law, not even the smallest part will pass away (5:18). Matthew portrays Jesus as the true and authoritative interpreter of the Law. He restores it to its original meaning: 'As you know, our ancestors were told... But I tell you...' (5:21)."[21]

It is well to remember, however, that religious differences between Jewish Christians and Jewish Pharisees at the *end* of the first century tell us nothing about the historical Jesus shortly after the *beginning* of the century. The task of excavating an original Jesus from the accumulated theological deposits of several decades has to start with identifying and separating out the earliest layers of the tradition. Modern scholarship sees Matthew as borrowing heavily not only from Mark but from a second source, Q (common to Matthew and Luke), and another called M (found only in Matthew), all of which were circulating before the final break between Judaism and Christianity, which imminent event gave Matthew his particular slant. What that leaves behind, of more interest to students of folk-lore than historians, is (i) Matthew's speculative (if not entirely invented) genealogy (1:1-17) tracing the descent of Jesus from Abraham through David to "Joseph the husband of Mary, of whom was born Jesus"; (ii) his distinctive version of the miraculous birth story (virgin conception, guiding star, three wise men, first-born killings, flight into Egypt); and (iii) elaborate expositions of Jewish scriptural texts proving, as Matthew sought to demonstrate to pious Jewish readers, that Jesus was the Messiah whose coming was foretold by the prophets. These are the glosses of the late first-century Matthew community, and important as they are in helping us understand the infancy of Christianity, most scholars would agree that they tell us nothing of significance in the quest for Jesus the Galilean born nearly a century before Matthew was written[22].

More problematic is Matthew's picture of Jesus, along with Mark's, as a prophet of the imminent end-time: apocalypse soon. Matthew evidently shares Paul's belief (or has perhaps learnt it from him) in an early second coming which will inaugurate a new epoch where "Christ" will reign with his saints. What is problematic, here as with Mark, is not whether Matthew's Jesus community believed this - it evidently did - but whether Jesus the man had himself believed and taught it.

Prominent in the Q material used by Matthew but not utilized by Mark (perhaps because it was unknown to him) are Matthew's five discourses or sermons of Jesus, beginning with what is now known as the Sermon on the Mount (chapters 5-7). These are clearly used to serve Matthew's polemical purpose. He too was writing theology, not history; so for the modern historian there remains hard analytical and interpretive work to be done in locating an original Jesus in the sayings, even when they have been tentatively surmised from embedded sources.

Luke

Luke's gospel is generally regarded as having been written a little after Matthew, probably before 100 CE (but a minority of scholars, including Burton Mack, have proposed a second-century date). Theissen and Merz suggest it was "composed in a large city west of Palestine", adding that "the author knows the Mediterranean well, and his horizon embraces the whole of the inhabited world". For him, "the sea" is the Mediterranean where for Mark it is Galilee, which Luke demotes to a lake[23]. The community Luke is addressing is very different from Matthew's Syrian or eastern constituency, and it has clearly evolved a significantly different theology. In Luke's community gentiles were strongly represented and probably dominant. One of the most fascinating and as yet unresolved puzzles is the relationship of these different Jesus schools or communities to each other. Were they geographically separated in such a way that they remained largely ignorant of each other, or at least of their theological differences? Or did they sometimes co-exist, easily or not, within the same town or city, much as today's Catholic, Baptist, Pentecostalist and Mormon churches face each other across the marketplace, vying for custom with their competing truths?

Once again, attribution of the third gospel to the physician Luke mentioned in the Colossians letter (2:11) is purely traditional, though scholars accept that the gospel and its sequel, Acts, were written by the same author. Both were addressed to an unknown Christian named Theophilus, and Acts refers in its opening words to "the former treatise", clearly meaning Luke's gospel. But major differences and contradictions between Acts' account of Paul's missions and Paul's own letters, coupled with Luke's striking refusal to count Paul an apostle, make it highly unlikely that the author was a companion and colleague of Paul, as tradition suggested.

Luke begins his gospel with an acknowledgment that by the time it is being written there were many other versions in circulation, in which eyewitnesses and "ministers of the word" had made "declaration of those things which are most surely believed among us"; but, he says, "it seemed good to me also, having had perfect understanding of all things from the very first", to write a new account to set the record straight. Whether Luke had read a copy of Matthew and decided that its emphasis needed correction we cannot know for sure, though it seems likely. But it is clear that, like Matthew, he knew Mark and Q, since these are strongly incorporated within his own work, along with a large amount of material which is peculiar to him, designated L by modern scholars. As for the "many" other gospels he dismisses in his opening sentence, all have been lost, unless early versions of some of the so-called "apocryphal" gospels were already circulating.

Luke is a leftist. His Jesus is a champion of the poor, the oppresssed, the exploited and mistreated, the outsider. As Robert Miller puts it, "Jesus congratulates them for belonging to God's kingdom (6:20-21) and warns against the spiritual dangers of wealth (6:24-25; 8:11-15; 12:13-21; 16:13-15, 19-31; 18:18-25). Among the outcasts are sinners, to whom Jesus' mission is especially directed (5:32; 19:10)... He uses the despised toll collectors and Samaritans as examples of positive religious behavior (10:29-37; 17:11-19; 18:10-14; 19:2-10)"[24].

Luke moderates the message of Mark, Matthew and Paul that Jesus was an apocalyptic prophet of the imminent end-time. He downplays ideas of an early second coming and the beginning of the end of the world. Where Mark had had Jesus warn that the kingdom of God was "at hand", Luke's parallel passage merely records that Jesus "taught in their synagogues" (4:15). Luke's Jesus tells his disciples the parable of the nobleman and the servants expressly to correct their mistaken belief that "the kingdom of God should immediately appear" (19:11-27).

Answering the Pharisees' taunting question as to when exactly this kingdom of God was going to arrive, Luke's Jesus answers quite differently from Mark's or Matthew's Jesus whose answer may be summed up as "any moment now". Luke's Jesus, on the contrary, says "The kingdom of God cometh not with observation: Neither shall they say, Lo here! or, Lo there! for, behold, the kingdom of God is within [or among] you" (17.20). Again, he tells his disciples not to panic when they hear of "wars and commotions": "the end is not by and by" (21:9), or in the Jesus Seminar's Scholars Version, "it doesn't mean the end is about to come". This flatly contradicts Mark's Jesus, who says that the "wars and rumors of wars" are indeed the prelude to earthquakes, famines and troubles which are "the beginnings of sorrows", or, Scholars Version, "mark the beginning of the final agonies" (13:6-8). Luke's Jesus (or Luke himself) has an altogether more subtle and nuanced view of the end-time and the nature of the kingdom of heaven.

Luke is also the first of the evangelists to introduces the idea of Jesus as "savior" (2:11), which Miller points out is "a Hellenistic title for divine deliverers". The contemporary cult of the Emperor Augustus declared the emperor himself both "savior" and "son of God". Miller draws attention to the author's strong emphasis on the universalism of Christianity, which he calls in Acts "the Way". "Jesus' offer of salvation comes first to Israel, but is meant for the whole world (2:30-32; 3:6; 13:28-29)... Luke's writing shows sensitivity for a Gentile audience. He regularly translates or omits Aramaic terms in his sources, and often substitutes Greek names for Semitic ones. He omits Mark's story about the Syro-Phoenician woman (7:24-30), the one story most likely to offend gentiles [since Mark's Jesus refers to them as 'dogs']. He depicts Jesus freely interacting with non-Jews and using them as positive examples in his teaching (4:25, 27; 7:1-10; 10:29-37; 17:11-19)"[25].

These very different first-century Jesuses are reflected in the very different Jesuses of twentieth and twenty-first century scholars. The Jesus Seminar Fellows reject a narrowly Jewish and anti-gentile Jesus, while for Geza Vermes it is precisely the most typically Jewish sayings which point to a fully kosher Jesus.

John

The fourth canonical gospel has been recognized by scholars since the eighteenth century as presenting a very different Jesus story from that of the three synoptic gospels. Indeed, this should be clear to a casual reader with no pretension to scholarship. John's Jesus is not born of Mary: he existed from the beginning of time. He was the *logos* or word, the essence or manifestation of God himself. In Mark and Matthew Jesus is a divinely appointed prophet, God's agent or "son", preaching the kingdom of God to the Jews. In Luke, by contrast, he is a radical wisdom-teacher and God's appointed savior of the world (perhaps in direct and deliberate challenge to the savior-title claimed by the Augustan dynasty). But in John he *is* God, and the kingdom of God is "my kingdom", the kingdom of Jesus (18:36).

Unlike the synoptics' Jesus, John's never uses parables. Far from inventing or re-inventing the genre, he knows nothing of it. He speaks like a Greek orator in long, literary discourses rather than popular aphorisms, has no "sermon on the mount" (or plain), has very little ethical teaching, performs no exorcisms, and has almost nothing to say about the "kingdom of God" (just the one reference in 3:3: "except a man be born again he cannot see the kingdom of God", and that in 18.36 already referred to, where the kingdom is not God's but his own). The synoptics' Jesus refuses to perform miracles simply to prove to doubters that he has divine or superhuman power. John's Jesus performs all his miracles expressly as "signs" to demonstrate that he is the incarnate Son of God. (John Dominic Crossan and Robert T Fortna have suggested that whoever wrote or compiled John drew his signs stories from a much earlier written source constituting a now lost "Signs Gospel"). John's Jesus even seems to live in a different age, one wholly lacking the mixed world of Sadduces, Zealots and scribes who give the synoptics' Jesus so much trouble, and equally absent are the poor, publicans and prostitutes befriended by Luke's Jesus in particular. John's altogether more lofty, literary and philosophical Jesus is clearly above such embarrassing vulgarities.

This Jesus is primarily concerned to tell the world who he is, while the synoptics' Jesus leaves his hearers to work that out for themselves - perhaps because the ambiguities which are inherent in the question had yet to be resolved by the church when they were written. Many of John's Jesus' lengthy discourses begin with "I am", which, as Robert Fortna says, "breaks upon its hearers with shock and rage" since it appears to deliberately invoke Yahweh's own self-description "I am that I am"[26]. "I am," says John's Jesus, the bread of life (6.35), the light of the world (8.12), he who existed even before Abraham (8.58), the good shepherd (10:11), the resurrection and the life (11.25), the true vine (15:1), and the way, truth, life and only means by which anyone can come to the Father (14:6). Jesus makes none of these claims in Mark, Matthew or Luke. The synoptics' Jesus just doesn't talk like that.

There is now all but total consensus among scholars that John was the last of the four biblical gospels to be written, no earlier than the very end of the first century and perhaps well into the second. John T Robinson of *Honest to God* fame put an argument for the priority of John, but it failed to convince his colleagues in either church or academy. Burton Mack has suggested that the two volume Luke/Acts may have been composed after John, but this too has failed to gather mainstream support. An early second-century date would account for the striking absence in his gospel of Sadduces and Zealots, both of which groups had by then faded from the scene. The gospel's fierce polemic against "the Jews" suggests a period after the final expulsion of Jewish Christians from the synogogues, a process which was certainly well under way but not yet complete when Matthew was written, but which forced them to join with gentile Christians in making a new religion, the process Luke is beginning to describe. Historians have suggested that this seems to have reached some form of climax or crisis in the 90s, most decisively in the Transjordan territories ruled by Agrippa II, where Jews functioned as magistrates and were in a position to order the expulsion of "Christians" as heretics.

This final break, no doubt enforced with great bitterness and ill-feeling, is seen by many scholars as explaining John's anti-Jewish rhetoric. Matthew had written his gospel while the status of Jesus was still a matter of dispute *within* Judaism, complicated by the rise of a parallel gentile Jesus movement; and the author's railings against "the Pharisees" and "chief priests" seem to reflect a polemic by one set of Jews against another. John's is a polemic of excommunicated Jews and their gentile allies against those who had finally kicked them out. Both writers, Matthew and John, unconsciously read back the conditions of their own times to the period of Jesus' ministry some three generations earlier, as if it had been Jesus himself who had forced the break[27].

Once again it is only early church tradition that names John as the author. Irenaeus (late second century) and Eusebius (late third and early fourth) assert that this was John the son of Zebedee, described in Matthew

(17.1) as one of the three disciples who was present with Jesus at his "transfiguration" on a high mountain, and thus one of his inner circle. The final chapter of John, clearly added later, simply ascribes the gospel to an unnamed "disciple whom Jesus loved" (21: 20-4), but Robert Fortna comments that "it is not altogether certain that this Beloved Disciple, as he has usually been known, was in fact a real person"[28]. Scholars are virtually unanimous in rejecting the tradition that a contemporary or disciple of Jesus wrote the book (or, indeed, the three New Testament epistles, the book of Revelation, and a non-canonical Acts ascribed to the same "John"). Not only would he have been very old indeed but he would have to have had a phenomenal memory to recall even the gist, let alone the wording, of those long and intricate speeches, which are recorded nowhere else.

The point is sharply made by Geza Vermes (who dates the gospel as late as 100 to 110) in *The Changing Face of Jesus*. Contesting the tradition originated by Irenaeus that the disciple John had lived to a great age in Ephesus and produced the fourth gospel there, Vermes notes the sophisticated, elegant, philosophical language and comments in his dry, understated way: "To envisage as the author... an 'uneducated and common' Galilean fisherman (Acts 4:13), who was a centenarian give or take a few years, yet not only still creative but fully at home in Hellenistic philosophical and mystical speculation, requires a leap of the imagination which seems to be beyond the reasonable... The total irreconcilability of the fourth gospel with the synoptics, combined with the late date of its composition, would strongly militate against an author who was an eye-witness of the historical Jesus... Judging from his work, [the author] was either an educated Jew of mystical leanings who also had some acquaintance with Hellenistic mysticism, or, considering the evangelist's violent detestation of the Jews, a cultured Greek who first toyed with Judaism and subsequently embraced Christianity"[29].

Vermes is equally dismissive of the popular church-sponsored explanation for the fourth gospel's distinctiveness, namely that it deliberately avoids repeating what had already been told in the synoptics, preferring instead to enrich their incomplete accounts with a divinely inspired spiritualized biography proving that Jesus was indeed God. "No critical reading of the four gospels justifies such an understanding of John. For it is obvious to any religiously unbiased reader that if the Fourth Evangelist is right, his forerunners must be mistaken or vice versa." Then, referring to specific contradictions between the two accounts, he continues: "The synoptics and John cannot be simultaneously correct when the former assign to Jesus a public career lasting a year, while John stretches it to two or possibly three consecutive Passover festivals during Jesus' ministry in Galilee and Judaea. Likewise, if John's dating of the crucifixion to the day *before* the Passover, i.e.14 Nissan [the Jewish Pesach or Passover month], is accurate, the synoptics who depict the last supper as a Passover dinner and place the events leading to the execution of Jesus on 15 Nissan must be in error. Or to Hebraize and suitably adapt the English proverb to the Passover situation, you can't have your unleavened bread and eat it!"[30]

Scholars are not agreed on whether John knew and consciously adapted the synoptic tradition or wrote independently of it. A few scholars have argued for John's knowledge of all three synoptics. Theissen and Merz suggest that, in taking over the narrative gospel form, John was "presumably indicating a knowledge of at least one synoptic gospel". Robert Fortna, probably speaking for most of his Jesus Seminar colleagues, inclines to a different assessment: "This gospel's uniqueness does not stem, apparently, from a deliberate intent to differ from the synoptic gospels, for it was probably independent of them literarily. It overlaps with them in the *narratives* - of Jesus' miracles and of his 'passion' and resurrection - but this overlap is probably due to common sources underlying the various gospels"[31].

Whatever their differences of detail, scholars are broadly agreed that John's gospel derives from a particular Jesus community, perhaps in Transjordan, Egypt or Asia Minor (modern Anatolia in Turkey), which cherished its own memories of Jesus and maintained its own sources, some unique to itself and some common to other Jesus groups. The community may have been led by a teacher who was understood by his followers to wear the mantle of Jesus' "beloved disciple". It was familiar with both Jewish tradition and Greek literature and philosophy. It was thoroughly Hellenized. It may have had links, suggested within its text, with other communities later condemned as heretically "gnostic". It had the confidence to assert its own version of the Jesus story, and its own interpretation of Jesus as fully God incarnate. After some initial hesitation, the gospel was adopted by the wider church as authentic and added to the canon. More than any other gospel or New Testament document, including Paul's letters, it profoundly influenced the development of church doctrine as it came to be defined in the official creeds: the doctrine of Jesus as the unique Christ, the second person of the Trinity, "very God, begotten, not created".

Mainstream scholars are agreed on something else. John's gospel is of far less value as a source for the authentic sayings and doings of the historical Jesus than its three synoptic predecessors. Its grandeur and beauty of expression, its high spirituality and lofty Christology have ensured it a permanent place in the hearts and minds of Christian believers (who long managed to remain blind to its incipient anti-semitism, at least until Mel Gibson used and abused its rhetoric in his notorious film *The Passion of the Christ*). It is an invaluable source on Christian, Jewish and Greek culture at the junction of the first and second centuries. But it comes far too late to carry anything other than the faintest echo of the words of a Galilean Jesus of the late 20s or early 30s, who would simply not have understood what John's sophisticated, philosophical Jesus was on about. John's Jesus is a haunting avatar, the "human form divine", beloved of generations of Christians. But he is John's inspired literary creation. His magnificent discourses come from John's own fertile imagination. The fourth gospel introduces us to a religious teacher of remarkable power and originality: but that teacher is John, not Jesus.

Cameo: Jews? Israelites? Judeans?

The New Testament polemic against "the Jews", particularly as presented in Matthew and John, has festered into virulent anti-Semitism in periods of Christian history right up to the present day (as exemplified in Mel Gibson's notorious box-office dollar-earner **The Passion of the Christ**)*. To counter ignorant racist readings, many scholars have been at pains to point out that it was Jews themselves who accused leaders of "the Jews" of rejecting and eventually killing Jesus. Thus one party of Jews accused another party of Jews of killing a Jew. Geza Vermes, writing in* **The Guardian** *newspaper (27/2/04), asks: "So can the New Testament as such be blamed for fomenting anti-semitism? A nuanced reply is that its stories about Jesus were not originally conceived as anti-Jewish: they were meant to describe a family row between various Jewish groups. But in non-Jewish surroundings they were liable to receive an anti-Jewish interpretation. Anti-semitism is not in the New Testament text but in the eyes and in the minds of some of its readers". This, however, seems a generous assessment by a Jewish scholar when we are faced with Matthew's account of the Jewish mob saying "His blood be on us, and on our children" (37:25).*

The Jesus Seminar's Scholars Version of John translates the stereotyped opponents of Jesus as "Judeans" rather than "the Jews". This is in line with the adoption by the Seminar of the following three-phase terminology for those practising the religion ascribed to Abraham and Moses.

• "Israel", "Israelites" and "Israelite religion" are used for the first temple period (prior to 586 BCE, when the southern kingdom of Judea or Judah was conquered by the Babylonians and Solomon's temple was destroyed);

• *"Judea", "Judeans" and "Judean religion" are used for the second temple period (520 BCE to 70 CE, when worship centered on the temple rebuilt about 520 BCE and greatly extended by Herod the Great between 34 and 4 BCE);*

• *"Jews" and "Judaism" are used for the post-70 CE period when, with Herod's temple destroyed, the religion of the rabbis, the Talmud and the synagogue replaced temple-centered forms.*

*These differentiated terms have seemed to some pedantic but they serve to remind us that there were different phases and tendencies in the religion of those who came to be lumped together as "the Jews". Thus, in the Scholars Version the placard over the cross reads "Jesus the Nazarene, the King of the Judeans", and it is "the Judeans" who demand his crucifixion. Robert Miller explains in **The Complete Gospels** (p 195): "This terminological adjustment has been a long time in coming. The failure to observe crucial transitions in the history of Judaism has contributed to the tragic history of anti-semitism among Christians, which the new terminology will help put to an end. Further, it will set the historical record straight."*

To summarize:

For their source material on the historical Jesus scholars have turned first to the earliest Christian documents, the letters of Paul and the narrative gospels. But while Paul's letters tell us a great deal about his own theology, they say remarkably little about the historical Jesus, whose life and sayings are of far less importance to him than his death and resurrection. The four gospels represent the first attempts to give Jesus something resembling a human biography, setting his reported words and deeds in a narrative framework. But the earliest of them was written some forty years and the latest some seventy years after the events they describe and interpret. By the time of their composition the Jesus movement had spread across the known world and was already culturally and theologically astonishingly diverse. Each of the gospels therefore has its own distinctive ideological or theological emphasis. These books remain prime sources for historical Jesus scholarship, but because they mix oral tradition, accumulated mythology and theological spin, the objective historian has a great deal of work to do in disentangling history from mystery in order to unearth the flesh-and-blood Jesus.

One approach has been to work out where the narrative gospels may have drawn on earlier texts, now lost. The earlier the text, the closer to the historical Jesus, the greater chance that it preserves the gist of his own teaching. In the following chapter we shall follow this line of enquiry, before turning to the Christian literature that never made it into the approved biblical canon.

Notes to Chapter 4

1 Crossan, *Historical Jesus*, 427, and Koester, *Introduction to NT* Vol 2, 112

2 Dates proposed by Koester and accepted by Crossan. Some scholars propose slightly later dates. Scholars are divided on whether the other letters bearing Paul's name were written by him. 1 and 2 Timothy and Titus are considered second-century "pious forgeries", and Hebrews makes no claim to be by Paul.

3 Theissen, *Historical Jesus*, 55

4 Bowker, *Dictionary*. Robert Eisenman seems to assume James's authorship in *James the Brother of Jesus*.

5 Vermes, *Changing Face*, 209

6 as above, 148

7 Bowker, *Dictionary*, 618

8 Sellew in *Complete Gospels*, 11

9 as above, 10, and Thiessen, *New Testament*, 97

10 Theissen, *Historical Jesus*, 27

11 as above, 27

12 Sellew in *Complete Gospels*, 10

13 Theissen, *Historical Jesus*, 27. For good measure they add that "the same goes for Luke, Mark and John", all shaped according to their author's theological premises rather than by a primary concern to get the history right.

14 Mack, *Lost Gospel Q*, 24. Mack is commenting on Schmidt's *Der Rahmen der Geschichte Jesu* ("The Framework of the Story of Jesus"), Trowitzsch, Berlin, 1919.

15 e.g. Crossan, various, and and Helmut Koester, 'History and Development of Mark's Gospel' in *Ancient Christian Gospels*, Philadelphia and London 1990.

16 Sellew in *Complete Gospels*, 9

17 Theissen, *New Testament*, 99-102

18 Ancient writings, especially religious scriptures, were written on scrolls made of lengths of parchment sewn together. These could be many feet long and were consequently far too unwieldy for easy circulation. By the late first century, however, writings began to be inscribed on papyrus sheets, not sewn together in a scroll but stitched together to make a book with wooden or leather covers. This innovation amounted to a revolution in written communication, since books were far more portable. It seems likely that the early gospel writers made use of the new technology, writing *books*, not *scrolls*.

19 Theissen, *Historical Jesus*, 30

20 Many scholars now believe that each of the biblical gospels and most of the early extra-biblical ones, such as Q and Thomas, are best understood as the product of a particular Jesus-movement community (or assembly, or church) which had developed its own distinctive theological emphases. The written gospel is seen as the community's attempt to put its own interpretation of the Jesus story on record, with authorship attributed to a particularly revered apostle or charismatic leader to give it the stamp of authenticity or inspiration.

21 Brandon Scott in *Complete Gospels*, 56-7, quoting from the Jesus Seminar's own translation (Scholars Version).

22 For two very different but equally illuminating analyses of the nativity stories see Vermes, *The Nativity*, and Miller, *Born Divine*.

23 Theissen, *Historical J*, 32

24 Miller in *Complete Gospels*, 116

25 as above, 117

26 Fortna in *Complete Gospels*, 198

27 Geza Vermes in *The Changing Face of Jesus* p. 30 emphasizes that "Christian commentators" are mistaken in supposing there was any formal break between the synagogues and Jesus in Jesus' own lifetime. "Synagogues were local places of worship, and in larger cities.... there were many of them. So exclusion from one could easily be followed by joining another. The joke about the shipwrecked Jew building two synagogues on his desert island so as to have one where he never sets foot may express a timeless truth." The break came in John's day, not Jesus'.

28 Fortna in *Complete Gospels*, 197

29 Vermes, *Changing Face*, 10

30 as above, 8

31 Theissen, *Historical Jesus*, 35. Fortna in *Complete Gospels*, 196

5

JESUS BEFORE CHRISTIANITY

In discussing the biblical gospels in the previous chapter we noted that each of them drew material from earlier sources now lost. For nearly two centuries scholars have tried to identify and isolate these sources in an effort to close that problematic gap between Jesus' life in the 20s and the gospel records of it written nearly half a century later.

No manuscript copies of any such sources have survived. But nineteenth-century scholars worked out that there are clear traces of them embedded in the gospels as they have come down to us. Not only their existence but, many scholars say, their detailed content can be inferred and reconstructed from a critical examination of the texts we do have. What are these lost works, and what is the process by which scholars claim to have at least partially recovered them?

1. *Q*, *M* and *L*

When the nineteenth-century pioneers began to analyze the contents of the gospels, only the four now familiar to us as part of the New Testament were available for detailed scrutiny and study. While it was known that other gospels had existed, it was generally accepted that these had been excluded from the canon for good reason, as unreliable or heretical.

It was to these canonical gospels, then, that the nineteenth-century German pioneers in "biblical criticism" devoted their attention, and they noted that Matthew, Mark and Luke contain much common material, often in strikingly similar or even identical wording. These three gospels were therefore described as "synoptic", meaning that they give parallel accounts of events from the same point of view or under the same general aspect. In this they are distinct from John, which was written even later and from a very different perspective, apparently using material from sources unknown to the others.

A consensus soon developed among textual analysts that Mark was the earliest of the three synoptics, and that material in Matthew and Luke which was identical or very similar to Mark was probably derived directly from the Mark text. But some of the material common to Matthew and Luke was not in Mark. Where did that come from? Scholars had come to the view by the end of the nineteenth century that the authors or compilers of Matthew and Luke drew on a very early common source, either not available to or ignored by Mark, a source since lost. This hypothetical or inferred text was called Q, a convenient abbreviation for the German word "quelle", meaning "source". The proposition that Matthew and Luke drew from Mark and Q was called the *two-source theory*.

However, if we subtract the material Matthew and Luke appear to have taken from these two sources we are still left with significant material that is peculiar to each of their respective accounts. That which appears in Matthew and nowhere else may have come from a lost third source (unless Matthew just made it up), and that peculiar to Luke from a fourth. The Matthew-only source is sometimes designated by source theorists as M and the Luke-only source as L. On this account we have a *four-source theory*: Matthew and Luke built their accounts from Mark, which has survived independently, and from Q, M and L which have only survived in their "embedded" forms.

Could this mean, then, that the first generation of Jesus-followers had written gospels or gospel-fragments before any of the canonical gospels as we now know them came into being? Or are all the stories and sayings common to Mark, Matthew and Luke drawn from a common oral tradition? There appears to be no way of telling whether M and L were *written* or *oral* traditions: they could be either. On the other hand, many scholars have found the evidence for a *written* Q very persuasive: if two different authors or editors quote the same sayings in strikingly similar or even identical wording there is a strong presumption that they are taking them from a stable written document rather than from word-of-mouth transmission, where every telling is likely to be a little different.

If these scholars are right, hidden in Matthew and Luke is the text of an earlier gospel, much closer to Jesus' own time than the late-first-century narrative gospels familiar to us. This source subsequently fell out of use and disappeared from view, probably because once it had been incorporated into the narrative gospels it was no longer copied by scribes as a separate work. One estimate is that of Mark's 661 verses over 600 are substantially repeated in Matthew and over 300 in Luke, but Matthew and Luke also share about 240 verses not found in Mark[1]. It is these verses, mainly consisting of sayings, including those collected together as the so-called "sermon on the mount", which specialists in the field assign to Q.

Burton Mack in *The Lost Gospel Q* tells how Q gradually came to assume such importance in the Jesus quest. Three German scholars contributed to its discovery. Karl Lachmann in 1835 drew attention to the fact that Matthew and Luke agreed in the order of their material only when they followed Mark. Christian Wilke in 1838 drew the obvious conclusion that Mark must have preceded the other two, overturning the ancient presumption that Matthew came first. In the same year Christian Weisse put the pieces together and proposed that Matthew and Luke had written independently of each other, each drawing on two sources, one being Mark and the other a lost collection of sayings of Jesus. It was this lost collection that Weisse was the first to call Q.

The theory at first caused barely a ripple on the then placid pond of early biblical criticism. Christian scholars were reluctant to abandon the priority of Matthew, since that is where it had always been positioned in the New Testament. But H J Holtzmann made the first exhaustive examination of the Q hypothesis in 1863 and concluded it was essentially correct. Other scholars began to take it seriously.

In 1907 Adolf von Harnack, who, says Mack, "wanted to see how the teachings of Jesus sounded when divorced from a setting of miracle and myth", published *The Sayings of Jesus* (English translation 1908) which was largely composed of Q texts. The lost source began to emerge from the shadows, but it was still far from being recognized as "a book of instructions with its own history, much less as a charter for a Jesus movement that did not have a narrative gospel". Those who wished to read and study it "did not have a single text to read, but had to work with a synopsis of the gospels, comparing readings in two columns, jumping back and ahead to get the sequences straight, and pondering material that may or may not have been part of the original text. Only those having great patience, thorough familiarity with the synoptic tradition, boxes of colored pencils, and a capacity for detailed analysis could even read Q, much less hope to argue for this or that refinement of the text or explore its genre, content, and composition"[2].

Not until the 1980s was it possible to dispense with the colored pencils. A series of studies beginning in the 1970s paved the way for what became the standard text of reference for Q. In 1988 John Kloppenborg published *Q Parallels* in Greek, with an English translation, discussion of variant readings, parallels from other sayings literature, and a Greek concordance. Burton Mack followed with his own more colloquial translation in *The Lost Gospel* in 1993.

Studies of the style and content of Q by Kloppenborg, James M Robinson, Stephen J Patterson, Jonathan L Reed and others suggest that it grew from smaller collections dating back to the 50s of the first century CE, or even late 40s. Summarizing the dating evidence, Theissen and Merz (independently of the Jesus Seminar and other American Q scholars) conclude that "Q certainly came into being before the Jewish War and the destruction of the temple... The temptation story has clear allusions to the surmounting of the Caligula crisis (39/40 CE). The image of the Pharisees as persecutors of Christians is to be located historically in the 40s and early 50s; the same goes for the preaching and mission orientated on Israel which is presupposed in Q"[3]. Moreover, as most place names in Q are towns and villages in northern Galilee (Chorazin, Bethsaida, Capernaum) or western Syria (Tyre, Sidon), it seems distinctly possible that the text originated with Jesus communities in or near his own home territory of Galilee[4]. It is on this evidence of time and place that Q eventually came to be recognized by a growing number of scholars as probably the earliest of all Jesus sources: the book of the Jesus movement before the Jesus movement went Christian (since "The center of Q's theology is not Christology [claims about Jesus' status, such as Messiah/Christ, Lord, Son of God, God incarnate] but the reign of God"[5]).

However, textual reconstruction or recovery of Q remains controversial, and interpretation of the hypothetical results even more so. If everything common to Matthew and Luke but not derived from Mark is assigned to Q, we have a complex document which seems to consist of several distinct parts. The greater part is "wisdom sayings" and aphorisms divorced from any narrative context, but there are also stories with a punch-line saying, and a number of prophetic utterances which appear to warn that the end-time is at hand. The latter proved something of an embarrassment to some Q supporters who had looked to Q to provide irrefutable evidence supporting their contention that the historical Jesus was not an end-time prophet.

This complexity, seemingly an incoherent jumble of different genres, interpreted in different ways according to different presuppositions, has made a number of scholars skeptical of the project of recovering an authentic Q, or doubtful about its value in providing a solution to such critical questions as whether Jesus was essentially a wisdom teacher, as the Jesus Seminar argues, or an end-time prophet, as Sanders, Vermes and others believe. In Burton Mack's view, Q proved "powerless to adjudicate such a conflict of images because it contained sayings that supported both views of Jesus"[6].

One way of addressing this problem is to interpret the different genres within Q as representing successive stages of its composition. James M Robinson, director of the International Q Project at the Institute for Antiquity and Christianity, Claremont, has argued that the "wisdom sayings" which make up the greater part of Q place it firmly in a literary genre or category familiar to first-century Jewish readers, including such

books as the *logoi* or wisdom sayings of Proverbs and the gospel of
Thomas. Helmut Koester and John Kloppenborg have pushed this further
by arguing that the sayings sections of Q probably represent Q's earliest
form (designated Q^1) with the punch-line stories (Q^2) and end-time
prophecies (Q^3) representing later additions, to make up the double-
layered text with which Matthew and Luke were apparently familiar[7]. But
critics of this approach say it is not clear why a reverse layering, making
the apocalyptic bits the earliest and the wisdom sayings the latest, is
necessarily ruled out. Hence Mack's view that Q scholarship has so far
proved powerless to adjudicate the conflict.

Another complication is that Matthew and Luke sometimes use
variant wordings, which suggests that they adapted Q to their own
viewpoints. Thus, Matthew's typical concern for righteousness is
expressed in the beatitude (5:6) "Blessed are they that hunger and thirst
after righteousness, for they shall be filled". Luke, on the other hand
(6:21) has "Blessed are you that hunger now, for you shall be filled",
expressing through the addition of the word "now" the Luke community's
more radical social concern that the problem of hunger - physical hunger
rather than a yearning for righteousness - be tackled with some urgency.
Michael Steinhauser, introducing the Kloppenborg translation of Q
published by Polebridge (linked to the Jesus Seminar), suggests that the
original probably read something like "Blessed are you that hunger, for
you shall be filled".

Similarly, where Matthew has a weak "Blessed are the poor in spirit",
Luke has a more robust and radical "Blessed are the poor", and where
Matthew has a softer "Whoever loves father and mother more than me is
not worthy of me", Luke's more shocking version is "If someone comes
to me and does not hate his own father and mother... he cannot be my
disciple". It is not easy to separate out later theological glosses from the
inferred original, which strengthens the view that Q reconstructions,
illuminating as they are, always need to be treated with critical caution.

Theissen and Merz, who emphasize the hypothetical nature of Q and caution against over-confident reconstruction, nevertheless accept that of these "wisdom sayings, prophetic and apocalyptic sayings, sayings about the Law, community rules and parables... some certainly go back to Aramaic logia [*logia*, "collections of sayings"] and thus to the beginnings of the tradition... Form-critically the logia source is to be described as a collection of sayings in which the teaching of Jesus has been preserved. The sayings were probably collected and disseminated by the earliest Christian itinerant charismatics, who continued the lifestyle and preaching of Jesus. The central concern of the preaching is to call people to discipleship of Jesus in the face of the kingdom of God which is breaking in"[8].

Noticeably absent from Q and therefore, it seems, from the theology of the early Jesus community which produced it, is a birth story or any biographical framework. There are no miracles, healings or exorcisms. There is no passion: no death, no resurrection, no ascension, no atoning sacrifice. Jesus is son of God and son of Man, but these terms seem not to have acquired the high Christological meanings attached to them by the later church. The Q community's Jesus appears to have been a divinely inspired and sanctioned teacher and prophet, a man of God but never described as God himself. This community, perhaps, did not seek to *define* his status but to *live* his way.

Even those historians who have been most enthusiastic in embracing Q reconstructions do not naively suppose or claim that every "Jesus saying" in this once-lost now-found collection was uttered by Jesus. It is widely conceded that some are likely to be later formulations by the community's leaders of what they understood Jesus to have said, or sayings formulated by the leaders themselves in the belief (which was also Paul's) that they were speaking or writing as Jesus' representatives and with his authority. It may be that, as James Dunn argues, some sayings were preserved in liturgical performance by which members of the community were able to evoke the living presence of their master. But at its core, wherever that may be located, Q specialists argue that the gospel of the Q community probably brings us closer to the essential teaching of the historical Jesus - whether wisdom instruction for living, or emergency preparation for the end-time, or both - than any other text.

The principal sayings and parables which are believed to make up Q are listed in the Cameo *Q Revealed* on page 89. The general reader already familiar with Jesus sayings from Matthew and Luke will get an impression of Q's content by glancing at the italicised sign-posting. More detailed study will require recourse to the Kloppenborg or Mack translations of Q.

2. *Thomas*

Until the middle of the twentieth century Q, M and L were the only early putative sources known to scholars, but in 1945 a Coptic (first century Egyptian) translation of a gospel previously known only in three Greek fragments was unearthed among the hoard of so-called "gnostic" documents found at Nag Hammadi in Egypt. (The entertaining story of the Nag Hammadi finds is told in chapter 6). This was the gospel of Thomas, which is made up of 114 sayings, including parables, ascribed to Jesus. According to an analysis in *The Five Gospels* by a group of Jesus Seminar scholars, "Thomas has forty-seven parallels to Mark, forty parallels to Q, seventeen to Matthew, four to Luke, and five to John. These numbers include sayings that have been counted twice. About sixty-five sayings or parts of sayings are unique to Thomas". Thomas is therefore regarded by the Jesus Seminar as "a fifth independent source for the sayings and parables of Jesus" - a fifth gospel of no less value to historical detectives than the four which made it into the New Testament. But there are many scholars who remain doubters when it comes to Thomas. No important early Christian text has been the subject of more heated controversy.

As with Q but quite unlike the biblical gospels, Thomas has no narrative, no context, no acts or miracles of Jesus. Christological titles for Jesus ("Christ", "Messiah", "Son of God") and references to his birth,

Cameo: Q revealed

*Q consists of the following sayings, numbered as in Kloppenborg's translation and with corresponding chapter and verse references as they appear in Matthew (Mt) and Luke (Lk). Texts marked * indicate the few sayings or incidents which have a narrative context. (Extracted from **Q/Thomas Reader**).*

* John the Baptist's preaching: Q3:7-9, 16-17 / Mt 3:7-12 / Lk 3: 7-9, 16-17
* Temptations of Jesus: Q4:1-13 / Mt 4:1-11 / Lk 4:1-13

Sermon on the mount - the blessings: Q6:20 / Mt 5:1-6, 11-12 / Lk 6: 12-23

On retaliation - "Love your enemies": Q6:27-35 / Mt 5:38-44 / Lk 6:27-35

"Judge not": Q6:36-37 / Mt 5:48; 7:1-2 / Lk 6:36-38

Blind leading the blind: Q6:39-40 / Mt 15:14 / Lk 6:39-40

Motes and beams: Q6:41-42 / Mt 7:3-5 / Lk 6:41-42

"By their fruits ye shall know them": Q6:43-45 / Mt 7:16-20; 12:33-35 / Lk 6:43-45

Building house upon a rock: Q6:46-49 / Mt 7:21-27 / Lk 6:46-49

* The believing centurian: Q7:1-10 / Mt 7:28-29 / Lk 7:1-10

John on Jesus and Jesus on John: Q7:18-28 / Mt 11:2-13 / Lk 7:18-28; 16:16

The kingdom seized by violence: Q16:16 / Mt 11:12-13 / Lk 16:16

"This generation like children": Q7:31-35 / Mt 11:16-19 / Lk 7:31-35

* Following Jesus: Q9:57-62 / Mt 8:19-22 / Lk 9:57-62

Sending laborers to the harvest: Q10:2-12 / Mt 9:37-38; 10:7-

15 / Lk 10:2-12

Woes to Galilee: Q10:13-15 / Mt 11:20-24 / Lk 10:13-15

"Whoever hears you hears me": Q10:16 / Mt 10:40 / Lk
  10:16

"Hidden from the wise and revealed to babes": Q10:21-22 /
  Mt 11:25-27 / Lk 10:21-22

"Blessing on eye-witnesses": Q10:23-24 / Mt 13:16-17 / Lk
  10:23-24

The "Lord's prayer": Q11:2-4 / Mt 6:9-13 / Lk 11: 2-4

"Ask...seek...knock": Q11:9-13 / Mt 7:7-11 / Lk 11:9-13

* *Exorcism by Satan: "Whoever is not with me is against me":*
  Q11:14-23 / Mt 9:32-34; 12:22-30 / Lk 11:14-23

"Last state worse than the first: Q11:24-26 / Mt 12:43-45 / Lk
  11:24-26

* *Pharisees ask for a sign:* Q11:16, 29-32 / Mt 12:38-42; 16:1-
  2,4 / Lk 11:16, 29-32

Light under a bushel: Q11:33-36 / Mt 5:14-15, 6:22-23 / Lk
  11:33-36

"Woe to you Pharisees": Q11:39b-44, 46-52 / Mt 23:4-
  7,13,23-36 / Lk 11:39-52

"Hidden and revealed": Q12:2-3 / Mt 10:26-27 / Lk 12:2-3

"Sparrows for a farthing... hairs on head numbered": Q12:4-
  7 /Mt 10:28-31 / Lk 12:4-7

Confessing and rejecting Jesus: Q12:8-10 / Mt 10:32-33,
  12:32 / Lk 12:8-10

The Spirit's assistance: Q12:11-12 / Mt 10:19 / Lk 12:11-12

"Ravens...lilies... seek ye first...": Q12:22-31 / Mt 6:25-33 /
  Lk 12:22-31

"Treasures in heaven": Q12:33-34 / Mt 6:19-21 / Lk 12:33-34

"Thief in the night": Q12:39-40 / Mt 24:43-44 / Lk 12:39-40

"Faithful and unfaithful servants": Q12:42b-46 / Mt 24:45-51 / Lk 12:42-46

"Not peace but a sword": Q12:49, 51-53 / Mt 10:34-36 / Lk 12:49-53

Signs of the times: Q12:54-56 / Mt 16:2-3 / Lk 12:54-56

Come to terms with an accuser: Q12:57-59 / Mt 5:25-26 / Lk 12:57-59

Mustard and leaven: Q13:18-21 / Mt 13:31-33 / Lk 13:18-21

Strait gate: Q13:24-27 / Mt 7:13-14, 22-23 / Lk 13:24-27

Gentiles in the kingdom - "the first shall be last": Q13:28-30 / Mt 8:11-12; 20:16 / Lk 13:28-30

Lament over Jerusalem: Q13:34-35 / Mt 23:37-39 / Lk 13:34-35

"Who humbles himself will be exalted": Q14:11, 18:14b / Mt 23:12 / Lk 14:11; 18:14

The kingdom like a wedding feast - "compel them to come in": Q14:16-24 / Mt 22:1-10 / Lk 14:16-24

Discipleship - requirement to "hate" father and mother: Q14:26-27, 17:33 / Mt 10:37-39 / Lk 14:26-27; 17:33

"Salt of the earth": Q14:34-35 / Mt 5:13 / Lk 14:34-35

"Lost sheep": Q15:4-10 / Mt 18:12-13 / Lk 15:4-7 [Lk includes lost coin, 15: 8-10, omitted by Mt]

Two masters, God and mammon: Q16:13 / Mt 6:24 / Lk 16:13

The kingdom and the law - divorce and adultery: Q16:16-18 / Mt 11:12-13; 5:18; 5:32 / Lk 16:16-18

"Millstone around the neck": Q17:1-2 / MT 18:7,6 / LK 17:12

"Forgive seven times seven": Q17:3B-4 / MT 18:15; 21:22 / LK 17:3-4

"Faith to move mountains": Q17:6b / Mt 17:20 / Lk 17:6

Coming of the Son of Man: Q17:23-37 / Mt 24:26-28, 38-41 /

> Lk 17:23-24, 26-30, 34-35, 37
>
> *Parable of the talents:* Q19:12-26 / Mt 25:14-30 / Lk 19:12 27
>
> *Disciples to judge Israel:* Q22:28-30 / Mt 19:28 / Lk 22:28-30

death, resurrection, ascension and second coming are conspicuous by their absence. (There is one reference to "son of man", but the context suggests this should be understood in its broadest sense of "son of Adam", a common term for "human being"). Again, like Q, Thomas has wisdom sayings, parables and brief dialogues, but unlike Q it has no apocalyptic sayings.

Commenting on Thomas, Stephen J Patterson reminds us that "the students of famous philosophers such as Epicurus or Epictetus often collected the wise and witty sayings of their tradition into *gnomologia*, or 'words of insight', which they might then use as they evangelized the public in the marketplaces and streets of the ancient world. Jews and other ethnic groups of the eastern empire also gathered the aphoristic wisdom of their sages into collections of *logoi sophon*, or 'sayings of the wise'... The gathering of Jesus' sayings into such a collection places him among the sages of the past, the prophets of Sophia (the feminine personification of wisdom in Jewish lore) sent into every generation with her saving words of wisdom"[9].

That Thomas really is a sayings gospel is clear enough, but if there remains much to resolve about Q, the dating and interpretation of Thomas is even more controversial. There are references to a gospel of Thomas in early-third-century writers (Hippolytus and Origen), so it was well known by then, and its composition cannot be much later than 200 CE. But fragments of a Greek version were already known to modern scholars from Greek papyri among the 19th century Oxyrhychus finds, and these appear to date from around 140 or 150 CE, indicating that the gospel was in circulation before the middle of the second century at the latest. As for the earliest possible date, at least one saying appears to refer to the destruction of the temple, which would indicate a date after 70 CE unless it is accepted uncritically as forecasting a future event. Until recently it was widely assumed that the gospel's gnostic flavor - its self-description as "*secret* sayings" - made a second-century date most likely, and many scholars, especially in Europe, continue to argue or assume that the sayings were compiled around 140 or 150 CE. (See Cameo: *'In the Know': Gnosticism and the Gospel of Thomas* at the end of this chapter).

But in the United States, and particularly among scholars associated with the Jesus Seminar, arguments for a much earlier date have won many followers. First, it is argued, the simple or primitive genre of *sayings collections* appears to precede the more complex genre of *narrative gospels* which began with Mark. In form, Thomas has much in common with Q, which clearly preceded the narrative gospels since its material was used in them. It therefore makes sense to propose a sequence in which oral memory of Jesus' sayings gave way to or was gradually consolidated into written sayings collections, and these in turn developed into narrative gospels which either subsumed or superseded the early collections.

Secondly, although half of Thomas's sayings are paralleled in the biblical narrative gospels, their order in Thomas (where they are arranged by a form of word association, with no trace of a narrative link) is completely independent of the canonical books. This strongly suggests that Thomas has not borrowed from the canonical gospel writers, as was originally assumed, but rather that they inserted traditional sayings at appropriate points in their narrative, picking them either direct from Thomas or from sources common to both traditions. Moreover, where there are such parallels, the Thomas version is often demonstrably more primitive and less theologically overlain than the canonical version. Theissen & Merz give telling examples, including Thomas's version of the parable of the wicked husbandmen, which is clearly more primitive and therefore, they argue, probably older than the familiar version in Mark 12:1-12.[10]

Thirdly, it is argued that "the collection must come from a period in which the church was still appealing to the authoritative position of particular apostles within particular communities as a way of guaranteeing the reliability of its traditions"[11]. Also, Thomas does not treat "the twelve" as "a unified, sanctified group of quasi-saints", as begins to happen in Acts (around 100 CE). On both these counts, this would make Thomas either earlier than, or more or less contemporaneous with, the canonical gospels, but no later.

All this assumes that Thomas can be treated as a stable text, written at an early date and continuing in a more or less unaltered state till it reached the libraries of Origen and Hippolytus in the third century. But few scholars now believe that any of the early texts, biblical or extra-biblical, enjoyed such stability. Today we can expect to read *Paradise Lost* or *David Copperfield* more or less as Milton and Dickens wrote them, but ancient texts were quite different. We have seen how Mark appears to have existed in a number of variant forms, Matthew and Luke were built from earlier sources, and John changed and "grew" till well into the first century. Thomas was almost certainly no exception.

This has led some scholars to suggest that the Thomas collection, like Q, is best understood as derived from a very early core, added to in several stages over the years. As Stephen J Patterson puts it, "Without the necessity of having to look after the narrative quality of the overall work, each new curator of the collection could have added new sayings, or sloughed away outmoded sayings, with little difficulty. Thus, such a collection would quite naturally have been a cumulative product, whose content might have easily changed from generation to generation". This recalls Geza Vermes's "scribal creative freedom". Patterson is foremost among those who confidently conclude that "Many of these sayings undoubtedly derive from the very earliest period of the Jesus movement, perhaps some even from Jesus himself"[12].

Who wrote or compiled this book? The opening line of the gospel describes it as sayings recorded by Didymos Judas Thomas. "Thomas" is the Semitic word for "twin", and "Didymos" is its Greek translation. Only Judas is a real name. The biblical gospels and epistles have several confusing references to apostles named Judas. Apart from Judas Iscariot, John 14:22 has a "Judas, not Iscariot", who becomes Judas Thomas or Judas the Twin in the Syriac translation of the same passage. Mark (6:3) and Matthew (13:55) have a Judas or Jude who is one of four brothers of Jesus, and the short epistle of Jude claims in its first verse to have been written by "Jude, the servant of Jesus Christ and brother of James". Then there are John's intriguing references to "doubting Thomas". The double-emphasis on the word twin, coupled with the evidence of a tradition that Jesus had brothers named Judas and James (who is singled out as a special authority-figure in the gospel of Thomas) has led Helmut Koester to suggest that the opening line of Thomas intends to claim as its author Judas the twin brother of Jesus[13]. (Koester does not argue, of course, that the claim is true. And the more skeptical Bart Ehrman has Thomas down as a plain "forgery"). Commenting on all this, Patterson concludes that, "however intriguing, all of these claims probably do not tell us much about the actual authorship of the Gospel of Thomas. They belong, rather, to the common early Christian phenomenon of assigning important accounts of the tradition to prominent apostolic figures as a means of asserting their reliability... It is likely that over time, and especially in Syria, the figure of Judas the brother of Jesus came to be identified with the apostle Thomas, perhaps since both were known in some circles as 'the Twin'. Such identification is not uncommon among the great legends and heroes of the past. For all practical purposes, we do not know who really wrote this gospel".[14]

Church tradition located the Judas-Thomas community in eastern Syria on the basis that several Syriac texts dating from the late-second or third century claim the authority of the apostle Thomas. According to Patterson again (in his contribution to *The Complete Gospels*), "Didymos Judas Thomas seems to have been a popular legendary figure from apostolic times, especially in Syria... In early Christianity the names of particular apostles often acquired special significance within specific geographical areas. For example, Peter is associated with Rome, John with Asia Minor, and James with Jerusalem. We cannot be certain whether such associations are grounded in historical memories of the evangelization of these areas, or are purely legendary. Thomas, or Didymos Judas Thomas, was apparently the patron apostle for Syria"[15].

But Patterson questions the assumption that the collection originated in Syria, asking "Could the Gospel of Thomas itself be partially responsible for bringing the Thomas tradition to eastern Syria in the first place, it having been composed earlier in another place?" Two factors, he suggests, support this notion. "First, as a collection of Jesus' sayings, a large part of its material, if not the collection as a whole, would have come originally out of Palestine, the center of activity for the earliest Jesus movement. Secondly... it is noteworthy that aside from Thomas, the other authority figure to which the Gospel of Thomas appeals is James the Just (saying 12), that is, James the brother of Jesus. He, in contrast to Thomas, was not associated with the east, but with Jerusalem... If one may assume that the sayings tradition, generally speaking, has its origins in Palestine with the emergence of the Jesus movement, then it seems that the best way to account for both the James and Thomas traditions in the Gospel of Thomas would be to postulate that at least part of the collection was assembled originally in Palestine. Later a group of early Christians would have taken the collection with it as it migrated east, to eastern Syria"[16].

If it were established that some sayings in the Thomas collection and others in Q originated in the very area in which Jesus was said to have preached and taught, and particularly if those sayings could confidently be identified and separated out from later additions, this would clearly be of immense historical importance. But neither Patterson nor the Jesus Seminar collectively claim that a Galilean origin for some sayings is more than a possibility with circumstantial support. On current evidence, the Jesus Seminar dates Thomas as we know it in its final redaction (or edition) to the 70s or 80s, a period when the *narrative* gospels were also beginning to take shape but had not yet been adopted by the church as uniquely authoritative.

Even this is far too early for Geza Vermes, who makes only a passing reference to the Thomas gospel in *The Authentic Gospel of Jesus* (2003), holding to the older consensus that supported a date "perhaps in the middle of the second century AD". Vermes is unpersuaded that the sayings are anything other than either reworkings of their parallels in the synoptic gospels or later sayings "tainted with heretical ('Gnostic') ideas"[17]. John Bowker's *Oxford Dictionary of World Religions* similarly holds to a date of "c.150", maintaining with Vermes that the sayings "are gnostic and depend mostly on the New Testament gospels", though Bowker accepts that "they may include some genuine words of Jesus preserved nowhere else, e.g. 'Love your brother as your soul [i.e. self], guard him as the apple of your eye' (saying 25)". Bart Ehrman also reads many of the sayings as "appearing to presuppose a Gnostic point of view", and argues that since gnostic teachings "cannot be dated with confidence prior to the beginning of the second century", the early 100s seem the most likely date for "the document as a whole". But despite his evaluation of the gospel as probably a second-century forgery, Ehrman acknowledges that "some of these sayings may be quite old - may, in fact, go back to Jesus himself"[18]. Thus even Thomas skeptics are reluctant to pronounce this enigmatic gospel as wholly disconnected from the teachings of an historical Jesus.

And if the dating of the book is difficult, how much more so is the task of uncovering its meaning. "The interpretation of the Gospel of Thomas", writes its specialist interpreter Stephen Patterson, "is still in its infancy. This gospel, unlike those of the New Testament, has only been available for study for a few decades. Its interpretation is complicated by the fact that the only surviving complete text... is in Coptic, a language which few scholars have mastered. Finally, there is the troubling issue of esotericism... Even a cursory reading of Thomas will reveal that many of its sayings are quite obscure, some perhaps intentionally so, often using paradox or obtuse metaphors to make their point... There is still much work to be done before this text is fully understood"[19].

Nevertheless, Patterson offers a concise guide to the Thomas sayings in his Introduction to the Jesus Seminar's translation in *The Complete Gospels*. (See Cameo: *Thomas without Doubts*, page 100). He describes the book as fitting into an ancient tradition of "wisdom literature" dating back to Proverbs and Ecclesiastes and still very much alive in first-century Judaism. The wisdom sayings traditionally spoke of "what is true about people, about life and the world... about what is worthwhile in the world, and what is wrong with it, about human wisdom and human foolishness". This gospel, however, is less traditional in that it reflects the influence of gnosticism. "In Thomas one sees an early Christian community taking its first steps in the direction of gnosticism, its counter-cultural wisdom a blossom of the anti-cosmic gnostic orientation that would reach its full flowering among Christians only in the second century"[20].

Without some understanding of the inner world of gnosticism, some of the Thomas sayings defy easy explanation or categorisation. What are we to make of the last in the collection, 114?: "Simon Peter said to them, 'Make Mary leave us, for females don't deserve life'. Jesus said, 'Look, I will guide her to make her male, so that she too may become a living spirit resembling you males. For every female who makes herself male will enter the domain of Heaven'."

Patterson and others relate this to a notion found elsewhere in gnostic literature and in Thomas itself which sees salvation consisting in a return to a state of primordial androgynous perfection. Saying 22, for instance, has the Father's domain or kingdom open to those who "make male and female into a single one, so that the male will not be male nor the female be female". But not everyone finds this convincing. Saying 114 does not advocate an androgynous perfection: on the contrary, most modern readers would find it breathtaking in its mysogyny. It would be a brave

Christian who would put such a saying in the mouth of "the living Jesus" today![21]. The obscurity of some sayings may be due to translation problems. The English translation is from the Coptic, which in turn is from the Greek, which, if the earliest sayings come from the first Jesus movement or from Jesus himself, must have originated in Aramaic. Where it is possible to compare the Coptic version with the surviving Greek fragments there are some significant differences. We may assume that changes, subtle or significant, will have occurred at each translation, and then again as each layer was edited and re-edited, copied and re-copied, over perhaps two hundred years. Such are the everyday problems of understanding and interpretation which face specialist Jesus detectives.

Scholars continue to debate the historical value of Q and Thomas. Some we have quoted remain unpersuaded that Matthew and Luke used a written sayings gospel. Despite their championing of Thomas as an early gospel containing sayings which may have originated with Jesus himself, the Jesus Seminar's consensus is that only 37 of the 114 sayings contain possible authentic words of the historical Jesus, of which only three are "red letter" sayings considered "undoubtedly" authentic. (For an explanation of the Seminar's color-coding, see chapter 7). Of the 37, no fewer than 35 are paralleled in one or more of the canonical gospels, 24 of them via Q, leaving only two "probables" with no parallels elsewhere. Geza Vermes, on the other hand, includes nothing at all from Thomas in his inventory of "authentic or probably authentic" sayings of Jesus. But if this has to be put down as yet another unresolved debate, it nevertheless seems that the Q/Thomas hypothesis has established itself as an interpretive tool that can no longer be dismissed out of hand. A sequence whereby oral memories become written sayings collections, which accumulate more sayings as they circulate, which eventually give way to narrative gospels in which they are embedded, seems a fitting and reasonable explanation of the way the texts developed. The skeptics will find this hypothesis hard to dislodge unless they can offer a more persuasive one.

Cameo: Thomas without doubts

What is Thomas all about? Stephen Patterson puts it in context. For convenience, I have added the text of sayings he refers to only by numbers.

"As an example of the genre **logoi sophon** ('sayings of the wise') the Gospel of Thomas belongs to a lively tradition in first century Judaism: Wisdom. This Wisdom tradition produced collections such as one finds in Proverbs, Ecclesiastes, or the Wisdom of Solomon. Many of Thomas' sayings seem quite at home in this tradition: they speak of what is true about people, about life and the world. They speak about what is worthwhile in the world, and what is wrong with it, about human wisdom and human foolishness. The Wisdom tradition, on the whole, is rather conservative. It tends toward the conventional, the tried and true. By contrast, Thomas frequently offers a rather uncommon wisdom, a wisdom that is "not of this age" (1 Cor. 2:6), to quote a contemporary of Thomas. Thomas' sayings can speak of renouncing the world:

10: Jesus said, 'I have cast fire upon the world, and look, I'm guarding it till it blazes';

they can ridicule prudence:

76: 'Jesus said, 'The Father's imperial rule is like a merchant who had a supply of merchandise and then found a pearl. That merchant was prudent; he sold the merchandise and bought the single pearl for himself. So also with you, seek his treasure that is unfailing, that is enduring, where no moth comes to eat and no worm destroys';

they can exclude the savvy of the world from God's realm:

64: a version of the Q parable in Matthew 22:1-10 and Luke 14:16-24 of the man whose supper invitations were refused with feeble excuses, ending 'Go out on the streets and bring back whomever you find to have dinner. Buyers and merchants will not enter the places of my Father';

and they can undermine conventional values such as home and family:

55: Jesus said, 'Whoever does not hate father and mother cannot be my disciple, and whoever does not hate brothers and sisters, and carry the cross as I do, will not be worthy of me';

and 99: The disciples said to him, 'Your brothers and your mother are standing outside'. He said to them, 'Those here who do what my Father wants are my brothers and my mother. They are the ones who will enter my Father's domain';

or undermine traditional piety:

14: Jesus said to them, 'If you fast, you will bring sin upon yourselves, and if you pray you will be condemned, and if you give to charity you will harm your spirits...';

and undermine respect for community leaders:

3: Jesus said, 'If your leaders say to you, "Look, the Father's imperial rule is in the sky", then the birds of the sky will precede you. If they say to you, "It is in the sea", then the fish will precede you. Rather, the imperial rule is inside you and outside you. When you know yourselves, then you will be known, and you will understand that you are children of the living Father. But if you do not know yourselves, then you live in poverty, and you are the poverty';

and 102: Jesus said, 'Damn the Pharisees! They are like a sleeping dog in the cattle manger: the dog neither eats nor lets the cattle eat'.

The wisdom one finds in Thomas is hardly conventional. In fact, if one is to recognize any common wisdom at all in Thomas' outlook, one must first, it seems, cultivate a way of thinking that subverts dominant cultural values. The theological underpinnings for Thomas' decidedly counter-cultural bent also go somewhat beyond those of standard Wisdom theology. The truth Thomas reveals about human nature extends beyond the rather ordinary observations that people tend to be selfish (41), vain (36), judgmental (26), foolish, and easily led astray (34):

41: Jesus said, 'Those who have something in hand will be given more, and those who have nothing will be deprived of even the little they have'. 36: Jesus said, 'Don't fret, from morning to evening and from evening to morning, about what you are going to wear'. [The Greek version of this saying, available in the fragment known as POxy 655, adds the words familiar in their Q-Matthew-Luke parallel, "You're much better than the lilies, which don't card and never spin..."] *26: Jesus said, 'You see the sliver in your friend's eye, but you don't see the timber in your own...' 34: Jesus said, 'If a blind person leads a blind person, both of them will fall into a hole'.*

People are this way because they have forgotten who they are, where they have come from. In 28 Jesus speaks as one who has come from God to remind the "children of humanity" of whence they have come and to where they shall ultimately return:

28: Jesus said, 'I took my stand in the midst of the world, and in the flesh I appeared to them. I found them all drunk, and I did not find any of them thirsty. My soul ached for the children of humanity, because they are blind in their hearts and do not see, for they came into the world empty, and they also seek to depart from the world empty. But meanwhile they are drunk. When they shake off their wine, then they will repent'.

Patterson suggests that this saying 28, and others like it,

reflects the early stages of the way of thinking that came to be known as gnosticism, in which freedom or salvation from an evil world ruled by the powers of darkness depended on an enlightened understanding or wisdom (*gnosis*) accessed via a God-sent messenger by the select few with "ears to hear". Mark and John similarly demonstrate early gnostic influence, as do Paul's letters, which suggests that it was part of the background thinking of at least some, and perhaps all, early Jesus movement communities before a more fully-developed and more explicitly esoteric gnosticism divided the church later in the second century and came to be persecuted by the proto-orthodox as heretical. Gnostic themes in Thomas include the deprecation of "the world and the flesh" (56 and 80); the requirement that the believer remove himself or herself from the ways of the world (21: 6), and, says Patterson, "perhaps a primitive catechism for the return home" (49 and 50):

56 : Jesus said, 'Whoever has come to know the world has discovered a carcass (or, in 80, a body), *and whoever has discovered a carcass, of that person the world is not worthy'.*

21:6: 'As for you, then, be on guard against the world.'

49-50: Jesus said, 'Congratulations to those who are alone and chosen, for you will find the Father's domain. For you have come from it, and you will return there again... If they say to you, "Where have you come from?" say to them "We have come from the light, from the place where the light came into being by itself, established itself, and appeared in their image". If they say to you, "Is it you?" say "We are its children, and we are the chosen of the living Father". If they ask you, "What is the evidence of your Father in you?" say to them, "It is motion and rest"'.

In Thomas one sees an early Christian community taking its

> *first steps in the direction of gnosticism, its counter-cultural wisdom a blossom of the anti-cosmic gnostic orientation that would reach its full flowering among Christians only in the second century. Thomas shares with gnosticism a basic concern for personal identity within a world which was widely perceived as brutal and mean. Thomas presents us with a Jesus whose words call one from out of the chaos into a quest, to seek and to find, and finally to discover one's true identity as a child of God. (**The Complete Gospels, p 301-4**)*

3. Signs

Some scholars have followed John Dominic Crossan and Robert T Fortna in detecting another hypothetical "lost" text, this time embedded in John, which has a collection of "signs" or visible demonstrations that Jesus was indeed the divine Christ as preached by John's community. Thus John 2:11 interprets the water-into-wine miracle at Cana as "the beginning of miracles" done by Jesus that "manifested forth his glory", with the intended consequence that "his disciples believed on him". Jesus Seminar scholars postulate an earlier version from a more literal translation: "This (was) the beginning of the signs Jesus did, and he (showed) himself, and his disciples believed in him". Further "signs" are described in Galilee (an official's son healed, 2:12 and 4:46-54; a huge catch of fish, 21:1-14; the feeding of the five thousand and walking on water, 6:1-25) and more in Jerusalem (Lazarus raised, 11:1-45; blind man given sight, 9:1-8; and crippled man healed, 5:2-9).

Noting inconsistencies and contradictions thrown up or highlighted by the inclusion of these "signs" stories, Robert T Fortna has proposed that the writer of the fourth gospel drew on an older document which was perhaps "so familiar and revered by John's audience that it could not be rewritten or even paraphrased, although it had undoubtedly become in some way obsolete". He suggests that "In the Signs Gospel, then, we have perhaps the earliest, certainly the most rudimentary of gospels"[22]. However, outside the Jesus Seminar the case for Signs as an independently originated and embedded source has yet to receive significant acceptance among scholars.

4. *The Didache*

There is another early document which may throw more light on the kind of person Jesus was than most of the non-biblical gospels. The only known full text was discovered in Istanbul in 1873 and published in 1883. Known today as the Didache, the Greek word for "training", its full title in translation is "The Training of the Lord Through the Twelve Apostles to the Gentiles", which makes clear that this is not a gospel but a manual for new converts, schooling them in morals and religious community practice. At first it was believed to have been compiled some time in the second century and assumed to be dependent on the New Testament gospels, particularly Matthew. But twentieth-century scholars began to draw attention to features suggesting a first-century date, notably the treatment of bishops and deacons as a somewhat novel order within the Jesus movement, only just beginning to replace apostolic and itinerant leadership.

Many scholars have interpreted the manual as a collage of texts from different periods in the first and second centuries. But in 2003 Aaron Milavec published two books, a thousand-page commentary, *The Didache: Faith, Hope, and Life of the Earliest Christian Communities*, and a shorter work, *The Didache: Text, Translation, Analysis, and Commentary*, arguing in both for a very early mid-first-century date, prior to the New Testament gospels and contemporaneous with the earliest Pauline letters and the earliest layers of Q and Thomas. Still controversial, Milavec's reading has attracted growing scholarly support, notably from John Dominic Crossan and some (but not all) members of the Jesus Seminar.

Milavec proposes that the Didache "outlines a comprehensive, step-by-step program of formation that was used by the early Jewish followers of Jesus to initiate non-Jewish candidates into their way of life as they awaited the unfolding of the Kingdom of God proclaimed by Jesus". But the Jesus of the Didache is not the Jesus of the New Testament, either that of the gospels or of Paul. First, he is not "the Lord" of the book's full title: the Didache's Lord, Milavec proposes, is God the Father. Jesus is described throughout as "God's servant", sent to reveal "the Way of Life". Although sometimes referred to as "Jesus Christ", he has no exalted titles and is associated with no miraculous deeds: here the title Christ (Milavec argues) appears to carry the sense of "God's annointed", "God's messenger", rather than divine status. "The document is entirely silent about Jesus dying for our sins (much like the early layers of the Q Gospel and the Gospel of Thomas). Nor does the Didache say anything about Jesus' vindication and exaltation through his resurrection and ascension" - in contrast to Paul, the New Testament gospels and Acts. It is this "primitive christology" of the Didache that persuades Milavec that it was compiled and used by some of the very earliest Jesus-movement communities, before Pauline theology gained its ascendance.

Thus the Didache gives us no biographical information about Jesus, but if Milavec and his supporters are right it shows us how the early Jesus movement understood Jesus before he was elevated by the church to divine status. The Jesus of the movement's first training manual was a man, a teacher, a servant or messenger of God, sent to preach a way of life rather than salvation from sin and death. This sounds like a very Jewish Jesus, a Jesus in the line of the Hebrew prophets, a son of God only in the sense that all who serve God are sons of God. This is the Jesus whose memorable sayings are recorded by the compilers of the first editions of Q and Thomas. But as Paul's exaltation of Jesus as a divine being, coupled with John's understanding of him as the Word who was not only *with* God but *was* God, came to dominate church theology, the Didache was quietly dropped or suppressed - till its re-emergence in Istanbul eighteen hundred years later.

5. *Peter*: the first passion story?

More intense scholarly controversy has attached to the so-called gospel of Peter, known from a seventh- or eighth-century papyrus codex discovered in 1886 in yet another Egyptian site, a grave at Akhmim, and from other scattered fragments which appear to come from the same work, the earliest of which has been dated to the second century. This gospel contains a version of the passion story broadly similar to those of the canonical gospels, leading most early commentators to assume that it was dependent upon them. But again, a number of modern scholars have disagreed, notably Koester, who proposes Peter's independence, and Crossan, who has advanced the radical thesis that Peter's passion narrative was the model for the canonical ones, rather than the other way round.

Theissen and Merz suggest it was "most probably composed in the first half of the second century", certainly some time between 70 CE (since the destruction of Jerusalem is presupposed) and around 190, when it is condemned as a forgery by the church fathers[23]. From this they adduce a likely dependence on Mark. But the distinguished Jesus Seminar scholar Arthur J Dewey takes a different tack. In a commentary which goes to the heart of the way we interpret not only extra-biblical gospels but also the church's canon, he shows how modern New Testament scholarship has undermined many of the old assumptions:

"The arguments both for dependence and for independence assumed the existence of some historical (that is, factual) account. Depending on how one reads the relationship between Peter and the canonical gospels, one could maintain that one or the other preserves an earlier, historical kernel. But, since the canonical gospels are witnesses to a very complex interpretive enterprise, both oral and literary, and were subject to the various formats and patterns of ancient communication, they cannot be simple historical reports. This means that the extracanonical gospels, such as Peter, must also be re-evaluated."

By this view, the quest for factuality, for a historical core or kernel, for "what really happened", is at worst misconceived and at best inadequate. All the gospel accounts bear witness to "a very complex *interpretive* enterprise". Peel away one layer of interpretation and you only reveal another. No amount of peeling-away will bring you to a pure kernel of historical truth, unmediated by interpretation. This viewpoint, with its explosive implications for the quest, is of particular interest as coming from a leading member of the fact-focused Jesus Seminar. Dewey continues:

"This rethinking has been based on the discovery that almost every sentence of the passion narrative of Peter appears to be composed out of references and allusions to the psalms and the prophets. In effect, 'scriptural memory' may well have been a major influence in the formation of this early passion narrative. Furthermore, recent studies which are not interested in searching for some historical core have tentatively established an original compositional layer whose form and content was shaped by the Jewish tradition of the suffering righteous one."

The argument here is that the passsion narratives, biblical and extra-biblical, have a common origin *not* in any factual historical event - a real arrest, trial, crucifixion and resurrection - but in a particular literary genre rooted in a particular culture. It is worth quoting Dewey at some length as he explains this "revisionist" thesis:

"The most important result established by this research is that the original stage of Peter may well be the earliest passion story in the gospel tradition and, as such, may contain the seeds of subsequent passion narratives [including those of the biblical gospels]. In contrast to those early interpreters of Peter who assumed some sort of factual account at the core, the recent revisionists find something other than sheer historical report. They contend that the passion tradition begins not as a simple historical description but as an imaginary response to the trauma of Jesus' fate, expressed in the stock form of the Jewish tale of the righteous one who is unjustly persecuted and subsequently vindicated.

"The story pattern of this tale... is as follows. The actions and claims of a righteous person provoke his opponents to conspire against him. This leads to an accusation (Peter 3:2?; 4:2?), trial (1:1), condemnation (2:3), and ordeal (3:1-4; 4:1; 5:2). In some instances this results in his shameful death (5:5). The hero of the story reacts characteristically (4:1), expressing his innocence, frustration, or trust in prayer (5:5), while there are also various reactions to his fate by characters in the tale (4:3-5). Either at the brink of death or in death itself the innocent one is rescued (5:5) and vindicated (5:6 - 6:1). This vindication entails the exaltation (5:5) and acclamation (8:1) of the hero as well as the reaction (8:1) and punishment (5:1, 3-4) of his opponents."[24].

Dewey's analysis would move the date of "the earliest stage of Peter" to the middle of the first century, around the time of Q and Paul's first letters and before Mark, Matthew, Luke or John had composed the gospels which included their own similarly-patterned passion stories. Thus the findings of the revisionists "challenge basic assumptions about the historical development of early Christian literature". For some they suggest a wholly mythological rather than an historical Jesus. For those not prepared to go that far, an early Peter joins Q, M, L, an early layer of Thomas and an early Didache in offering glimpses of both a pre-Christian Jesus and the very process by which he begins to be transformed into one whose meaning and purpose is to be found not in his life and wisdom-teaching but in the cosmic magic and mystery of his death.

Notes to Chapter 5

1 *QT Reader*, 8. There are, of course, no chapter and verse divisions in the early manuscripts. They were imposed much later.

2 Mack, *Lost Gospel*, 19-22, where full references are given for all citations.

3 Theissen, *Historical Jesus*, 28

4 Introduction to *QT Reader*, vi, by Michael G Steinhauser. See also Jonathan L Reed, *Archaeology and the Galilean Jesus,* Trinity Press International, Harrisburg PA, 2000.

5 Kloppenborg, *Excavating Q*, 391-2

6 Mack, *Lost Gospel*, 31

7 The history and development of Q scholarship is summarized in the Introduction to *QT Reader* by Michael G Steinhauser.

8 Theissen, *Historical Jesus*, 28

9 Patterson in *Complete Gospels*, 301-2

10 Theissen, *Historical Jesus*, 39

11 Helmut Koester, cited in *QT Reader*, 89

12 Patterson in *QT Reader*, 89

13 Koester as cited by Patterson in *QT Reader*, 91

14 Patterson in *QT Reader*, 91

15 Patterson in *Complete gospels*, 302

16 Patterson in *QT Reader*, 92-3

17 Vermes, *Authentic Gospel*, xiii

18 Ehrman, *Lost Christianities*, 20

19 Patterson in *Complete Gospels*, 304. The Coptic version of Thomas is assumed to be a translation from a Greek original, of which only a few fragments have been found.

20 as above, 304

21 The Jesus Seminar scholars put this saying firmly in the black, rejecting it as an authentic Jesus saying. (For an explanation of the Seminar's color-coding, see chapter 7). As the Seminar's commentary to *The Five Gospels* notes (p 532), "The Petrine tradition is not notably kind to women... Peter's question reflects a debate in developing Christianity over the place of women in the community, and especially concerning their leadership roles. These issues do not belong to the ministry of Jesus, but to the Christian movement as it developed into an institution in a culture that did not accord women public roles". That culture, once established within the church, was to survive for two thousand years and more.

22 Fortna in *Complete Gospels*, 175

23 Theissen, *Historical Jesus*, 49

24 Dewey in *Complete Gospels*, 400-1

Cameo: 'In the know': Gnosticism and the gospel of Thomas

Gnosticism is often misunderstood as a distinctively Christian heresy, not least because from the late-second-century onwards it was persecuted as such by a proto-catholic or proto-orthodox tendency within the church. But gnosticism was a fluid movement influencing many middle-eastern religious traditions, including Judaism and mystery cults as well as the Jesus movement. It should not be misunderstood merely as an aberrant version of Christianity.

In its fully developed form, gnosticism saw the world as irredeemably evil because it was the creation not of the High God, the one true God, but of an evil demiurge or fallen angel. Most men and women are prisoners of this evil, material world and its sins of the flesh (which figured large in the gnostic imagination). But it was possible to escape the world, the flesh and the devil by accessing a secret wisdom or esoteric knowledge, "gnosis", which the High God made available through savior figures or redeemers. These divine messengers were believed to descend from the High Heaven into the world to scatter wisdom for those who had ears to hear, and then ascend again to their heavenly realm.

Those who picked up the gnosis thought of themselves as descendants of the High God stranded in enemy territory, sparks of divine light trapped in the material world as stars appeared to be trapped in a dark sky. Their goal, their salvation, was to acquire enough secret knowledge to enable them to spring the trap, break free of the material world, and ascend to their true home in Heaven. Gnostics were thus "those in the know" or "those who know" (which inspired T H Huxley to coin the word **agnostic** *for those who don't).*

It is easy to see how the early Jesus movement would hold some attraction for both Jews and gentiles already affected by gnostic ideas. Jesus could easily be interpreted as a Christ, a messiah, the latest savior-redeemer who came to share his secret wisdom through his teaching in order to save believers and bring them to their heavenly home. Early suggestions of what appear to be gnostic influence are apparent in the theology of Paul's letters, Mark, John, and Thomas. These early-gnostic features appear to have become part of much late-first and early-second century forms of Christianity, but by the late second century, when gnostic metaphysics had become more fully developed, it began to be challenged as heretical by the proto-orthodox tendency within the church , and was subsequently persecuted virtually to extinction.

One argument for an early date for Thomas is that its gnosticism is weak and undeveloped. As the editors of the Jesus Seminar's **The Five Gospels**, *put it (p 501), "Perhaps it is best to describe Thomas as reflecting an incipient gnosticism. There are, after all, a number of ways in which Thomas is not gnostic at all. Thomas has no doctrine of the creation; it provides no account of the fall. It contains nothing about an evil creator god. Moreover, Thomas seems to know Judaism in its basic, orthodox form [rather than in its gnostic variants]... Thomas is rooted in the Jewish wisdom tradition, such as we find in Psalms and Proverbs. It is a wisdom gospel made up of the teachings of a sage. But it is moving off in the direction of gnostic speculation such as we find in later gnostic documents. In these respects, Thomas represents an early stage in Christian gospel writing and theologizing, quite comparable to what we find in the New Testament, especially in Paul and the Gospel of John".*

6

THE UNOFFICIAL FACES OF JESUS

Luke, writing shortly before the end of the first century, acknowledges that "many" before him had taken up the task of writing accounts of "things which are most surely believed among us" as passed on by "eye-witnesses and ministers of the word" (1:1-2). "Many" implies that there were more pre-Lukan gospels in circulation than have survived, for we only have Mark, Matthew, the earlier writings which appear to be embedded in Matthew and Luke, a possible early version of Thomas and fragments of gospels which are difficult to date with certainty.

However, several gospels written soon after Luke do survive. The best-known, of course, is John, since it is the only one eventually chosen for inclusion in the New Testament. But over the next two centuries dozens of narrative gospels were produced by different Christian commu-nities, and for many years these were regarded by some churches as no less "holy scripture" than the four which made it into the canon. Most disappeared as one particular church faction, with its own preferred books, came to dominate the others. Gospels and other Christian writings considered by this dominant faction "heretical" or "unorthodox" ceased to be copied and circulated, or were destroyed. But some were hidden away by Christians who continued to revere them and hoped for a day when the theological tide would turn in their favor.

Many centuries later, in modern times, collections of these books have been, literally, dug up and re-examined. They have radically changed our view of early Christianity. What they tell us is that by the second century there was not one Christianity but a plethora of Christianities, not one understanding of who Jesus was and what he had said and done, but many. If most scholars find less reliable evidence for the historical Jesus in most of these gospels than in the New Testament collection it is not because they regard them as "less inspired" or less theologically "correct": these are judgments which belong to religious faith rather than evidence-based historiography. Rather, their reliability as accurate records of what Jesus really said and did is assumed to diminish as the time gap between the historical events and the recording of them grows. If there are problems with matching the canonical gospels' late-first-century accounts to early-first-century events, they clearly multiply when the accounts come from the second, third or later centuries.

We shall look at some of these late gospels shortly and summarize what scholars have made of them as historical Jesus sources. But before doing so it may be helpful to make a couple of short digressions.

Digression 1: the game of the name

First, what should we call these gospels and early Christian writings? The terms most commonly used are "apocryphal", "unorthodox", "non-canonical" and "gnostic", but there are problems with all these labels.

Apocryphal derives from a Greek word meaning "hidden". In this literal sense it seems a good description of these books, which were indeed hidden for centuries in caves, jars and the dry sands of Egypt. But they were not written to be hidden. The word was first applied to those books of the Hebrew scriptures that were excluded from the Hebrew canon which became the Christian "Old Testament". Such books are still printed in some versions of the Bible as "the Apocrypha". By analogy, Christian books excluded from the New Testament came to be seen as a new Apocrypha, and "apocryphal" took on the meaning of "spurious", "false", "sham", "of doubtful authenticity". But of course this was not how such books were seen by those who wrote them and by the communities that revered them as holy writ. To call these books "apocryphal" is to fall into the trap of viewing them exclusively through the eyes of a faction that disowned them and tried to write them out of history.

Unorthodox takes us right back into the same flawed perspective. None of these books were unorthodox when they were written and widely used in private and public worship, because there was no such thing as an agreed orthodoxy. Every competing Christianity was orthodox in its own eyes: all the others were the ones out of step. If this sounds familiar in a twentyfirst-century world filled with Christianities as diverse as those of Roman Catholics and Plymouth Brethren, Anglicans and Adventists, Methodists, Mormons and Moonies, Baptists and Branch Davidians, Marxist liberation theologians and Uganda's fascist Lord's Liberation Army, it is salutory to be reminded by the contemporary literature that the religion which claimed to derive from Jesus was no less diverse, and no less mutually hostile, nearly two thousand years ago when it was still in its infancy.

Consideration of the term "orthodoxy", incidentally, throws up another problem: What are we to call the faction which eventually won out in this ideological dog-fight and became the Roman Catholic Church? That is, what are we to call it as we watch it emerge in the second and third centuries, before it established itself as orthodox or could proclaim itself "catholic"? In many parts of the Christian world at this time it was actually the weaker faction, considered "heretical" by rival Christian churches. I propose to follow those scholars who refer to this group - the faction of Ignatius, Clement, Tertullian and Athanasius - as "proto-orthodox". Their position would eventually become "orthodox", but that was in the future[1].

Non-canonical may seem to us a fair description of these books - I have already used it several times, and will sometimes do so again - but we need to keep reminding ourselves that in the early centuries there was no fixed canon: rather, there were competing collections of "approved" books. The word *canon*, derived from the Greek for "measuring rod" or "standard", was originally used by the Greeks in a secular sense to refer to canons of correct spelling or correct musical chords. Even when second and third-century Christian writers used the word it was to refer to a "canon of faith", a "canon of truth" or a "canon of our holy tradition", never a canon of books[2]. The "father of ecclesiastical history", Eusebius, writing early in the fourth century, goes to great pains to guide his readers to "approved" and "authentic" books and distinguish these from "rejected" writings, but Athanasius, bishop of Alexandria, was probably the first to list the 27 books that became the New Testament and describe them as "the canon". He did so in a letter written in 367, asserting that "in these alone the teaching of godliness is proclaimed. Let no-one add to these; let nothing be taken away from them"[3]. But even then Athanasius's selection was not universally accepted and some branches of the church continued to proclaim their own. The debate continued into the fifth century and beyond, and not until the mid-sixteenth-century at the Council of Trent was the Athanasian canon formerly ratified by the Roman Catholic church. Most Protestant churches followed suit, though Martin Luther queried the inclusion of James's epistle. To call certain books "non-canonical", then, is to read back into the second century judgments made hundreds of years later.

Gnostic brings a different set of problems. Some of these books were gnostic, but some were not. Gnosticism actually predated the Jesus movement and aspects of its mythology were gradually absorbed into a diverse range of Christian theologies. Gnostic Christians believed the material world was not created by the supreme God but by an inferior deity or devil, and was irredeemably evil. Salvation came not by faith in Jesus' atoning sacrifice at his death but by acquiring the "secret knowledge" believed to be hidden in Jesus' teachings during his life. When hitherto unknown gospels came to light at Nag Hammadi in 1945 they all tended to be dubbed "gnostic". But subsequent scholarship has shown that gnostic influences may be detected in the letters of Paul and the biblical gospels, while some late gospels of the second and third century show no sign of gnosticism. Indeed, some scholars have come to argue that the range and diversity of books in which a special "saving knowledge" of Jesus is to be found is so wide that there may be said to be many gnosticisms - or none. This robs the term of any useful meaning when lazily applied to all gospels which were rejected by the divines who approved the New Testament.

In what follows, then (when we are done with these digressions), I shall try to remember to refer to "late gospels", meaning all those generally assumed to have been written or compiled after the last of the New Testament gospels, John. Even this relatively value-free term will at times be problematic, since some scholars argue that some "late" gospels (such as Peter, discussed in the last chapter) may in fact be early, possibly first century! But we have to call them something to distinguish them from those which eventually came to be privileged by inclusion in the New Testament when the proto-orthodox faction won out and proclaimed itself orthodox and all other positions heretical[4]. Since most are not fully attested until the second, third, fourth or fifth centuries, "late gospels" seems appropriate. Otherwise, I shall simply refer to "non-biblical" books, and ask readers to bear all the above qualifications in mind.

Digression 2: "pious forgeries"

When we come to look at these late gospels and other contemporary Christian books we shall see that a number of them include within their text the claim that they were written by one of the apostles. The Secret Book of James begins "James, writing to..." and continues in the first person. A separate work known to scholars as Proto-Gospel of James claims to have been written by James the brother of Jesus. The Gospel of Peter is also written in the first person: "I, Simon Peter, and Andrew, my brother...". The Gospel of Thomas begins "These are the secret sayings that the living Jesus spoke and Didymos Judas Thomas recorded...". The so-called Secret Gospel of Thomas (another book entirely) begins "I, Thomas the Israelite, am reporting to you...". And there are Acts of John, of Paul, of Peter, of Thomas; letters claiming to be by Paul, Peter, James and Titus; Apocalypses of Paul and Peter; a Secret Book of John... and so on. No scholar who has studied these books in their surviving manuscript copies believes that any of them were written by the apostles or their companions. But that is often the claim made within the text itself. Are they then plain forgeries?

Many scholars - particularly those working with Christian academic affiliations - prefer to use the term "pseudonymous", meaning "written in the name of". "Pseudonymity of this type was conventional in Antiquity", argues Donald Rappe, discussing Secret Book of James; and Stephen J Patterson, commenting on the Gospel of Thomas, adds that "the ascription... to an apostolic figure probably derives from an urge to guarantee the reliability of the tradition"[5]. In this view, pseudonymity did not necessarily involve deliberate deception. The writer or compiler wrote from within a particular apostle's tradition, perhaps the apostle or evangelist who was believed to have founded the community producing the book. Second-century or later readers would understand this. In any case, they would not have had a "modern" view of such matters, where to write in someone else's name in order to embue your own work with their authority would be denounced as plainly dishonest.

But a harsher view is taken by Bart D Ehrman. "Almost all of the 'lost' Scriptures of the early Christians," he writes, "were forgeries". To refer to them as pseudonymous writings is to prefer "a more antiseptic term. But it does little to solve the problem of a potential deceit, for an author who attempts to pass off his own writing as that of some well-known person has written a forgery". Ehrman flatly discounts the argument that the ancients had no concept of forgery: "People in the ancient world did not appreciate forgeries any more than people do today. There are numerous discussions of forgery in ancient Greek and Latin sources. In virtually every case the practice is denounced as deceitful and ill-spirited"[6].

Ehrman tells a good story about the second-century Roman physician Galen who heard two men at a bookstall arguing about a book prominently marked "by Galen". One insisted it was a forgery, the other maintained it was genuine. Galen's response was to write a book called *On His Own Books*, describing how one could distinguish books by Galen from books forged in Galen's name[7]. (Presumably *On His Own Books* really was by Galen!)

Forgeries were often committed for money. Such deception was widely condemned. But Ehrman notes that second-century followers of the classical Greek philosopher Pythagoras often wrote their theses in the name of Pythagoras, who had lived seven hundred years earlier. "Why? Because, they claimed, their own ideas were simply elaborations of the system devised by the greatest mind the world had ever seen. To sign their own names would have been an act of hubris and, in a somewhat ironic sense, a false attribution"[8]. It seems likely that something like this is what was sometimes happening when second-century and later Christians wrote in the name of first-century apostles. If their writings were forgeries, they were "pious forgeries", written by men convinced that they knew the mind of the apostle. This would also apply to New Testament books like the late-first-century letters written in Paul's name by unknown authors to Timothy and Titus, as well as to the much later non-biblical letters, again claiming Paul's authorship, to the churches of Laodicea and Alexandria, and a third letter to the Corinthians: books which never made it into the final canon. On the other hand, it would not apply to, say, Matthew's gospel or the epistle to the Hebrews, neither of which claimed to be written by the author to whom they were later attributed.

With these digressions and clarifications out of the way, we may turn to the late books themselves to see what, if anything, scholars have extracted as reliable evidence on the historical Jesus. There are several guides, but among the best and most recent are *The Complete Gospels*, edited by Robert J Miller, and Bart D Ehrman's *Lost Christianities* and *Lost Scriptures*. A slightly older guide-book is Helmut Koester's *Ancient Christian Gospels* published in 1990: an exceptionally detailed study, of particular use to specialist students.

1. Buried treasure: the Nag Hammadi hoard

Several gospels of critical interest to Jesus detectives only came to light in 1945. Ehrman scarcely exaggerates when he enticingly describes their discovery as "a story of serendipity, ineptitude, secrecy, ignorance, scholarly brilliance, murder, and blood revenge"[9]. As with all good stories, there are several versions. Here I weave together two, those of Ehrman in *Lost Christianities* and Elaine Pagels in *The Gnostic Gospels*. In December 1945 some Egyptian peasants were digging for nitrate fertiliser in caves under a cliff by the banks of the Nile, just outside the hamlet of al-Qasr and near the village of Nag Hammadi, about forty miles north of Luxor. Their spades hit what turned out to be a large red earthenware jar about two feet high. At first they were frightened of opening it in case it contained an evil genie. On the other hand, it might contain gold... Greed or curiosity got the better of fear and they broke it open, to find nothing but bundles of old and crumbling leather-bound books.

Old books were not gold, but the peasants knew there were strange men in far-away Cairo who might be persuaded to part with a coin or two for such finds. So the books were divided among the group, which involved ripping some of them apart to ensure fair shares. As the books disintegrated, most of the group decided they were worthless and abandoned their share. But the leader - graced, as serendipity would have it, by the name Mohammed Ali - gathered most of the scattered remains in his turban and took them home. After his mother had used a few brittle leaves to light the fire, the rest were piled up in the animal shed.

There they might have rotted away unrecognized and unread except for a blood feud and a triple murder. Six month's earlier Ali's father, employed as a night guard, had shot and killed an intruder. The intruder's family then killed Ali's father to satisfy family honor. About a month after the discovery of the jar of old books Ali and his brothers exacted their revenge on their father's killer, hacking him to death while he lay asleep at the roadside. For good measure (though readers may not feel the need to know this) they cut out his heart and ate it. Aware that he'd be a prime suspect and that his home was likely to be searched, Ali gathered up some of the old documents from the goat shed and asked a local priest to look after them until the trouble blew over. The priest had a brother-in-law who offered to take the documents to a Cairo dealer for sale on the black market, but when the Egyptian authorities got wind of the find they confiscated the lot. Eventually, after much haggling, the authorities licensed a sale to the Coptic Museum, where the leaves were finally recognized as ancient Christian documents. Most of the rest of the pile, which had been dispersed by Mohammed Ali, was tracked down, and an international team of experts under an American scholar, James Robinson, was assembled to photograph, translate and publish them.

What Ali and his friends had unearthed turned out to be by far the most important collection of early Christian writings to be discovered in modern times. Reassembled, the papyrus leaves made up twelve leather volumes and some leaves left over. The experts disentangled 46 different works - gospels and other treatises - of which several were duplicated. Some were already known of from fragments found elsewhere or from references in other early writings. Some were wholly new to scholars. All were in the ancient Coptic language but appeared to be translations of Greek originals. The copies were unusually easy to date, since some of the leaves had been written on merchants' receipts conveniently dated 341, 346 and 348, indicating that the scribes had made these copies in the mid-fourth century. The Greek originals were obviously earlier.

Why were these copies stuffed into a jar and buried under a cliff shortly after 348? Ehrman points out that they were hidden away just as Bishop Athanasius of the Egyptian province of Alexandria (which included Nag Hammadi) was successfully urging the churches under his jurisdiction to adopt his 27-book canon - our New Testament. Ehrman speculates that monks at a nearby monastery "felt the pressure from on high and cleaned out their library to conform with the dictates of the powerful bishop of Alexandria"[10]. Rather than burn books they had long held to be sacred, they sealed them in a jar and buried them in the wilderness for safe-keeping until, as they hoped, the tides of scriptural preferences shifted. And there they remained for 1500 years till

Mohammed Ali and his gang dug them up, passed them to a local priest to avoid their being confiscated as potential evidence in a police murder hunt, and managed to off-load them on a Cairo museum. History moves in mysterious ways...

The Nag Hammadi documents are of incalculable value in fleshing out our knowledge and understanding of the diversity of the early church. But what clues do they offer scholars whose focus is not church history but the historical Jesus? That is the question we need to keep in mind as we look over the detectives' shoulders while they peruse the most important of these texts, one by one.

The Secret Book of James

More than half a century after its discovery there is still no scholarly consensus on the significance and dating of this "apocryphon" or "secret book", which purports to tell of a private revelation imparted by Jesus to James and Peter a few days after the resurrection and prior to the ascension. It begins with an account of how "the twelve disciples [used to] sit all together at the [same time], remembering what the Savior had said to each of them, whether secretly or openly, and setting it down in books". This is a striking description of the process assumed by many scholars, whereby Jesus' sayings and teachings were first "remembered" by disciples, creating an oral tradition, which then came to be "set down in books" that derived their authority from attribution to a particular disciple or close associate. According to Donald Rappe, this "witness to the compiling or 'remembering' of sayings traditions, the conspicuous deference to James and Peter, and the primitiveness of much of its content suggest that [the Secret Book of James] may well have been written in the first half of the second century"[11]. The adventurous John Dominic Crossan once again proposes an even earlier date, "late-first-century or early-second century", but this has not won widespread support. While the Secret James sayings and parables often have parallels or similarities to those in the synoptic gospels, scholars such as Ron Cameron[12] and

Helmut Koester[13] consider that they are not directly dependent on the synoptics but are derived independently from the pool of oral traditions. But even assuming the early-second-century dating proposed by Rappe, which would make it roughly contemporary with John, the Secret Gospel of James is generally regarded as too late a composition or compilation to afford scholars any reliable new information on the historical Jesus.

The Dialogue of the Savior

Like the Secret Gospel of James, much of the so-called Dialogue of the Savior is written in the form of a series of conversations between Jesus and his disciples. To these dialogues are added lengthy theological reflections on baptism, metaphysics and an apocalyptic vision of the journey of the saved soul. Julian V Hills proposes that these somewhat disparate elements were edited together around 150[14], but Koester and Pagels propose a much earlier date for the dialogues themselves. Koester argues that in the form in which they appear in the Nag Hammadi copy - the only one known - they "most likely [date from] the beginning of the second century" and are based on an earlier "dialogues gospel" that "may have been composed during the last decades of the first century". This would make their compilation more or less contemporary with Matthew and Luke, perhaps prior to John.

Against so early a date, the recorded words of Jesus (apparently a post-resurrection Jesus) in the Dialogue bear little relation to the aphorisms, beatitudes and parables remembered in Q, Mark, or any other first-century composition. Instead, they read like the words of a Jesus invented as a mouthpiece for the early-gnostic theology of an unknown teacher/editor. As such, they are judged by most scholars to yield no significant information on the flesh-and-blood Jesus of Galilee. As Crossan notes wryly, where the "biography gospels" give us twenty chapters of Jesus' life before his death, the "dialogues gospels" give us twenty chapters after it[15].

The Gospel of Philip

Virtually unknown until it was found at Nag Hammadi, Philip has attracted some notoriety as a result of the cavalier use made of it in *The Da Vinci Code*. Dan Brown's novel elevates this and the Gospel of Mary to a status above that of the canonical gospels, suggesting that they were excluded by proto-orthodoxy, not because they were considered historically unreliable but because they told a truth about Jesus which had to be suppressed, namely that he had married Mary Magdalene and raised a family with her. The novel quotes two passages from Philip, one describing Mary as "the one who was called his companion" and the other saying he loved his companion more than his disciples, as evidenced by the statement that he kissed her "on the mouth".

As the millions of readers of this novel will be well aware, Dan Brown's fictional "expert" Leigh Teabing claims that the word translated as "companion" is an Aramaic term which really meant "spouse". Teabing, or Brown himself, is evidently ignorant of the fact that Philip is known only in Coptic, not Aramaic. He makes much of a tentative translation which has Jesus "often" kissing Mary "on the mouth"; but the Nag Hammadi Philip, which is the only known manuscript, is full of holes where the text has been chewed away by mites and time, and the most accurate translation of this passage reads "... the companion of the [*small hole*] Mary Magdalene [*bigger hole*] her more than [*small hole*] disciples and used to kiss her [*hole*] on her [*hole*]. The rest of [*big hole*] said to him 'Why do you [*hole*] her more than all of us...". That the author of Philip has Jesus loving Mary is clear. That he has him kissing her is equally clear. But "on the mouth"? Sexually? This particular hole could well have contained cheek, forehead, hand, foot. Even taking into account some mysterious references in Philip to an otherwise unknown sacrament known as "bridal chamber", which some have suggested could refer to an initiation rite involving sex, it would seem to take an enflamed imagination, coupled with flagrant disregard for historical methodology, to see in these incomplete passages from a third-century gospel hard evidence of the historical Jesus' love life.

But the controversy offers a graphic illustration of the problems textual scholars continually face. It is from a combination of serendipities - a casual dig by Ali and his companions, Ali's mother stoking the fire on a cold night, the feeding habits of Ali's animals, the wear and tear of time - that inventive minds have conjured up a sexually active Jesus who married his favorite companion and went on to sire a line of French kings! *The Da Vinci Code*, despite its notorious claims to documentary authenticity, is a novel, fiction not history, and may perhaps be seen in much the same light as some of the third- and fourth-century gospels which elaborated a Jesus story for the sake of a good read and a handsome royalty. (See Cameo: *Did Jesus have a Love Life?*, page 128).

Returning from whimsy to scholarship, even Bart D Ehrman, who tries hard, finds Philip "notoriously difficult to understand in its details". It is unlike either the biographical gospels in the canon or the dialogue and sayings gospels with which it was found. Ehrman describes it as "a collection of mystical reflections that have evidently been excerpted from previously existing sermons, treatises and theological meditations, brought together... under the name of Jesus' disciple Philip"[16]. Its theology is clearly gnostic, where Jesus saves by imparting secret knowledge. Scholars date it to the late-second or early third century and the real-life ones, unlike the fictional Mr Teabing, are in general agreement that it tells us nothing about the human Jesus - his words, deeds, or even his private life.

The many other books in the Nag Hammadi jar, including a Gospel of Truth, an Apocalypse of Paul and an Apocalypse of Peter, likewise tell us much about early Christian diversity but nothing reliable about the historical Jesus. The one possible exception is the Gospel of Thomas, which we have looked at separately. For the rest, as Elaine Pagels describes them, they range from "secret gospels, poems, and quasi-philosophic descriptions of the origin of the universe, to myths, magic and instructions for mystical practice". But Nag Hammadi was not the only hiding place for gospels which were getting the thumbs-down from the proto-orthodox.

2. Finds before and after Nag Hammadi
The Gospel of Mary

This gospel has attracted enormous interest since the publication of Karen King's study and translation *The Gospel of Mary of Magdala* and, of course, *The Da Vinci Code*. A fifth-century Coptic translation was discovered in obscure circumstances in the 1890s but not published till 1955, and two additional early-third-century Greek fragments came to light in the twentieth century. Even so, only about half the original is known to us.

The gospel strikingly asserts the authority of Mary Magdalene as Jesus' principal disciple and interpreter and offers a clear example of women's leadership roles in some parts of the early church before male supremacy became entrenched. Karen King describes its dating as "highly tentative but [it] may arguably have been written sometime in the late first or early second century"[17]. Clearly it was not written by the historical Mary Magdalene, and Mary is always referred to in the third person. Nor does it explicitly claim to have been written by a woman. The emphasis is gnostic: Mary reveals Jesus' secret teachings to male disciples who are not sufficiently spiritually advanced to understand them without patient explanation. Once again, Mary is important (and relevant) for what it tells us of how Jesus' teachings were interpreted in one group of churches around the turn of the first century, a group distinguished by its resistance to the leadership's growing marginalization of women, rather than for any echoes of the authentic words and deeds of the historical Jesus.

The Infancy Gospel of Thomas

This is one of several "infancy gospels" (not to be confused with the Gospel of Thomas) that tell stories of Jesus' boyhood, attempting to fill

Cameo: Did Jesus have a love life?

It is not surprising that many writers, and latterly film-makers, have raised questions about Jesus and sex. Apart from the well-known links between religious and erotic ecstasy which are not far below the surface in most religious traditions, Jesus is unusual among religious teachers of ancient times in his reputation for mixing freely with men and women rumored to be not entirely respectable. While there is no evidence whatever to support the tradition that Mary Magdalene was a prostitute, reformed or not, let alone any shred of fact to support the fantasy that she was Jesus' lover, wife or mother of his children, speculation about whether or not Jesus was a sexual being has been around since the second century. Morton Smith and Dan Brown are only among the latest to recycle this ancient theme.

Prurience may be a common motivation for such speculations, but questions of whether or not Jesus was a sexual being were bound to be raised, however discreetly, by the fundamental controversies within the church over his cosmic status. Was he human, or divine, or both? Some early Christians insisted that he was wholly divine, a spirit who had merely appeared to take on human form. Others maintained that he was wholly human, a prophet of God but not God himself, and a son of God only in the sense that he was a chosen servant of God, or even in the wider sense in which all were seen as God's children. Yet others - the proto-orthodox group who would eventually win out - argued that he was uniquely and mysteriously both fully human and fully divine, "very God, begotten not created". It is not difficult to see how these controversies raised questions about Jesus' sexuality.

If Jesus was wholly spirit, a human being in appearance only, he could be assumed to be sexless, without desire - and, like *angels, without genitals. On the other hand, if he was fully human (either because he was **only** human, not divine, or because in some ineffable way he was both fully human and fully divine) he must have shared in everything that makes humans human. As a normal man he must have felt hunger and thirst, heat and cold, pleasure in the company of loving companions, delight in the company of children, anguish at betrayal - and, at the end, the physical agony of being strung up on a cross. That is what it was to be fully human. But, as everyone knows from their own experience, there was something else. If Jesus was really fully human, a man of flesh and blood, he must have known sexual desire. Not just what sexual desire was, as a piece of head knowledge, but the intimate experience, how it felt, what happened to the body, the rush of blood and hormones, the irrepressible fantasy, the struggle between repression and satisfaction.*

*The church's insistence on devotion to Jesus as the Christ, the Word of God who from the beginning was both **with** God and **was** God, had the inevitable effect of denying Jesus the man who, because he was human, knew what we know, experienced what we experience, and shared our natural desire to find a mate and increase and multiply. It was in the nature of what became church orthodoxy that Jesus the man, the Galilean peasant whose reported words and deeds had started it all, had to be neutered, theologically castrated. But it was also in the nature of dissent that Jesus the eunach would never be universally credible. There would always be Christian writers, artists and film-makers who would give the son of man who taught us to love our enemies a love life of his own - or at least the capacity, emotional and physical, to be a fully operational sexual being.*

the gap between his birth and his visit to Jerusalem as a 12-year-old prodigy as recounted in Luke 2: 41-52. Although the oldest copy known is a Syriac manuscript dated to the sixth century, Irenaeus appears to refer to it in his treatise *Against Heresies*, written about 185, indicating that it was probably composed mid-second century. As summarized in *The Complete Gospels*, "The initial episodes portray a petulant Jesus at play, a sometimes hot-tempered lad ready to use his remarkable abilities in destructive or self-serving ways, and a prodigy at school, impatient with the limitations of his merely human teachers. As time progresses, he becomes a child devoted to his parents and siblings, finally eager to use his powers to help and to heal those in need... This gospel affords us a view of how Jesus was regarded in the unsophisticated religious imaginations of ordinary early Christians, rather than in the more abstract theological affirmations of Christian intellectuals"[18]. Although attempts have been made to argue that some stories in the genre of "infancy gospels" could be based on memories passed down within the family, for instance by Jesus' brothers, they have not proved convincing to any significant branch of mainstream scholarship.

The Infancy Gospel of James

Another work in the same genre, this is similarly dated to the mid-second century. It tells a nativity story clearly based on Luke, but is largely taken up with asserting the perpetual purity and virginity of Mary. Ronald F Hock in *The Complete Gospels* comments that "The increased focus on purity and virginity derives from one of the cultural trends of the period. In both philosophical and more popular literary sources there is an increasing value placed on the cardinal virtue of *sophrosyne*, self-control of the tongue, the belly, and, to use the euphemism of the day, the things below the belly. It is clearly control of what is below the belly that is most admired. Mary is very like the heroines of the romance, the most popular literature of the day. The romance features characters who preserved their chastity against all odds. But even in the romances the heroines remain chaste only outside of marriage. In this respect Mary exceeds them and remains always a virgin, and thus perfectly pure"[19]. This gospel clearly tells us something of interest about the origins of the Virgin Mother cult, but, to quote John Bowker in *The Oxford Book of World Religions*, this and other infancy gospels "are important for the study of iconography, legends and Christmas carols, but devoid of historical value".

The Gospel of Judas

There was much excitement in the popular press when a Gospel of Judas was exhibited by the National Geographic Society in Washington in April 2006. The papyrus was found in an Egyptian cave in 1978, circulated among traders for a while, during which it rapidly detereriorated in condition, then locked in a safe deposit box in New York until it was bought by a Swiss dealer in 2000 who handed it over to the Maecenas Foundation for Ancient Art in Basel for authentification, reconstruction of the separated fragments, and translation. Fragments were sent to the University of Arizona and carbon-dated to between 220 and 340 CE. The text, in Coptic, is presumed to be a translation of a Greek original referred to and condemned as "heretical" by Bishop Irenaeus of Lyon in 180 CE, which suggests a mid-second century date for its composition.

Just as the gospel of Mary appears to be the product of a Jesus community that reverenced Mary Magdalene as Jesus' closest companion, ranked higher than any of the male disciples, so Judas would seem to indicate the existence of a community that gave a similarly exalted status to the odd one out among the disciples. The gospel has Jesus telling Judas to step away from the others so that he can tell him "the mysteries of the kingdom". Judas is promised that he will "exceed all of them". The kiss in the garden by which Judas betrays his master is presented as a divinely ordained set-up, necessary to God's plan for Jesus to die a sacrificial death. In any case, Judas is promised by Jesus that he will only be sacrificing "the man that clothes me", the human body, not the divine spirit. This emphasis on "the mysteries of the kingdom" and

Jesus as a spirit in man's clothing strongly suggests a community heavily influenced by gnostic mythology/theology.

The rehabilitation of Judas may also represent a subtle rejection of Christian antisemitism by a surviving band of Jewish Christians. That Judas, meaning "the Jew", was pictured by other Jesus communities as the betrayer of the Christ was perhaps perceived within this gnostic group as part of the campaign (already well under way in John's gospel) to blame "the Jews" as a whole for putting the Messiah to death. The gospel of Judas may thus represent an attempt to justify Judas's apparent treachery as an act of obedience to God's will, thereby exonerating "the Jews" from blame. Modern thinkers and writers have been fascinated by the moral ambiguities of the Judas-betrayal story. (Was Judas Satan's agent in the destruction of Jesus, or God's chosen instrument in fulfilling Jesus' redemptive destiny?). The Judas gospel shows that this conundrum exercised at least one Jesus community as early as the second century.

As to its usefulness as an historical-Jesus source, Geza Vermes voiced the consensus of scholars in commenting in a *Guardian* newspaper review: "The document is of interest for the ideas of the gnostics but it almost certainly adds nothing to our understanding of what happened 150 years before it was written." Like Mary, Philip and the others, it enriches our knowledge of the diversity of early Christianities but tells us nothing about the human Jesus and his place in human history. It should not be confused with a concoction by one "Benjamin Iscariot as recounted by Geoffrey Archer", shamelessly published by Macmillan in 2007 as *The Gospel According to Judas*, which served to demonstrate once again that there's good money to be had in bad Jesus-history.

3. Fragments

Fragments of more lost gospels are included and translated in Miller's *Complete Gospels*. They include manuscripts known to scholars as the Egerton Gospel, Gospel Oxyrhynchus 840 and Gospel Oxyrhynchus 1224. None of these consist of more than a single page of modern text.

What remains of the Egerton Gospel (named after the man who funded its purchase) exists on two small fragments carbon-dated to the second half of the second century, making it one of the very earliest extant Christian manuscripts. (The dating of most documents relies on scholarly guess-work based on style and content rather than carbon-dating of the papyrus itself). Its actual composition is also thought to be very early, *The Complete Gospels* suggesting "the second half of the first century, approximately at the same time that the related narrative gospels were being drafted"[20]. Some scholars have argued that Egerton could have been a source for the biblical gospels, particularly John, with which its fragmentary text appears to have close parallels; but others consider it more likely that its author was drawing on the ever-expanding pool of divergent traditions available to the other gospel writers. It might, for instance, be a fragmentary survivor of those "many other" accounts referred to in Luke's introduction to his own gospel. At present, not enough has survived to settle the argument. Jon B Daniels, however, suggests that, small as they are, the Egerton fragments can offer an insight into ways the narrative gospels emerged, providing "significant evidence about early variations in the formulation and transmission of written or oral traditions about Jesus"[21]. Specifically, like its contemporary proto-orthodox or biblical gospels, Egerton appears to have been constructed by taking stories which had already assumed a fixed form in oral or early written tradition, and arranging them in a literary framework designed to further a particular theological purpose.

However, the only story in these fragments which is seemingly without parallel elsewhere is one in which Jesus appears to take a handful of water from the Jordan and scatter it on the ground to produce a miraculous growth of fruit. But the text is so fragmentary at this point that a number of different readings are possible - all of them seemingly more legendary than historical.

Other fragmentary gospels were discovered in a series of excavations between 1897 and 1934 in old rubbish dumps at the Egyptian village of

Behnesa. Thousands of bits of papyri were unearthed, including Greek, Latin and Egyptian texts, all labelled "Oxyrhynchus" after the ancient name of the village, and allocated a number. Oxyrhynchus 840 consists of some 45 lines of text in which Jesus is rebuked by a priest for taking his disciples into the temple court without any external purification ceremony. Philip Sewell in *The Complete Gospels* proposes as an "educated guess" a composition date "sometime before 200", while Theissen and Merz tentatively suggest it "could well come from the first century"[22]. Here, as so often, expert assessments differ so starkly that the lay Jesus-detective is reminded that the dating game is often down to intelligent guesswork.

These differing assessments are almost reversed in the case of Oxyrhynchus 1224 which contains two fragments of Jesus sayings. Because sayings collections are assumed to be an earlier genre than narrative gospels, Robert J Miller suggests it may belong to the layer of Jesus writings which includes Q and early-Thomas: "It could be as early as the 50s when Christians first began to create books about what Jesus had said and done". But Theisssen and Merz conclude that it is in such a fragmentary state that "no certain reading can be made"[23]. One of the two fragments is about 6 x 13 cm (think postcard), with not a single line complete. The other is even smaller, just over 3 x 4 cm (think credit-card), with just five incomplete lines and four full words. The sayings, in so far as they can be deciphered, include an injunction to "pray for your enemies, for the one who is not against you is on your side [and] the one who today is at a distance, tomorrow will be near you". This appears to be a variant of the familiar "love your enemies" in Q, embedded in Matthew and Luke, and Miller comments that later Christian writers tended to prefer the "pray for" form, which "might be taken as a softening of a too-difficult injunction"[24]. So even a tiny scrap of papyrus dug out of a rubbish tip can present the Jesus detective with a conundrum. Did the historical Jesus tell his followers to do the difficult thing and *love* their enemies? Or did he merely ask that enemies be *prayed for* on the politic basis that today's enemies might be tomorrow's friends? Did his later followers soften a too-hard injunction, or toughen up a too-soft one?

When these gospel fragments were first discovered the tendency among theological scholars was, again, to assume they were simply reworkings and elaborations of the biblical gospels. Where they duplicated a biblical-gospel story or saying they were judged reliable, because the Bible itself was assumed to be reliable. Where they introduced a new story or saying, these were assumed to be heretical or fanciful additions. Thus John Bowker as late as 1997 in *The Oxford Dictionary of World Religions*: "Apocryphal gospels more or less followed the model of the New Testament ones, but contribute little or nothing of historical value"[25]. But it is now clear that much modern scholarship takes them more seriously. As we have noted, some scholars have speculated that Egerton, far from being derivative of John, could have been the source from which John, or even the authors of the synoptics, put together their narratives. And Oxyrhynchus 1224 could be the model for Q and the earliest sayings gospels. This would certainly raise their historical significance. Theissen and Merz, in *The Historical Jesus*, cite some scholars who see Egerton as dependent on all four canonical gospels (e.g. J Jeremias, *Unknown Sayings of Jesus*), some who see particular dependence on John (e.g. C H Dodd, *A New Gospel*), and some who see an independent tradition (e.g. G Mayeda, *Das-Leben-Jesu fragment*, H Koester, *Ancient Christian Gospels*, and J D Crossan, *Four Other Gospels*)[26]. But so long as these tantalising versions of the story are known to us only in these tiny, holey fragments the debate is likely to continue without resolution.

4. Jewish-Christian and other gospels

Among other second-century texts are three that are usually labeled the Jewish Christian gospels. The Gospel of the Nazarenes or Syrian Gospel is an Aramaic version of Matthew, with some elaborations. It was in use among a community of Jewish Christians in Aleppo, Syria. Of greater interest is the Gospel of the Ebionites, used by Jewish Christians in Transjordan. This too is based on Matthew, with some material from Luke and Mark but with significant deletions and amendments. The infancy narratives are omitted, which led proto-orthodox church leaders to charge that the Ebionites denied the miraculous conception and divinity of Jesus (which they evidently did: but Mark also omits a miraculous conception story). The Ebionites were vegetarians: their John the Baptist is on a locust-free diet, his Matthean "wild honey and locusts" becoming honey and pancakes. Origen suggested the Ebionites (a faith-community, not an ethnic group) derived their name from the Hebrew term *ebyon*, meaning "poor": he mocked them as "poor in understanding". But Ehrman may be closer to the mark in suggesting they perhaps continued the practice of the early Jerusalem church, as described in Acts 2:44-45 and 4:32-37, of abandoning private possessions in order to embrace the poverty of Jesus himself[27]. After all, if Jesus was taken seriously in blessing "the poor", the *ebyonites* had a claim to be regarded as his true disciples.

The Gospel of Hebrews, also early-second-century, is again known only from tiny fragments and quotations in Clement and Origen, which suggest that it was gnostic in theology and used among Jewish Christians in Egypt. Once again it may be said of these gospels that they expand our knowledge of a theologically diverse second-century church but add little or nothing to what we can know of the historical Jesus. The same appears to be true of other gospels circulating at the same time among groups of gentile Christians. The Gospel of the Egyptians was used, as its name implies, by Egyptian Christians, as was a fragmentary Coptic gospel known as the Gospel of the Savior. A Gospel of Truth was discovered among the Nag Hammadi finds and is not so much a narrative life as a celebration of the joys of salvation brought by Christ's revelation of secret knowledge. A Gospel of Nicodemus appears to be of fifth century origin. No doubt more await discovery, accompanied by exaggerated claims, followed by scholarly argument.

5. More buried treasure: the Dead Sea Scrolls

The extraordinary story of the making, hiding, discovery, translation, dating and interpretation of the Dead Sea Scrolls has been told many times - and in a number of different versions. It began one day in the late 60s CE when members of an ancient Jewish religious community at Khirbet Qumran, on the western shore of the Dead Sea and eight miles south of Jericho, packed their entire library of scrolls into huge earthenware jars and carried them out for temporary hiding in nearby caves. No doubt they intended to come back and collect them when the Jewish-Roman war that threatened their community was over. But they never did come back, and the jars lay undisturbed for nearly 2000 years till a young Bedouin shepherd, Muhammed edh-Dhib, climbed into one of the caves in 1947 and stumbled on the scrolls. This set off a massive search of local caves over the next ten years by both archaeologists and native Arabs ("who nine times out of ten outwitted their professional rivals"[28]), resulting in the discovery of many thousands of fragments and a quantity of scrolls, mostly containing hitherto unknown texts assumed to be connected with the nearby ruins of what was soon identified as an Essene community.

Amid much controversy, the scrolls were dated to the Second Temple period, the earliest from the second century BCE and the latest from the mid-first century CE. Geza Vermes writes that "The principal novelty provided by the manuscripts consists of cryptic allusions to the historical origins of the Community, launched by a priest called the Teacher of Righteousness, who was persecuted by a Jewish ruler, designated as the Wicked Priest"[29]. Inevitably there was intense scholarly and public interest once it became apparent that the manuscripts overlapped with the rise of the Jesus movement. What new light could they cast on the origins of Christianity, and even on Jesus himself?

In the event, there was soon almost unanimous agreement among scholars that the principal scrolls were pre-Christian. Geza Vermes was the first to propose, in 1952, that the conflict between the Teacher of

Righteousness and the Wicked Priest as described in key scrolls known as the Damascus Document and the Habakkuk Commentary (carbon-dated to no later than 5 BCE) related to events in the Maccabean revolt between 166 and 134 BCE[30]. (He suggested that the Wicked Priest was Jonathan Maccabee, executed in 142 BCE, while the Teacher of Righteousness was probably an idealized figure rather than an historical person). The Maccabean context was soon adopted by most scholars working on the scrolls, though a persistent dissenting voice has been that of Robert Eisenman who has continued to argue for CE datings of major manuscripts, on which basis he has proposed an entirely new theory of Christian origins and the identity of the historical Jesus (see chapter 10). But it is clear that the overwhelming majority of scholars have held to the earlier datings, and if they are right it follows that this second hoard of buried treasure, following so close on the Nag Hammadi discoveries, has much to tell us about religious life before the birth of Jesus but nothing about Jesus himself.

We have seen, then, that most scholars, having applied their forensic tools to every jot and tittle of every ragged fragment, have concluded that with a few important exceptions these mostly-second-century or later documents appear to offer hardly any reliable clues about the historical as distinct from a mythologized Jesus. This is not because they are considered intrinsically less reliable, less truthful or less "inspired" than the biblical gospels, but because so many are in a fragmentary state, and most date from a century or more after the events they purport to describe. This critical assessment does not fit comfortably into the agenda of the conspiracy theorists who have found ready audiences for sensationalist claims that the "amazing truth" about Jesus is to be found (usually in code) in these long-suppressed documents rather than in the biblical gospels. The fact is that all the gospel narratives, biblical and non-biblical, early and late, were written to preach a version of "the gospel", not to provide latter-day scholars with objective historical data.

What can confidently be said about the later documents is that they can provide valuable information on the process of gospel compilation which can be applied to the critical evaluation of the earlier materials. In this way they have played a crucial part in helping scholars sift mythical from historical truth, legendary story-telling from factual reporting, ideological or theological accretion from community tradition, all of which plays a part in any determination of who on Earth Jesus really was.

All the documents we have considered so far (apart from the Dead Sea Scrolls which largely pre-date Jesus) are the products of early Christian communities. We turn next to non-Christian Jewish and secular Roman records. Can they tell us anything more about our elusive quarry, the man Jesus?

6. Early Jewish references to Jesus

Scholars have searched long and hard for non-Christian Jewish references to Jesus in the first and early-second century, finding it puzzling that a trouble-maker who had to be put to death, and whose followers went on to form an heretical Jewish sect which eventually broke with Judaism altogether, would apparently go unrecorded in Jewish literature until the third or fourth centuries. But with the possible exception of one dubiously dated text, the search has proved fruitless. One reason may be the loss of records in the destruction of Jerusalem in 70 CE, another may be the comparative lack of cohesion in first-century Judaism prior to its reorgan-isation and reformation in the rabbinic period. Some scholars have attributed a Jesus origin to sayings or stories associated in rabbinic liter-ature with later Jewish teachers. Others have cited the silence as evidence that the Jesus stories are early Christian fictions rather than historical facts.

'Yeshu the Nazarene'

The earliest Jewish reference in rabbinic sources is found in a document referenced as "bSanh 43a" in *Jesus Christ in the Talmud, Midrash, Zohar and the Liturgy of the Synagogue* by G Dalman, first published in 1893.

Dated broadly between the early-second and early-third century, the text describes how, some time in the past (no date is given), "Yeshu the Nazarene" was stoned, then hanged, on the eve of the Passover "because he practised sorcery and enticed Israel to apostasy". Dalman assumed this referred to Jesus (Yeshu being the Hebrew version of the name), but a modern scholar, John Meier, argues that Yeshu the Nazarene was a different and later deviant teacher. Meier concludes that "Analysis of the context, and study of the tradition, the material, the motifs and the form suggest that there is not a single rabbinic 'Jesus passage'... up to c.220 CE"[31], but that where the name Jesus or Yeshu does occur, as in the above text, it refers either to someone else of the same name (which was common) or was inserted during the slow process of putting together what became the Talmud. (On rabbinic literature and the Talmud see Cameo *The Mishnah and the Talmud* in chapter 10).

There is a continuing scholarly argument as to whether there are any Jesus references, direct or indirect, in the Talmud and Mishnah. Geza Vermes and Hyam Maccoby argue that some miracle stories in third and fourth-century literature have close parallels with the miracles of Jesus as reported in the gospels; and some wisdom-sayings from the same period, even the parable form itself, look to some like a throw-back to, or memory of, Jesus. We shall look more closely at this argument when we come to focus on these two scholars in chapter 10. Suffice it to emphasize here that the rabbinic writings include no clearly-attested reference to Jesus of Nazareth. However essentially Jewish Jesus was in his own time, by two or three centuries later when the rabbinic writings were collected, edited and fashioned into an orthodoxy, his place in Judaism was that of just another false messiah, the heretical founder of an entirely new religion, and therefore unworthy of more than a rare tangential reference in the new body of Jewish scriptures that became the Talmud.

Jesus written in stone

It has been claimed that, while there are no first-century Jewish

Cameo: Essenes and the Jesus movement. Any connection?

*While the Dead Sea Scrolls of the first century BCE can give us no biographical information about a Jesus believed to have lived and died in the first century CE, there are some striking similarities between the Essenes of the Scrolls and the early Christians of the New Testament, some of which suggest that the Jesus movement may have modeled itself on the Qumran community. It is possible that Jesus himself knew something of the community and of the Teacher of Righteousness. Geza Vermes in **The Complete Dead Sea Scrolls in English** (pp 22-23) lists the relationship between the Scrolls and the New Testament under three headings:*

"1. We note (a) fundamental similarities of language (both in the Scrolls and in the New Testament the faithful are called 'sons of light'); (b) ideology (both communities considered themselves as the true Israel, governed by twelve leaders, and expected the imminent arrival of the Kingdom of God); (c) attitude to the Bible (both considered their own history as a fulfilment of the words of the Prophets). However, all correspondences such as these may be due to the Palestinian religious atmosphere of the epoch, without entailing any direct influence.

"2. More specific features, such as monarchic administration (i.e. single leaders, overseers at Qumran, bishops in Christian communities) and the practice of religious communism in the strict discipline of the sect and at least in the early days in the Jerusalem church (cf. Acts 2:44-5), would suggest a direct causal connection. If so, it is likely that the young and inexperienced church modeled itself on the by then well-tried Essene society.

"3. In the study of the historical Jesus, the charismatic-escha-

tological aspects of the Scrolls have provided the richest gleanings for comparison. For example, the Prayer of Nabonidas... concerned with the story of Nabonidas' cure by a Jewish exorcist who forgave his sins, provides the most telling parallel to the Gospel account of the healing of a paralytic in Capernaum whose sins Jesus forgave. The second example is the so-called Resurrection fragment... In this poem, the age of the eschato-logical kingdom is characterized, with the help of Psalm 146:7-8 and Isaiah 61:1, by the liberation of captives, the curing of the blind, the straightening of the bent, the healing of the wounded, the raising of the dead and the proclamation of the good news to the poor. Likewise, in the Gospels, victory over disease and the devil is viewed as the sure sign of the initial manifestation of God's reign. Jesus is reported to have announced: 'If it is by the finger of God that I cast out demons, the Kingdom of God has come upon you' (Luke 11:20). Similarly, to John the Baptist's inquiry whether Jesus was the final messenger the following reply is sent: 'Go and tell John what you hear and see: the blind receive their sight, and the lame walk, lepers are cleansed and the deaf hear, and the dead are raised up, and the poor have good news preached to them' (Matt.11:4-5)." Did Jesus know the Prayer of Nabonidas, or were Nabonidas and Jesus both drawing on the Psalms and Isaiah?

documents mentioning Jesus by name, there may be inscriptions or artefacts. In October 2002 the Israeli Antiquities Authority (IAA) issued a licence to a well-known Israeli collector of antiquities, Oded Golan, allowing him to lend an ossuary (a stone casket containing burial bones) to the Montreal museum in Canada. Shortly after its arrival, the IAA began to receive phone calls enquiring about the inscription on the lid of the ossuary: "James, son of Joseph, brother of Jesus".

It seemed, then, that officialdom in Jerusalem had unwittingly licensed the shipment of a unique artefact providing a physical link to Jesus via the bones of his brother. For millions of uncritical Jews, it was one more proof of their ancient right to the land of Israel. For millions of uncritical Christians, it was proof, inscribed in stone, that their faith was grounded in history. The *Wall Street Journal* opined that "The simplest explanation is the likeliest... the James ossuary is what it seems, the earliest recorded reference to Jesus of Nazareth". *Newsweek* declared breathlessly that "biblical archaeologists may have found their holy grail". The tabloid Toronto *Sun* was more graphic, screaming across its front page "Oh, my God!"

Nor was it merely the general public and press who accepted the inscription as authentic. Internationally acclaimed experts gave it their seal of approval. French Aramaic scholar Andre Lemaire, who first revealed the existence of the ossuary after he had been invited to inspect it, declared it "almost certain that the inscription referred to the Jesus of the Bible". John Dominic Crossan suggested that it was "the closest we come archaeologically to Jesus". The founder and editor-in-chief of *Biblical Archaeology Review*, Hershel Shanks, and Ben Witherington III, writer of a series of works on the Jesus quest, jointly authored what became a best-selling book, *The Brother of Jesus*, marshalling the arguments for the ossuary's authenticity and dismissing the growing voices of doubt.

On its return to Israel early in 2003 at the end of the loan period, Golan was required to hand over the ossuary to the IAA. The inscription was deciphered and the reference to Jesus confirmed. But the IAA decided to subject the relic to forensic tests, and it quickly transpired that the ancient patina characteristic of first-century stone objects had been artificially contrived. The inscribed ossuary was a clever fake - a forgery hardly less audacious than the Hitler diaries, and one that had fooled historians of international repute.

Golan's premises were searched and more fakes and false patinas discovered. Four men were charged with him, including a former head of the antiquities laboratories at the Israel Museum in West Jerusalem and an inscriptions expert at Haifa university. A key witness told the IAA that he had been asked to help prepare thousands of fake artefacts. All five men named have protested their innocence as the investigations dragged on. Precisely who made the fakes may remain unresolved, but what is not in doubt is that the Joseph/Jesus ossuary is not what it seems. Equally inauthentic, according to virtually all specialist scholars, is another group of ossuaries dug up in Jerusalem in the 1960s and claimed in 2007 as the burial boxes of the whole Jesus family - his mother, father, wife and children. These were merely the latest in a long line of forgeries - not even "pious forgeries", but fakes made to satisfy an immensely lucrative market. While both "discoveries" certainly made headlines around the world, they did nothing to challenge the hard fact that in early Jewish literature - on paper, parchment or stone - the historical Jesus remains tantalisingly invisible.

7. Roman references to Jesus

It is sometimes claimed that, if Judaism succeeded in airbrushing Jesus out of its first-century records, there are at least significant references to him in contemporaneous secular Roman literature. In fact, there are none prior to the destruction of Jerusalem in 70, some 40 years after his execution. There is no mention of him or of anything which could be identified as a possible reference to the early Jesus movement in the writings of Jesus' contemporary Philo, who is often cited (without reference to any specific source) as a witness to Jesus' historicity. Every secular reference we know of not only postdates Paul's epistles and the early sayings collections of the 50s and 60s but also (with the possible exception of the Mara text, which we shall look at shortly) Mark's gospel of the 70s. But this is hardly surprising, since Christian literature probably had no circulation beyond the communities to which it was addressed until the second century.

Such few references as there are come after 73, and most after 100

CE, when some perfunctory knowledge of Christianity as one cult among many began to be reflected in passing mentions in letters and books. The most important of these, in date order, are

(i) a letter by Mara bar Sarapion probably written soon after 73;

(ii) the famous and much disputed references to Jesus by name in *Jewish Antiquities* by the historian Josephus Flavius, written in the 90s but known only in later edited versions;

(iii) two mentions of "Christus" by Pliny the Younger in or shortly after 111;

(iv) a mention by the historian Tacitus in 116 or 117, and

(v) a reference to "Chrestus" by Seutonius around 120.

We shall look at each of these in turn, except that the Josephus references, which are both the most explicit and the most controversial, will be left till last.

The Mara letter

An otherwise unknown Syrian Stoic, Mara bar Sarapion, wrote a letter to his son from the Roman prison where he was apparently awaiting execution some time before the end of the first century. The letter was unearthed and published by a German scholar, A Baumstarck, in 1897, but was little noticed until Theissen and Merz drew attention to it and suggested a composition date "soon after 73 CE"[32]. Mara commends the cultivation of wisdom while noting ruefully that wisdom does not safeguard against the persecution of the righteous, citing three wise men unjustly put to death: Socrates, Pythagoras and an unnamed "wise king" of the Jews.

"What good did it do the Athenians to kill Socrates?" he asks, "for which deed they were punished with famine and pestilence. What did it avail the Samians to burn Pythagoras since their country was entirely buried under sand in one moment? Or what did it avail the Jews to kill their wise king, since their kingdom was taken away from them from that time on?... The Jews were slaughtered and driven from their kingdom, everywhere living in the dispersion. Socrates is not dead, thanks to Plato; nor Pythagoras, because of Hera's statue. Nor is the wise king, because of the new law which he has given"[33].

Although Jesus is not named in the reference to the Jews' "wise king", it seems likely that Mara was aware of the accusation by the Christian community that the recent destruction of Jerusalem and deportation of Jews was God's punishment for their role in the killing of Jesus. If this is so, the final sentence may be read as the earliest (unconscious!) formulation of a liberal interpretation of the resurrection: that Jesus lives, not as a risen god, but exactly as Socrates and Pythagoras continue to live, in the power of their teachings and their works. In each case, their special wisdom has vindicated them and ensured that they live on. Mara is neither a Jew nor a Christian since he writes elsewhere in the letter of "our gods", but it may well be that his own situation as victim and prisoner inclines him to a sympathetic view of Jesus as fellow innocent sufferer.

Theissen and Merz, in their discussion of the letter, suggest that Mara got what knowledge he had of Jesus from earliest Syrian Christianity, particularly Matthew's gospel, which has the "wise men" seeking the new-born "king of the Jews", and which interprets the events of 70 CE as punishment for what "the Jews" had done to Jesus. But this would suggest either an earlier date for Matthew, which most scholars consider unlikely, or a later date than the "soon after 73" they suggest for composition of Mara's letter. On the current scholarly consensus, Mark is the only one of the canonical gospels which may have been written by the early or mid-70s, and Mark's passion story also emphasizes that Jesus was executed as "king of the Jews". But Mara bar Sarapion could perhaps have heard the "king of the Jews" birth and death stories from sources which Mark had used and Matthew would draw on again a few years later.

Clearly by the time Mara wrote his letter some awareness of early Christian tradition was percolating through to the pagan world, but as Theissen and Merz conclude, "we probably do not have testimony about

Jesus independent of synoptic Christianity, but [we do have] evidence [in this letter] that the 'king of the Jews' depicted by Matthew also attracted pagan sages, as is depicted in legendary form" in the Matthew birth story.

Pliny the Younger, Tacitus and Seutonius

Pliny, Tacitus and Seutonius were not victims like Mara but pillars of Roman imperialism, and their brief references to Jesus, such as they are, reflect their position as senior Roman officials. Around 111 Pliny was appointed by the emperor Trajan as imperial legate in the province of Pontus where he was required to deal with subversive Christians. In a series of letters to the emperor he explains the difficulties he faces in pinning criminal activity on the Christian community. He writes that "it was their habit on a fixed day to assemble before daylight and recite by turns a form of words to Christus as a god". In another letter he refers to the Christians' "perverse and extravagant superstition". He never refers to Jesus by name and clearly regards "Christus" as "a cultic deity... a kind of anti-god to the Roman state gods"[34].

Rome was famously burned down by the emperor Nero in 64 CE, and it is sometimes assumed or claimed that this was blamed on Christians *at the time*, which would give us our earliest secular reference to Christianity (though again no mention of Jesus himself). But the earliest record we have of the suggestion that the fires were part of a pogrom against rebellious Christians is a passage by Tacitus in his *Annals*, written in 116/117. Tacitus here actually doubts that Christians were responsible, though he regards them as guilty of "hatred against the human race" and therefore deserving of "the most extreme punishment". Writing long after Nero's death, however, at a time when it was safe for a Roman aristocrat to acknowledge the emperor's notorious cruelties, he accepts that "it was not, as it seemed, for the public good, but to glut one man's cruelty that they were being destroyed".[35]

Where Pliny had taken the Christian's "Christus" to be just another cultic god, Tacitus understands that this upstart and troublesome religion was derived from a man who had lived in Judea at the time of Tiberias. "Christus, from whom the name had its origin, suffered the extreme penalty during the reign of Tiberias at the hands of one of our procurators, Pontius Pilate, and a most mischievous superstition, thus checked for the moment, again broke out not only in Judea, the first source of the evil, but even in Rome"[36].

Seutonius Tranquillus was a highly placed lawyer who used his access to the legal archives to write his famous lives of the emperors, *De Vita Caesarium*, probably between 117 and 122 CE. Seutonious writes that Claudius (emperor from 41 to 54) had expelled the Jews from Rome, an event also reported in Acts 18:2 ("Claudius had commanded all Jews to depart from Rome"). The reason given by Seutonius for Claudius's action is that "the Jews, stirred up by Chrestus, continually caused unrest".

Theissen and Merz[37] point out that "Chrestus" was a common name among Greek slaves, and "Chrestiani" was a term sometimes used by Tertullion, Justin and others to mean "useful ones" or slaves in general. But the context clearly suggests that Seutonius is referring to a particular agitator remembered for having stirred up Jewish unrest in Rome. He gets the title (or name) wrong, and mistakenly supposes his Chrestus to have been in Rome in person. But, combined with the reference in Acts, this does seem to reflect a distorted memory of disruptive Christian activity in Rome in the late 40s, perhaps occasioned by the first visit of Christian missionaries to the Jewish community there.

None of these authors - Pliny the Younger, Tacitus and Seutonius - refer to Jesus by name. They tell us that a religious movement or cult that they associate with the Jews and vaguely know as Christianity was making trouble in Rome and the provinces around the end of the first and beginning of the second century, but nothing in their writing conveys any significant information on Jesus himself.

Josephus

We are on slightly firmer territory with the works of the historian

Josephus Flavius, who lived from around 37 to about 100 CE. Josephus was commander of the Jewish forces in Galilee during the revolt against the Romans of 66-70, but as defeat loomed he dramatically changed sides in 69, shortly before the destruction of Jerusalem. After having the good fortune to prophesy correctly that Vespasian would be the next emperor, he was rewarded with imperial protection, a pension and a safe house in Rome where he wrote his two principal histories, *The Jewish War* in the late 70s and *Jewish Antiquities* in the 90s. The two works together provide a wealth of information, albeit from a turn-coat's perspective, on religious, political and social life in Galilee and Judea in the first century.

Not surprisingly, as it is primarily an account of the war of 66-74, the first book makes no reference to Jesus or his followers (unless, as one scholar has argued, his "Jesus son of Ananias" can be linked to the Christians' Jesus, which theory we shall look at shortly). But there are two passages in *Antiquities* which do refer to the Christians' Jesus by name. The first is the much-quoted "Testimonium Flavianum" or "Jesus Notice". In a passage devoted largely to the misgovernment of Pontius Pilate, the text in English translation runs:

"Around this time there lived Jesus, a wise man, if indeed one ought to call him a man. For he was one who did surprising deeds, and a teacher of such people as accept the truth gladly. He won over many Jews and many of the Greeks. He was the Messiah. When Pilate, upon hearing him accused by men of the highest standing among us, had condemned him to be crucified, those who in the first place came to love him did not give up their affection for him, for on the third day he appeared to them restored to life. The prophets of God had prophesied this and countless other marvellous things about him. And the tribe of the Christians, so called after him, have still to this day not died out."[38]

Church fathers from Eusebius in the fourth century on frequently quoted this passage as testimony (hence "Testimonium Flavianum") of Jesus' historicity. If a Jewish/Roman historian said Jesus seemed to be more than a man, asserting unequivocally that he was the Messiah, crucified and raised from the dead on the third day as prophesied in the scriptures, who could question its veracity? But doubts about the authenticity of the passage began to be raised when *Antiquities* came to be studied afresh in the sixteenth century.

It was noticed that when Origen referred to Josephus, a century earlier than Eusebius, he specifically stated that Josephus did not believe that Jesus was the Messiah; which suggests that he did not have the text as we have it today. Almost all modern scholars now believe this passage was worked over by Christian editors in the late-third or early-fourth century and that the specifically "Christian" passages are interpolations. It is argued in particular that no Jew outside the Jesus movement (and Josephus was clearly no Christian) would baldly assert that Jesus was the Messiah, or report without question that after his crucifixion he rose from the dead. These are Christian doctrines and they would have been anathema to a late-first-century Jew, particularly one brought up as a Pharisee, as Josephus claimed to be.

On the other hand, there are indications that some parts of the passage do derive from the original text. The description of Jesus as a "wise man" fits with other "wise man" references by Josephus, and "reflects the picture of Jesus which was going the rounds in Palestine as a popular tradition"[39]. His description of Jesus' miracles as "surprising (or startling) deeds" is also typical, and "accept gladly" is said to be a favorite phrase of Josephus. The somewhat derogatory phrase "tribe of the Christians" is unlikely to have been written by a later Christian editor, unless we are to credit him with a double-bluff. Finally, a second mention of Jesus by name later in the book seems to assume the reader's knowledge of him from an earlier reference, which could only be this "Jesus notice".

For these reasons, many scholars now conclude that Josephus did indeed write about Jesus but that Christian "improvements" were added in the third or fourth century. A proposed reconstruction of Josephus' original by J P Meier has won wide acceptance:

"At this time appeared Jesus, a wise man. For he was a doer of startling deeds, a teacher of people who receive the truth with pleasure. And he gained a following both among many Jews and among many of Greek origin. And when Pilate, because of an accusation made by the leading men among us, condemned him to the cross, those who had loved him previously did not cease to do so. And up until this very day the tribe of Christians (named after him) has not died out."[40]

The second of Josephus's two Jesus references occurs a little later in *Antiquities*[41] where the killing of James in 62 CE is recorded. Josephus reports that the Sanhedrin under the high priest Ananus condemned James and others for unspecified transgressions of the Law and had them stoned to death. Josephus indicates that the process was illegal, that it was condemned by "those faithful to the Law" (presumably his fellow Pharisees) and that the events caused so much division among Jerusalem Jews that Ananus was shortly afterwards deposed. James is not described as the leader of the Jerusalem church, but Josephus does call him "the brother of Jesus who is called Christ" (or "the so-called Christ"). The authenticity of the text is assumed by almost all scholars, and, as indicated above, it has been cited as evidence for the authenticity of at least the de-Christianized version of the earlier Jesus reference, since Josephus, having done so already, would not consider it necessary to explain again who this Jesus was.

What conclusions, then, do scholars draw from the secular references to Jesus, from Mara bar Sarapion and Josephus to Pliny, Tacitus and Seutonius? Clearly all these writers were aware of a Jewish or mainly Jewish religious movement called Christians, and some knew that the movement worshipped someone named Jesus. Mara in the 70s, somewhere in a Roman prison, had heard the story that the destruction of Jerusalem was divine punishment for the Jews having killed their wise and innocent king. Josephus, writing in Rome in the 90s, had heard that the James wrongly condemned and killed by the Sanhedrin in 62 was believed by Christians to be the brother of Jesus, a wise man and wonder-worker who had gained a following among Jews and gentiles and had been executed on a cross on the authorization of Pontius Pilate after accusations had been made against him by Jewish leaders. Pliny in the early-first-century knows nothing of Jesus, only that a subversive group opposed to Roman state religion worshipped one Christus. Tacitus has heard that one Christus was executed under Pilate but that his "mischievous superstitions" had continued to gain ground in Judea, where they had begun, and had spread to Rome. Seutonius only knows that one "Chrestus" and his followers were wrongly blamed for the burning of Rome under Nero.

While all this, coming as it does from quarters unfavorable to Christianity, may amount to significant evidence for the *existence* of an historical Jesus, it does not give us original or independent data on his life and teaching. All these passing references come in books and letters written between half a century and a century after the period of Pilate's prefectship, by which time the synoptic gospels and some of the "many other" lost gospels referred to by Luke were in circulation. Theissen and Merz conclude that Josephus, the most explicit of all these writers, may well have drawn on Luke's gospel or the tradition that produced Luke/Acts. "His picture recalls that of Jesus in the Lukan writings. In both places Jesus is called 'man'. In both places there is a report on him in summary form and a distinction is made between his Jewish accusers and Pilate's responsibility... Perhaps Josephus had contact in Rome with a Christianity of a Lukan stamp. But his roots in Palestine make it seem possible that he also used reports and popular traditions current in Jerusalem"[42]. However that may be, it would seem that the secular references, scanty and late as they are, do little more than indicate that by the end of the first century some awareness of the fast-spreading Christian religion and its supposed originator had percolated through to some parts of the empire's literary and political elite. These isolated references cannot be made to add up to independent evidence of the teachings of an authentic historical Jesus, on which they are wholly silent.

8. Postscript: another Jesus?

Before we leave Josephus it is worth a short detour into another aspect of recent Jesus/Josephus scholarship, briefly referred to above. Although the historian's first book, *The Jewish War*, contains no reference to Jesus of Nazareth, it does include in Volume 6 paragraphs 300-309 a story about another prophetic Jesus, said to have suffered and died at the hands of the Jewish people and a Roman governor during the war which culminated in the destruction of the Jerusalem temple.

In 1994 and 1995 Craig A Evans drew attention to the story, offering an abridged translation of the passage from *The Jewish War* as follows:

"Four years before the war [of 66-70 CE]... there came to the feast, at which it is the custom of all Jews to erect tabernacles to God, one Jesus son of Ananias, an untrained peasant, who, standing in the Temple, suddenly began to cry out... 'A voice against Jerusalem and the sanctuary... a voice against all the people'... Some of the leading citizens, angered at this evil speech, arrested the man and whipped him with many blows. But he, not speaking anything in his own behalf or in private to those who struck him, continued his cries as before. Thereupon, the rulers... brought him to the Roman governor. There, though flayed to the bone with scourges, he neither begged for mercy nor wept... When Albinus the governor asked him who and whence he was and why he uttered these cries, he gave no answer to these things... Albinus pronounced him a maniac and released him... He cried out especially at the feasts... While shouting from the wall, 'Woe once more to the city and to the people and to the sanctuary...' a stone [from 'one of the engines', i.e. a Roman catapult]... struck and killed him."[44]

Evans pointed up the parallels with the Jesus passion story in the gospels. Both Jesuses came to Jerusalem at Passover and spoke out against the temple leaders. Both were arrested, examined and beaten by Jews before being hauled before the Roman governor. Both remained silent before their accusers. Both found the governor reluctant to convict. Both died as a result of their supposedly blasphemous words and deeds, albeit in different circumstances and by different means.

However, in weighing up the possibility of direct literary relationship between Josephus' story and the Christian passion tradition, Evans decided there was insufficient common vocabulary to support the hypothesis. "There is no indication", he concluded, "that the story of one Jesus influenced the telling of the story of the other Jesus".

Eight years later the question was revisited by Theodore J Weeden Sr. in an extensive paper for the Fall 2003 meeting of the Westar Institute Jesus Seminar. Weeden argued that the Josephus passage taken in full, rather than in Evans's abridged version, presented many more parallels than Evans had acknowledged, listing 19 in all. He went on to argue that Mark had built his story of the trial of Jesus of Nazareth on the Josephus account of the trial of Jesus son of Ananias, and Matthew, Luke and John had followed suit. Thus the evangelists' passion story was essentially "fictive".

One implication of the hypothesis, as Weeden's Jesus Seminar colleagues pointed out in discussion of his paper, is that the composition of Mark would have to be re-dated from the early 70s to the late 70s or 80s, since *Jewish War* was almost certainly not written and circulated until 78 or 79. An alternative possibility was that the 70s edition of Mark, like Q and Thomas, omitted a passion story and only acquired one by editorial addition inspired by the Josephus story of Jesus son of Ananias. But most Seminar Fellows were not persuaded, concluding that the supposed parallels in the sequence of events were no more than one might expect: offence, arrest, trial, conviction, death. It seemed to them more likely that Josephus was deliberately parodying the tradition of mad prophets, particularly, as one Fellow put it, when the mad prophet's "Woe is me" is followed by a precision strike from a ballistic missile! The Seminar voted down Weeden's thesis. But his hypothesis that the passion story is best understood as a "true fiction" rather than a factual history has parallels with the theory that the key elements of the story are derived from literary sources such as the Hebrew prophets and the psalm writers. It stands as a challenging alternative to mainstream faith in factual history, and we shall look more fully at this school of scholarship in chapter 11.

In this and the preceding chapters, then, we have looked at a complex tangle of texts from different authors and editors, writing from different geographical centers, at different times, with widely different cultural and theological emphases. None of it is written by objective historians or biographers as we would understand these disciplines today. Miracle and magic jostle with the mundane, spirit with flesh and blood, legend with stories of everyday life, the metaphysical with the physical. Whatever there is to be known about a real-life Jesus of Galilee is buried somewhere at the heart of these ancient codices and literary scraps. It is time to move on in Part II to see what some of the world's leading historians, literary analysts and scholarly specialists have made of this material.

Notes to Chapter 6

1 I have deliberately avoided describing it as the faction of Paul or of the Apostles since most second- and third-century Christianities claimed to follow Paul, and all asserted their allegiance to some or all of the original apostles. I am reminded of a conversation I had in China with a former member of the Red Guards. Knowing how the Guards had been riven with violent factionalism, I enquired of the comrade which faction he had belonged to. Without hesitation he answered "I was on the side of Chairman Mao"!

2 Dungan, *Constantine's Bible*, 29

3 Metzger, *The Canon of the New Testament,* Clarendon Press, Oxford, 1987

4 The original meaning of heresy was "choice"!

5 Relevant introductions in *Complete Gospels*, 332 (Rappe) and 302 (Patterson)

6 Ehrman, *Lost Christianities*, 9

7 as above, 30

8 as above, 31

9 as above, 51

10 as above, 54

11 *Complete Gospels*, 332

12 Cameron, *Sayings Traditions*

13 Koester, *Ancient Christian Gospels*

14 *Complete Gospels*, 343

15 *The Dialogue of the Savior* is not to be confused with a quite different *Gospel of the Savior*, a sixth-century Coptic copy of which was discovered in Egypt in the 1960s, described in Ehrman, *Lost Scriptures*.

16 Ehrman, *Lost Christianities*, 38

17 *Complete Gospels*, 360

18 as above, 369-70. See also Miller, *Born Divine*

19 *Complete Gospels*, 37

20 as above, 413

21 as above, 413

22 *Complete Gospels*, 418 and Theissen, *Historical Jesus*, 51

23 *Complete Gospels*, 422 and Thiessen, *Historical Jesus*, 51

24 *Complete Gospels,* 424

25 Bowker, *World Religions*, 384

26 Theissen, *Historical Jesus*, 44-5 with full citations.

27 Ehrman, *Lost Christianities*, 100

28 Vermes, *Complete Dead Sea Scrolls*, 5

29 as above, 3

30 as above, 4, 54-6

31 Theissen, *Historical Jesus*, 74-5

32 as above, 77

33 Theissen and Merz, *Historical Jesus* 77. T & M comment that the reference to

Pythagoras is "historically extremely inaccurate" in that Mara appears to confuse Pythagoras the philosopher with a namesake sculptor.

34 as above, 81

35 Tacitus, *Annals* 15.44.5, cited by Theissen, *Historical Jesus*, 82

36 Tacitus, *Annals* 15.44.3. Tacitus mistakenly used the title *procurator*, which belonged to his own day. The proper term in Pilate's time was *prefect*.

37 Theissen, *Historical Jesus*, 82n

38 Josephus, *Jewish Antiquities*, 18, 63f

39 Theissen, *Historical Jesus*, 74, quoting Geza Vermes. *Historical Jesus* includes a thorough review of the debate on this passage.

40 Meier, John: *Marginal Jew*, Vol 1

41 Josephus, *Jewish Antiquities*, 20:200

42 Theissen, *Historical Jesus*, 74

43 Craig A Evans in an article, "Jesus in Non-Christian Sources" in *Studying the Historical Jesus*, eds. Bruce Chilton and Craig A Evans, 1993, and the following year in a book, *Jesus and his Contemporaries*. The English text here is his translation from Josephus's *The Jewish War*.

PART II

INTERPRETATIONS

7

THE JESUS SEMINAR

Both old and renewed quests for the Jesus of history were characterized by scholarly individualism. From Reimarus via Schweitzer to Perrin and Sanders, Jesus detectives tended to work individually, pursuing their own researches and writing up their own conclusions in books published under their name alone. Of course, they talked to each other, got together in conferences and academic associations, read each other's papers, criticized their rivals and were criticized in turn. But research into the historical Jesus was rarely a team effort. Jesus detectives tended to turn every one to his own way.

This changed with the formation of the Westar Institute's Jesus Seminar, which held its first meeting in Berkeley, California, in March 1985, moved to Sonoma in 1986 and to Santa Rosa in 1994. In his book *Honest to Jesus* the Seminar's founder Robert Funk tells of his growing disenchantment, first with the church, then with theological seminaries, then with the secular universities. Starting out to be a parish minister, he "soon learned that passion for truth was not compatible with that role", so he turned to teaching in theological seminaries for two decades, only to conclude that "theologians should abandon the cloistered precincts of the church and seminary where nothing real was on the agenda". Following his own disenchanted advice he took a post at the University of Montana, which taught him "another hard lesson: universities are much like churches, replete with orthodoxies of various kinds". Seeking to escape such orthodoxies, Funk brought together a group of scholars to look afresh at the parables of Jesus, which he saw as the core-carriers of Jesus' message. This led to the formation of a Parables Seminar in the early 1970s and a specialist journal, *Semeia*, launched in 1974, both linked with the US-based Society of Biblical Literature. In 1981 Funk and his wife

Charlene Matejovsky started their own publishing house, Polebridge Press, and it was through these groupings that Funk attracted the scholars who came together to form the Westar Institute and its Jesus Seminar.

Westar's declared aim was the promotion of "religious literacy". "The level of public knowledge of the Bible borders on the illiterate," wrote Funk in *The Five Gospels*. "The church and synagogue have failed in their historic mission to educate the public in the fourth 'R', religion[1]... The public is poorly informed of the assured results of critical scholarship, although those results are commonly taught in colleges, universities and seminaries"[2]. The implication that the churches had become dishonest in preaching what they knew to be untrue is made plain in Funk's *Honest to Jesus*, which picks up the theme in similarly evangelical language: "In this enterprise, we are mounting a frontal assault on a pervasive religious illiteracy that blinds and intimidates, even those, or perhaps especially those, in positions of authority in the church and in our society"[3].

Initially, on Funk's personal invitation, some thirty scholars signed up to the enterprise and became the founding Fellows of the Westar Institute. Over the next few years, as it began to attract publicity and attention, more than two hundred were involved at different points in the Institute's work. Of these, a core group of nearly 80 Fellows were listed on the roster of those who worked on Westar's primary project, the Jesus Seminar (76 on the Jesus sayings, 79 on the Jesus acts). All but a handful were US Americans (the others coming from Canada, South Africa, Germany, Australia and New Zealand) and all but five were men. Admission as Fellows was open to "critical scholars", defined as those who "make empirical, factual evidence the controlling factor in historical judgments... Critical scholars adopt the principle of methodological skepticism: accept only what passes the rigorous tests of the rules of evidence. Critical scholars work from ancient texts in their original languages, in the case of the gospels, in Greek, Coptic, Aramaic, Hebrew, Latin, and other tongues. Critical scholars practice their craft by submitting their work to the judgment of peers. Untested work is not highly regarded".

Most Fellows professed continuing allegiances to church or synagogue, or came from religious backgrounds, but they distanced themselves from "non-critical" scholars, "those who put dogmatic considerations first and insist that the factual evidence confirm theological premises"[4]. Westar soon came under attack from those it characterized as "non-critical", particularly conservative Christian groups. Funk has claimed that at least one Fellow lost his academic post as a result of his membership[5] and others were forced by institutional pressure to withdraw. Rigorous inquiry had always threatened theological orthodoxy. Rigorous inquiry on an organized, collective scale upped the ante. But, as we shall see in due course, the Seminar also came under attack from some scholars who shared its disdain for uncritical theology but criticized its skeptical methodology.

1. The method: beads and ballots

Westar's first project was the big one: a new but this time *collective* quest for the authentic Jesus of history, pursued through the Jesus Seminar. Funk thought the best starting point was an evaluation of all the words and deeds *attributed* to Jesus in the first two hundred years of the church, but was surprised to discover that no-one had ever drawn up a comprehensive collection. This became the Seminar's first task, and it arranged to meet in full session twice a year to pool expertise and debate technical papers circulated in advance. The Seminar collected more than fifteen hundred versions of around five hundred reported sayings of Jesus (the precise number depends on how clusters of sayings embedded in longer narratives are counted). The inventory naturally drew on all the surviving gospels of the period, not just biblical books, as the Fellows adopted the rule that "canonical boundaries are irrelevant in critical assessments of the various sources of information about Jesus". This alone put them at odds with church tradition and its conservative defenders.

Meanwhile, the Seminar scholars were working together on a new translation of all the gospels, biblical and extra-biblical, starting with the canonical four and Thomas. The *Scholars Version* or SV broke with the long tradition of translating into literary or liturgical language, seeking English (or American) figures of speeech where there are Greek colloquialisms in the originals. In the SV's Mark 1: 41 Jesus tells the leper "Okay, you're clean!" In Matthew 23:13 he addresses scholars and Pharisees as "you imposters! Damn you!", instead of the King James Version's archaic "woe unto you"; and in Luke 10:15, where the KJV has "thrust down to hell" and the Revised Standard Version has "brought down to Hades", the SV has Jesus telling Capernaum "you'll go to Hell". Where a literal translation sounds odd in English, as with "He that hath ears to hear, let him hear", which faithfully reproduces a Greek saying without quite managing to convey its sense, the scholars looked for a less stilted English equivalent. One translator suggested the proverb "A wink is as good as a nod to a blind horse". They settled for "Anyone here with two good ears had better listen!" The SV is certainly fresh, lively, readable and determinedly colloquial. As Funk explained, "Every expression that did not strike the ear as native was reviewed and revised, not once but many times"[6]. However, what is "native" to some is by definition foreign to others. The colloquialisms of the SV make it a very American, even a very Californian version. The first five gospels were first published as *The Five Gospels* and the full set as *The Complete Gospels*. Whatever view is taken of the "native" style, the enterprise represents a remarkable achievement, unique in the long history of Jesus scholarship.

Once the new translations were under way and a working inventory of reported Jesus-sayings was completed, the sayings were sorted into four categories: parables, aphorisms (pithy sayings and riddles), dialogues and stories. The Seminar then began to test what it had found. "The goal... was to review each of the fifteen hundred items and determine which of them could be ascribed with a high degree of probability to Jesus. The items passing the test would be included in a database for determining who Jesus was. But the interpretation of the data was to be excluded from the agenda of the Seminar and left to individual scholars working from their own perspectives"[7]. This left each contributor free to formulate and publish their own distinctive profiles of Jesus, and, as we shall see, many went on to do so. Critics often make the mistake of ascribing a common view to all the Seminar's members. In fact, the Seminar embraced a wide variety of scholarly conclusions and opinions.

After what Funk calls "agonizing review", a phrase which no doubt covers much scholarly argument, the Seminar agreed on the mechanism by which it would arrive at the best available consensus on the authenticity of each saying. Scholars would bring to the table their particular expertise in textual criticism, form criticism, oral transmission and first-century Jewish and Mediterranean history and argue out the historical reliability of each saying and deed, text by text. They would then take a vote.

However, while simple majority voting may serve to determine who is in and who is out in politics, it was always recognized by the Seminar as far too crude a mechanism to produce an adequate reflection of scholarly opinion on the authenticity of Jesus' reported sayings and doings. Funk and his colleagues therefore came up with the "colored beads and boxes" system which became the trademark of the Seminar, admired by supporters for its ingenuity and derided by opponents for its "populism" - often seen as a cardinal sin by those who have chosen to cloister themselves within the academy, where scholar speaks only with scholar.

Under Funk's system Fellows first cast their vote by placing a colored bead in a box (later amended to marking a color-coded card).

• A *red* vote indicated either "I would include this item unequivocally in the database for determining who Jesus was", or "Jesus undoubtedly said this or something very like it".

Cameo: Robert Funk on "The Aim of the Quest"

"The aim of the quest is to set Jesus free. Its purpose is to liberate Jesus from the scriptural and creedal and experiential prisons in which we have incarcerated him. What would happen if the 'dangerous and subversive memories' of that solitary figure were really stripped of their interpretive overlay? Were that to happen, the gospel of Jesus would be liberated from the Jesus of the gospels and allowed to speak for itself. The creedal formulations of the second, third and fourth centuries would be de-dogmatized and Jesus would be permitted to emerge as a robust, real, larger-than-life figure in his own right. Moreover, current images of Jesus would be torn up by their long affective roots and their attachment to pet causes severed. The pale, anemic, iconic Jesus would suffer by comparison with the stark realism of the genuine article.

"This forecast, I am acutely aware, stands in strong contrast to what many scholars of the gospels take the quest to be all about. Many scholars perceive the quest as primarily a historical puzzle without any real significance for other questions, especially theological issues. A quest without consequences is a legacy of older posturing born of painful struggles to come clean within the confines of the church... [But] isolating a single face in a Galilean crowd is more than a challenging puzzle. It has far-reaching implications for the Christian faith." - **Honest to Jesus. pp 300-301.**

• A *pink* vote indicated either "I would include this item with reservations (or modifications) in the database", or "Jesus probably said something like this".

• A *gray* vote indicated either "I would not include this item in the database, but I might make use of some of the content for determining who Jesus was", or "Jesus did not say this, but the ideas contained in it are close to his own".

• A *black* vote indicated either "I would not include this item in the primary database", or "Jesus did not say this; it represents the perspective or content of a later or different tradition".

One member suggested what Funk calls an "unofficial but helpful interpretation":

red: That's Jesus!
pink: Sure sounds like Jesus!
gray: Well, maybe.
black: There's been some mistake.

Once the beads were in the ballot box, a consensus was determined by weighted average. Red counted 3 points, pink 2, gray 1 and black 0. The points were added up and divided by the number of votes, then converted to percentages. A 75% and upwards score gave the item a red "That's Jesus!" ranking, between 50% and 75% a pink "Sure sounds like Jesus", between 25% and 50% a gray "Well, maybe", and below 25% a black "There's been some mistake". As Funk explains, "In a system that made the dividing line between pink and gray a simple majority, nearly half of the Fellows would lose their vote. There would only be winners and losers. Under weighted averages, all votes would count". While the weighting system meant that black votes in particular could readily pull an average down, "this shortcoming seemed consonant with the method-ological skepticism that was a working principle of the Seminar: when in sufficient doubt, leave it out".

The Seminar eventually published two volumes of color-coded texts in its own SV translation. The first, *The Five Gospels*, included a detailed evaluation of each Jesus saying, and the second, *The Acts of Jesus*, covered his reported deeds. Responding to critics who ridiculed the notion of voting to determine historical authenticity, Funk emphasized in his introduction to *The Five Gospels* that "voting does not, of course, determine the truth; voting only indicates what the best judgment is of a significant number of scholars sitting around the table". Moreover, there was nothing new in counting votes in biblical scholarship. "Committees creating a critical text of the Greek New Testament under the auspices of the United Bible Societies vote on whether to print this or that text and what variants to consign to notes. Translation committees, such as those that created the King James Version and the Revised Standard Version, voted in the course of their deliberations on which translation proposal to accept and which to reject".

Even color-coding itself wasn't new. Funk cites a fourteenth-century manuscript of the four canonical gospels in which the narrative is written in vermilion, the words of Jesus in crimson, and the words of everyone else in black. There was also a "red-letter" edition of the New Testament published in America by Louis Klopsch around 1900, after Klopsch had invited scholars in America and Europe to "submit passages they regarded as spoken by Christ on earth" for printing in the color of his blood. Thus, says Funk, Klopsch "convened the first Jesus Seminar (by mail) and produced the first red-letter edition"[8].

The Seminar's co-chair for many years, John Dominic Crossan, has pointed in *The Historical Jesus* to a closer and more recent precedent. In preparing its third edition of *The Greek New Testament* in the 1970s the United Bible Societies' panel of scholars, evaluating the merits and likely authenticity of disputed readings, voted on a four-fold scale. The Introduction to the edition explains that "By means of the letters A, B, C, and D the Committee has sought to indicate the relative degree of certainty, arrived at on the basis of internal considerations as well as the external evidence, for the reading adopted as the text. The letter A signifies that the text is virtually certain, while B indicates that there is some degree of doubt. The letter C means that there is a considerable degree of doubt whether the text or the apparatus contains the superior reading, while D shows that there is a very high degree of doubt concerning the reading selected for the text". There were often majority and minority opinions. Crossan comments: "Grading by color or grading by letter makes no substantial difference to the process. Beads or ballots, hands raised or heads nodded, does not change the ultimate fact of scholarly reconstruction"[9].

These explanations, disclaimers and precedents have not prevented critics, including other scholars as well as conservative theologians, from mocking the methodology of the Seminar and tut-tutting at its breezy Californian disdain for solemnity and stuffiness. In particular, critics persist in representing the Seminar as claiming that scholars' votes can determine historical truth, an absurdity that Funk and his Fellows have clearly and repeatedly repudiated. However, the tendency of some Seminar scholars to write and speak of what they - or sometimes, more loosely, just "scholars" - have "found" or "determined", does tend to imply more certainty than the complexities of the quest can warrant. Interpreting a particular consensus as a factual finding plays into the hands of those whose own certainties are derived from dogma rather than critical enquiry.

Before the scholars cast their beads, however, they had to arrive at their decisions by agreed rules of evidence, defined as "standards by which evidence is presented and evaluated in a court of law". One of the Seminar's most important and most welcome innovations is that it set out its rules of evidence clearly, for public perusal and evaluation, rather than clasping them close to its scholarly bosom as academic trade secrets. The large public readership at which the Seminar aimed was not told "These are our conclusions. We are scholars, so you must accept what we tell you". Rather, the rules were set out clearly and explained in detail, with examples. An important aim in encouraging religious literacy was to clarify not only *what* conclusions had been arrived at but *how* they had been reached.

2. Rules of written evidence

Funk has explained the Seminar's agreed rules for evaluating the sayings, dividing them into rules of written and oral evidence. Although the rules are said to be based on "the methodology of two hundred years of Jesus scholarship", they clearly draw on more recent scientific refinements. I list them here in italics, each followed by my own summary drawn from Funk's explanatory notes[10].

• *The evangelists frequently group sayings and parables in clusters and complexes that did not originate with Jesus.*

Example: Sayings and parables which may have originated separately were brought together in groups or clusters by the evangelists (the authors or editors of the gospels), often using a memory device such as a key word which links them. Thus, the sayings in Mark 10:17-31 ("sell all you have", "rich cannot enter the kingdom", "camel and the eye of a needle", "rewards of leaving everything to follow Jesus") are clustered around the key word "money" or "wealth". This clustering, in the Seminar's view, is likely to be the evangelists's doing, not the work of Jesus.

• *The evangelists frequently relocate sayings and parables or invent new narrative contexts for them.*

Example: Jesus' first disciples cannot be expected to remember the particular occasions on which sayings were first uttered and stories first told. Jesus probably repeated his best stories many times. His followers would remember the story but not necessarily a specific context. When it came to compiling a narrative gospel, the story would have to be placed in a context, which would tend to be one which best fitted the evangelist's own message or theological emphasis. Sometimes the context was simply invented. For instance, Jesus is reported in Mark 2: 27 as saying "The sabbath was made for man, and not man for the sabbath". Mark places this as the climax of a story in which the Pharisees criticize the disciples for plucking grains of corn as they walk through the fields of Galilee on the sabbath. But many scholars now think that the Pharisees were almost exclusively a Jerusalem-based party in Jesus' time and cannot have played any significant role in Galilee, though they had spread into the area by the time Mark was written. This casts a query over Mark's narrative. And if Mark's context is questionable, what are we to make of the saying itself? Does it come from Jesus or the author of Mark?

• *The evangelists frequently expand sayings or parables, or provide them with an interpretive overlay or comment.*

Example: When asked why Jesus and his followers didn't fast, as John the Baptist did, Jesus quips in Mark 2:19 that you don't fast at a wedding when the bridegroom is still around! But in the next verse, Mark has him add that it will be time to fast "on the day when the groom is taken away". Mark's problem is that his community of the Jesus movement in the 70s believed in maintaining Jewish fasting customs. A non-fasting Jesus was an embarrassment, so Mark expands the saying to make it conform to his own teaching.

• *The evangelists often revise or edit sayings to make them conform to their own individual language, style, or viewpoint.*

Example: Mark records the parable of the sower in 4:3-8. But he then makes Jesus give the disciples a lengthy and uncharacteristically labored exposition of its meaning (4:10-20) which only makes sense within a context of Mark's strange conviction, not shared by the other evangelists, that while Jesus preached publicly he reserved his secret meanings for his closest disciples alone. The parable itself is in the "Sure sounds like Jesus" (pink) category, but the esoteric explanation sounds more like Mark's own gloss (black).

• *Words borrowed from the fund of common lore or the Greek scriptures are often put on the lips of Jesus.*

Example: Funk argues here that the concept of plagiarism, though not unknown, was not understood in the ancient world as it is today. Commonly used words of wisdom, or sayings regarded as sacred, were frequently attributed to legendary sages such as Solomon or Socrates, and the early church continued the practice by sometimes putting such sayings in the mouth of Jesus. The saying that it's not the healthy but the sick who are in need of a physician is attributed by Mark to Jesus (2:17), but is also found in secular sources, attributed to Plutarch and Diogenes Laertius. In particular, the Greek version of the Hebrew scriptures, the Christian Old Testament, was used, especially by Matthew, as a source for sayings attributed to Jesus - most famously his words on the cross, which are a direct quotation from the Psalms.

• *The evangelists frequently attribute their own statements to Jesus.*

The gospel writers (and especially John) tend to summarize Jesus' message in their own words, although these are attributed to Jesus. This is clear from the very different styles of language used by each of the evangelists.

• *Hard sayings are frequently softened in the process of transmission to adapt them to the conditions of daily living. Variations in difficult sayings often betray the struggle of the early Christian community to interpret or adapt sayings to its own situation.*

Examples: Matthew and Mark both report Jesus as saying "the last will be first and the first last", presumably taken from oral memory. But this is uncomfortable for those who consider themselves among "the first", or the better sort. So Mark 10:31 softens it to "*many* of the first will be last, and of the last *many* will be first". Matthew, however, retains the harder version. Similarly, when Mark reports Jesus' advice to the rich young man to sell all his goods and give the proceeds to the poor, adding for good measure that it is easier for a camel to squeeze through a needle's eye than for a rich person to get into God's domain, he adds a get-out clause: "Everything's possible for God" (10:21-27). So it's not so hard after all! Funk adds: "Modern interpreters have been in the softening business too: some literalists have located a caravan pass, called the needle's eye, which a camel can squeeze through with difficulty, if it is not loaded with baggage; others have imagined a tight gate in the wall of Jerusalem, through which a camel can barely pass. These are feeble and misguided attempts to take the sting out of the aphorism and rob Jesus's words of their edge".

• *Sayings and parables expressed in "Christian" language are the creation of the evangelists or their Christian predecessors. Sayings or parables that contrast with the language or viewpoint of the gospel in which they are embedded reflect older tradition (but not necessarily tradition that originated with Jesus). The Christian community develops apologetic statements to defend its claims and sometimes attributes such statements to Jesus.*

As Funk reminds us, "Jesus was not the first Christian. However, he is often made to talk like a Christian by his devoted followers. The contrast between Christian language or viewpoint and the language or viewpoint of Jesus is a very important clue to the real voice of Jesus. The language of Jesus was distinctive, as was his style and perspective, if we take the bedrock of the tradition as our guide. The inclination of the evangelists and other Christians was to make Jesus himself affirm what they themselves had come to believe". For example, the earliest known summary of "the gospel" is an oral version quoted by Paul in 1 Corinthians 15:3-5: Christ died for our sins, was buried and rose on the third day "according to the scriptures". Mark repeats this summary, but reports that Jesus himself, rather than "the scriptures", predicted these events and expressed his gospel in these terms (8:31, 9:31, 10:33). Both Paul's and Mark's version are composed in "Christian" terminology (that is, the terminology of those within the Jesus movement who came to believe that Jesus was the divine Christ predicted in the scriptures), but Mark attributes his Christian version to the pre-Christian Jesus.

• *Sayings and narratives that reflect knowledge of events that took place after Jesus' death are the creation of the evangelists or the oral tradition before them.*

Example: Jesus is sometimes made to give detailed predictions of events, such as the persecution of his followers, or the destruction of the temple, that happened later in the first or second centuries, when the gospels were written. "Whenever scholars detect detailed knowledge of postmortem events in sayings and parables attributed to Jesus," says Funk, "they are inclined to the view that the formulation of such sayings took place after the fact".

3. Rules of oral evidence

If the Seminar tends to doubt that Jesus originated the sayings that are attested elsewhere (in secular sources or the Old Testament), or are couched in later Christian language, or appear to have been "softened", or fit too comfortably into the theology of the evangelist, or appear to show detailed knowledge of later events, what does it consider reliable? Funk answers that with this "fundamental axiom":

• *Only sayings and parables that can be traced back to the oral period, 30-50 CE, can possibly have originated with Jesus.*

Sayings that critical analysis demonstrates as having been formulated by the gospel writers in their own *late*-first-century language are eliminated from contention. Scholars look, instead, for evidence that a particular saying antedates the written gospels and can be located in the two decades after Jesus' death. Four "rules of attestation" were formulated by the Seminar to determine which sayings could be assigned with a high degree of probablity to this early oral period:

• *Sayings or parables that are attested in two or more independent sources are older than the sources in which they are embedded.*

• *Sayings or parables that are attested in two different contexts probably circulated independently at an earlier time.*

• *The same or similar content attested in two or more different forms has had a life of its own and therefore may stem from old tradition.*

• *Unwritten tradition that is captured by the written gospels relatively late may preserve very old memories.*

The first three of these rules make it possible to isolate a body of sayings that is almost certainly older than the written gospels. The fourth recognizes that oral tradition continued well into the second century, so that scholars need to be on the alert for stray tradition that could go back to the early period. As we noted when first considering oral tradition in Chapter 3, the spoken word in the form of stories and aphorisms repeated conversationally or in the memorized litanies of the early church was far more influential than the written word in a largely illiterate society. Funk reminds us that "copies of the first gospels were undoubtedly rare and difficult to use once acquired. It is not an easy thing to look up a passage in a sixteen-foot scroll (unrolling and rolling the parchment until one came to the desired text). Codices were just coming into use (a codex is a stack of sheets bound at one side like a modern book), but sacred books continued to take the form of the older scroll, as they do in Judaism to this day". Hence the persistence of oral memory, and the critical importance to the Jesus scholar of detecting it where it is embedded in the later written record.

4. What did Jesus really *say*?

But it is one thing to isolate sayings from the early oral tradition, and another to confidently ascribe them to the historical Jesus of Galilee himself. Here the Seminar applies a controversial criterion, that of *distinctiveness*. As Funk puts it, with characteristic breeziness, "Jesus undoubtedly said a great many very ordinary things, such as 'hello' and 'goodbye', and whatever he hollered when he hit his thumb in the carpenter's shop or stubbed his toe on a rocky road. But if we are to identify the voice of Jesus that makes him the precipitator of the Christian tradition, we have to look for sayings and stories that distinguish his voice from ordinary speakers and even sages in his day and time". Admonitions to love your neighbor, to keep the kosher laws, to honor your parents, to keep the sabbath, could be found on the lips of any and every itinerant Jewish teacher/preacher. But some of the reported sayings of Jesus cut right across the grain of social and religious custom and contemporary political correctness, such as the earthy assertion that it's not what you eat but what you excrete that makes you filthy (Mark 7:15), and the distinctly off-message advice to travelling disciples to eat whatever their host puts before them rather than insist on kosher food (Thomas 14:4).

Other reported sayings are not only distinctive but shocking. The parable of the Samaritan (Q in Luke 10:30-35), the vineyard laborers (Matthew 20:1-15), the prodigal son (Luke 15:11-32), and the injunction to lend without expectation of any return (Thomas 95:1-2), all "call for a reversal of roles, or frustrate ordinary, everyday expectations". There are two ways of interpreting these out-of-step sayings. One is to say that precisely because they are so contrary, so opposed to the religion and morality of the day, they are *unlikely* to be the authentic words of a contemporary Jewish teacher. The other is to say that their very distinctiveness, originality and bare-faced effrontery is what made them memorable and gives them the mark of authenticity. The shock value, exaggeration and humor is what made his stories and one-liners so memorable that they were retained and retold again and again by his followers until they began to be collected and recorded in writing. The Seminar went decisively for this second framework of interpretation.

Having examined 1330 reported sayings of Jesus (420 in Matthew, 177 in Mark, 392 in Luke, 140 in John and 201 in Thomas), the Seminar voted 29 red, 184 pink, 381 gray, and 736 black. Of the red sayings, 11 were found in Q/Matthew, 14 in Q/Luke, 1 in Mark, none in John, and 3 in Thomas. Pink sayings broke down as 60 from Q/Matthew or Matthew's M source, 65 from Q/Luke or Luke's L source, 65 from Mark, and 40 from Thomas. Altogether 213 sayings were voted red (29) or pink (184) and 1117 gray or black[11].

The sayings that picked up the most red votes were:

Q/Matthew 5:39 ("turn the other cheek"),

Q/Matthew 5:40 ("when sued for your coat, give your cloak too"),

Q/Luke 6:20 ("blessed are the poor" [Matthew's weaker version,

"blessed are the poor in spirit", mustered only a pink]),

Q/Matthew 5:41 ("go the second mile"),

Q/Luke 6:27 ("love your enemies").

This is the contrary Jesus, the outrageous, radical, revolutionary Jesus, the Jesus who captivated with riddles and aphorisms, a Jesus who defied common sense and challenged his hearers to attempt the impossible. It is also, according to the Seminar's dating criteria, the Jesus of the very earliest sources, particularly the Jesus of Q: a Jesus who preceded, and is therefore more historically grounded than, the Jesus of the narrative gospels and the divinized Christ-Jesus of Paul and John.

When published in 1993 in *The Five Gospels: What did Jesus Really Say?* the Seminar's proposals - boldly claimed as "findings" - unleashed a hail of criticism. Conservative Christians, especially in the USA, were scandalized by the denial of authenticity to the whole of John and the exclusion of all explicitly "Christian" sayings (that is, those considered by the Seminar to betray a later origin and a late-first-century christology) in the synoptic gospels. Other scholars, not all of them conservative, lamented the negative emphasis by which only 213 out of 1330 sayings were granted any significant degree of historical authenticity, and a mere 29 of these the full red-letter endorsement. But Mark Allan Powell, in his well-balanced commentary in *The Jesus Debate*, argues that, given the Seminar's maxim "When in sufficient doubt, leave it out", the overall results "can be read in a way that is surprisingly positive". Pointing out that some scholars voted black almost every time, that even a few black votes could pull down the weighted average of a saying's final score, and that gray sayings frequently functioned as an "I'm not sure" rather than a "probably inauthentic" vote, he finds the proportion of reds and pinks impressively high. He comments:

"The story that, by and large, went unreported was this: two hundred historians, relying on investigative techniques of critical scholarship, affirmed the authenticity of some 18 per cent of the sayings attributed to Jesus in books that were written a generation after his death by people who made no pretence of being objective or unbiased in what they wrote. The media, however, missed this story, reporting instead the rather bland and predictable instances in which critical scholarship was unable to affirm convictions of religious piety"[12].

5. What did Jesus really *do*?

After six years' intensive work on the sayings, the Seminar turned in 1991 to Jesus' reported *acts*: the events, healings, miracles and human encounters, including the birth and passion stories, which constitute the narrative elements of the gospels. This was to take another six years. The Fellows examined 387 reports of 176 events where Jesus was the principal or a substantial actor. Once again, as with the sayings, the

Seminar's key forensic tool was the established date-line. For at least twenty years after Jesus' death, all reports of his acts had existed only in oral tradition, shaped and re-shaped by followers less concerned with our modern notions of historical truth than with preaching a message and expressing a theological conviction. Even when the sayings began to be written down in collections like Q, the acts and deeds continued to circulate only in oral form for another twenty years, until the author of Mark produced the first surviving attempt to link them in a written narrative. And at least another ten or twenty years passed before Mark's narrative was elaborated by other gospel writers (at least the biblical ones). Not surprisingly, therefore, where Q had been taken as the best available repository of the sayings, Mark was favored as more likely than his successors to carry some residue of historical authenticity when it came to the stories of what Jesus had done.

But the Seminar took the well-established view that the author of Mark was not himself an eye-witness of the events he recounts. At best, "he is reporting information conveyed to him by a third person or persons, who themselves were quite possibly not eye-witnesses... Since he doesn't name those from whom he gets his information, his sources are anonymous". Thus "the foundation of the critical approach to the gospels is the recognition that much of the information... is based on hearsay". Moreover, what survives and is recorded of this hearsay "has been assimilated to a set of typifications developed over time by those who shared their convictions about [Jesus] with each other through storytelling. Believers reinforced their convictions by subtly molding their stories - without being conscious of doing so - to conform to their beliefs"[13].

This is the process by which folklore, rather than history, is made. As folklore, these stories - and those in the rest of the Bible - have been "wrapped in memories that have been edited, deleted, augmented, and combined many times over many years. Sorting out the fact from the fiction is a task for the well-informed and patient sleuth". And the intelligent sleuth must take into account the likelihood that at least some of those who told stories about Jesus may indeed have been "telling stories", in the modern colloquial sense of imaginative fictions. As Funk explains in the Introduction to *The Acts of Jesus*,

"There are at least five conditions that might have prompted them to employ their imaginations.

• They might have created stories to fulfil a prophecy or to match scriptural language.
• They might have invented stories to assist in marketing the messiah to the larger world.
• They might have made up tales to give expression to their own convictions about who Jesus was and what he did and said.
• They might have imagined scenes to justify practices adopted by themselves or by their communities.
• And they might have put into a fictive story form claims that they were making on their own behalf or on behalf of their leaders".

Funk adds that the evangelists "did not, of course, wilfully distort the historical truth; rather, they were merely indulging the human proclivity to adjust inherited oral traditions to their own controlling perceptions born of faith"[14].

Given this approach, based on the conviction that it is the historian's business to evaluate evidence critically and with due skepticism, it is not surprising that only ten of the 176 reported Jesus-events examined by the Seminar were voted red (meaning that the event's historical reliability was considered "virtually certain" as "supported by a preponderance of evidence" and that Fellows "unequivocally" supported its inclusion in "the database for determining who Jesus was"). Another 19 were voted pink (meaning Fellows concluded the event "probably occurred"). The combined reds and pinks, 29 in all, amounted to 16% of the total: slightly lower than the 18% making up the reds and pinks among the sayings.

Once again, however, the real story of the Seminar's "findings" is not the broad swathe of blacks and grays but the fact that a substantial group of critical historians with no common theological agenda affirmed in red a real live historical Jesus: a man who was born in Nazareth (not Bethlehem) during Herod's reign, to a mother named Mary and a natural human father; had brothers named James, Joses (or Joseph), Judas and Simon, and unnamed sisters; was baptized in the Jordan by John; preached the kingdom of God or "God's good news" as an itinerant teacher in the villages of Galilee, winning followers or disciples; successfully healed some sick people, including Mary of Magdala; was believed to cast out demons as an exorcist; kept company with social outcasts; and was flogged and crucified by the Roman authorities during the prefecture of Pontius Pilate (26-36 CE).

The resulting pared-down, de-supernaturalized, *humanized* Jesus - no virgin birth, Bethlehem stable, wise men or shepherds, flight into Egypt, miracles, "I am" soliloquies, last supper, betrayal by Judas, bodily resurrection, post-resurrection appearances, ascension (all weight-voted black) - has not satisfied those who by faith affirm the biblical gospel records as factual history fully guaranteed by divine inspiration. It has also seemed disappointingly thin to many who have come to love the beautiful literary and philosophical discourses of John's highly sophisticated and spiritualized Jesus, who remains unremittingly black in the SV. Indeed, as we shall see in subsequent chapters, it has also seemed too reductionist to some historians outside the Seminar whose credentials and objectivity are as well-attested as those of the Seminar's Fellows.

But the Jesus Seminar's resonant affirmation that there was an historical Jesus is also a challenge to those scholarly skeptics who have argued that he was wholly mythical or legendary, an invention of the late-first-century religious imagination. In fact, the Seminar's findings on both acts and sayings - and particularly its evaluation of Q - have persuaded some radical skeptics in the scholarly community to rethink their arguments and concede that there probably was, after all, a flesh-and-blood Jesus who trudged the dusty lanes of ancient Galilee, threw in his lot with the despised and rejected, promised them that God was on their side, won a reputation as a miracle-worker, and was killed off as a dangerous trouble-maker. We shall note this effect of Q scholarship in chapter 11.

A mere summary of the Seminar's conclusions (see Cameo: *The Red and Pink Jesus,* page 185) hardly does justice to the huge amount of collaborative detective work involved. As with the color-coded sayings, every single one of the color-coded acts - gray and black as well as red and pink - is examined in detail. A single phrase may merit several pages of detailed analysis, including not only the Seminar's own conclusions but those (often different) of other distinguished scholars such as John P Meier and E P Sanders. Moreover, a single story is often broken down and evaluated part by part, some parts one colour, others another. Take the first eight verses of Mark, which relate that (a) the "good news of Jesus" began with Isaiah's prophecy of a coming messenger, understood to be John the Baptist, (b) John appeared in the Judean wilderness and called for baptism, (c) crowds followed him, (d) John wore a mantle of camel hair and a leather belt, (e) he announced that someone more powerful would succeed him, whose sandals he was not fit to untie, and (f) that while he, John, baptized with water, his successor would baptize with the holy spirit. For the Seminar, this is a multicolored story: (a) is black, (b) red, (c) pink, (d) gray, (e) pink and (f) gray. Two and a half pages of analysis explain how and why the Fellows reached each of these color-conclusions.

This kind of detail on the "acts of Jesus" is followed through for some five hundred pages. As with the sayings volume, the student or general reader may learn not only what decision the Seminar reached on any particular reported action, but what arguments were taken into account, how a finding was reached, and even, in some cases, how the Seminar's conclusion compared with that of other scholars. Westar's evangelical passion for "theological literacy" informs every page of these two milestone works, *The Five Gospels: What did Jesus Really Say?* and *The Acts of Jesus: What did Jesus Really Do?*

6. Jesus and Apocalypse

The Seminar's excavation of Jesus revealed a human rather than a heavenly being, not so much the divine Word as a sage who had a divine way with words. This was its challenge to the churches. But the Seminar also posed a challenge to the rest of the scholarly community. It centered on what many saw, and continue to see, as the single most important question about Jesus, his message and his mission. As Robert J Miller puts it, "Did the historical Jesus teach that God would put an end to the world as we know it and create a new world of justice and peace? And did Jesus teach that God would do this *soon*, within the lifetime of his own generation? In other words, was the historical Jesus an apocalyptic prophet?"[15]

As our summary of earlier quests showed, Johannes Weiss and Albert Schweitzer at the beginning of the 20th century established a view of Jesus that dominated historical Jesus scholarship for nearly a hundred years. The Jesus they found at the end of their quest was not a figure who could be accommodated to the modern world and its Enlightenment values and ideals. He was a man of his own times, and those times were decidedly pre-modern. Jesus was one of a number of doomsday prophets who proclaimed the imminent end of the world as it was known. For this Jesus, Israel's God was about to make a cataclysmic intervention in human history, replacing the kingdoms of the world with direct rule from heaven. Israel's God would depose and replace Rome's emperor and rule as king and judge in a world supernaturally transformed. This was the apocalypse, and Jesus believed it was his mission to proclaim it, and then to die as a "ransom" for the sins of those who had heard the warning and heeded it with repentance. His death would clear the way for the ultimate act of God, the coming of his kingdom on earth, as it was in heaven.

There are many reported sayings of Jesus focusing on "the kingdom" (of God or of heaven), usually translated in the Jesus Seminar's SV as "God's imperial rule", "God's realm" or "God's domain". Some clearly emphasize the imminence of kingdom come, some seem to mean that the kingdom has already arrived, while others are ambiguous. Mark 9:1, for instance, has Jesus saying: "I swear to you: Some of those standing here won't ever taste death before they see God's imperial rule set in with power" (SV). On a plain reading it is hard to interpret this as meaning anything other than that the apocalyptic arrival of the kingdom, its being "set in with power", is an event predicted by Jesus to happen within the lifetime of his listeners. In the same vein is Mark 13:30: "I swear to you, this generation certainly won't pass into oblivion before all these things take place", and Matthew 10:23, where Jesus sends his disciples out into the countryside, promising them: "I swear to you, you certainly won't have exhausted [or won't make it through] the cities of Israel before the Son of Man [or Adam] comes".

But against these "kingdom soon" promises/warnings are a number of "kingdom now" statements that seem to flatly contradict them. Luke 17:20-21 has Jesus saying "You won't be able to observe the coming of God's imperial rule. People are not going to be able to say, 'Look, here it is', or 'Over there!' On the contrary, God's imperial rule is right there in your presence". Thomas 113:4 has "The (Father's) imperial rule is spread out upon the earth, and people don't see it". Luke 11.20 and Matthew 12:28 have Jesus saying "If by God's finger I drive out demons, then for you God's imperial rule has arrived". Thomas 3:1-3 has Jesus poking fun at the idea that the kingdom is in the sky, emphasizing that it is within and among his disciples: "If your leaders say to you, 'Look the (Father's) imperial rule is in the sky', then the birds of the sky will precede you. If they say to you, 'It is in the sea', then the fish will precede you. Rather, the (Father's) imperial rule is within you and it is outside you".

So did Jesus believe and teach that the kingdom was an apocalyptic event that was about to happen in his own day, or that in a more subtle sense it was a present reality capable of transforming the world by stealth? Or did he sometimes suggest the one thing and sometimes another? Or is one set of sayings a true reflection of what Jesus taught and the other set a misinterpretation? If so, which is the authentic voice of

Jesus and which the misinterpretation?

As we have seen, prior to the Jesus Seminar, through most of the 20th century, the scholarly (if not the ecclesiastical) consensus was with Weiss and Schweitzer: Jesus was convinced that God was about to miraculously intervene in history to impose his kingdom, and that is what his teaching and preaching was all about. What should be made, then, of the passages that seem to flatly contradict or subvert this message? Such passages, it was argued, represented not the words of Jesus but the misinterpretations of later gospel writers who were increasingly embarrassed by the fact that, although the disciples had been promised that they would not complete their mission or taste death before the kingdom arrived, they *had* completed their mission and *had* died - and the kingdom had not come. The evangelists could not omit entirely the "apocalypse now" warnings since they were so well attested in oral tradition, but they were softened or neutralized by added sayings or new interpretations suggesting that the kingdom could be understood in different ways: as a coming event, but no-one knew when or how, or as an event already come, already present in the world, particularly in the Jesus movement as it was being transformed into the church.

The Jesus Seminar turned this interpretion on its head. Jesus may initially have shared the apocalyptic view of kingdom-come as preached by John the Baptist and other Jewish prophets, it proposed, but as he began his own independent ministry as a sage and story-teller he came to speak in parables and riddles of an alternative reality, one that challenged and subverted the political, social, religious and family values of what was conventionally understood as the "real world". The promised kingdom, God's domain, was this alternative to our default reality. It was not a kingdom *of* this world (though it was *in* this world), rather a vision of how the world might be. It was "right there in your presence", under your very noses, if only you could see it! The texts that reported Jesus in this vein, the Seminar argued, were most likely the more authentic, precisely because they flatly contradicted the current expectation of imminent apocalypse as

Cameo: The Red and Pink Jesus

Ten acts or events involving Jesus were voted red ("virtually certain"):

*1. Jesus was born, a "descendant of Abraham", i.e. a Jew, and named Jesus by Joseph (**Matthew 1:1, 24-25, 2:1, Luke 2:21**), who was generally assumed to be the father (**Luke 3:23**).*

*2. Jesus' mother was Joseph's wife Mary (**Matthew 1:16**), to whom Joseph was engaged at the time of conception (**Luke 2:5**).*

*3. Jesus had brothers and sisters (**Mark 6:3, Matthew 13:55-57**).*

*4. Jesus came from Nazareth and was baptized in the Jordan by John (**Mark 1:9, Matthew 3:13, Luke 3:21**).*

*5. Jesus came to Galilee, including Capernaum, proclaiming God's good news (**Mark 1:14,21, 6:6, Matthew 4:12, Luke 4:14,31**).*

*6. One of Jesus' companions was Mary of Magdala (**Luke 8:1-2**).*

*7. Some said Jesus drove out demons in the name of Beelzebub (**Q in Luke 11:15**).*

*8. Jesus shared meals with social outcasts ("toll collectors and sinners") (**Mark 2:15-16, Matthew 9:10-11**).*

*9. John the Baptist was regarded by Jesus and others as a genuine prophet (**Mark 11:32, Luke 20:6**).*

*10. Jesus was crucified by Roman soldiers under Pilate (**Mark 15:24, Matthew 27:26, 35, Luke 23:33, John 19:16**).*

Some 19 pink acts fill out the Seminar's portrait of "the shadowy figure pictured in snapshots". The Fellows say: "We are quite confident that a person Jesus of Nazareth once existed, in spite of a few skeptics who believe that all the stories about Jesus are pure myth. We are confident that he began as a disciple of John the Baptist, that he quit John at some point and returned to Galilee where he launched his own career as an itinerant sage. We believe he spoke about God's domain or God's imperial rule in parables and short, pithy sayings and attracted a substantial following. There is little doubt that he was also a charismatic healer and exorcist and that he was eventually put to death by the Romans around the year 30 CE.... Beyond these meager facts, there is very little hard detailed information. Yet it is easy to imagine a story that joins these facts together in a single, sequential narrative. The evangelists did so by asking why Jesus met the fate he did and what his life meant to them. They employed scripture and their own convictions as guides in fashioning a story that accounted for the death of a suffering and righteous hero...

"Jesus was evidently an itinerant sage, wandering about from place to place, teaching and healing and living on handouts. Jesus was active during his public career in the towns and hamlets of Galilee." Galilee was a "semi-pagan" province "whose inhabitants, because they were often of mixed blood and open to foreign influence, were not highly regarded by the Judeans living to the south... Dividing the two provinces was the [hostile] territory of Samaria, through which Jesus may have occasionally passed on his way to and from Jerusalem...

"We are not certain that Jesus deliberately formed a group of disciples, but it is clear that followers, including women, gathered around him... Jesus was popular with the people, although the evangelists tend to exaggerate that popularity. However, Jesus was not well received in his hometown. He was also opposed by some religious authorities in both Galilee and Jerusalem, though much of the controversy in the gospels between adherents of the new sect

and Judaism may reflect later conditions subsequent to the destruction of Jerusalem and the temple (70 CE) when the budding church was competing with the synagogue.

"We do not know how long his public career lasted, but the narrative gospels imply a relatively short period, from one to three years. As a final act, Jesus went to Jerusalem, either spoke or acted against the temple and the temple authorities, and was executed by the Romans."

Jesus as social deviant

"We are confident that Jesus was a social deviant - he regularly infringed the social codes in force in his society. He consorted openly with social outcasts... did not observe kosher... did not practice fasting... infringed the sabbath codes occasionally... did not observe other purity codes, such as washing his hands before eating. He was at odds with his family; he advocated adopting 'true relatives' as part of his extended family."

Jesus' language and literacy skills

"Jesus' native tongue was a dialect of Aramaic current in Galilee that Judeans apparently could distinguish from their own form of speech... We do not know whether Jesus could read or write; the story of Jesus in the synogogue reading from Isaiah may well be a fiction invented by Luke." The story of Jesus *"stooping down and 'drawing' in the sand... cannot be taken as evidence that Jesus could read and write. The critical reader must be constantly alert to fictional embellishments in the gospels. We do not know whether Jesus knew Hebrew, in his day only a literary language. There is now evidence that suggests he may have been bilingual; Greek was probably his second language, learned from the pagan*

> *environment that surrounded him in Galilee, especially in Sepphoris, a hellenistic city located only four miles from his home village. In any case, the written gospels were all composed in Greek, and judging by the poetic shape of much of the language, it seems certain that the Jesus tradition took its formative shape in Greek as well. If Jesus did not speak Greek, very few of his original words have come down to us."* - ***"What Do We Really Know About Jesus?", in "The Acts of Jesus", pp 527ff***

preached by the Baptist and the Essenes. Those texts that had Jesus seemingly promising an imminent kingdom imposed by divine intervention reflected his followers' misplaced assumption that Jesus shared these conventional apocalyptic expectations. Both authentic and misinterpreted versions of kingdom teaching found their way into different strands of the early oral tradition and came to sit side by side in the gospels.

But in this matter, as with all the reported Jesus sayings on all topics, "the task of historical criticism is to analyze this complex blend of memory and interpretation in order to distinguish what should be attributed to the historical Jesus and what should be attributed either to progressive elaboration by the rank and file of early Christians who passed on stories about him, or to the focused creativity of the individual gospel writers"[16]. And the Seminar concluded (almost but not quite unanimously) that the "present kingdom" sayings were authentic, the apocalyptic sayings misinterpretations. Jesus hadn't, after all, got it wrong as Weiss, Schweitzer and a following wind of twentieth-century critical scholarship had supposed. On the contrary, they had got *him* wrong.

Thus Mark's unequivocal "this generation certainly won't pass into oblivion before all these things take place" was voted black on the basis that it was "taken by most Fellows as Mark's remark to his own audience, rather than as something Jesus said earlier to his disciples"[17]. Matthew's "you won't make it through the cities of Israel before the Son of Man comes" was also rated black, as reflecting "the eschatological intensity of Matthew's vision", which was "far removed from Jesus' perspective". Mark's "some of those standing here won't ever taste death before they see God's imperial rule set in with power" ended up with a gray. Some Fellows voted black, attributing the formulation to Mark rather than Jesus, while others voted pink on the basis that Jesus meant that the kingdom was arriving during the lifetimes of the disciples and was "set in with power", or made apparent, by what were believed to be his successful exorcisms. Here the black and pink mixed into a somewhat sludgy gray.

On the other hand, Luke's "God's imperial rule is right there in your presence" (or "the kingdom of God is within you" in the familiar King James Version) got a pink. The Fellows noted that it is paralleled in Thomas 113:4, which was also voted pink. Why? "The rule of evidence invoked in this instance is that [this formulation of the saying] does not fit the tendencies of the unfolding tradition, which were predominantly apocalyptic. The best explanation for the presence of sayings like these in the gospel record is that they originated with Jesus, who espoused a view unlike that of his predecessors and successors"[18]. On the same basis, Luke's version of the first three beatitudes in the "sermon on the mount" (though Luke has it delivered "in the plain") gets the full red treatment: Jesus really did tell the poor, the hungry, the suffering, "God's domain belongs to you" - though whether he meant they would inherit it after God's own revolution or that it was already present with them rather than with the rich and powerful remained ambiguous.

Since publication of the color-coded *Five Gospels* and *Acts of Jesus* Westar and the Seminar have strengthened their emphasis on an historical Jesus understood as "eschatological" (meaning concerned with the fulfilment of what Jesus saw as God's end-plan in a broad sense) but not "apocalyptic" (meaning the belief that God was about to impose his rule through a cataclysmic supernatural intervention). Ironically, their view finds more favor in the liberal churches, since it avoids Schweitzer's disturbing conclusion that, since the apocalypse never happened in his own time and is still awaited two thousand years later, Jesus got the timing badly wrong. But the non-apocalyptic Jesus has yet to be established in a new scholarly consensus. The scholarly community outside the Seminar remains deeply divided between those who read the sources as indicating that Jesus was indeed a prophet of apocalyptic doom whose teachings had to be modified by the church when his prophecies failed to materialize, and those who conclude that Jesus used "the kingdom" or "God's domain" as a metaphor for an alternative reality, to be tasted here and now, which teaching was misunderstood and muddled by his followers and the recording evangelists.

The divide is of critical importance to all who look to Jesus as teacher and shaper of their world view - and, perhaps, to those who look on and witness the battle of words from a secular or humanist perspective. We shall return to the debate in Chapter 12, after we have looked at what a broader range of scholars have made of the sayings and doings of Jesus.

7. The Seminar and its critics

If, as is sometimes charged, the Jesus Seminar often set out to court controversy, it cannot have been disappointed. Rationalist and Jewish critics, from their different perspectives, have criticized it for failing to free itself from a Christian paradigm. Christian scholars and church-people have accused it of furthering a secular, humanistic agenda with intent to undermine the faith. Scholars who have not themselves succeeded in escaping the academy and its specialist publications complain of its populism and the success it had, particularly in its early days, in grabbing media attention. Its claim that the views of a scholarly community carry more weight than those of any individual scholar is countered with the charge that the community is self-selected from a like-minded liberal-skeptical elite. Its basic assumption that it is possible to excavate at least a kernel of historical "truth" about Jesus is criticized by postmodernist scholars as a final fling of old-fashioned Enlightenment "modernism". Some scholars who do not question the integrity of the

Seminar's work nevertheless criticize many of its assumptions and research methods - particularly its heavy reliance on a stratified model of hypothetical gospel Q and its eager embrace of inconclusive arguments for an early date for Thomas.

Westar as "destroyers of Christianity"

To its own scarcely-concealed delight, the Seminar's conservative critics have sometimes accorded the Westar Fellows a degree of influence that they themselves could only dream of. In an "Advent Meditation" preached on December 15 2006 in the Redemptoris Mater Chapel of the Apostolic Palace (the Vatican), to a congregation that included Pope Benedict XVI and the Roman Curia, Father Ramiero Cantalamessa, Pontifical Household Preacher, attacked as "painful" for the Christian believer today

"...the systematic rejection of Christ in the name of an objective historical research... We are watching a race to see who succeeds in presenting a Christ who best measures up to the man of today, stripping him of every transcendental aspect... The temptation to clothe Christ in the garb of our own epoch or ideology has always existed. But in the past the causes were arguably serious and of a wide scope: Christ the idealist, the romantic, the liberal, the socialist, the revolutionary... Our time, obsessed as it is with sex, cannot but think of him as troubled by certain problems of desire."[19]

Jesus has been "modernised, or better, postmodernised", and Father Cantalamessa knows who is to blame.

"It is good to know the origin of these recent currents which make Jesus of Nazareth a testing ground for the postmodern ideals of ethical relativism and absolute individualism (called deconstructionism) that are, directly or indirectly, inspiring novels, films and events and also influence historical investigations of Jesus. We can trace it to a movement that emerged in the United States in the final decades of the last century and that in the 'Jesus Seminar' had its most active form... The aim of these scholars is no longer simply to correct but to destroy, as they say, 'that mistake called Christianity'[20]...

"The truly sad thing is not that these things have been written (you need to invent something new if you want to continue to write books) but rather that, once published, hundreds of thousands, if not millions, of these books are sold. It seems to me that the incapacity of historico-philological research to link the Jesus of reality with the Jesus of the Gospel and ecclesiastical sources has to do with the fact that it ignores and does not concern itself with studying the dynamic of spiritual or supernatural phenomena. It would be like trying to hear a sound with your eyes or see colors with your ears..."

But Cantalamessa comforts himself and his Vatican audience with the suggestion that the work of critical scholars in general and the Jesus Seminar in particular has had its day.

"Fortunately, it seems that a chapter in the studies of Jesus is finally closing and the page is being turned. In a work entitled *Christianity in the Making*, destined to be a watershed as his previous studies have been, James Dunn, one of the best living scholars of the New Testament, after a careful analysis of the results of the last three centuries of research, comes to the conclusion that there was no rift between the Jesus who preached and the Jesus who was preached, between the Jesus of history and of faith. This faith was not born after Easter but in the first encounters with the disciples, who became disciples precisely because they believed in him, even though at the beginning it was a fragile faith, naive about its implications."

James Dunn: *What the Seminar missed*

The Vatican hierarchy's enthusiastic endorsement of James Dunn's work is significant. Dunn has indeed provided conservatives, both Catholic and Protestant, with a scholarly critique of some of the most important presuppositions of liberal historians. Since his challenge has been hailed as counter-reformation to the Jesus Seminar's reformation it is worth setting out the crux of his argument here.

The Emeritus Lightfoot Professor of Divinity at the University of Durham argues at length in *Jesus Remembered* (2003), the first in a projected trilogy on "Christianity in the Making", and more concisely in *A New Perspective on Jesus: What the Quest for the Historical Jesus Missed* (2005), that all questers, old and new, have been locked into a "literary paradigm" in which the sayings of Jesus, transmitted orally for twenty years or more, are now treated as if they had been composed as written texts and subjected to continuous editorial revision. Dunn proposes a different approach to the oral tradition, one that he argues is supported by recent research into the way oral story-telling works in modern Middle Eastern villages.

The earliest written collections of Jesus-sayings, as incorporated into the gospels, should be understood, he suggests, not as the work of evangelists plying the trade of literary editor at the end of a twenty-year game of Chinese whispers, but as a *memorized* litany of teachings which the disciples began putting together *during his ministry*. The litany was not written down: Dunn is with those scholars who think the disciples and Jesus himself were probably illiterate. But it was committed to memory, and the memory was consolidated by constant repetition and *performance*, a practice continued within the Jesus movement for many years until the litanies were eventually committed to written texts as authorized and reliable sayings-collections.

Dunn does not claim that these litanies give us a word-for-word account of "what Jesus actually said". Rather, they convey "the *theme* of the story, or... its *core* element" (his emphasis)[21]. Ironically for one who is otherwise a trenchant critic of the Jesus Seminar and all its works, Dunn calls the Seminar's founder to his aid. "On this point", he continues, "Robert Funk agrees: under the heading 'Performance as gist; nucleus as core', [Funk] observes the 'general rule in the study of folklore that oral storytellers reproduce the gist of stories in their oral performances... As a consequence, historical reminiscence is likely to be found in the nucleus of stories, if anywhere'".

So Funk at one end of the spectrum and Dunn at the other both agree that there were about twenty years of oral transmission before anything was written down, and that what was transmitted was the *theme*, *core*, or *gist* of the sayings, rather than a word-for-word Greek translation of what Jesus had said in Aramaic. In what respect, then, do these two scholars (and two different schools of scholarship) differ in the deductions they make from this agreed assessment?

Funk and his colleagues insist on the *instability* of oral transmission. The gist of the original saying, its essential message - and especially its punch-line - might be remembered fairly accurately at first, but it is unlikely to have remained frozen in form and content for twenty years. Additions, interpretive changes and amendments made to fit theological convictions would subtly shift the content so that what came to be written down after a long gap might differ significantly from the gist of what Jesus had actually said. For Funk, then, the essence of the scholars' task is to examine each saying, one by one, subjecting it to a series of analytical techniques in an attempt to separate out the original and authentic from the embellished and corrupted. This can only be done by addressing the orally transmitted sayings in their *written* versions, for *that is all we have to work on*. Unless and until anthropologists discover in a hitherto unexplored corner of the Sinai desert a group of illiterate Christians who have never seen a written text and have memorized sayings, parables and miracle stories by telling them to each other over and over again around the camp fire, we cannot avoid recourse to the literary paradigm.

For Dunn, on the other hand, oral transmission is remarkably *stable*. He proposes that in Jesus' own lifetime, or immediately after his death, the disciples collected the sayings and stories and wove them into spoken litanies, repeated or recited at what would evolve into local church gatherings. The very action of *repetition* and *performance* guaranteed stability. Therefore, when the litanies came to be written down and circulated in scrolls or codices, they may be assumed to have reliably and accurately reflected the core of what Jesus had said. Where for Funk the object is *Jesus reconstructed*, for Dunn it is *Jesus remembered* - hence the title of his book.

Seminar scholars would no doubt see Dunn's view as the product of faith (Father Cantalamessa's "dynamic of spiritual or supernatural phenomena") rather than of critical historical enquiry divorced from church dogmas and pre-scientific supernaturalism. It rescues Jesus from the darkness of the Enlightenment and hands him back, intact, to the church. Dunn replies that faith is not an alternative to history. "If we are to 'get back to Jesus of Nazareth' in any confident degree, we have no choice other than to use *well-informed historical imagination* to attempt to enter into what was happening to the Jesus tradition during that initial stage"[22] (my emphasis). The stakes are high, and the debate is likely to intensify.

Thomas Altizer: No Christ, no passion

The Jesus Seminar has been no less vigorously attacked from the opposite end of the theological spectrum. Thomas Altizer, professor of religious studies at the State University of New York, Stony Brook, was an early proponent of "death of God" theology in the 1960s, when his "Gospel of Christian Atheism" scandalized the faithful. As a disciple of William Blake and admirer of Friedrich Nietzsche (whose *The Antichrist* he describes intriguingly as "perhaps the most original and certainly the most radical unveiling of the historical Jesus"), Altizer's approach is romantic and mystical rather than a product of Enlightenment rationalism. He sees Jesus as "the first purely apocalyptic prophet", whose death and "resurrection" [his quotation marks] were understood by Blake as an apocalyptic "self annihilation of God", where "the death of God [is] the final advent of apocalypse itself"[22].

From this perspective, the Jesus Seminar is mocked as a "scholarly magisterium" which "has given us a graded gospel" with its guts surgically cut away. Its fileted Jesus is "removed from any possible historical ground, as the Jewish world of Jesus of Nazareth now becomes virtually invisible and unheard, except insofar as it is a world under assault". The Seminar's conviction that an early stratum of Q and Thomas bring us closer to the real Jesus than the narrative gospels "means that only wisdom parables and sayings are acceptable, despite the fact that this reduces them to a very prosaic level of meaning indeed". In comparison, "the Cynics were far more radical, to say nothing of the prophets".

Despite Funk's warning against finding a congenial Jesus, says Altizer, "it would appear that the Jesus discovered in the Jesus Seminar is wholly congenial to the Fellows of that seminar, or at least to the majority of those Fellows", who appear to "have little awareness of any world outside their own, and certainly little theological awareness". And if the Seminar "is wholly indifferent to the question of the relation between Jesus and God, and proceeds as though the question of God is of no real significance at all in the language of Jesus, it is difficult to imagine how it would be possible to create a more nonhistorical Jesus". For Altizer, this represents a sad failure to fulfil the early promise of Crossan and Funk, who had produced "extraordinarily powerful studies of the parables, revolutionizing our understanding of the parables in the past generation, unveiling the parables as effecting profound reversals of every possible expectation or understanding". But the Jesus who is left after their Seminar has done him over is a Jesus in whom "the Christ of passion is wholly absent". Altizer the atheist, for whom God has been put to death for God's sake, prizes the Jesus story for its imaginative depth and epic significance to the human condition, and it is (as he sees it) the absence of these cosmic qualities in the Seminar's Jesus that leads him to dismiss them in terms reminiscent of Blake's passionate contempt for the dispassionate Newton.[23]

Liberal apostasy or group experiment?

But let us end this chapter with a more positive assessment of the Jesus Seminar, again from Mark Allan Powell, himself an authority on narrative criticism. He sums up its achievements as follows:

"The Jesus Seminar needs to be evaluated for what it is. It is not a collection of liberal apostates conspiring to undermine the Christian faith, nor is it a think tank of objective historians dispassionately following the strictures of academic research to see what they will reveal. It is a group of like-minded scholars testing a set of hypotheses regarding Jesus as a figure in history. The fact that they begin with hypotheses rather than with a blank slate does not invalidate their work. All serious historians do so... What marks the Jesus Seminar as unique - probably the *only* thing that marks them as unique - is that they are a group. Though other scholars may confer with colleagues, only the Jesus Seminar has invested the time, money, and energy to meet so regularly and under such circumstances that their publications can truly be termed the work of the whole group. This is not an inconsiderable accomplishment, and this fact alone earns them the attention they have received... Although the group seems early on to have established parameters that limited consideration to hypotheses that fit within a particular interpretative scheme, its research was genuine in terms of fine-tuning and revising those hypotheses in the crucible of critical debate. Thus, the group may represent only one of several available positions on the historical Jesus, but it represents that position well, having presented it with intense attention to detail."[24]

Within that "one position", however, are a variety of emphases. As noted earlier, when the Seminar started its work it was agreed that while the authentification of historical data was the task for the group working together as a collective, "the *interpretation* of the data was to be excluded from the agenda of the Seminar and left to individual scholars working from their own perspectives". It is to the perspectives of individual scholars within the Seminar that we turn next, before we move on to look at the interpretations of major players outside it whose conclusions are often very different.

Notes to Chapter 7

1 *The Fourth R* was adopted as the title of Westar's bi-monthly magazine.

2 Funk, *5 Gospels* 34

3 Funk, *Honest* 6

4 Funk, *5 Gospels* 34-5

5 John Lown taught at Nazarene College, San Diego. When he joined the Seminar his college demanded that he choose between his job and the Seminar. He chose the Seminar.

6 Funk, *Acts* xviii

7 Funk, *5 Gospels* 35

8 as above, 37

9 Crossan, *Historical J* 425, citing Aland, K, et al, *The Greek New Testament*, 3rd ed. pp xii-xiii, New York, United Bible Society pp xii-xiii

10 Funk, 5 *Gospels* 16-33

11 *Forum* 6 No 1, 1990. *Forum* is the bi-annual journal of the Westar Institute.

12 Powell, *Debate* 80. Powell's "200 historians" includes all Westar Fellows. In fact, those who participated regularly in the Jesus Seminar numbered just over 70.

13 Funk, *Acts* 4

14 as above, 6

15 Miller, *Apocalyptic* 1

16 as above, 2

17 Funk, *5 Gospels* 113

18 as above, 365

19 The transcript of Cantalamessa's sermon as published at *http://www.zenit.org/english/visualizza.phtml?sid=100024*

20 as above. Although Cantalamessa gives references for most of his quotations, "that mistake called Christianity" is unsourced.

21 Dunn, *New Perspective* 52

22 as above, 53

23 Altizer, *Contemporary J* 17 and 19-32

24 Powell, *Debate* 91

8

DIVERSITY IN UNITY: A RANGE OF JESUS SEMINAR PORTRAITS

Where Robert Funk has frequently likened the investigative work of the Jesus Seminar to that of the detective or sleuth, Roy W Hoover, co-editor with Funk of *The Five Gospels*, has characterized it as analogous to an archaeological dig. "We, along with other scholars," Hoover wrote after publication of *The Five Gospels* and *The Acts of Jesus*, "had recognized that several levels of tradition are present in the gospel texts (corresponding metaphorically to the levels of occupation that become exposed in the course of excavating the site of an ancient city) and we had made it our particular aim to distinguish 'the Jesus level' of the evidence from the later compositional levels that were the creations of the gospel authors and of their written sources. In finding 'the Jesus level' of these sources we were able to retrieve a number of 'artifacts' embedded in them that are very probably, in some cases almost certainly, traceable to the Jesus of history: sayings, stories, activities typical of him, and certain events of his life"[1].

The question that arises once the excavation has been concluded is whether any meaningful portrait of Jesus can be constructed on the basis of the recovered 'artifacts'. "Is it possible", Hoover asks, "to find in the authentic 'Jesus level' materials, together with other information about first-century Palestine and the wider Roman world, evidence sufficient to enable one to sketch a profile that would credibly resemble the Jesus of history?"

The Seminar had produced broad agreement among its Fellows on a number of fundamental propositions: that Jesus did not refer to himself as the Messiah, did not claim to be a divine being who descended to earth from heaven to die as a sacrifice for the sins of the world, did not teach that God was about to make an apocalyptic intervention in history by replacing the rule of men with direct rule from heaven. Rather, "at the heart of Jesus' teaching and actions was a vision of life under the reign of God... in which God's generosity and goodness is regarded as the measure and model of human life... a vision of what life in this world could be, not a vision of life in a future world"[2].

But beyond this broad level of agreement there were significantly different emphases and nuances. Funk had made it clear from the start of the enterprise that once "the Jesus layer" had been identified and its "artifacts" unearthed, individual Fellows would be free to develop and publish their own interpretations of what they had collectively discovered. Nevertheless, when Roy Hoover proposed a follow-up volume of individual Jesus profiles, there were misgivings. As Funk's co-chair John Dominic Crossan put it baldly: "There could be hopeless disagreement. Bob Funk's Jesus is quite different from mine". But Hoover's project was endorsed by Fellows who were perhaps glad to take a break from the constraints of collegiality, and fourteen, including Crossan, contributed to *Profiles of Jesus*, a mosaic of Jesus portraits offering a fascinating variety of emphases and viewpoints derived from study of the same data but with different interpretive strategies[3].

These different strategies, Hoover recognized, could be reduced to two distinct categories. The first was a methodology in which the profile was based primarily or entirely on "the authentic words of Jesus" as agreed (in red or pink) by the Seminar. What Jesus had *said* was who and what he *was*, or at least what we can recover of who and what he was. Profiles by Funk, Hoover, James Robinson, Brandon Scott, Charles Hedrick and Mahlon Smith fell into this category.

The second approach placed less emphasis on the supposed authentic words of Jesus and more on the social world Jesus inhabited. This involved reliance not only on texts but also on sociological and anthropo-logical models, and on studies of comparative religion, to give Jesus a context in time, place and culture. As Hoover put it, "The implicit or explicit claim of this approach is that the meaning of Jesus' words can be discerned only through the lens of his social location and intention. It follows that the social meaning of Jesus' teaching emerges as of first importance, or as what stands out, accompanied as it is by religious affirmations and legitimations"[4]. The profiles by Crossan, Marcus Borg, Stephen Patterson and Hal Taussig are in this category.

The distinction is significant, but, says Hoover, it is not hard-edged or absolute. "All of the contributors who have based their work primarily on Jesus' words would agree that discerning the relation between Jesus' teaching and the social world in which it took place is an important part of the task of reconstructing his profile; and the contributors who use that social world as their principal focus also make considerable use of Jesus' words". The difference is one of emphasis. "Ultimately one is [either] persuaded to see Jesus as first of all a religious visionary or as first of all a social reformer, however earnestly one tries to find a balance between his religious message and its social implications, or between his social reform and its religious legitimations and meaning"[5].

How, then, do the Fellows of the Jesus Seminar answer the question, Who on Earth was Jesus? We shall look in turn at some of the profiles they have produced, always bearing in mind that what I present here are only summaries of brief distillations of what is often a life-time of intensive study and scholarly investigation. The reader whose appetite is stimulated is referred to the scholars' books as listed in the bibliography at the end of Part III.

1. Robert W Funk's Jesus as stand-up comic

Funk not only founded the Westar Institute and its Jesus Seminar, he also largely funded it and was its prime mover and shaker until his death in 2005. Not surprisingly, then, his Jesus "emanates from a compendium of parables, aphorisms, and dialogues the Jesus Seminar has isolated from the mass of tradition that accrued to his name"[6]. The Seminar's work may be a collective enterprise but it is also Funk's own personal legacy. Nevertheless, when he feels free to write entirely on his own behalf, rather than as the official voice of the Seminar or its parent Westar Institute, his Jesus is fresh, distinctive, witty and wise, wholly human, not in the least supernatural. Funk's book *Honest to Jesus* gives the most fully nuanced version of the Jesus he has discovered in a long career of dedicated and intricately detailed scholarship, but his pithy four-and-a-half page contribution to *Profiles* is a masterpiece of compression, presenting as it does a human Jesus of genius who challenges today's world as he did the world of his own time and place.

This Jesus is a wandering teacher of wisdom expressed in striking, colorful, poetic but everyday language. He is a "a master of the short, pithy witticism known as an aphorism", and of the "fantasy about God's domain" expressed in the form of a parable. An aphorism, says Funk, is different from a proverb. Proverbs express conventional wisdom: what everyone already knows. An aphorism subverts or contradicts conventional wisdom. As examples of modern aphorisms Funk cites Oscar Wilde: "We wouldn't be so concerned about what people thought of us if we realized how seldom they do"; and Flannery O'Connor, who, when asked if she thought the universities stifle writers, replied "Perhaps, but they don't stifle enough of them".

The parable, on the other hand, is a "fantasy" in the sense that it is about "an order of reality that lies beyond, but just barely beyond, the everyday, the humdrum, the habituated". This "barely beyond" reality is not a mere fairy-tale, an unrealizable and unachievable fiction. Nor is it a future mode of being in an apocalyptic kingdom-come or a heavenly realm entered after death. "The parable is... an invitation to cross over, to leave the old behind and embrace the new", and to do so now, in this world, this life, this time. Funk adds that "the ability to cross over will depend, of course, on both the tenacity with which one holds to the inherited scheme of things, and on one's willingness to cut the ties to comfortable tradition. The parable is pitted against the power of the proven. Making the transition under such circumstances does not come easily".

Funk's Jesus challenges his audience by offering them options that consistently run counter to their normal way of looking at life. "Both his parables and aphorisms regularly frustrate the expectations of his hearers. Jesus develops a consistently rhetorical strategy that matches the content of his message. First, he depicts and then distorts the everyday world he and his Galilean neighbors inherit and inhabit - the received world. Second, his parables and witticisms transform and transcend that world. He adopts and then distorts the received world in order to hint at a new horizon. The result is a fleeting glimpse of what lies beyond the boundaries of the everyday; his language and deeds constitute a knot-hole in the cosmic fence". Jesus' language is always concrete and specific, never abstract. He describes the kingdom of God in mundane terms: "dinner parties, travelers being mugged, truant sons, the hungry and tearful, toll collectors and prostitutes, a cache of coins". This Jesus does not make theological statements. "He would not have said, 'All human beings have sinned and fallen short of the glory of God'. He would not have confessed, 'I believe in God the Father Almighty'... He would not have said 'God is the ground of being'... He does not make philosophical generalizations. He would not have said, 'I think, therefore I am', or 'Homo sapiens is the only animal that has language'". This Jesus "did not have a doctrine of God; he had only experience of God".

He is no literalist. Jesus' language is "highly figurative or metaphorical". His listeners know the parable of the leaven is not about breaking bread, and stories of mustard seeds and sowers are not advice for gardening enthusiasts and cereal farmers. Jesus' audiences know he has some other, much more significant subject in mind. "They know this... because his exaggerations, his caricatures, resist literal interpretation... A slave has a debt of ten million dollars cancelled, but he is unable to forgive a debt of ten dollars. The contrast is ludicrous" - and precisely because it is ludicrous it is memorable.

Jesus often makes his point by countermanding usual expectations. It is the poor and hungry rather than movers and shakers who are to be blessed, or congratulated, the prodigal truant rather than the thrifty and loyal son who is welcomed home like royalty. And Jesus makes free use of parody and humor. Have you heard the one about the woman who loses a coin, spends ages searching for it, then when she eventually finds it goes and loses it again by spending it on a celebration? "Jesus may be described as a comic savant. He was perhaps the first stand-up Jewish comic. A comic savant is a sage who embeds wisdom in humor, a humorist who shuns practical advice. 'If someone sues you for your coat, give him the shirt off your back to go with it.' That is not practical advice: to follow it is to go naked. Comic wisdom refuses to be explicit."

Comic wisdom is also a quality recommended to Funk's fellow scholars. Of his seven "ground rules for the quest", the sixth insists that "Our investigations, our quest for truth, should be sprinkled with humor. We must not take ourselves too seriously. As serious as this business of the Bible and Jesus and religion really is, we should remember that we are all buffoons of one sort or another, clowns strutting about on life's stage or waiting in the wings, as Paul suggests in his second letter to the Corinthians". And the fallibility and inconclusivity of scholarship is underlined in his rule seven: "No matter how many illusions we dispel, no matter how firm the conclusions we reach this time around, we will turn out to be wrong in some way, perhaps in many ways, down the road. Someone, somewhere, sometime will have to come along and correct our mistakes while adding their own... Human knowledge is finite"[7].

Funk summarizes his profile this way: Jesus as sage "constructs a new fiction that becomes the basis for... action... He was undermining the immense solidity of the received world with a vision of an alternative reality... In his parables and aphorisms is embedded a world coming into being". But Funk sounds a warning that has not gone down well with the churches. Not only is this Jesus not God (whatever that might mean), but even as a peasant-sage he is not unique. He is "one of the great sages of history, and his insights should be taken seriously but tested by reference to other seers, ancient and modern, who have had glimpses of the eternal, and by reference to everything we can learn from the sciences, the poets, and the artists. Real knowledge, divine knowledge, is indiscriminate in the vessels it elects to fill"[8]. And although this very human Jesus is "a Jesus for a New Age", this doesn't mean "Jesus for crystals and channeling, for auras and chakras, meditation and yoga, astrology and harmonic convergences, or even holistic medecine". Funk's "new age" is "the end of the Christianized era" in the sense that "the Christianized, industrialized West can no longer pretend to sponsor the only game on planet earth"[9].

Funk probably failed his own test (printed in red in the color-coded *Five Gospels*), "Beware of finding a Jesus entirely congenial to you"! But he cannot be accused of falling into another elephant trap, that of supposing he has got Jesus neatly boxed and labeled, fully explained, comprehensively interpreted and finally understood. He acknowledges that, in the parables, aphorisms, dialogues and correlative acts discerned as authentic in his and the Seminar's sifting of ancient fragments, he has caught and we can hope to catch no more than a mere glimpse of Jesus' vision.

"Visions come in bits and pieces, in random stunning insights, never in continuous, articulated wholes. Yet from these fragments of insight we can begin to piece together some sense of the whole. Together those fragments provide us with glimpses of the historical figure. Since his vision was neither more nor less than a glimpse, the best we can hope for is a glimpse of his glimpse".

2. Bernard Brandon Scott's Jesus as visionary poet

Where Funk derives his profile of Jesus from the full range of Jesus' sayings (as authenticated by the Seminar), Brandon Scott, Darbeth Distinguished Professor of New Testament at the Phillips Theological Seminary, University of Tulsa, Oklahoma, derives his primarily from the

> ## Cameo: Funk on "Demoting Jesus"
>
> *"Give Jesus a demotion... He asked for it, he deserves it, we owe him no less. As divine son of God, coeternal with the Father, pending cosmic judge seated at God's right hand, he is insulated and isolated from his persona as the humble Galilean sage. In the former there is not much left of the man who loved to laugh and talk at table,... who never seemed to maintain a trace of social distance in the conversation. A demoted Jesus then becomes available as the real founder of the Christian movement. With his new status he will no longer be merely its mythical icon, embedded in the myth of the descending/ascending, dying/rising lord of the pagan mystery cults, but of one substance with us all. We might begin by turning the icon back into an iconoclast" - **Honest to Jesus, p 306**.*

parables. Scott was a pioneer of parable studies before the Jesus Seminar was formed, influenced by two early monographs by Funk, *Language, Hermeneutic, and the Word of God* (1966) and *Jesus as Precursor* (1975). As noted earlier, Funk had formed a Parables Seminar in the 1970s and a parable studies journal, *Semeia*, in 1974. Scott's own major contributions at this stage were *Jesus, Symbol Maker for the Kingdom* (1981) and *Hear Then the Parables* (1989).

To Scott, Jesus is a revolutionary of a special kind. "He revolts in parable." There is no evidence that he was leading a political revolution or had any social program in mind. He was neither a social worker nor an activist. "Jesus the oral storyteller seems to me closer to a poet"[10]. His parables are his poems.

Scott not only sees the parable as a distinctive literary form but insists that Jesus' own parables are themselves distinctive *within* the form. "Despite various assertions to the contrary, there is no evidence of parable tellers contemporary with Jesus. The rabbinic parable develops after the destruction of the temple in 70 CE and follows a very different stereo-typed use"[11].

But Scott's poetic Jesus is not a "tweedy poetaster" weeping over fading daffodils or waxing lyrical over lilies of the field. He is (it seems to me, though Scott himself does not say so) closer to Shelley's view of poets as "the unacknowledged legislators of the world". Strikingly, Scott cites a modern poet, Seamus Heaney, to exemplify the role of poetry in offering visionary gleams or glimpses of an "alternative reality":

"...In the activity of poetry... there is a tendency to place a counter-reality in the scales - a reality which may be only imagined but which nevertheless has weight because it is imagined within the gravitational pull of the actual and can therefore hold its own and balance out against the historical situation. This redressing effect of poetry comes from its being a glimpsed alternative, a revelation of potential that is denied or constantly threatened by circumstances. And sometimes, of course, it happens that such a revelation, once enshrined in the poem, remains as a standard for the poet, so that he or she must then submit to the strain of bearing witness in his or her own life to the place of consciousness estab-lished in the poem"[12].

Scott applies this striking insight to Jesus' parables about the kingdom, or realm, of God. "Jesus's vision is not an alternative to the default world in the sense that it is a replacement. It is a counterweight, a counter-reality in Heaney's terms. Thus, it is always dialogically related to that default world. The default world will almost always win in the long run, because it *is* the default. That is why Jesus' own language betrayed him in the end. Jesus's parables are 'a glimpsed alternative, a revelation of potential that is denied or constantly threatened by circumstance', or in my terms, constantly threatened by the default world. A glimpsed alternative is not a worked out program. It is always temporary, glimpsed. It is a possibility, not a reality... The redress of the parable is hope and hope has power - not because it is a concrete program, a worked out plan or blueprint, but because it creates the counter-reality to the default moral world. It says things do not have to be this way." Heaney's insight illuminates Jesus' deeds as well as his oral poetry. The poet, says Heaney, "must then submit to the strain of bearing witness in his or her own life to the place of consciousness established in the poem". Scott comments that "In Jesus' parables his consciousness is established and his life bears witness to that consciousness. Thus the parables provide the coordinates for understanding Jesus' deeds".

Scott recognizes and answers two criticisms of his view of Jesus. One is that a poet-Jesus offering glimpses of an alternative way of living, much as any visionary poet might do, hardly measures up to a unique master-teacher whose appearance in history gives birth to a new religion. "Such a view of Jesus appears too ephemeral for what came afterwards: Christianity and the church triumphant". But, says Scott, Jesus wasn't responsible for what came afterwards. He had no plan for a new religion or a new church. "With my view, Jesus remains firmly attached to Judaism and is engaged in an argument within Judaism. He is part of a continuing debate. To put it too boldly, he is against the Deuteronomist and sides with Job and Qohelet". That is to say, he is against religious rules and regulations, codified into "thou shalts" and "thou shalt nots", and stands in the poetic wisdom tradition of the writers of Job and Ecclesiastes (also called Qohelet).

The second criticism Scott acknowledges and answers is that of E P Sanders, who commented that it is hard to see why anyone should be put to death merely for spouting poetry, a view expressed even more trenchantly by John P Meier, who made the "tweedy poetaster" jibe I borrowed earlier. "A tweedy poetaster who spent his time spinning out parables and Japanese koans, a literary aesthete who toyed with first century deconstructionism, or a bland Jesus who simply told people to look at the lilies of the field - such a Jesus would threaten no-one, just as the university professors who create him threaten no-one"[13]. Ouch!

Scott responds that language is more dangerous than Sanders and Meier imagine. "Socrates... died because of his provocative language; and the fate of Salman Rushdie in our own day demonstrates the power of words in a traditional society. Poets still have power." (This explains Scott's earlier statement: "The default world will always win in the long run, because it is the default. That is why Jesus' own language betrayed him in the end"). But "the redress of the parable is hope", and Scott invokes Vaclav Havel, who was imprisoned for his poems and plays - forms of words which inspired the "velvet revolution" against Communist dictatorship - and became president of post-Communist Czechoslovakia, later the Czech Republic. Hope, wrote Havel, is "a state of mind, not a state of the world... and it's not essentially dependent on some particular observation of the world or estimate of the situation... it transcends the world that is immediately experienced, and is anchored somewhere beyond its horizons... It is not the conviction that something will turn out well, but the certainty that something makes sense, regardless of how it turns out"[14]. Scott summarizes his profile like this: "Jesus revolts in parable and the parables create a counter-world, a hoped for world that redresses the world as it is and surely makes sense, regardless of how it turns out, even if it turns out to be his crucifixion".

Funk's and Scott's views of Jesus are similar. Both derive from what they consider are most likely to be the historically authentic sayings of Jesus, as distinct from the sayings put in Jesus' mouth by his later followers as they pursued their own christocentric agendas. Both speak of "glimpses" and "alternative realities". Funk's concentration on the aphorisms evokes a peasant sage always ready with a cracking one-liner. Scott's emphasis on the parables produces a poet with a vision of the kingdom of God, understood not as apocalypse soon but as a glimpsed alternative or counterweight to our default reality. So similar, so different.

3. John Dominic Crossan's Jesus as social revolutionary

If Funk and Scott each produced a Jesus congenial to them (and perhaps to Democrat-voting west coast liberals), John Dominic Crossan discovered a decidedly unsettling Jesus he confessed himself unable to follow. In *Jesus: a Revolutionary Biography*, he imagines meeting up with the object of his studies, who tells him: "I've read your book, Dominic, and it's quite good. So, now you're ready to live by my vision and join me in my program?". Crossan answers, "I don't think I have the courage, Jesus, but I did describe it quite well, didn't I, and the method was especially good, wasn't it?" "Thank you, Dominic", says Jesus, "for not falsifying the message to suit your own incapacity. That at least is something". "Is it enough, Jesus?" asks Crossan. "No, Dominic", says Jesus, "it is not"[15].

An ordained Roman Catholic who left the priesthood in order to marry, Crossan is probably the most widely-read of all historical-Jesus scholars, with more than twenty books to his name, both specialist and popular, some of them long-standing best-sellers. A former chair of the Historical Jesus Section of the Society of Biblical Literature, he was also co-chair of the Jesus Seminar in the 1990s. Despite his close association with these collegiate bodies, however, he has always maintained his own distinctive methodology, resulting in a highly personal perspective on Jesus which has occasionally resulted in friction between him and fellow scholars, including some in the Jesus Seminar enterprise.

While collaborating with his Seminar colleagues - and, indeed, co-leading them with Funk and Hoover - in the attempt to isolate the probably-authentic sayings, Crossan always insisted that a credible Jesus could never be reconstructed from his words alone. In this, his emphasis was different from that of Funk (which no doubt explains his warning quoted above: "Bob Funk's Jesus is quite different from mine"). Crossan's Jesus is more than a peasant sage or a visionary poet offering glimpses of an inspirational but unattainable alternative world. He was more than a wise man gifted with a wonderful way with words. "I emphasize as strongly as possible," Crossan writes, "that Jesus was not just a teacher or a preacher in purely intellectual terms, not just part of the history of ideas. He not only discussed the Kingdom of God: he enacted it, and said others could do so as well. If all he had done was talk about the Kingdom, Lower Galilee would probably have greeted him with a great big peasant yawn. But you cannot ignore the healings and the exorcisms, especially in their socially subversive function. You cannot ignore the pointedly political overtones of the very term *Kingdom of God* itself"[16].

And in what looks like a pointed criticism of some Seminar colleagues he adds: "It is, unfortunately, one of the abiding temptations of pastors and scholars to reduce Jesus to words alone, to replace a lived life with a preached sermon or an interesting idea. To remove, however, that which is radically subversive, socially revolutionary, and politically dangerous from Jesus' *actions* is to leave his life meaningless and his death inexplicable". In his earlier and more comprehensive book *The Historical Jesus* he makes the point twice, in identical language, within the space of a short introduction or "Overture". Jesus' sayings, he insists, "are not a list to be read. They are not even a sermon to be preached. They are a score to be played and a program to be enacted"[17].

Crossan played a key part in the decision-making that produced the Seminar's color-coded *Five Gospels*, but even before that enterprise was completed he had offered his own "reconstructed inventory" of the words which, in his personal judgment, "actually go back to the historical Jesus". It includes 106 sayings from Mark, Q in Matthew/Luke, and Thomas, in his own translation. The metaphor of *reconstruction* is important here. Crossan deliberately avoids the words *quest* and *search*: "Those terms seem to indicate a positivistic process in which we are going to attain an answer once and for all forever." Reconstruction, on the other hand, "is something that must be done over and over again in different times and different places, by different groups and different communities, and by every generation again and again and again. In order to emphasize that viewpoint, I talk hereafter only of reconstructing the historical Jesus as best one can at any given place and time"[18]. This does not mean "*mere* reconstruction, as if reconstruction invalidated somehow the entire project". It means "there is *only* reconstruction"[19].

In line with this rejection of a modernist "positivism" and in tune with a 1990s postmodernist sensibility, Crossan has insisted that he does not claim for his methodology "a spurious objectivity, because almost every step demands a scholarly judgment and an informed decision. I am concerned, not with an unattainable objectivity, but with an attainable honesty"[20]. Denial of the possibility of objectivity, however, never leads with Crossan to an undervaluation of rigorous critical methodology. His profile of Jesus is thoroughly grounded in critical assessment of the evidence contained in or deduced from the available data, but he himself gives it a more provisional status than the corporate profile produced by the Seminar and other self-described questers. Not so much Behold the man we have sought and *discovered* in the texts, more Behold the man as we have so far been able to *reconstruct* him from all the available data.

So where most textual scholars (precisely because they *are* textual scholars) begin with surviving documents, Crossan chooses to begin *The Historical Jesus* with what he can discover about the entire culture - geography, politics, economy, power relations, religion, class structure, purity codes, sexual mores, magic and mystery systems, health and healing structures - of early first-century Lower Galilee. He acknowledges the daunting problems of such an undertaking, not least the fact that the period is obscured from contemporary view by what he calls "three giant filters". First, "the past is recorded almost exclusively in the voices of elites and males, in the viewpoints of the wealthy and the powerful, in the visions of the literate and the educated". Second, even this elite-focused record is known to us only in bits and pieces that have survived largely through "the vagaries of chance and luck, fate and accident". We have only a few odd pieces of the giant jigsaw from which to construct our picture. Third, this already doubly-filtered past is further filtered through the limitations imposed by where we stand as observers in our own particular present - "let us say in individualistic, democratic, urban, middle-class America, often with ethnocentric presumptions it is not even aware of projecting".

So how is it possible to imagine the face of a Mediterranean Jewish peasant with such incomplete data and across two millennia? Crossan cites three major sets of sources he has drawn on to counter the obscuring effects of the filters. "First, on the macrocosmic level, there are anthropological or sociological studies and models, especially those using trans-temporal and cross-cultural disciplines. Next, on the mesocosmic and more local level, there are archaeological digs and discoveries. Finally, on the microcosmic level, there are papyrus documents and archives, documentary texts predominantly from Egypt in which ordinary peasants have preserved an individual voice and a personal presence normally denied them by their illiteracy and their poverty"[21]. Crossan plunges with gusto into all these scholarly disciplines to build his reconstructed historical Jesus.

From his "macrocosmic" or large-scale level - the anthropological, sociological and cross-cultural disciplines - he begins to reconstruct a Jesus who is clearly a child of his own time and place. The place is a peasant community in the Lower Galilee area of the eastern Mediterrannean, a community with the essential characteristics of all Mediterranean peasant communities two thousand years ago. Thus Crossan emphasizes the similarity of such communities rather than the distinctiveness of Judaism. Ninety percent of the population lived in villages or isolated settlements and ten in the few towns and cities. Of this ten, fewer than two percent belonged to the elite class. Death was a daily fact of life. Probably a third of the live births died before they reached the age of six, nearly two thirds before 16, three-quarters before 26, nine out of ten before 46. Fewer than one in 30 reached the age of 60. (If Jesus lived for about 33 years he was already a senior citizen, well into the oldest quarter of the population, at the time of his ministry and execution).

The other inescapable fact of life was taxes. The 98 percent of

Mediterranean peasantry and urban artisans paid with their labor and its produce to support the lavish life-styles of the two percent who made up the Greco-Roman elite. "In general, resources extracted from the tax base were mostly redistributed to the men of the apparatus - who mostly invested their official gains in large estates. Taxation was generally regressive... [The elite] took a larger share...than did the elites in more primitive societies before them, or in industrial societies after them." Such gross inequality and impoverishment of the masses made for deep resentment, and resentment made for revolt.[22]

Revolt came in many forms. Violent resistance was one, but it was only sporadically successful, and was always followed by terrible retribution. Another strategy was that of the Cynics. Not to be confused with the negative way we use the words *cynic* and *cynicism* today, the Cynics of the Hellenized Mediterranean revolted in wit and wisdom, satire and mockery, aphorisms and clever one-liners. But Cynicism "involved practice and not just theory, life-style and not just mind-set in opposition to the cultural heart of Mediterranean civilization, a way of looking and dressing, of eating, living, and relating that announced its contempt for honor and shame, for patronage and clientage. They were hippies in a world of Augustan yuppies"[23]. Jesus, says Crossan, fits that tradition - but only up to a point. Greco-Roman Cynics were educated towns-people, centered on the marketplace rather than the farm. Like twentieth-century hippies, they showed little sense of collective discipline and no interest in developing a program or strategy for social change. They were content to mock.

Jesus, on the other hand, was good on mockery but he also had a program. This is apparent, says Crossan, in the stories of his deeds as well as those of his sayings as collected in Thomas, Q and Mark. His program centered on "the reciprocity of open healing and open eating, shared miracle and shared table... Things are shared in common. The healers are not to receive alms or handouts, let alone payments or wages. They bring with them a free, open and shared healing. In return they are to receive a free, open, and shared eating... Sharing was... a strategy for building or rebuilding the peasant community on radically different principles from those undergirding an honor/shame society, a society based on patronage and clientage. Jesus' strategy was based on an egalitarian sharing of spiritual and material power at the most grassroots level... Here, I think, is the heart of the original Jesus movement, a shared egalitarianism of spiritual and material resources. I emphasize this as strongly as possible and I insist that its material and its spiritual aspects, the fact of it and its symbolic representation, cannot be separated"[24]. And on this egalitarian sharing-in-common was built a "kingdom-of-God movement as Jesus and his first companions lived in radical but nonviolent resistance to Herod Antipas's urban development and Rome's rural commercialism in Lower Galilee of the late 20s"[25].

Crossan's Jesus, then, is "a peasant Jewish Cynic" - with a social program. He did not see himself as "the new broker of a new God", for "he was neither broker nor mediator but, somewhat paradoxically, the announcer that neither should exist between humanity and divinity or between humanity and itself. Miracle and parable, healing and eating were calculated to force individuals into unmediated physical and spiritual contact with God and unmediated physical and spiritual contact with one another. He announced, in other words, the brokerless kingdom of God"[26].

In seeking to understand (or reconstruct) Jesus' "kingdom" teachings, Crossan reaches into his "mesocosmic" or archaeological and historical source material to remind us of another line of kings, saviors and sons of God. Rome had declared Julius Caesar divine after his assassination in 42 BCE. His adopted son, Octavius, thereby became a son of god. In 27 BCE this son of god was renamed Augustus, meaning reverenced or worshipped one - "not quite divine but close enough for now" writes Crossan - and within a month of his death in 14 CE he was formally declared "*divus* in his own right, son of a god and a god as well". Horace had already acclaimed Augustus as "descended, across more than a thousand years, from the Trojan Anchises and the goddess Aphrodite or Venus". Seutonius, in his *Lives of the Caesars*, written a century or so after Augustus's death, added a story of the future emperor-god's miraculous conception. His mother Atia had fallen asleep during a solemn service in the temple of Appollo, and a serpent had glided into her bed. "When she awoke," according to Seutonius, "she purified herself, as if after the embraces of her husband... In the tenth month after that Augustus was born and was therefore regarded as the son of Appollo". For good measure, Crossan cites an inscription on marble tablets in the temple of Augustus: "Providence... has... adorned our lives with the highest good, Augustus... and has in her beneficence granted us and those who will come after us [a Savior] who has made war to cease and who shall put everything [in peaceful] order... with the result that the birthday of our God signaled the beginning of Good News for the world..."[27]

Thus, argues Crossan, the Romanized world into which the historical Jesus was born was a world that already had a "king of kings" (emperor), proclaimed as a divine son of God, a Savior, a bringer of the Gospel ("Good News") and a prince of peace who had "made wars to cease". In preaching and practising an alternative kingdom, Jesus and the Jesus movement were challenging the state and its chosen god, daring to offer an alternative. The new kingdom of a new God, a kingdom which could be lived here and now, under the noses of the imperial apparatus, promised a very different Good News, not for the two percent elite but for the 98 percent oppressed. The means by which the Roman emperors had "made wars to cease", the so-called "Pax Romana", a peace enforced by bloody conquest and ruthless occupation, was to be banished in favor of a peace in which men, women and children, clean and unclean, Jew and God-fearing gentile, would eat at the same table and share and share alike. (We are reminded of the evangelist John's Jesus: "Peace I leave with you, my peace I give unto you. Not as the world giveth give I unto you..." - 14:27) This was not John the Baptist's future kingdom, to be inaugurated at any moment by a dramatic divine intervention which would topple the emperor and install God's chosen people on his throne. It was a kingdom already come, by which the kingdoms of this world would be subverted and sidestepped.

Finally, on the "microcosmic" level, there are the texts. For Crossan, as for other Jesus Seminar scholars, the earlier a particular saying or story can be dated and the more often it is "attested" in documents that appear to be independent of each other, the more reliably and historically "authentic" it would appear to be. Crossan divides the writings into different chronological strata, numbering them 1 to 4. Then he counts the number of times each saying of Jesus occurs throughout the strata, numbering them again, 1 for a single attestation, 2 for two, and so on. A saying in the earliest stratum but with four attestations is thus inventoried as 1/4, and a saying in the latest stratum with only one attestation is 4/1. So a 1/4 saying, very early and frequently attested, is deemed far more likely to be historically authentic than a 4/1, late and reported only once.

In the first stratum, anything before 60 CE, he places Paul's four undoubtedly authentic letters (1 Thessalonians, Galations, 1 Corinthians and Romans), Thomas, Q, a few fragments, and other materials which, like Q, he believes to be embedded in later works. The four Pauline letters he dates respectively to 50, 52-3, 53-4 and 55-6, broadly in line with most recent scholarship. For Thomas, he lines up with scholars who discern at least two layers, but he dates these earlier than most. The first, he suggests, was "composed by the fifties CE, possibly under the aegis of James's authority", and the second "possibly as early as the sixties or seventies" after the martyrdom of James in 62, when "the collection and maybe also its community migrated to Syrian Edessa". Q he also dates as "composed by the fifties, and possibly at Tiberias in Galilee". To these he adds the 87 lines of the so-called Egerton Gospel, two more tiny fragments (the "Fayum Fragment" and P. Oxy. 1224) and a Gospel of the Hebrews known only from quotations by third- and fourth-century writers, which he dates again to the 50s.

More important than these fragments, however, are the three collections Crossan controversially argues are embedded in later works. These are a "Miracles Collection" he believes was used by Mark and John, an "Apocalyptic Scenario" found both in the Didache and Matthew, and, most important (and most controversial), a "Cross Gospel" embedded in a later Gospel of Peter. Many scholars even within the Jesus Seminar, and probably most outside it, remain unconvinced by Crossan's contention that these are pre-60 writings embedded in the later documents. If he is right about the Cross Gospel in particular, the earliest narrative account of the crucifixion and events leading up to it is not that of Mark, post-70, but an independent account written up to twenty years earlier, known to and used by the four New Testament gospel writers. Alternatively, a single early crucifixion narrative was drawn on by Mark, John and the Gospel of Peter. Either way, if Crossan's proposed dating were to carry the academy, perhaps after another pot-luck excavation in the Egyptian sands, conventional understandings of the origins and historical authenticity of the passion narrative would be overturned.

In a second stratum, dated 60-80, Crossan places Mark (the end of the 70s); the second letter to the Colossians, "written most likely not by Paul himself but posthumously by one of his students and in his name"; a so-called "Signs Gospel" he finds embedded in John, a "Dialogue Collection" embedded in a later Dialogue of the Savior; and the "Secret Mark" unearthed by Morton Smith . The embedded materials have, again, failed to convince many scholars, and "Secret Mark", as we have seen, has been under heavy suspicion as a forgery since Bart Ehrman's account of its "discovery".

In his third stratum, 80-120 CE, Matthew is dated to around 90, Luke "possibly as early as the nineties", John to "very early in the second century", but with additions made between 120 and 150, and the Revelation/Apocalypse "towards the end of the first century". To this stratum Crossan also attributes the First Letter of (yet another) John, the First Letter written in the name of Peter around 112, and the letter in James's name, around 100. In the fourth stratum, 120-150, he controversially places the Acts of the Apostles (usually dated with Luke to the 80s or 90s), 1 and 2 Timothy, 2 Peter, and, among other writings that did not make it into the New Testament, the Gospel of Peter with its embedded Cross Gospel.

As indicated earlier, Crossan draws most of his "authentic" sayings of Jesus from the first stratum (Q in Matthew and Luke, and Thomas), and a little from Mark in the second. From these he constructs his profile of a Jesus who makes revolutionary demands for a revolutionary purpose. A key set of texts here is the story Jesus tells, in versions found in Thomas, Q-Matthew and Q-Luke (inventoried, therefore, as 1/2, since Q counts as a single source), of the man who sends servants out to invite guests to a feast. The servants report that each of the guests has an excuse for declining the invitation. One has a business meeting, one (in the Thomas version) has just bought a house (or, in Luke's version from Q, five yoke of oxen), another is busy arranging a wedding feast (for a friend in Thomas, for himself in Luke) and another will be out collecting his rents. Matthew's invitees actually seize, abuse and kill the servant. The minor differences are of little consequence: Crossan sees them as interesting but not crucial examples of how the same story can be retold or elaborated in different ways to underline the writer's own polemical purpose. What is critical, for Crossan, is the denouement. The would-be host, not to be done out of his dinner party, tells his servant: "Go out on the streets and bring whomever you find to have dinner" (Thomas and, virtually identically, Matthew), or more elaborately but with the same intention, "Go out quickly into the plazas and alleys of this city and bring the poor and maimed and blind and lame here... Go out onto the roads and hedges and compel them to enter, so that my house may be full" (Luke).

Crossan comments on this extraordinary punch-line: "For the servants to execute that order they would have to create an open and shared table, a meal in which poor and rich, female and male, single and married, slave and free, gentile and Jew, might all end up eating together. And that as anyone knows, in the first as in the twentieth century, is no way to have a meal, no way to give a dinner party... A person might give a feast for society's outcasts as a special event. That could easily be understood in the honor/shame ideology of Mediterranean society as the act of a benefactor... But if one gave such feasts persistently and exclusively, there would undoubtedly have been some very negative social repercussions... It is the indiscriminate character of that 'anyone' which negates the social function of the table, which is to establish a social ranking by what one eats, how one eats, and with whom one eats. It is the random selection of guests and the open table that is the most startling element of the meal depicted in the parable. At this feast, one could easily have classes, sexes, ranks, and grades all mixed up together. The social challenge of an egalitarian table is the radical threat posed by the parable and is the content of Jesus' ecstatic vision"[28].

Crossan's Jesus, then, is a Mediterranean Jewish peasant - and he gives equal emphasis to "Mediterranean" (meaning "under the Roman Empire"), "Jewish", and "peasant"[29]. The elite would have classed him among the despised and rejected, whose privations he knew and shared. He revolted, not in violence but in offering a vision of a different way of living, where there would be no elite and no underclass, no master and no servant, no conqueror and no conquered, no clean and no unclean: a way of living where all would be shared among equals. He drew on a tradition of prophetic language to call this new way of living the "kingdom of God" or "kingdom of heaven", a kingdom of peace which he boldly offered as an alternative to the empire of Rome and its peace by force. He not only preached and practised this way of life, he offered a social program for its realization. This was revolutionary, and revolution was treason. So he was executed. But you can nail a body to a wooden post: you cannot so easily extinguish an ecstatic vision and the program to which it gives concrete expression.

Cameo: Crossan on Jesus as "permanent performance"

"In the beginning was the performance; not the word alone, not the deed alone, but both, each indelibly marked with the other forever. He comes as yet unknown into a hamlet of Lower Galilee. He is watched by the cold, hard eyes of peasants living long enough at subsistence level to know exactly where the line is drawn between poverty and destitution. He looks like a beggar, yet his eyes lack the proper cringe, his voice the proper whine, his walk the proper shuffle. He speaks about the rule of God, and they listen as much from curiosity as anything else. They know all about rule and power, about kingdom and empire, but they know it in terms of tax and debt, malnutrition and sickness, agrarian oppression and demonic possession. What, they really want to know, can this kingdom of God do for a lame child, a blind parent, a demented soul screaming its tortured isolation among the graves that mark the edges of the village? Jesus walks with them to the tombs, and, in the silence after the exorcism, the villagers listen once more, but now with curiosity giving way to cupidity, fear, and embarrassment. He is invited, as honor demands, to the home of the village leader. He goes, instead, to stay in the home of the dispossessed woman. Not quite proper, to be sure, but it would be unwise to censure an exorcist, to criticize a magician. The village could yet broker this power to its surroundings, could give this kingdom of God a localization, a place to which others would come for healing, a center with honor and patronage enough for all, even, maybe, for that dispossessed woman herself. But the next day he leaves them, and now they wonder aloud about a divine kingdom with no respect for proper protocols, a kingdom, as he had said, not just for the poor, like themselves, but

for the destitute...

"Even Jesus himself had not always seen things that way. Earlier he had received John's baptism and accepted the message of God as the imminent apocalyptic judge. But... Herod Antipas moved swiftly to execute John, there was no apocalyptic consummation, and Jesus, finding his own voice, began to speak of God not as imminent apocalypse but as present healing. To those first followers from the peasant villages of Lower Galilee who asked how to repay his exorcisms and cures, he gave a simple answer, simple, that is, to understand but hard as death itself to undertake. You are healed healers, he said, so take the Kingdom to others, for I am not its patron and you are not its brokers. It is, was, and always will be available to any who want it. Dress as I do, like a beggar, but do not beg. Bring a miracle and request a table. Those you heal must accept you into their homes.

"That ecstatic vision and social program sought to rebuild a society upward from its grass roots but on principles of religious and economic egalitarianism, with free healing brought directly to the peasant homes and free sharing of whatever they had in return. The deliberate conjunction of magic and meal, miracle and table, free compassion and open commensality, was a challenge launched not just at Judaism's strictest purity regulations, or even at the Mediterranean's patriarchal combination of honor and shame, patronage and clientage, but at civilization's eternal inclination to draw lines, invoke boundaries, establish hierarchies, and maintain discriminations. It did not invite a political revolution but envisaged a social one at the imagination's most dangerous depths. No importance was given to distinctions of Gentile and Jew, female and male, slave and free, poor and rich. These distinc-

tions were hardly even attacked in theory; they were simply ignored in practice.

"What would happen to Jesus was probably as predictable as what had happened already to John. Some form of religiopolitical execution could surely have been expected. What he was saying and doing was as unacceptable in the first as in the twentieth [or twentyfirst] century... And it is now impossible for us to imagine the offhand brutality, anonymity, and indifference with which a peasant nobody like Jesus would have been disposed of.

"What could not have been predicted and might not have been expected was that the end was not the end... Jesus' own followers, who had initially fled from the danger and horror of the crucifixion, talked eventually... of resurrection. They tried to express what they meant by telling, for example, about the journey to Emmaus undertaken by two Jesus followers, one named and clearly male, one unnamed and probably female. The couple were leaving Jerusalem in disappointed and dejected sorrow. Jesus joined them on the road... unknown and unrecognized... Later that evening they invited him to join them for their evening meal, and finally they recognized him when once again he served the meal to them as of old beside the lake. And then, only then, they started back to Jerusalem in high spirits. The symbolism is obvious, as is the metaphoric condensation of the first years of Christian thought and practice into one parabolic afternoon. Emmaus never happened. Emmaus always happens." - **John Dominic Crossan, "The Historical Jesus", pp xi-xiii**

4. Marcus Borg's Jesus as revolutionary mystic

Marcus Borg is Hundere Distinguished Professor of Religion and Culture at Oregon State University. A former chair of the Historical Jesus Section of the Society of Biblical Literature and president of the Anglican Association of Biblical Scholars, he has written a dozen books, of which *Meeting Jesus Again for the First Time* (1994) has remained for more than ten years a best-selling account of Borg's own relationship with a Jesus he sees in both historical terms ("the pre-Easter Jesus") and as a present reality ("the post-Easter Jesus"). Borg's commitment to historical and cultural scholarship is underpinned by a parallel commitment to a modern Christianity that is both rational and mystical, liberal and "ecstatic". His many followers have been mocked as "Borg-again believers" - and have appropriated the jibe as a badge of honor.

Borg's popularity owes much to his ability to build bridges between the densely detailed and jargon-ridden world of the academy and the wider world beyond the academy's walls, where the shape of the wood is perceived as more important than the micro-ecology of individual trees. In his published work he has laid more stress on his conclusions than on detailed explanations of the methodology by which those conclusions have been reached. Broadly, his methodology is that of the Jesus Seminar (particularly the group within the Seminar who emphasize the importance of social location and religious typology) but with some important varia-tions. With most of his Seminar colleagues, his primary sources for Jesus' sayings are the early layers of the synoptic gospels as preserved in Q, and what he takes to be the earliest redaction of Thomas; but in contrast to Funk and most Seminar Fellows he accepts Mark as a broadly reliable source for narrative material.

With Crossan, he constructs his profile of the "pre-Easter" Jesus not only from the texts but from anthropological, archaeological and cross-cultural studies - "everything we can know about the social world of Jewish Palestine in the first third of the first century"[30]; but he adds studies of "the phenomenology of religious experience and a typology of religious figures" which turn Funk's sage and Crossan's social revolutionary into a Jewish mystic with a mission, a visionary whose vision endures in the "post-Easter" Jesus, where Borg insists it is no less relevant today than it was two thousand years ago. This is not to say that Borg's Jesus is the heaven-sent Savior of conservative theology. "[First], in all likelihood, the pre-Easter Jesus did not think of himself as the Messiah or in any exalted terms in which he is spoken of. Second, we can say with almost complete certainty that he did not see his own mission or purpose as dying for the sins of the world." Nor was his message "about himself or the importance of believing in him"[31]. Jesus as God's blood sacrifice or as John's "Word made flesh" has no more credence with Borg than with his post-Christian colleagues in the Seminar.

In an important summary of his views written for Westar's *Fourth R* journal in May-June 1994 and included in Roy Hoover's *Profiles of Jesus* in 2002, Borg describes his picture as a "five-stroke sketch of Jesus". Each of the five "strokes" corresponds to "a type of religious figure known in many cultures: the ecstatic, the healer, the wisdom teacher, the social prophet, and the movement initiator". We shall look at each of these in turn, though not in Borg's order.

Borg's *wisdom teacher* is essentially the sage of the Seminar as a whole: an oral teacher who spoke in parables, aphorisms and "great one-liners". His sayings were "not only memorable, but invitational: they invite a new way of seeing very different from acculturated ways of seeing". The content of Jesus' wisdom "subverts conventional wisdom, and is an invitation to an alternative way or path, which may be spoken of as the eye of a needle, the narrow way, the road less traveled".

Borg is also one with his Seminar colleagues in insisting that Jesus' teaching on the kingdom of God or heaven was non-apolcalyptic. "Jesus did not expect an imminent divine intervention in which the objective state of affairs would change so dramatically that everybody would have to say, 'Yes, the Kingdom of God (or the Messianic Age) has arrived'."

The scholarly tradition of Jesus as prophet of God's day of judgment, running from Weiss and Schweitzer through Rudolf Bultmann and Gunther Bornkamm to E P Sanders today, is dead. "To think that [Jesus] could have held such a dogmatic and literalistic view of the future when he had such an enlightened view of the present is difficult for me to imagine. Perhaps I don't want to believe that Jesus was a proclaimer of 'The end is coming soon!'. But more than that, I find it hard to believe that such eschatological literalness could be part of the consciousness of an enlightened one." (However, in what was perhaps an unguarded moment, Borg confessed that it was the anti-apocalyptic viewpoint of the Jesus Seminar that attracted him to them in the first place. So he did not reach this position in the process of collaborative research. Rather, he was attracted to the collaborative research because it appeared to corroborate a viewpoint he already held.)

But Borg adds another color to the palate from which Funk's portrait of a sage is painted. "It seems likely that an enlightenment experience was the source of the transformed way of seeing things reflected in Jesus' alternative wisdom. An enlightenment experience is a particular kind of mystical or peak experience in which the cognitive aspect is especially strong. Combining such mundane factors as the personality type of the recipient with his or her natural intelligence and gifts and modes of expression, we get an enlightened teacher. Such was Jesus, and in this respect he was like Lao Tzu, the Buddha, and Socrates." Not just Funk's stand-up comic, then, nor even simply Brandon Scott's visionary poet, but a *mystical* master of comic wisdom, and a poet who has undergone a life-transforming experience of enlightenment which he offers to those with two good ears to hear.

The *healer* is another religious type common to a range of cultures. "We know of many such persons near the time of Jesus, both in the broader Mediterranean world and within Judaism", for example Rabbi Haninah ben Dosa who, according to the Talmud, expelled demons and healed sickness at a distance. Within this cross-cultural framework of "ecstatic healers" Borg is persuaded that "the gospel traditions about Jesus as healer and exorcist reflect historical happenings". He distinguishes between the so-called "nature miracles" - water into wine, walking on water - which he sees as myths, and the healings and exorcisms which, however they are interpreted today, appear to refer to historical events.

There is an important distinction, however, between Borg's view of Jesus' healings and exorcisms and Crossan's. As we have seen, Crossan draws on medical anthropology to make a sharp distinction between *healing illness* (the social meaning placed upon a physical condition) and *curing disease*, which is the organic condition itself. Crossan thinks Jesus did the former but not the latter, "healing" the leper by removing the taint of "uncleanness" in both the leper's own eyes and the eyes of his community, but not curing the physical lesions. This isn't good enough for Borg, who is "not inclined to engage in psychosomatic 'reductionism'... Whatever complexity of psychosomatic relationships might be involved, I think he did both. Not only does the gospel tradition indicate that, but it is difficult to imagine that simply healing illness (without organic, physical cure) could have made much of an impression within a peasant milieu." So Borg concludes that Jesus "effected healings that struck people as remarkable, and performed what both he and his contemporaries experienced as exorcisms. It seems likely to me that one reason he attracted attention and a following was his reputation as a healer".

When we come to the third and fourth "strokes" of Borg's sketch, Jesus as *social prophet* and as *movement initiator*, he appears at first to agree with Crossan's picture of Jesus as social revolutionary and initiator of a program of transformation. Certainly his view of the political context is similar to Crossan's in its emphasis on the vast inequalities of wealth and power. This type of society had lasted in ancient Israel since the tenth century BCE, the only changes being the substitution of foreign for native elites. "In the time of Jesus, the peasant society was structured as a purity system or a 'politics of purity', which was the ideology of the ruling elites; in that sense it was the 'dominant consciousness' of his social world. The society was manifestly oppressive. The governing class, the top one percent of the population, received about fifty percent of the wealth. The top ten percent (the governing class plus retainers and merchants) received about two-thirds. The remaining ninety percent (mostly peasants) produced most of the wealth, yet retained, due to taxation and land ownership by the elites, only about one-third of their production"[32].

But where Crossan's Jesus revolts against all this inequality and injustice as a peasant revolutionary who happens to be Jewish but has much in common with peasants everywhere in the Hellenized Mediterranean world, Borg's Jesus is a very Jewish revolutionary in the line of the Jewish prophets Elijah, Amos, Hosea, Micah, Isaiah of Jerusalem, and Jeremiah. "They were all ecstatics with a vivid experiential sense of the reality of God, and they all passionately criticized the urban ruling elites who exploited an oppressed peasantry and at the same time legitimated their place in society with religious ideology and ritual." Jesus championed the cause of the poor and heaped threats and "woes" on the urban ruling elite, directing his indictments against "wealth, religious ideology, the purity system, hierarchy and patriarchy, the temple and Jerusalem itself - not as the center of Judaism, but as the center of the urban ruling elites, who were also the temple and purity elites". It was Jesus the prophet and instigator of social revolution who was killed by those whose supremacy he challenged and threatened. "The most plausible understanding of Jesus' arrest and execution is that he was perceived as troublesome by the elites." Lest this be misunderstood as an echo of Christian antisemitism, Borg emphasizes that "it was not 'the Jews' or 'the Jewish people' who rejected Jesus; rather, it was some of the Jewish aristocratic elite, who are more accurately seen as oppressors, not representatives, of the Jewish people".

What distinguishes Jesus from many other social revolutionaries, Borg argues, is the ecstatic dimension. "There is a kind of ecstatic experience that radically minimizes cultural distinctions by disclosing their artificial character: the distinctions are a humanly created grid imposed on reality, and not an order built into reality itself (that is, not decreed by God). Yet, on another level, those distinctions do matter, for they are one of the central causes of human suffering throughout history. Because their artificial character is apparent, they are even more intolerable. Almost (but not quite) paradoxically, these distinctions are relativized even as they become the target of passionate indictment and compassionate creation of an alternative vision". The ecstatic dimension, that "separation from one's ordinary state of being", both shows up and dissolves class, caste and gender distinctions imposed by local cultures.

Again, where Crossan gives Jesus a program (which requires a movement to see it through) Borg sees Jesus as a *movement founder, initiator or catalyzer* (which implies a program to be followed). And where the program of Crossan's Jesus is overtly universal, that of Borg's Jesus is specifically Jewish. Borg does not mean that Jesus was "the founder of Christianity in the sense that he intended to generate a new religion", but rather the initiator of or catalyzer for "a Jewish movement whose purpose was a social and religious transformation within Judaism". Borg argues that the movement-within-Judaism which Jesus initiated is evidenced by his forming a group of twelve followers (Mark 3:14 and Q/Matthew 19:28 and Q/Luke 22:30), the number being a symbolic reconstitution of the twelve tribes of Israel. (The Essenes had done the same, with the same symbolic intent)[33]

In regarding the choosing of the twelve as "one of the most certain facts of Jesus' ministry", he breaks sharply with the consensus of Seminar scholars, who color all three references an unambiguous black[34]. "Fellows were divided on whether Jesus actively recruited disciples", according to the commentary in *The Acts of Jesus* (p 71). "But there was general agreement... that the number 'twelve' in connection with an inner circle of disciples is a fiction". The general agreement clearly did not include Borg, who sees the deliberate recruitment of a body of disciples as evidence that Jesus was not content with mere social criticism but was concerned to spread a vision of social action, particularly in relation to subverting and breaking the purity codes which made outcasts of many, and doing so by what Crossan calls "open commensality" and Borg calls "inclusive table fellowship".

At the heart of Jesus' program is "the centrality given to compassion as the core value of a life lived in faithfulness to God: 'Be compassionate as God is compassionate'". The Jesus movement, asserts Borg, was not started by those who came after him, followers of the post-Easter Jesus who created the Christian church. It began with Jesus himself, the pre-Easter historical Jesus, as the means by which his social program was intended to take effect. "By speaking of [Jesus] as a movement catalyzer, I am affirming that his social vision was not a discarnate ideal but was already, in embryo, incarnate in his following during his lifetime."

It is striking that Borg attaches words like "enlightened" and "ecstatic" to each of his four "strokes": his Jesus was an *enlightened* wisdom teacher, an *ecstatic* healer, an *ecstatic* prophet, and his social program was driven by his *ecstatic* experience. This is so important to Borg that he makes it into a fifth stroke in its own right - and the first of the five, as he lists them. He emphasizes that "the description of Jesus as ecstatic... is central to my construction of an historical image of Jesus; within the scholarly community it is the most distinctive element of my historical reconstruction. Though other scholars do not necessarily deny that Jesus was an ecstatic, few make it so centrally important."

The word ecstasy simply means separation from one's ordinary state of being. "A religious ecstatic or mystic is a person who frequently experiences non-ordinary states of consciousness which are felt to be disclosures of another, deeper, or 'more real' level of reality than that known in ordinary states of consciousness." Borg chooses his words carefully. The "non-ordinary states of consciousness" are *felt to be* disclosures of a deeper reality. Borg recognizes the subjective and interpretive nature of the experience. Just as he refuses to be drawn into "pychosomatic reductionism" when discussing Jesus' healings and exorcisms, so he avoids making judgments as to whether what is "felt" by the ecstatic or mystic has some independent, objective reality. The *experience* is what counts, however it is interpreted.

"Jesus seems to have been one of these ecstatics. He was a Jewish mystic. The conclusion seems inescapable when one realizes that there really are people who have experiences like these; that the Jewish tradition has many such figures at its center... [and] that so much in the gospels points to his being a Jewish ecstatic: the language of 'Spirit', the hours of prayer (best understood as meditation or contemplation), and his healings... Moreover, such experience seems the best explanation of what else we see in the traditions about Jesus: his subversive wisdom, the ground of his passion and courage as a social prophet, and the source of his radical social vision".

This emphasis on a mystical, almost magical Jesus, is more common in the churches than in the cool cloisters of academe. It seems to many to be out of step with the rational, scientific spirit of our times. But to Borg-again Christians and students who find that his portrait speaks to their condition more powerfully than most, it is Borg's strength that he positions an historical Jesus in his own historical period and social location, not ours. Moreover, Borg's mystic is no less the child of rigorous scholarship than Funk's sage and Crossan's holy subversive. Borg has trawled through scholarly studies of non-western religions, religious and humanist studies of the varieties of religious or mystical experience, religious psychology, and the sociology and typology of religion, drawing on each to illuminate the study of the texts he has worked over with his Jesus Seminar colleagues. In the liberal churches of North America it is Borg's wholly human but no less holy Jesus who is being "met again for the first time".

Cameo: Borg on "ecstatic religious experience"

"The range of ecstatic religious experience is broad. **Visions** *involve seeing into another level of reality, and* **shamanistic experiences** *add to this a sense of journeying into another level.* **Unitive or mystical experiences** *involve a strong sense of connectedness (union or communion) with 'what is'. They can be introverted experiences ('eyes closed') or extroverted ('eyes open', as in nature mysticism) and can occur in meditative solitude or in the midst of activity in the world.* **Encounter experiences** *include a vivid sense of the sacred becoming present (sometimes, but not always, in visionary form), and are marked not by connectedness as much as by confrontation with 'otherness', challenge, and sometimes commissioning.*

"The varieties and nuances of ecstatic religious experience (as well as the broad sense in which I define the notion) are suggested by the various phrases used to characterize them: Rudolf Otto's experience of the numinous which is also the **mysterium tremendum et fascinans***, Abraham Maslow's 'peak experiences', R M Bucke's 'cosmic consciousness', Abraham Heschel's 'radical amazement', and Martin Buber's 'I-Thou/I-You' moments which contrast sharply with the 'I-It' (subject/object) quality of our ordinary experience. These experiences also include such widely differing states as the 'shamanic state of consciousness' described by cultural anthropologists, and the 'enlightenment experience' of the Buddha. Jewish thought and history includes such phenomena as the 'throne mysticism' of a mystical tradition preceding the time of Jesus, the 'call visions' of the classical prophets, the 'other-worldly journey experiences' lying behind at least some of the apocalypses, a nature mysticism which seems to lie behind charac-terizations of the world as 'filled with the glory of God' (radiant*

presence), and the reported trance-like state of some Jewish healers of Jesus' time.

"All of these forms of ecstasy share an experienced sense of 'the sacred', of 'what is', of 'the ultimate', of 'the way things really are'. For ecstatics - those with intense or frequent episodes of this sense - 'the sacred' is not an article of belief, but an element of experience.

*"Such people know God. This statement, provocative and possibly problematic, leads to a final comment about ecstatic religious experience. Scholars studying the phenomenon report that persons having such experiences consistently describe them as a state of knowing, not just a state of feeling. William James spoke of such experiences having a **noetic** quality: not just feelings of joy and ecstasy, but a cognitive sense of **knowing** something one didn't know before. Abraham Maslow identified the same quality as 'B-cognition', a somewhat unhappy term, sounding like a class of cognition inferior to some 'A-class cognition'. Peak experiences, according to Maslow, are not only affective 'highs' but include a strong sense of knowing. What is known is Being-itself; 'B-cognition' thus means 'cognition of Being'. Whatever the terminology, the point is the same: for ecstatics, the experience of 'the sacred' carries with it a vivid sense of epiphany - a strong subjective sense that what one has experienced is indeed a disclosure of reality.*

"For ecstatics, religious conviction is not the result of strong belief in 'secondhand religion' (William James's term for religious beliefs one learns about from others). Cognition is the product of

*firsthand religious experience. Ecstatics are those who can say, as did Job at the climax of his divine epiphany, 'I had heard of thee by the hearing of the ear, **but now my eye beholds thee'** (Job 42:5). God becomes an experiential reality, and it is in this sense that an ecstatic knows God."* - **Borg's "Jesus: a Sketch"** *in* **Profiles of Jesus, *ed. Roy W Hoover, pp 130-132.***

5. A less congenial Jesus

Most Jesus Seminar Fellows present a Jesus who, despite Funk's warning, is likely to be congenial to themselves and their readers: a Jesus wise, enlightened, charismatic, visionary, radical, of his own time but timeless, of his own culture but relevant to every culture. Some Seminar scholars, however, have found their researches have brought them face to face with a Jesus less comfortable and congenial. We shall look briefly at two such dissenting profiles.

(i) Kathleen Corley's Jesus: "A foundation myth for Christian feminism"

The number of women Fellows of the Jesus Seminar during its work on the sayings and acts of Jesus was never more than half a dozen. They included Kathleen Corley, a theology professor at the University of Wisconsin-Oshkosh, whose major work is *Women and the Historical Jesus: Feminist Myths of Christian Origins*. More than a hundred pages of this 250-page study are given over to scholarly references. As the title indicates, Corley's focus is Jesus' attitude to women. Was he a proto-feminist? Did his radical egalitarianism extend to women? The sub-title indicates her answer: such an optimistic and fashionably liberated view amounts to a "feminist myth".

Like Crossan and Borg, Corley draws on cross-cultural studies of first-century Mediterranean and Jewish society, but with particular reference to the roles of women. She concludes that "Jewish women, both in the Diaspora and Palestine, lived in freer circumstances than has previously been supposed. Some Jewish women enjoyed certain legal freedoms, joined men for communal meals and became leaders and patronesses of their synagogues. Jewish women's lives thus probably differed little from those of their Hellenistic and Roman sisters living in similar economic and social circumstances during the Roman period. Thus, neither the presence of women among Jesus' disciples, nor the inclusion of women among his table companions necessarily differentiates Jesus from a Greco-Roman or Palestinian environment"[35].

If women were generally present and played a part in Jewish and Greco-Roman society, and if it was not particularly unusual for them to mix with men socially and at table, it is less likely that the presence of women among Jesus' associates reflects a determination to defy convention and insist on the equality of women as part of the proclamation of God's kingdom. Nor can what we would now call a feminist message be detected in or adduced from Jesus' sayings, writes Corley. "An analysis of Jesus' teachings commonly considered authentic makes this clear. The bulk of Jesus' teaching shows attention to other matters, particularly in its concern for the poor and the enslaved: the issue of gender can be seen as secondary to other interests: social and economic justice, the true Fatherhood of God and a reform of class and rank structures"[36].

Corley notes that when Jesus is attacked for associating with "tax-collectors", "sinners" and "whores", he does not respond by challenging this abusive and insulting language. Indeed, he adopts the language of his slanderers, telling them (in Q/Matthew 21:31) "Truly I say to you, the tax collectors and the harlots go into the kingdom of God before you". Corley comments that "To claim an insult robs it of its power", and suggests that Jesus accepted the label of the women around him as "whores" "possibly in bitter jest, even as the basis of a bitingly sarcastic riposte"[37]. The term "whore" or "prostitute" was commonly levelled at low-status women who were often assumed to be sexually promiscuous and "available", particularly if they hung out with predominantly male groups, and also at higher-class women suspected of being socially progressive or "liberated". A woman like Mary Magdalene may have been characterized as a whore simply because she was low-class (probably a fisherwoman), and the probably higher-class Joanna slandered as a prostitute because she was liberal and open in her choice of male and female companions.

But while "claiming the insult" to rob it of its power may point to a recognition by Jesus of an underlying tension aroused by the presence of women among his followers, and his use of a style of bitter humor may seek to "relieve the tension through laughter, while at the same time serving to incorporate women in a predominantly male group", Corley (with evident reluctance) finds it impossible to read into it a positive feminist message. Jesus does not use such opportunities to make a ringing declaration of the equality of women, or denounce their oppression. The poor and enslaved are specifically "blessed", and no doubt that included women; but Jesus did not single them out for liberation. Significantly, none of his women followers were appointed to "the twelve", or given leadership positions in the revolution to bring about the kingdom of heaven.

Corley argues that her Seminar colleagues Crossan and Borg, and the pioneering Christian feminist theologian Elizabeth Schussler Fiorenza (not in the Seminar), are all mistaken in interpreting the parable of the Feast (Matt. 22:2-13, Lk. 14:16-24, Thom. 64:1-12) as evidence of a feminist ethic. Their view is that by opening up the banquet of the kingdom to the unclean, Jesus overturned purity regulations by eating with women. But Corley disputes that the target of the parable is purity regulations. Jesus, she says, "may not have been overly concerned with purity outside of the Temple". Purity issues arose within rabbinic Judaism later and were not emphasized in Jesus' time. Moreover, even the purity-conscious sectarians of the Qumran community seem to have allowed women to join certain ritual meals. "Thus concern over Jesus' table practice is more likely to have been a matter of propriety than purity". If purity is not the issue, "the point of the parable of the Feast does not hinge on... gender, but on... class and rank. Any application of the parable to the situation of women would therefore have been strictly secondary. One could argue that women are invited as those among the poor, the sick, and the street people, but the point of the parable is not to invite *women* to the Feast, but the underclasses. Jesus here does not defend the right of women to join him at table"[38].

Again, Corley finds nothing radically "feminist" about the story of Jesus dining with Mary and Martha (Lk.10:38-42). While Martha busies herself in the kitchen, Mary sits at Jesus' feet, and is commended by him as having "chosen that good part". But the "good part" consists of receiving instruction in a posture reflecting "a more conservative, matronly role", and she remains silent throughout. "The more radical stance", writes Corley, "would have been to invite Mary to recline with him like an equal on a banquet couch, as Jesus does with Salome in the gospel of Thomas (61)". Of Luke's stories in general involving Jesus and women, "Jesus does not appear radical in his relationships with women; it is the women who are bold, not Jesus"[39].

Corley disputes the feminist construction put by some modern historian-theologians on other parables of Jesus. "Since the parables use images drawn from everyday Palestinian life, women and women's activities occasionally figure as the point of comparison to the Kingdom of God. This leads certain scholars to posit an anti-patriarchal or egalitarian ethic for Jesus' teaching overall. Upon closer analysis, however, the images and roles of women in Jesus' parable are unexceptional. Stories involving women simply reflect the presence of women in Jesus' social environment; they are told to make points about the Kingdom of God, not the status of women... The evidence of the parables reveals that Jesus was part of the patriarchal society in which he lived and that he evinced similar patriarchal biases". The 104 parables and sayings in Matthew include 85 characters: 73 are men and 12 women - of whom five are foolish maidens! The 94 parables and sayings in Luke have 108 characters: 99 are men and nine women. This alone suggests that "Jesus, like other speakers and writers of his day, was by nature predisposed to re-imagine in his narratives a world dominated by men and their concerns and shows little interest for women and women's concerns"[40].

Corley examines each of the five parables which specifically revolve around women's activities or utilize images of women: the Leaven, the Lost Coin, the Empty Jar, the Unjust Judge and the Prodigal Son. She concludes that "it is difficult to argue that the first three demonstrate any subversion of gender roles... Rather, [they] underscore common gendered roles from antiquity by creating images of women engaged in everyday activities... [The] images of women... are hardly complimentary. One loses a coin worth two days sustenance, another spills her grain without noticing it, another overproduces bread; the point of the parable is made at each woman's expense... Insofar as gender issues are concerned, the above parables do not substantiate modern feminist claims for Jesus. Rather, they suggest a male-centered outlook that tends to portray women characters in less than complimentary ways"[41]. Scholars have too easily assumed that the historical Jesus elevated the status of women, only to have the church put them back where the men thought they belonged. Corley's closely argued analysis "challenges this reconstruction of the purpose and message of Jesus and labels it a foundation myth for Christian feminism... Jesus' teaching contains a critique of class distinctions and slavery in his culture, [but] that critique is not extended to gender distinctions or sex discrimination". Corley acknowledges that this makes for a less congenial Jesus than many would like to find in the texts. "Some may be disappointed with the conclusions of this study. In the midst of a changing world, many women and men look to Jesus as a potential model for equality between the sexes." But if they cannot find such a Jesus they can at least build on the implications of his broader radical egalitarianism. "That women numbered among Jesus' disciples is still noteworthy, as not all religious, philosophical and social institutions in antiquity included them, although many did. That Jesus did challenge ancient assumptions about social rank is also still important, as few in his time made a similar critique of ancient culture." But in the end "the impulse towards equality stands on its own without needing to appeal to an ancient man, however influential he may still be"[42].

(ii) Gerd Lüdemann's "almost ridiculous" Jesus

Where Kathleen Corley found a Jesus who was rather too *male*-centered for modern liberal tastes, Gerd Lüdemann found a *self*-centered Jesus who "makes the mistake of so many religious people: he sees himself at the center of the world" - and thereby makes himself "almost ridiculous".

If Corley is in a tiny minority of Seminar Fellows as a woman, Lüdemann is in an even smaller one as a non-American. Lutheran professor, first of New Testament Studies, then of the History and Literature of Early Christianity, at Gottingen University, Germany, he is the author of an exhaustive study, *Jesus nach 2000 Jahren: Was er wirklich sagte und tat*, published by SCM Press, London, in an English translation by John Bowden as *Jesus after Two Thousand Years: What he Really Said and Did*. It concludes with a full inventory of Lüdemann's own version of "all the authentic sayings and actions of Jesus", with those that have "a very high degree of probability" italicised and those with "a relatively high degree of probability" in standard Roman. The inventory often parallels that of the Seminar's color-coded consensus, but conspicuously parts from it on some crucial issues.

Lüdemann takes pride in having held a chair with a long and illustrious record of radical scholarship in historical Jesus and New Testament studies. Gottingen University was founded in 1737 and came to play a central role in the development of historical biblical criticism. Former occupants of theology chairs include pioneers whose work remains important today: Johannes Weiss and William Wrede in the nineteenth century, Ernst Troeltsch, Walter Bauer and Ernst Käsemann in the twentieth. "Their uncompromising concern with early Christian texts in a strictly historical spirit, subject to no dogmatic compulsions, soon led to charges that they were radicals", described by one student as "a horde of iconoclasts who wanted to smash everything to pieces". Lüdemann disarmingly adds: "I see myself as being in the tradition of this school"[43].

Lüdemann was always going to be his own man, and it was soon clear that he wasn't able to accept the overwhelming consensus view of the Seminar that the warnings of an imminent apocalypse scattered through the gospels, from Q to John, expressed the beliefs of the early church and were no part of Jesus' message. Lüdemann not only included the apoca-lyptic sayings in his inventory of the authentic words of Jesus, but he interpreted them as Jesus' biggest mistake.

This dissenting view did not result in a break with the Seminar, which has always been relaxed about accommodating minority views provided they are not represented as the Seminar's collective position. In any case, an apocalyptic Jesus continues to have many advocates outside the Seminar, particularly among German scholars. But Lüdemann's views and his chosen way of expressing them cost him his New Testament chair at Gottingen. The immediate cause of this academic fracas was a "Letter to Jesus" he circulated in 1998 and subsequently published in his book *The Great Deception*[44]. Lüdemann did not contribute to Hoover's *Profiles*, but his "letter" gives us in summary his own "warts and all" profile of the Jesus he found he had uncovered after twentyfive years of research.

It begins "Dear Lord Jesus", with Lüdemann explaining that that is how he had been taught to address Jesus as a child, and how he found himself still addressing Jesus, "as a magical formula", although the recipient of his prayers and his letter had "become quite strange to me". He tells Jesus what conclusions he has come to in his research: "You didn't say or do most of the things which the Bible tells us that you said or did... you aren't at all the one depicted by the Bible and church tradition. You weren't without sin and you aren't God's Son. You didn't at all want to die for the sins of the world. And what was particularly painful for me, you didn't institute the eucharist which for years I celebrated every Sunday in memory of you."

Instead, "You drove out demons like a magician and saw in this the advent of the kingdom of God. You had intimate contact with the devil and finally saw him falling like lightning from heaven. You expected the collapse of the whole world in the near future... Despite profound experiences with your God, whom you called a father to be trusted and from whom you expected almost everything, your hopes for the future... died. They clashed with brutal reality. At the latest on the cross you had to learn what it means to become a godforsaken victim. And had not your followers... proclaimed belief in your resurrection, all your words and deeds would have blown away like leaves by the wind... [They] proclaimed your imminent return for judgment and eternal salvation... But you did not return, because your resurrection did not even take place, but was only a pious wish".

Jesus is told that he must take the blame for "all the crimes that have been committed in your name from your death to the present day... Don't say that it was all a mistake and a falsification of your message!" Jesus had inspired the church and had to be held accountable for its atrocities. "Therefore [in a side-swipe at his own scholarly profession] we really cannot get down to the business of the day and from now on proclaim your true message as though the last 2000 years had not happened." And, Lüdemann tells Jesus, he had trouble with Jesus' God. "The image of the creator God which you and your contemporaries had was shaped far too much from a human perspective, and that applies to a far greater degree to the servants of your church today... And since you will perhaps ask in alarm how I deal with the reality which you and your followers call God, I want to tell you a dream which freed me from this super-father, not to say superstition. I struggled with God. He was strong and wanted to drag me down into a chasm in which paralysis, guilt and anxiety were awaiting me... With the last of my strength I pushed God himself down into the mire and at last became free."

Clearly referring to his continuing scholarly work, Lüdemann tells Jesus that even after this dream "I made another attempt to separate the essence of your message from the time-conditioned features of your preaching. And I clung to your code of behaviour and the basis for it. I thought that elements of your preaching of non-violence, love of enemy and openness to the outcast remained valid. But these ethical maxims were also developed by others before you and are not unique. Moreover they presuppose the expectation of the imminent rule of your God, and that has proved an error."

So, Jesus is told, he no longer had authority, which made the quest for an authentic Jesus meaningless. "I doubt whether the investigation of history, including your preaching, leads to the formation of a moral code which can be binding in the present day. The historical method which I have practised hardly provides a universal ethical meaning or guidelines for action. My previous belief in that evidently rested on projections or on a presupposition behind which I could not investigate. I cannot go on believing in the normative power of history or of historical facts without presenting my own subjective notions in the guise of scholarship... So, Lord Jesus, an end to all that. I can no longer bear the totally confused situation of theology, the church and the Bible. Remain where you are, in the Galilee of the first century. Then you will again become far more credible as a charismatic exorcist and distinguished teacher, and we can again enter into a normal relationship with you, as we have done with other normative figures of antiquity, like Buddha, Confucius and Socrates. Your exaltation above all human possibilities was too much and derives from boundless fantasies of immortality and longings which must now be brought down to earth."

So the affair is over. "As far as religion is concerned, there must be a final end to things between us... [But] I shall continue to investigate your preaching and the Christian interpretations attached to it - with the aim of enlightening contemporaries... in understandable language about the real origin of our Western culture. For the Enlightenment, which is grounded in reason, with all its criticism of claims to revelation and privileged knowledge of every kind, remains a firm ingredient in the modern world". Enlightenment or reason, not Jesus and his God, "makes possible a constructive dialogue between the members of the different nationalities and cultures, and it alone would be in a position in the coming millennium to make peace between people of the most different ideologies and religions."

Lüdemann soon had a response - but not from Jesus[45]. The Confederation of Protestant Churches in Lower Saxony called for his immediate dismissal from his post at Gottingen. On April 22 1998 the university Dean convened an extraordinary session of the Collegium of Professors of the Theological Faculty at which Lüdemann was asked to explain his "renunciation of Christianity". Subsequently the Collegium unanimously concluded that "in making statements of this kind, Professor Lüdemann is in flagrant conflict with the character and tasks of the theological faculty", and he was invited to "reflect upon his membership" in the spirit of "the truthfulness that he always calls for". Lüdemann duly reflected, and decided not to resign. Consequently, the university resolved on November 18 that by fundamentally questioning the "intrinsic truth [the English translation in *The Great Deception* reads "intrinsic *right*", but the better reading is *truth*] of Protestant theology" he had terminated his membership in the theological faculty. Instead, it was recommended that a place be offered in another faculty where he was promised he could continue his scholarly work without responsibility for training future pastors and teachers of religion.

But this proposal fell foul of legal complications peculiar to Germany, where university theological faculties are governed by treaties between the churches and the state. With Catholic appointments the church has rights of veto, and it is not unusual for the church to black-ball scholars whose loyalty is suspect: the case of Hans Küng is the best known. The Protestant (Lutheran) church to which Lüdemann belongs has legal rights which fall short of the right of veto, but professors and lecturers seeking faculty appointments must take an oath which reads: "I commit myself to presenting the theological disciplines honestly, clearly and thoroughly in agreement with the principles of the Evangelical Lutheran church"[46]. Lüdemann argued, and has continued to argue, that "to tie theology to the church in this way goes against its claim to be a scientific discipline". The scholar's vocation is the search for truth as he or she sees it, not the confirmation of truth as the church decrees it.

Eventually a compromise was reached. Lüdemann was removed from his chair in New Testament studies, and thus from his responsibilities in training pastors, but retained in the theological faculty with a new chair, that of the History and Literature of Early Christianity, which has enabled him to continue his work as a professor of theology appointed by the state. His case has highlighted the inherent conflict between modern scientific historical scholarship and an ancient discipline - theology - built on assumptions of divine revelation, inspiration or guidance. Lüdemann quotes the sociologist Max Weber to the effect that theology as traditionally understood necessarily called for "a sacrifice of the intellect in favor of an unconditional religious surrender". Lüdemann refused to surrender, and paid a price for finding that a lifetime of historical enquiry led him to a Jesus very different from the exalted Lord of the churches, a man it was hard to distinguish from the many nameless hairy holy men who had wandered the wildernesses of Palestine uttering woes and blessings, commanding demons to go back where they belonged, and warning anyone who would listen to repent their sins or prepare to meet their doom: a most uncongenial Jesus.

6. Jesus and "The Powers that Be"

I selected the preceding six scholars for fuller treatment, but readers wishing to explore the full spectrum of the Jesus Seminar's unity in diversity will want to read more widely: for example, Robert T Fortna on John's gospel [47]; Lane C McGaughy, who argues that Jesus' sayings alone were subversive enough to threaten the authorities and have him put to death, since he "dwelt in a world in which language was potent, a world in which words could move the gods to change their plans [a world of prayers and curses] and word-pictures could enlighten and empower marginalized peasants"[48]; and Hal Taussig, who challenges both ecclesiastical and academic faith in a relevant Jesus, arguing that "The religious and intellectual significance of this historical Jesus [Jesus the sage] is consistently overstated. Even after demythologizing Jesus, it is important to stay grounded in the historically relative place he had in the development of Christianity and western consciousness. Neither his teachings, nor his prayers, nor his deeds can claim a central place in contemporary meaning schemes"[49]. But I'll draw this chapter to a close with brief notices of two more of the Seminar's most influential Jesus-questers.

(i) Roy W Hoover: Q's Jesus "as good as it gets"

Roy Hoover, whose work as an editor has been noticed earlier, summarizes his own view of "Jesus' ordering vision" as best attested in two blocks of sayings in the "sermon on the mount": the passage beginning "Don't react violently against the one who is evil... Love your enemies and pray for your persecutors" (Matt.5:39-42, 44-8, Scholars Version, with parallels in Luke 6:27-36 and Thomas 95:1-2); and "No one can serve two masters... You can't be enslaved to both God and your bank account!... Don't fret about your life... Notice how the wild lilies grow... If God dresses up the grass in the field, which is here today and tomorrow is thrown into an oven, won't God care for you even more?" (Matt.6:24-30, parallels Lk.12:22-31 and Thom. 36:1-2). These sayings above all, says Hoover, "convey to us... a sense of Jesus' ordering vision, that view of things that furnished his teaching with its coherence and guided his course of action". And because they originate in the Q layer apparently going right back to Galilee, they "may well be evidence about Jesus' teaching that comes as close to bridging the distance between the authentic Jesus tradition in the Gospels and the historical figure about whom they were written as we can ever hope to come. They are as early as any gospel tradition we know of, they are at the heart of the theology of the earliest layer of our earliest Gospel, Q, and they reflect a social setting like that of Capernaum and/or other similar nearby villages which was also the social location of Jesus' public activity. In other words, these passages probably take us as close as does anything preserved in our sources to 'hearing' the voice of the Jesus of history. To use the vernacular, this is as good as it gets"[50].

(ii) Walter Wink's non-violent Jesus

Walter Wink, Professor of Biblical Interpretation at Auburn Theological Seminary, New York, also finds the essence of Jesus' teaching in his revolutionary challenges to power and violence. Wink's thesis is developed in a trilogy of books, *Naming the Powers* (1984), *Unmasking the Powers* (1986), and *Engaging the Powers* (1992), and a shorter work abridging the trilogy, *The Powers That Be* (1998). Jesus exposed the power of "the Domination System" and challenged those who heard him to embrace the alternative power of his gospel. But the "Domination System" is still very much with us - and so too, says Wink, is Jesus' visionary alternative. Pursuing that alternative beyond the walls of the academy, Wink took a sabbatical in 1982, travelling to Chile to contact the resistance to General Augusto Pinochet's murderous dictatorship, then moving on through South and Central America, staying in *barrios* and *favelas*, talking with priests and nuns who were struggling for human rights and political freedom. What he saw and heard brought him close to physical and mental breakdown. But four years later he took another sabbatical year, this time in apartheid-ridden South Africa. Here he "discovered a remarkable variety of effective nonviolent actions... in perhaps the largest grass roots eruption of diverse nonviolent strategies in a single struggle in human history"[51].

Wink described his experiences in a book, *Violence and Nonviolence in South Africa* (1987), published in South Africa in innocuous brown covers under the deceptively bland title *Jesus' Third Way* and mailed individually to 3,200 South African clergy, black and white. No sooner had he completed his sabbatical year and returned to America when peace organisations invited him back to conduct a nationwide program of workshops on nonviolence. The South African powers that be refused him an entry visa, so he entered illegally, ran workshops in Lesotho, Johannesburg and Pretoria, and attended the historic Emergency Convocation of Churches before turning himself in to the authorities and being expelled from the country. The churches of the Emergency Convocation took a strong line in favor of nonviolent direct action, and one set of powers was confronted by the other. It was the powers that be that gave way, with "the release of Nelson Mandela from prison, power sharing, the election of a black president, and the drafting of a model constitution. Apparently the Powers can sometimes be transformed"[52]. Wink went on to become Peace Fellow at the US Institute of Peace, Washington DC, 1989-90.

Wink is a prime example of the activist-scholar, never content to excavate a dead Jesus but inspired to apply the authentic gospel to the real world and its problems. "Nonviolence", he insists, "is an aperture open to God. It is intercession in action. It appeals, as the Quakers say, to 'that of God' in the other. It invites a miracle"[53]. And "In a world sinking into ever-deeper injustice and violence, Jesus offers an alternative to the Domination System that just cries out to be tried"[54]. For Wink, the Jesus of history is alive and well, still calling disciples in a 21st century world ravaged by war and and abuse of power.

Too often overlooked by commentators, this variety of opinion within the Jesus Seminar reminds us that what binds them together is not a new party line on Jesus but a common commitment to critical scholarship with the aim of increasing religious literacy and challenging dumb fundamentalism. But they are not alone in such aims, and we turn next to scholars no less critical who have studied the same data, only to arrive at quite different conclusions.

Notes to Chapter 8

1 Hoover, *Profiles* 1

2 as above, 3-4

3 Most of the fourteen contributions had been previously published in *Forum*, *The Fourth R* and other collections and were revised for *Profiles*. Hoover gives details in his Preface, p vii.

4 Hoover, *Profiles* 5

5 as above, 5

6 All quotations in this section are from Funk's essay "Jesus: A Voice Print" in *Profiles* 9-13, unless otherwise noted.

7 Funk, *Honest* 26

8 as above, 302-3

9 as above, 297

10 All quotations in this section are from Brandon Scott's essay "The Reappearance of Parables" in *Profiles* 19-40, unless otherwise noted.

11 Among those who have made "assertions to the contrary" is Geza Vermes, who argues that some of the parables found in post-70 rabbinic literature may have originated much earlier, perhaps before the first century CE. Those who argue that rabbinic parables are not attested until the second century or later are open to the riposte that Jesus' parables also are known only from texts compiled after 70 CE .

12 Seamus Heaney, *The Redress of Poetry*, Faber, London, 1990

13 Meier, *Marginal Jew*, vol 1, 177. Sanders, *Jesus and Judaism*, 4: "It is difficult to make [Jesus'] teaching offensive enough to lead to execution".

14 Vaclav Havel, *Disturbing the Peace* 181, Faber, London, 1990

15 Crossan, *Revolutionary* xiv. Originally published in *Christian Century*, Christmas 1991.

16 as above, 93. With regard to the healings, Crossan accepts as authentic many of the stories of Jesus curing illness. He interprets these in the light of medical anthropology, where a distinction is made between disease and illness, disease being the physical condition and illness the social meaning attached to the condition. In this understanding Jesus dispelled illness but did not necessarily cure the disease: a leper was deemed clean and readmitted to society without necessarily losing his sores. On exorcisms, Crossan insists that while Jesus and his observers evidently believed that exorcists cast out real live spirits, we may interpret these events as psychosomatic healings.

17 Crossan, *Historical J* xiii and xxvi

18 Crossan, *Birth* 43-4

19 Crossan, *Historical J* 426

20 as above, xxxiv

21 as above, 3-4

22 as above, 3-4. Crossan cites Bruce J Malina, *The New Testament World: Insights from Cultural Anthropology*, Atlanta, John Knox Press, 1981, p 72, for town/country and class distribution; and Thomas F Carney, *The Shape of the Past: Models and Antiquity*, Lawrence KS, Coronado Press, p 88 for the death statistics and p 341 for the tax system.

23 as above, 421

24 Crossan, "Jesus as a Mediterranean Jewish Peasant", in *Profiles* 167-168

25 Crossan, *Birth* x

26 Crossan, *Historical J* 422

27 Crossan. For the inscription, *Historical J* 31. For the miraculous conception, *Birth* 28. For the progressive deification of Augustus, *Birth* 413-4

28 Crossan, *Profiles* 162-4

29 In correspondence with the author, Crossan writes: "It was a Jesus within homeland Judaism under the Roman Empire I was trying to reconstruct. To simply say that Jesus was Jewish is true but inadequate - like saying I am Irish! The statement of his Jewishness is insignificant *until* you specify where he is to be located within the spectrum of first-century homeland Judaism".

30 All quotations in this section are from Marcus Borg, "Jesus: a Sketch" in *Profiles* 129-36

31 Borg, "Portraits of Jesus" in Shanks (ed.),*The Search for Jesus* 87

32 Note that the relative percentages cited by Borg (without sources in his *Profiles* essay) are a little different from those cited and sourced by Crossan, but there is evident agreement on the oppressive nature of the society.

33 On "the twelve", Geza Vermes has pointed out that, before the Jesus movement, the Essenes looked forward to a time of renewal when "twelve chief priests shall minister at the daily sacrifice," and "below them... shall be the chiefs of the Levites to the number of twelve, one for each tribe" (*Complete Dead Sea Scrolls in English* p 26, citing the *War Scroll*). This would seem to support Borg's argument: if the number twelve was already a symbol of renewal based on a restoration of the twelve tribes of Israel, Jesus' use of it is more likely to be historical than fictional. On the other hand, Vermes criticizes Borg's understanding of Jesus as challenging or subverting the purity codes, which, he maintains, never created a caste system in Judaism as it has done in some cultures, such as Hinduism.

34 The Q text is the promise to the disciples that they would sit on twelve thrones and judge the twelve tribes of Israel. The Jesus Seminar concluded (*Acts of Jesus* p 71) that this did not belong to the earliest layer of Q. Thomas has no Twelve, Paul has a single reference (1 Cor.15:5). Much later, John has Jesus appoint "twelve" (Jn.6:70) but names only ten. The Seminar took the view that "The role of the 'twelve' is associated with the eschatological self-consciousness of the Christian community, which thought of itself as the new Israel living at the endtime, just before the final judgment". It therefore doubted that "such a notion originated with Jesus". Borg's dissent from this position indicates that he presumably voted red where the majority of his colleagues went black.

35 Corley, *Women* 141

36 as above, 142

37 Corley, "Gender and Class in the Teaching of Jesus" in *Profiles* 145. This is a chapter excerpted from *Women and the Historical Jesus*.

38 Corley, *Profiles* 142-3

39 as above, 143

40 as above,138-9. Corley cites Nicola Slee, "Parables and Women's Experience", *Modern Churchman* 26 (1984), pp 21-31, for the man/woman counts in the synoptic gospels.

41 Corley, *Profiles* 139-42

42 Corley, *Women* 141 and 146

43 Lüdemann, *Deception* ix-xi

44 as above, 1-9

45 I follow Lüdemann's own account in *Deception* xii-xx

46 The oath dates from 1848. It was suspended in the 1960s but reintroduced in 1995.

47 See for instance "The Gospel of John and the Historical Jesus" in *Profiles* 223-30. Fortna's most important books include *The Gospel of Signs*, 1970; *The Fourth Gospel and its Predecessors*, 1988; and *Jesus in Johannine Tradition*, 2001).

48 McGaughy, "The Search for the Historical Jesus: Why Start with the Sayings?" in *Profiles* 127

49 Taussig, "Jesus in the Company of Sages" in *Profiles* 193

50 Hoover, "The Jesus of History: A Vision of the Good Life" in *Profiles* 50-3

51 Wink, *Powers That Be* 8

52 as above, 10

53 as above, 122

54 as above, 11

9

JESUS AS PROPHET OF THE

APOCALYPSE

Virtually all the modern historians whose work we have so far been picking over (with the sole exception of Gerd Lüdemann) propose, discover or reconstruct a Jesus who preached a "kingdom of God" (Mark and Luke) or "kingdom of heaven" (Matthew) that exists, or *could* exist, in this world and this age, either as (i) a presently-available alternative way of living based on personal transformation, or (ii) a revolutionary social program that will transform the world itself; or perhaps both. But we have seen that this Jesus and this interpretation of his kingdom-teaching as non-apocalyptic directly challenged the view that had prevailed at least since publication in 1906 of Schweitzer's *Quest of the Historical Jesus*, which had presented Jesus as prophesying an imminent miraculous act of God by which the kingdoms of this world would be swept away and replaced by God's direct rule.

The two interpretations of the kingdom teachings, and therefore of the kingdom teacher himself, could hardly be more different. But although the kingdom-now emphasis of the Jesus Seminar scholars shook the older consensus it did not create a new one. Many scholars, including most in Europe and not a few in America, continued to read the kingdom sayings as prophesying an imminent apocalyptic event by which God himself would impose his own direct rule on earth, as it was in heaven. In this chapter we shall look at the work of some of the most influential historians who, although they differ among themselves on other points, are united in their view of Jesus as both eschatological (concerned with the end-time) *and* apocalyptic (the end-time or transformation understood as a miraculous act of God).

It may be asked how it can be that scholars can arrive at such startlingly different interpretations of the reported sayings, and thereby produce such very different profiles of Jesus himself. The fact is that kingdom sayings in the gospels are many, complex, and sometimes contradictory. Scholars are faced with several problems (which by now should be familiar to those who have read so far). Are all these kingdom sayings the authentic words of Jesus? If so, how do we reconcile the complexities and contradictions? If not, how do we decide which really are the teachings of the historical Jesus and which are the elaborations or misunderstandings of his later followers? Did Jesus preach kingdom-now, only to be misunderstood by some followers as preaching kingdom-come; or did he predict kingdom-come, only to have his followers re-write the script when the kingdom failed to come on cue?

The conflicting answers of different schools of scholarship arise from prior assumptions based on different methodologies. As we have seen, the Jesus Seminar dates Thomas, or at least an "early layer" of Thomas, as contemporary with, or even earlier than, Mark, Matthew and Luke. That makes available an additional documentary source, which, as it happens, often appears to go out of its way to contradict apocalypticism. The Seminar also isolates an early layer of Q, where apocalyptic sayings are thought to be absent (though they are to be found in what are held to be later layers, which prompts the skeptic to ask: are the apocalyptic references assigned to later layers because they inconveniently contradict the interpretation of Q as early and non-apocalyptic, or does the mixture of apocalyptic and non-apocalyptic sayings indicate that even this earliest collection of sayings includes conflicting interpretations of the originals?).

Another important Seminar criterion is that of "dissimilarity": if Jesus said something that stood out from the conventional wisdom of his time, this was likely to stick in the memory of his followers and find its way into the sayings collections when they came to be written down. These criteria, along with the others we have noted as important to the Seminar and its allies, make possible a process whereby every single saying and act of Jesus may be assessed, one by one, for likely authenticity. Out of this process emerged the consensus view of the Jesus Seminar scholars that the kingdom-now sayings seem more likely authentic than the kingdom-come ones (because they seem to be earlier and challenge conventional Jewish apocalypticism), and more in keeping with the wider picture that emerged within the Seminar of an enlightened, wisdom-teaching and social-reforming Jesus rather than a wandering god made flesh.

The scholars we are about to discuss, however, have worked with different assumptions. They are not persuaded that any part of Thomas is first-century and they therefore tend to rely primarily, if not exclusively, on the three synoptic gospels as their documentary sources. Even here, they tend to make less of the embedded Q materials and be skeptical of theories identifying earlier and later layers. Rather than assessing the authenticity of each saying and act of Jesus one by one, they are inclined to build their profiles from the broad sweep of the gospel narratives. This broad sweep, they conclude, contains too many unambiguously apocalyptic sayings for them to be easily dismissed as crude misunderstandings by Jesus' followers. Finally, the criterion of dissimilarity has little weight for them. Rather, they argue that the fact that the apocalyptic sayings appear to broadly accord with the end-time expectations of first-century Judaism actually makes their authenticity more rather than less likely. If, say these scholars, this produces a less modern, less Enlightenment-friendly, less socially radical Jesus than liberal sophisticates find congenial, a Jesus who really goofed and got it badly wrong, that's just too bad! It is the historian's task to tell it as it is according to the evidence, not to reconstruct a Jesus who slots neatly into the liberal, progressive agenda.

1. E P Sanders: Jesus and the end of history

E P Sanders came to the historical Jesus via a dazzling series of studies of first-century Judaism and the place of Paul within it[1]. No less dazzling was his academic record: a graduate in turn of Gottingen, Jerusalem, Oxford and New York, he went on to hold staff or visiting lectureships and professorships at Oxford, Cambridge, Ontario, North Carolina and Trinity College, Dublin. Add to these a doctorate from the University of Helsinki and membership of the British Academy and you can be in no doubt that Sanders is a specialist who has won the approbation of his peers. But if he has proved himself a brilliant scholar among scholars, he has shown himself equally capable of communicating with a wider lay readership in lucid, jargon-free language that has won him acclaim from critics as dissimilar in their views as the Roman Catholic journalist Paul Johnson and the Humanist Jesus-quester George Wells. His most widely read book, *The Historical Figure of Jesus* (1993), was a best-seller throughout the English-speaking world, praised for its honesty, lack of dogmatism, and disinclination to indulge in point-scoring contests with scholars with whom he disagreed.

Like Crossan and Borg, Sanders places great emphasis on the social and cultural context within which the man Jesus must be located. Indeed, Sanders goes further: this, rather than individual sayings or acts in the gospels, is his point of departure. But the world of early first-century Galilee that he uncovers is a world away from Crossan's and Borg's highly Hellenized Mediterranean. Sanders proposes that Jewish culture, Jewish religion, Jewish customs, Jewish local government and Jewish hopes were the overwhelmingly dominant factors governing the lives of the people who lived in Galilee's villages. Moreover, the Judaism within which they lived, moved and had their being was not at all the Judaism depicted in the New Testament by Christian writers, embittered as they had become towards the end of the first century by mainstream Judaism's growing hostility to the Jesus movement. Judaism as portrayed in the gospels is a corrupt religion dominated by puppet leaders, hypocritical Pharisees, luxury-loving Sadducees, money-grubbing "scribes" (or scholars) and self-serving priests. It is a religion obsessed by law, custom and the dead hand of tradition. Its people are oppressed by Roman occupation and taxation, but its religious and political leaders collaborate with their oppressors, demanding Roman justice for those who challenge their devolved authority. Above all, the Jews profess to expect deliverance by an anointed messenger of God, a messiah, but stubbornly refuse to recognise him when he shows up. Instead, to preserve their own petty powers and a comfortable status quo, their leaders bully a harrassed Roman prefect into having Jesus killed as a threat to the empire and to their privileged place within it, and as a blasphemer to boot.

Sanders finds this New Testament depiction of early first-century Judaism a caricature. First, he insists, there were important aspects in which Jews were little different from their gentile neighbors. Almost everyone in that world at that time believed in supernatural beings who were to be worshipped by the sacrifice of animals and various rites and purification ceremonies. There was common agreement on the big ethical issues: murder, theft and adultery were wrong, whether you were Jew or Greek. Jews, on the whole, were no more law-obsessed, no more given to "empty" ritual, and no more (or less) corrupt than the people around them.

In the northern province of Galilee in Jesus' life-time, the Jews were *not* "occupied" by the Romans: within the empire they actually had an unusual degree of self-government. In this they differed from Judea in the south, which the Romans ruled directly through a military governor. On the death of Herod the Great in 4 BCE, the emperor Augustus had divided the Jewish kingdom, appointing Herod's son Antipas "tetrarch" or client-king of Galilee, the small but fertile territory on the western shore of the lake. Antipas ruled throughout the life of Jesus (he died in 39 CE), under Roman protection but without any Roman troops stationed within the province - in sharp contrast to Roman-ruled Judea to the south which was well garrisoned with perhaps 3000 troops at the governor's disposal. Paradoxically, the Jewish sub-king Antipas had more freedom to rule Galilee as he wished, provided he maintained public order and paid tribute to the emperor, than the Roman governor on his southern border. He minted his own coins - "one of the principal signs of 'independence'" says Sanders, and "the institutions in the towns and villages in Galilee were thoroughly Jewish", with synagogues in every community. "Schools were Jewish, and Jewish magistrates governed according to Jewish law... Antipas was a good tetrarch... Consequently Rome did not have to interfere in Galilee... Josephus records no instance in which Antipas had to resort to force in order to suppress an uprising... Galileans in Jesus' lifetime did not feel that the things most dear to them were seriously threatened: their religion, their national traditions, their livelihoods"[2]. Even the one exception to the rule that Herod Antipas (confusingly referred to as "King Herod" by the author of Mark) was, in Sanders' view, a good Jewish king as Jewish kings went, actually emphasizes just how independent Galilee was. When John the Baptist denounced him (for abandoning his wife to pursue a liaison with his brother's wife Herodias, according to Mark 6: 17-29, or for inciting revolt, according to Josephus), Antipas had him executed. In Josephus's version, Antipas's rejected wife fled to her father, Aretas, an Arab king, who mounted a punitive raid on Galilee. When Antipas engaged him in battle it was with his own Jewish army: Roman troops were not involved[3]. Thus, even when Galilee's territorial integrity was violated, the Romans considered it Antipas's own business to defend his own semi-independent territory. If Sanders is right in suggesting that, "as far as we can tell, on the basis of the gospels, Jesus knew only one real city, Jerusalem"[4], it may well be that Jesus and his disciples scarcely ever set eyes on a Roman soldier until they crossed the border into occupied Judea and encountered a very different power-politics in the short and fateful entry into a Jerusalem which was virtually a foreign capital.

On Galilee's semi-independent status there is no substantial controversy among historians. Sanders simply emphasizes it more than most. But the picture he draws of economic and social life in the province is very different from those of Crossan and Borg, who emphasize the exploitation of the peasants and artisans who made up the majority of the population. Sanders points up the fertility of the soil, a climate ideal for agriculture, and, particularly on the Sea of Galilee itself, well-established trading networks for agricultural produce: walnuts, figs, olives, grapes - and, of course, fish. The small towns and villages - Capernaum, Magdala, Chorazin, Bethsaida and Nazareth - would have been overwhelmingly Jewish, with only a tiny gentile population, and such communities were evidently Jesus' prime targets. Antipas's capital before he built Tiberias in 25 CE was the old Greek city of Sepphoris, little more than an hour's walk from Nazareth, and its proximity has suggested to historians who favor a more Hellenized and less Jewish context for Jesus that he and others in the villages of the hinterland must have spent time there, where they could listen to Greek philosophers, attend the theatre and generally acquire cosmopolitan polish. "This is exceptionally improbable," says Sanders. "Village life was dominated by work. People worked six days a week, and on the sabbath travel was limited to 1000 yards or so". Even if some of them took their produce to the market, rising before dawn, grinding the grain, loading the donkey, leading it to the city market, trading all day, they would need to get home before dark. They did not earn enough to allow them to enjoy the theatre and stay overnight. In short, villagers then, like villagers ever since, at least until the age of fast and cheap travel, lived out the greater part of their lives in their village[5].

From correcting the picture of Jewish/Roman politics inferred from the New Testament (and popularized by *Monty Python's Life of Brian*), and questioning the assumption of some scholars of a cosmopolitan Galilee, more Greek than Jewish, Sanders turns to the gospel-writers' sour view of first-century Jewish religion, finding it equally wanting. In particular, their characterization of it as a web of restrictive laws and commandments, a religion of rigid observance rather than charity and neighborliness, is shown as somewhat less than objective. "Because modern New Testament scholars often attack - the word is not too strong - first-century Jews for observing some of these laws (especially the commandments governing sacrifice, food and purity), I wish to emphasize that these criticisms amount only to saying that ancient Jews were not modern Protestant Christians or secular humanists - a point that could be made with less animosity and self-righteousness than such scholars display when they discuss Judaism. Jews were not unique for having laws and customs, or for having laws and customs that covered these topics. More or less everyone did"[6].

What irritated their gentile neighbors was that they would not assimilate to the common culture - declining to pay even nominal respect to the gods of Greece and Rome, avoiding pork (the most popular food in Mediterranean countries), and refusing to work on the sabbath. This resistence to assimilation has an obvious explanation, says Sanders, and the explanation reveals the quality of Judaism that was most distinctive. "The Jewish 'customs' were commanded in the law that God gave to Moses on Mount Sinai. While everyone had conventional food laws, Jews had divine commandments governing food. *The most striking point about Jewish law is that it brings the entirety of life, including civil and domestic practices, under the authority of God...* 'Religion' in Judaism was not only festivals and sacrifices, as it was in most of the Graeco-Roman world, but rather encompassed all of life... *Judaism elevated all of life to the same level of worship of God...* It attributed to God the view that honesty and charity were as important as purification"[7] (Sanders'emphases).

Jews believed they had a special relationship with their god, the one God. They were a "chosen people" and God had given them the land of Israel. But, says Sanders, they did not claim to have *deserved* this special relationship: it was God's doing, and the covenant or agreement they had with him was a covenant of grace. He would look after them, and they would obey his commandments: that was the deal. Disobedience required repentence, marked by bringing a sacrifice, and reparations if their misdeeds harmed others. Failure to repent and make reparations merited God's punishment - perhaps sickness for the unrepentant individual, and a shared humiliation (such as the Babylonian captivity) for the backsliding nation. But there was faith that "God would always redeem his people, and, despite lapses, they would remain true to him"[8].

The religion of the Jews in Jesus' time, then, was more closely integrated with civil and domestic life than the religion of their gentile neighbors, no less and perhaps more charitable in practice than the secular moralities of the Greeks and Romans, and professedly more philanthropic. Sanders emphasizes this last point. "Today, most people who evaluate religions do so in terms of humanism: a good religion is one that inculcates human values." First-century Jewish thinkers were ready to defend their religion on humanistic grounds, claiming for themselves the widely-praised virtue of *philanthropia*, "love of all humanity". Their God-given law required them to love their neighbor, and Josephus pointed out that this necessarily extended to showing humane consideration to enemies even in war (though his own histories chronicle many a failure in this regard). Josephus, and before him Philo, even extended *philanthropia* to cover not only compassion towards fellow-humans but the welfare of animals, plants and the soil - a view Sanders summarizes thus: "The universe is God's garden; humans are not his only creatures"[9].

Although Sanders doesn't emphasize the point himself, this may help account for the fact that Jewish religion and ethics were widely admired in some sections of gentile society. It was by no means unknown for gentiles to wish to convert to Judaism, even though this entailed (for men) a painful and humiliating surgical operation. There were also sympathizers referred to by the Jews as "God-fearers": gentile men and women, usually well educated, who were attracted to Jewish monotheism, piety, and a religious sensibility that looked to them to be more rational than the cults of self-divinized emperors.

Sanders does not suggest that, even in semi-independent Galilee, all Jews were perfectly content to accept Roman suzerainty. Probably all but the few whose power was wholly dependent on Roman goodwill looked forward to a day of liberation when, with God's help, they would get the empire off their backs. But "the nature and scope of the longed-for change varied a good deal, as did views about how God would bring the change about. Relatively few people expected a Davidic Messiah who would liberate the Jews by defeating the Roman army. Some people expected a very grand sign that the time of liberation had arrived (such as the collapse of Jerusalem's walls), while others probably expected no more than that God would strengthen the hands of the righteous and strike terror into the hearts of Roman soldiers"[10]. How the day of liberation, the restoration of a Jewish kingdom and the idea of the "kingdom of God" fitted together was never settled but continuously debated among priests, Pharisees, Sadducees, Essenes and, not least, lay leaders, teachers and prophets who from time to time stood up and claimed to speak in God's name. "In general terms, this is where Jesus fits. He was an individual who was convinced that he knew the will of God"[11].

When it comes to working out more precisely who Jesus was within this context, Sanders adopts a very different approach from that of the Jesus Seminar. First, having established his own reconstruction of the local and contemporary context, he does not proceed to a text-by-text analysis of what Jesus is reported to have *said* but embarks on an overview of what Jesus is reported to have *done*. Second, he accords the three synoptic gospels a much higher degree of general reliability than do the Seminar scholars, privileging them as pretty well the only sources of any value. He does not consider Thomas an early work, and although he concedes that "some of [its] sayings are worth consideration" he actually gives it very little and lumps it in with later "apocryphal" gospels as "legendary and mythological"[12]; nor does he show anything more than an occasional passing interest in the Q hypothesis. This approach, which some scholars see as a throw-back to traditional methodologies, inevitably produces a Jesus according to Sanders with a strong family likeness to the Jesus according to Mark, Matthew and Luke.

This doesn't mean, however, that Sanders arrives at a wholly conventional Christian Jesus, nor should his evaluation of the gospels as the most reliable sources available to us be misunderstood as a naive and uncritical submission to traditional theological notions of some kind of divinely underpinned biblical authority. As we have seen, Sanders can be (quietly) scathing about the distorted view of first-century Judaism that he finds not only in much modern scholarship but deeply embedded within the gospels themselves, so any characterization of him as one who supposes that everything in the gospels must be gospel-truth would be wide of the mark. To Sanders no less than to Funk, Crossan and Burton Mack, the gospels are human records written many years after the events they describe, and edited with a polemical purpose. They have to be interrogated, investigated, critically analyzed. But for Sanders they are the best we have, the place we have to start when we ask who on Earth was Jesus. "We should trust this information", he writes, "unless we have good reason not to do so; that is, unless the stories in the gospels contain so many anachronisms and anomalies that we come to regard them as fraudulent. That is not the case"[13]. This is the opposite of the Jesus Seminar's declared practice of taking nothing for granted unless it is supported by positive evidence. Or, as Mark Allan Powell puts it, tending "to regard Gospel tradition as guilty of fabrication unless proven innocent"[14].

Soon after Jesus' death, Sanders suggests, the disciples came to believe that "in some sense" he had "risen" and would very soon return to inaugurate the kingdom. While awaiting this second coming they told stories of what he had said and done. The stories had a purpose: to convince others that Jesus was the messiah. "Thus, negatively, Jesus' words and deeds were pulled out of their original context (in his own career) and thrust into another context, the disciples' preaching and teaching". At first the self-contained stories, technically called *pericopes* (meaning cut-outs, or isolated units) were passed on orally, but at some point they began to be collected into larger groupings dealing with similar topics like healings, miracles or debates with opponents, and written down on sheets of papyrus, copied, and circulated among the growing number of communities of the Jesus movement. Sanders emphasizes that we do not *know* the chronology for sure, and what we think we know should be clearly distinguished from what we think we can *infer*. With this important caveat he suggests the following possible sequence of developments:

"Next, these groupings were put together to form what we now call proto-gospels - works that told a connected story, but not the whole story. A proto-gospel, for example, might consist of a series of pericopes dealing with conflict between Jesus and other Jews, and conclude with his arrest, trial and execution. Or a proto-gospel might be a large assemblage of sayings relevant to the ongoing life of Christian communities (ethics, questions of rank, sayings about missionary work and the like). Finally, the first gospel as we have it was written. Most scholars think that this was Mark. Subsequent authors used Mark and incorporated other materials, such as proto-gospels or topical collections that the author of Mark had not included."

We may recognize in these hypothesized "proto-gospels" the Q, M and L of the so-called "four source theory", and even such controversial proposals as Crossan's "Signs" gospel. Sanders does not commit himself that far, and is slightly more conservative than many scholars in dating the final versions of the biblical gospels to between 70 and 90 CE.

A critical factor in the making of these gospels, then, was the technique employed by each author or editor of taking pericopes from the tradition and placing them in whatever sequence best strengthened the author's argument. The gospel writers were not narrative historians. They took events and sayings out of their original context and gave them a new one that fitted their own polemical purpose some forty to seventy years later. But the gospel writers did more than move the pericopes around a bit. They also revised them. This, says Sanders, was inevitable, and should not be misinterpreted as corrupting some original core of pure wisdom and thereby rendering it inauthentic. "The alternative to introducing minor alterations to make a pericope relevant to a new audience and a new situation would be embalming it. The Christian material was kept alive and fresh, even though it was used over and over again, by being applied to living issues - not all of which were the issues of Galilee between 25 and 30 CE." I emphasize again that, in this view, alterations made by later generations to Jesus'original sayings are not *inauthentic* versions of an authentic original but *necessary revisions* to meet new situations. This distances Sanders from both the Jesus Seminar, which does tend to equate early with authentic Jesus and late with church corruption, and from James Dunn who argues that Jesus' sayings were indeed preserved - "embalmed" in Sanders' word - throughout the oral period.

Moreover, says Sanders, "the early Christians also created new material; they made things up". He insists this does not mean they cheated or acted dishonestly. Rather, they sometimes attributed to Jesus words they believed they had heard in prayer or by revelation. Modern Jesus detectives may want to distinguish the words of the living Jesus on Earth from those of the crucified Jesus in Heaven, but early Christians believed that the Jesus who had walked through Galilee and the Jesus who was waiting "above" to make a triumphant second descent was one and the same, so that the words they heard from heaven were no less "authentic" and authoritative to them than those remembered and retold as the words of Jesus in Galilee. Paul, more than twenty years after the crucifixion, quotes Jesus as telling him, "My grace is sufficient for you, for my power is made perfect in weakness" (II Cor.12:7-9). But Jesus the man is not recorded as using these words to anyone, let alone a Saul of Tarsus he never met. Paul is quoting Jesus the spirit, and for him the man and the spirit are one and the same. This is an example in the New Testament epistles of what Sanders refers to as "new" or "made up" material, but he does not think there is much of it in the gospels themselves, compared with the many alterations in context and "minor adjustments".

Like the great majority of modern scholars, Sanders largely excludes

John's gospel as an accurate source of the sayings and acts of Jesus. The long meditations on the person and work of Christ, presented in the first person as if Jesus had spoken them in discourses with his disciples or the crowd, were the literary creations of a very literary (and late) gospel writer. John presents Jesus as promising to send a "Spirit of truth" to guide his followers, and it is this spirit, speaking through John, who announces that he is the light of the world, the way, the truth, the life, the true vine, and so on. John "would not have agreed that historical accuracy and truth are synonymous, any more than he thought a true vine was a vegetable". John says plainly that he is giving his readers new teachings of a Jesus who has come to John after the crucifixion, resurrection and ascension. On John's own premise, then, the fourth gospel is not and was never meant to be a reliable *historical* source for the words and deeds of Jesus on Earth.

So, says Sanders, "the synoptic gospels are to be preferred as our basic source of information about Jesus". But this does not mean we can treat them as objective reports of "what actually happened". "Their authors too were theologians and were capable of creativity. Just as we cannot pose an absolute alternative between the legendary and mythological apocryphal gospels and the historical canonical ones (since there are legendary and mythological elements in the gospels of the New Testament), so also we cannot make a clean division between the theological Gospel of John and the historical synoptics, since the synoptics are also the work of theologians. *There are no sources that give us the 'unvarnished truth'; the varnish of faith in Jesus covers everything*"[15] (my emphasis).

We shall come shortly to what Sanders finally makes of Jesus, but there is one more preliminary point he emphasizes: none of the gospels are *biographies* as we understand biography. There is "no development, seldom a concrete setting (such as 'this was an important issue just then because...'), just short accounts stitched together with an introductory word or phrase". The gospels "lack most of the things that we now expect in the story of someone's life. Looks, personality, character - we know very little... Mary Magdalene has appealed enormously to people who have imagined all sorts of romantic things about her: she had been a prostitute, she was beautiful, she was in love with Jesus, she fled to France carrying his child. For all we know, on the basis of our sources, she was eighty-six, childless, and keen to mother unkempt young men." And if this is true of the supporting cast it is no less true of Jesus himself. "We have a general outline of his life, plus brief stories, sayings and parables, and from them we can learn quite a lot, but we cannot write 'the life of Jesus' in the modern sense."

So what *can* be done? Sanders answers:

"I am an academic, a professional scholar, and a historian by inclination and education. I shall do what I can to fill in the gaps and to make coherent sense of the bits and pieces that we have. This effort... is somewhat like reconstructive surgery: breaking comes before rebuilding. Unlike the surgeon, however, I do not start out with a picture of what our subject originally looked like. Nor do I have a fixed view of what he *should* look like when the operation is over. I start out with the results of plastic surgery that aimed at glorification and that often did not preserve the original place and significance of the individual bits. *I aim at recovering the historical Jesus. But the difficulties will always mean that results are partial at best. A true title of the project would be 'basic information about Jesus: important aspects of what he did, what he thought, and what others thought of him'"*[16] (my emphasis).

We may compare this with Robert Funk's "the best we can hope for is a glimpse of [Jesus'] glimpse".

In the first of his two major Jesus books, *Jesus and Judaism* (1985), Sanders anticipates the Jesus Seminar (which began its color-coding project the same year) in stratifying "what may be known about Jesus" into distinct categories: "virtually certain", "highly probable",

"probable", "possible", "conceivable" and "incredible". But where the Seminar first sought to evaluate the authenticity of Jesus' *sayings* in this way, Sanders is estimating the reliability of reported *facts*. He begins with a list of what he then regarded as "almost indisputable facts about Jesus":

- Jesus was baptized by John the Baptist.
- Jesus called disciples *and spoke of there being twelve.*
- Jesus *confined his activity to Israel.*
- Jesus was a Galilean *who preached and healed.*
- Jesus *engaged in a controversy about the temple.*
- Jesus was crucified *outside Jerusalem by the Roman authorities.*
- After his death Jesus' followers *continued as an identifiable community.*
- *At least some Jews persecuted at least parts of the new movement.*

But Sanders evidently came to view some of these "almost indisputable facts" as more disputable than they first appeared. In *The Historical Figure of Jesus*, written six years later, he makes a number of changes, altering or omitting some and adding others. In this first list, above, I have italicised each of the facts he subsequently changed. In his later list, below, I bold-italicise the new material he added or changed.

- ***Jesus was born c.4 BC, near the time of the death of Herod the Great.***
- ***He spent his childhood and early adult years in Nazareth, a Galilean village.***
- Jesus was baptized by John the Baptist.
- He called disciples *[omitting "and spoke of there being twelve"].*
- He ***taught in the towns, villages, and countryside of Galilee (apparently not in the cities).***
- He preached ***"the kingdom of God"*** *[but "healed" is omitted].*
- He ***created a disturbance in the temple area.***
- ***He had a final meal with his disciples.***

- *He was arrested and interrogated by Jewish authorities, specifically the high priest.*
- He was executed *on the orders of the Roman prefect, Pontius Pilate.*
- *His disciples at first fled.*
- *They saw him (in what sense is uncertain) after his death.*
- *As a consequence, they believed he would return to found the kingdom.*
- After his death, his followers *formed a community to await his return and sought to win others to faith in him as God's Messiah.*
- *[The statement that parts of the new movement were persecuted by at least some Jews is omitted].*

For Sanders, these facts - whether the shorter and earlier list or the longer, later and more nuanced one - can only be interpreted and understood by reference to what we can know *or infer* about the social and religious context of Jesus' preaching. That is why he has begun by studying and laying out the context as he sees it, one that is thoroughly Jewish, specific to first-century Galilee, and with an unremitting focus on "restoration eschatology": the conviction that God is about to intervene in human history by scattering Israel's enemies, ending the kingdoms of the world and replacing them with his own kingdom of heaven. A credible historical Jesus is, for Sanders, one who "fits into the general framework of Jewish restoration theology... [as] the founder of a group that adhered to the expectations of that theology"[17].

Of all the "almost indisputable facts" in Sanders' two lists, those that most closely fit the "restoration eschatology" framework are (i) Jesus' connection with and baptism by John, whose message was a call to repentance in preparation for the coming kingdom; (ii) the calling of disciples referred to as "the twelve"; (iii) his preaching "the kingdom of God"; (iv) his engagement in controversy, or creating a disturbance, in the temple area; and (v) the disciples' evident belief that he would return to found the kingdom.

On two of these points, the different ways in which Sanders recorded the facts has more significance than is at first apparent. In *Jesus and Judaism* Jesus calls *twelve* disciples and merely *engages in controversy* about the temple. In *The Historical Figure of Jesus* he simply *calls disciples* (without specifying the number) and creates a *disturbance* in the temple area. Both points have a special significance in restoration theology.

According to the Jewish scriptures, Israel had originally consisted of twelve tribes. Ten of these were lost when the kingdom split after the death of David. That God would one day miraculously restore the twelve tribes was an article of faith among first-century Jews in Palestine. Thus, Jesus' deliberate choice of twelve disciples was a signal that the time of deliverance had come. Matthew's gospel has him tell the twelve that in the coming kingdom they will each rule over the reconstituted twelve tribes. The Jesus Seminar scholars voted this a solid black, meaning that in their view Jesus never said it; rather, it represents the view of the Matthew community nearly seventy years later. Sanders, by contrast, reasons in *Jesus and Judaism* that the saying must have originated with Jesus as the church would never have invented such a prediction, given the unhelpful tradition that the traitor Judas was one of the twelve, and the equally embarrassing fact that the ten lost tribes were still as lost as ever when the gospels were written.

Sanders modifies this in his second book, where he tends to interpret "the twelve" as a symbol rather than a literal number. He notes the New Testament's confusion over who the twelve disciples actually were: their names are listed differently in different places and add up to either 14 or 15 (according to whether "Matthew" and "Levi" are counted as the same person)[18]. But this does not affect his argument. He concludes that, even if Jesus did not designate precisely twelve followers as disciples, he used the term "the twelve" symbolically to emphasize his message that the day of judgment and restitution was at hand, and that he and his disciples were God's agents in hastening the miracle.

The second significant point where Sanders' two lists differ is the question of what happened when Jesus visited the temple at Jerusalem. The earlier list is cautious: Jesus "engaged in a controversy about the temple". The later list is more concrete, and closer to the gospel accounts: Jesus "created a disturbance". Some scholars interpret the overturning of tables and stalls as an expression of fury that the holy temple area had been allowed to become so commercialized. The Jesus Seminar gives a pink ("probably true") rating to the statement that Jesus chased vendors and shoppers out of the temple forecourt, and a skeptical gray to the overturning of money-changers' tables, proposing that Jesus' demonstration was a protest against "the commercialization of the temple cult". Sanders, on the other hand, sees the story as recording a symbolic fulfilment, or preliminary to fulfilment, of Jewish scriptural prophecies of the destruction of the temple, which reinforces the picture he is building of Jesus as a prophet of the end-time and the impending miracle of kingdom-come.

In *Jesus and Judaism*, then, Jesus's kingdom teaching is interpreted by Sanders as being very much in line with that of John the Baptist and other prophets of doom-and-restoration theology. The "day of the Lord" was at hand, when the God of Israel would make a cataclysmic intervention in human history, destroying the temple, restoring the twelve tribes, liberating his own people and reversing the social order to put down the mighty and raise the poor, the outcast and the repentant. All that Jesus was doing and saying, Sanders suggests, fits what we know of what other Jewish prophets and teachers were saying and doing. "We cannot say that a single one of the things known about Jesus is unique: neither his miracles, non-violence, eschatological hope, or promise to the outcasts. He was not unique because he saw his own mission as of crucial importance, nor because he believed in the grace of God... We cannot even say that Jesus was a uniquely good and great man"[19].

But this somewhat stark summary belongs to Sanders' earlier work and is considerably nuanced and modified in the later *Historical Figure of Jesus*. Here, in a chapter of central importance, "The Coming of the Kingdom", Sanders canvasses all the kingdom sayings in the synoptic gospels and separates them out into six sub-divisions.

• First, "the kingdom of God is in heaven: it is a transcendent realm, to which people may look for inspiration and into which they will individually enter at death or at the great judgement". Sanders cites Mark 9:47, Matthew 18.9, Mark 10.15, Luke 18:17, where he understands Jesus to use "kingdom" in this sense.

• Second, "the kingdom of God is a transcendent realm now in heaven, but in the future it will come to earth. God will transform the world so that the basic structures of society (physical, social and economic) are maintained but remoulded. All people will live as God wills, and there will be justice, peace and plenty". Here the "Lord's prayer" (Matthew 6:10, Luke 11.2) serves as an example.

• Third is "a special subcategory of sayings [that] looks forward to a future realm that will be introduced by a cosmic event... [indicating] *how* the kingdom will come to earth". Sanders cites Mark 13:24-27: "But in those days, after that tribulation, the sun will be darkened, and the moon will not give its light, and the stars will be falling from heaven... And then they will see the Son of Man coming in clouds with great power and glory. And then he will send out the angels, and gather his elect from the four winds, from the ends of the earth to the ends of heaven".

• Fourth, there are the "drawn near" or "at hand" passages where, as in Mark 1:14-15, the message of Jesus is summarized as a pronouncement that "the time is fulfilled, and the kingdom of God is at hand". Here the emphasis is on the imminence of the event: it is to happen not just some time in the future but any day now, as when Jesus assures his followers that they "will not taste death" (Mark 9:1) until they see that the kingdom has come.

Each of these four categories emphasizes the kingdom as miraculous. It is primarily transcendent or supernatural, a kingdom ruled from another world, about to break on this one at some time in the near future. This is the kingdom teaching Sanders has focused on in his earlier book. But in *The Historical Figure of Jesus* he is prepared to acknowledge two more categories that bring the kingdom closer to home, here and now.

• Fifth, "it is possible in some passages that the kingdom is a special 'realm' on earth, one that consists of people who are dedicated to living according to God's will and that exists both in and side by side with normal human society". As Sanders comments, "In the centuries after Jesus' death, this is the way Christians have often seen themselves". There are no gospel sayings with precisely this meaning, says Sanders, but some come close: "the kingdom is like leaven, which cannot be seen but which leavens the whole loaf (Matthew 13:33, Luke 13.20f). In Luke17:20f the kingdom is 'among you'"[or, in the AV, 'within you'] - and the teaching that it is to come in the future, accompanied by signs and portents, is specifically repudiated by Jesus himself.

• Sixth and last, there are two passages which have been interpreted by many scholars as indicating that Jesus identified the kingdom with his own miracle-ministry. In Matthew 12:28 and Luke 11:20 Jesus says that "if it is by the Spirit of God [Luke: finger of God] that I cast out demons, then the kingdom of God has come upon you". And when John the Baptist is reported (Matthew 11:2-6) as sending word by his disciples to ask Jesus if he was "the one who is to come", Jesus tells the messengers to cite the evidence: "the blind receive their sight, the lame walk, the lepers are cleansed, the deaf hear, the dead are raised, and the poor have good news brought to them"[20].

In summarizing his conclusions, Sanders first draws attention to the way scholars have tended to pick and choose among these divergent, if not flatly opposed, meanings. Schweitzer and Weiss went for the cataclysmic cosmic event, Bultmann for a kingdom which, "although it is entirely future, wholly determines the present". C H Dodd relied most heavily on Sanders' sixth category: the kingdom had arrived in Jesus' own ministry. Norman Perrin argued that Jesus himself thought both that the kingdom was future and that in some unspecified sense it was also present in his own words and deeds. And "in very recent years a few American scholars have decided that Jesus did not expect the kingdom to come in the future at all... Jesus was actually a political, social and economic reformer, and he did not expect God to do anything dramatic or miraculous in the future".

Then Sanders delivers his own considered verdict:

"It is my own view that we cannot recover Jesus' view merely by picking and choosing among the sayings... but I do not think that a historical reconstruction should depend on the notion that we can definitely establish what Jesus did *not* say. If we calmly survey all of the kingdom sayings, we shall see that most of them place the kingdom *up there*, in heaven, where people will enter after death, and *in the future*, when God brings the kingdom to earth and separates the sheep from the goats." Perhaps forgetting his own assertion that we cannot definitely establish what Jesus did *not* say, Sanders suggests that the one saying in the synoptic gospels where Jesus says the kingdom is "among you" and is not to be looked for in cosmic signs and portents, is best read as an invention of Luke rather than a true saying of Jesus: "I believe that Luke wrote these two verses all by himself, unaided by a transmitted saying of Jesus... One cannot take Luke 17:20f as cancelling the large number of sayings about the future kingdom - including those that immediately follow in Luke"[21].

Sanders concedes that "The simplest and in some ways the best view to take of the complicated question of the kingdom in the teachings of Jesus is that he said *all* the things listed above [in the six categories] - or things like them. There is no difficulty in thinking that Jesus thought that the kingdom was in heaven, that people would enter it in the future, *and* that it was also present in some sense in his own work"[22]. But it is hard not to read this as something of a sop to those of his critics who had taken him to task for his previously expressed and more single-minded view of Jesus as foreteller of the apocalypse. In fact, a close reading suggests that the concession, if that is what it is, does not in the end really modify his earlier conclusion. Sanders is gently scornful of the view that the apocalyptic Jesus was the creation of followers who simply misunderstood him as preaching the same judgment scenario as John the Baptist - and less gently scornful of scholars who reject an apocalyptic Jesus as simply distasteful and unattractive to modern sensibilities. He also distances himself from the theological view (based on the sayings in the sixth category) that Jesus saw the kingdom as fully and exclusively present in his own miracle-ministry - a view, he says, for which there is simply a "lack of good evidence".

If, in the end, Sanders in *The Historical Figure of Jesus* endorses his own earlier view that Jesus preached a kingdom of God or kingdom of heaven that was primarily apocaplyptic, he does so not by studying the individual sayings and pronouncing on their authenticity but by reference to the context of the movement that began with John the Baptist. "John expected the judgement to come soon. Jesus started his career by being baptized by John. After Jesus' death and resurrection, his followers thought that within their lifetimes he would return to establish his kingdom. After his conversion, Paul was of the very same view. The Christians very soon, as early as I Thessalonians (c.50 CE) had to start coping with the troublesome fact that the kingdom had not yet come. It is almost impossible to explain these historical facts on the assumption that Jesus himself did not expect the imminent end or transformation of the present world order. He thought that in the new age God (or his viceroy) would reign supreme, without opposition." This is not to say that Jesus expected "the end of the world in the sense of destruction of the cosmos. He expected a divine, transforming miracle. As a devout Jew, he thought that God had previously intervened in the world in order to save and protect Israel. For example, God had parted the sea so that Israel could escape the pursuing Egyptian army, he had fed the people with manna in the desert, and he had brought them into the land of Palestine. In the future, Jesus thought that God would act even more decisively: he would create an ideal world. He would restore the twelve tribes of Israel, and peace and justice would prevail. Life would be like a banquet... The future was depicted, as in many other cultures, as a return to the beginning, or to an idealized 'golden age' - not the dissolution of the cosmos"[23].

In which case, Jesus got it wrong - unless, fully two thousand years later, we can accept the ingenious explanation of the unknown author of the "second epistle of Peter", writing roughly a century after Jesus' predictions. "Scoffers", he scoffed, would ask "Where is the promise of his coming?" The fools had failed to understand that "one day is with the Lord as a thousand years, and a thousand years as one day" (II Peter: 3-8). The kingdom that was "nigh", "at hand", and would come before Jesus' followers tasted death, was still a future event in which "the heavens shall pass away with a great noise, and the elements shall melt with fervent heat, the earth also and the works that are therein shall be burned up" (v. 10). By this account, hopes and expectations of "the Rapture" were kept alive indefinitely - and remain the defining mark of millions who understand it as the most fundamental of Christian fundamentals.

As Sanders puts it, "The Lord is not really slow, but rather keeps time by a different calendar"[24].

2. John P Meier: Jesus as mentor, message-bringer and miracle-maker

A Catholic priest and professor of New Testament at University of Notre

Dame in South Bend, Indiana, Meier too is a scholar's scholar. He "wins the prize for length", writes Mark Allan Powell. "Quantitively, at least, he has exceeded all other Jesus scholars, ancient and modern"[25]. His three-volume work *A Marginal Jew: Rethinking the Historical Jesus* examines every reported saying and fact about Jesus and runs to some 2500 pages. Meier may lack the popular touch of Funk, Crossan, Borg and Sanders, but he figures in more scholarly footnotes than most other workers in the field. Powell comments that "for those who are not truly committed the presentation can become tedious, but one thing is always clear: if, at the end of a discussion, you do not agree with Meier's conclusion, you can see exactly how he reached it, and identify at what juncture you parted company, and why. This, his academic peers affirm, is traditional (his critics say 'old-fashioned') historical criticism at its best"[26]. *A Marginal Jew* is published under the benign eye of the Roman Catholic church, to which Meier remains scrupulously loyal: he affirms his belief in the virgin birth, the miracles and the resurrection of Jesus. For him, the church's "Jesus of faith" is "the real Jesus", but as an historian claiming "academic objectivity" he distinguishes this "real Jesus" from "the historical Jesus", defining the latter as "that Jesus whom we can recover or reconstruct by using the scientific tools of modern historical research". Where, for most historians, the historical Jesus *is* the real Jesus of history, Meier's historical Jesus is "a scientific construct, a theoretical abstraction of modern scholars that coincides only partially with the real Jesus of Nazareth, the Jew who actually lived and worked in Palestine"[27].

In his first volume, Meier devotes two hundred pages to an explanation of his methodological procedure. Much of it is common to most modern scholarship, but he gives more prominence to three criteria than many of his colleagues. First, he argues that if a saying or act of Jesus embarrassed the gospel writers and the early church (for instance, the promise that the kingdom would come before the disciples tasted death) it is most likely to be authentic, since the natural inclination would be to omit or gloss over failed prophecies and challenges to conventional respectability. Second, reports of Jesus being rejected and executed as a criminal must be authentic, since the evangelists are unlikely to have invented negative stories about their master. Third, Meier uses the common criterion of multiple attestation in a distinctive way, suggesting that the case for historical authenticity is enhanced not only by multiple sources, as most scholars have recognized since the nineteenth century, but also by multiple forms. Thus, the fact that there are both narratives and sayings about Jesus' miracles makes it more likely that Jesus did indeed perform miracles, or acts that were regarded as miracles.

In his meticulous attention to detail and his methodical examination of the data saying by saying, deed by deed, fact by fact, Meier appears at first glance to have much in common with the Jesus Seminar. But this impression soon fades. The Seminar scholars on one hand and Meier on the other make very different evaluations of what "the data" properly consists of. Where the Seminar sees no ground for distinguishing between gospels that were eventually accepted into the Catholic canon and those that came to be deemed by church councils to lack divine inspiration and theological correctness, Meier effectively dismisses all but the four New Testament gospels as of any value in providing reliable source material. Thomas, accorded by the Seminar both contemporaneity and equal value with the synoptic gospels, is lumped by Meier along with all the other "late" and "apocryphal" gospels as virtually worthless. On the other hand, where the Seminar prints nearly all of John in inauthentic black, Meier, while recognizing the lateness of its composition and its developed christology, finds much that he deems authentic. For instance, he considers that John is right in portraying Jesus' ministry as lasting longer than the synoptics' single year, with more visits to Jerusalem than the one fateful trip recorded in Mark, Matthew and Luke.

This reliance on the biblical source material puts Meier closer to Sanders than to the Seminar, and it is therefore no surprise that Meier's Jesus, like Sanders', emerges as primarily a prophet of the miraculous coming kingdom of God. Jesus began his public life as a disciple of John the Baptist who, in an established tradition of Jewish prophecy, proclaimed an imminent fiery judgment on apostate Israel. John urged individual repentance, signified by a ritual immersion in Jordan's waters that would symbolically extinguish the flames about to consume the unrepentant. Since Jesus accepted John's baptism he evidently saw himself as one of John's disciples, a member of the locust-and-honey-eating wilderness circle, in which case he must have accepted John's message of imminent cosmic catastrophe for all but those who repented and allowed John to wash away their sins. Jesus the penitent? Indeed, says Meier, but not the introspective and individualistic penitence of the (Protestant?) West. Meier's understanding of Jesus' confession and repentence, as Powell helpfully summarizes it, "would have involved humble admission that he was a member of a sinful people (the rebellious and ungrateful nation of Israel), accompanied by a resolve to be different"[28].

At some point, however, Jesus left John's circle and launched out on his own. Meier does not think (as Crossan and Borg have suggested) that his move towards an independent ministry involved any critical disagreement with John or his message. Rather, Jesus came to develop a more nuanced and perhaps more gentle concept of the coming kingdom, one he felt compelled to take to the villages of Galilee rather than isolating himself in the wilderness and expecting people to make the journey to him. Jesus shifted the emphasis from God's fiery judgment to his mercy and forgiveness. Where John had preached and no doubt practised a life of ascetic renunciation, Jesus preached and practised open fellowship with "publicans and sinners". Where John had merely *warned* of the coming kingdom, Jesus *demonstrated* what it meant: sight to the blind, hearing to the deaf, leaping to the lame, healing to the leper, power to the poor.

But, Meier insists, Jesus never abandoned John's message of a *coming* judgment, an imminent apocalyptic day of reckoning. Like Sanders, he finds it impossible to read the collected kingdom sayings as indicating anything other than that Jesus himself expected God to make a miraculous, spectacular intervention in human affairs by bringing the world under direct divine rule. Like Sanders, Meier dismisses the view of the Jesus Seminar scholars that all the many apocalyptic sayings are inauthentic misinterpretations by later Christians who failed to see the difference between John's message of kingdom-come and Jesus' kingdom-now. But if Jesus never abandoned the message of John and the Jewish apocalyptic tradition, Meier argues that he made it very much his own. In particular, while the kingdom of God was, for Jesus as for John, a future cosmic event, Jesus most skilfully and evocatively gave it a whole range of secondary meanings. Like Sanders in his later *Historical Figure of Jesus*, Meier concludes that both kingdom-come and kingdom-now sayings are authentic words of the historical Jesus, though "the precise relationship between the coming and present kingdom remains unspecified"[29]. He grants that Jesus saw signs that the kingdom was already breaking out, already in some sense being realized, in his own ministry of healing miracles and open table fellowship, but he insists that the emphasis in Jesus' message was on a kingdom about to arrive. If Jesus saw his own ministry in kingdom terms, it was as "a partial and prelim-inary realization of God's kingly rule, which would soon be displayed in full force"[30]. Meier's Jesus, then, is like the Jesus of Sanders a Jewish prophet of the end-time, but Meier sharply dissents from Sanders' view that, in the end, there is nothing unique about this Galilean itinerant teacher. There had been and would be other prophets of a future kingdom, had been and would be other moral teachers, had been and would be other miracle-makers, healers, exorcists and holy men. But "it is the explosive convergence and mutual reinforcement of all these usually distinct figures in the one Jesus of Nazareth that made him stand out"[31].

Meier the academic historian stops short of explicity asserting with Meier the Catholic priest that the Jesus who uniquely stands out from all the rest is Peter's "Jesus the Christ, the son of the living God". We turn now to another Christian historian/theologian who unashamedly closes that gap.

3. N T Wright: Jesus as son of Israel's god

If there is one contemporary scholar who challenges John Meier when it comes to a "prize for length" it is N T Wright, dean of Lichfield and canon of Coventry cathedral before his elevation to the number three spot in the Church of England hierarchy as bishop of Durham. Wright's 760-page book *Jesus and the Victory of God* is merely one volume (the second) in a projected five- or six-volume series (in progress) under the umbrella title *Christian Origins and the Question of God*. But Tom Wright, as he is known to his friends and admirers, dispenses his immense erudition in an admirably clear and engaging writing style, and his work has consequently won the attention of both general readers and fellow scholars on both sides of the Atlantic - and particularly of those who have looked to modern scholarship to reclaim a scientifically validated historical Jesus for the church.

Like his fellow Durham historian/theologian James Dunn, Wright is critical of all previous historical Jesus studies, particularly those of the Enlightenment tradition up to Schweitzer and the late-modern methodologies of the Jesus Seminar. The first eighty-or-so pages of *Jesus and the Victory of God* are devoted to a robust demolition of all the schools of scholarship we have considered so far. Against these older quests, and what he sees as their mistaken attempts to uncover a wholly human Jesus fit for modern liberal humanist consumption, Wright set himself the task of launching what he called a "Third Quest", aiming, as he explains in the preface, "to denote one particular type of contemporary Jesus-research, namely, that which regards Jesus as an eschatological prophet announcing the long-awaited kingdom, *and which undertakes serious historiography around this point*". Wright complains that the term "Third Quest" has been hijacked by others to denote a wide range of current Jesus studies, but, he says, "I see no need to abandon my original sharper meaning"[32]. This sharper meaning appears to be encoded in the phrase I have italicized. For Wright, "serious historiography" centered on Jesus as proclaimer of the kingdom produces a Jesus who turns out to be just what the church has always claimed him to be: not simply a man in a *moment* of history but the divinely appointed pivotal point of the *whole* of human history. If it doesn't do that, it can't be "serious historiography" in Wright's book.

His methodology is much closer to that of Sanders than to that of the Jesus Seminar or Meier. He rejects a saying-by-saying approach as faulty historiography: we wouldn't try to recover the historical Julius Caesar by examining his reported speeches and testing them for authenticity. Rather, historians take into account everything written about Caesar as well as by him, and evaluate such data in the wider context of what can be ascertained about the world he inhabited. If that's how we study the historical Caesar, Wright asks, why study the historical Jesus differently?

Where, then, do we find the most reliable source material for the Jesus traditions? Wright is one of those who thinks it unnecessary to look much further than the three synoptic gospels. He has little time for the proposal that Thomas is an early and reliable source: like Sanders and Meier, he treats it as a late and "apocryphal" gospel. Nor is he much interested in sifting out early proto-gospel material such as Q. ("The proposal of a 'Q-and-Thomas' early Christianity is extremely tenuous")[33]. He acknowledges, of course, that the synoptic gospels were written many years after the events they report, but he ingeniously turns this into a virtue rather than a defect. His argument is that what he calls "the mindset of Jesus" is best understood by interpreting his reported words and actions in relation to *two* contexts. The first is the context of what *preceded* him: the milieu of first-century BCE Judaism. The second is the context of what *followed* him: the milieu of the first-century CE church, as reconstructed from the New Testament writings in general and the synoptic gospels in particular. Wright calls this criterion for authenticity the "double criterion of similarity and dissimilarity": "When something can be seen to be credible (though perhaps deeply subversive) within first-century Judaism, *and* credible as the implied starting point (though not the exact replica) of something in later Christianity, there is a strong possibility of our being in touch with the genuine history of Jesus".

The first context, that of first-century Judaism, was well-explored by Sanders, Vermes, Borg and Crossan in their different ways, if with different results. But Wright is not satisfied with their findings - any of them. He devotes most of his first volume, *The New Testament and the People of God*, to proposing a new reconstruction of the Jewish world in which Jesus lived. This new reconstruction is not much concerned with the social conditions of the Jewish peasantry (Crossan and Borg) or even the religious practice of devout Jews in fulfilment of the "covenant of grace" (Sanders), but is founded on three factors that Wright sees as central to understanding where Jesus came from.

The first and most important of these is "the hope for YHWH's return", followed by "the speculation that YHWH's agent would be exalted to share his throne, and the symbolic language used for YHWH's activity in the world"[34]. This conviction of a coming kingdom was both Jesus' inheritance and his bequest.

The Second-Temple/first-century hope of YHWH's return, Wright suggests, "has not received as much attention as I think it should". He points to an early Jewish commentary on the book of Isaiah known as the Isaiah Targum which highlights prophecies of "the return of the king" to inaugurate what it calls "the kingdom of god". (For Wright's spelling of god with a small g, see note 34).Whether or not Jesus knew and made use of the Targum, Wright argues, he would certainly have known the passages in Isaiah and other prophets that announce the rule of YHWH, since these hopes and expectations were deeply embedded in Jewish consciousness. Wright draws attention to and quotes at length from no fewer than nineteen such passages - nine from Isaiah, one from Ezekiel, one from Haggai, three from Zechariah, one from Malachi, and three drawn from the Psalms. Together they announce an imminent end to Jewish exile and the dawning kingdom under YHWH's direct rule, when Israel's god "will reign on Mount Zion and in Jerusalem" (Isaiah 4:2-6), and "the eyes of the blind shall be opened, and the ears of the deaf unstopped; and the lame shall leap like a deer, and the tongue of the speechless sing for joy... and sorrow and sighing shall flee away" (Isaiah 35:3-6). When this joyful day comes, people will know about it: "the moon will be abashed and the sun ashamed... every valley shall be lifted up, and every mountain and hill be made low... for he will come like a pent-up stream that the wind of YHWH drives on... darkness will cover the earth, and thick darkness the people... for YHWH will come in fire, and his chariots like the whirlwind, to pay back his anger in fury, and his rebuke in flames of fire... But who can endure the day of his coming, and who can stand when he appears? For he is like a refiner's fire... Thus saith YHWH: I am coming to gather all nations and tongues; and they shall come and see my glory..." (Isaiah 24:23, 40:3-5, 59:19-21, 60:1-3, 66:12-16, Malachi 3:1-4, Isaiah 66:18-19)[35].

"This catalogue is impressive in its range and scope", says Wright, "and indicates that the theme would have been well known" in Jesus' time. "YHWH would return; the promises would be fulfilled; the people would be victorious". True, the exile had ended without any sign of the return of the king and the inauguration of the kingdom, but that hadn't diminished the sense of expectation. It is still there in the post-biblical writings (the books written after the Hebrew Bible or Old Testament, and before the New), in 1 Enoch, Testament of Moses, Jubilees and the Qumran (Dead Sea) scrolls. "There is thus ample evidence that most Second-Temple Jews who gave any thought to the matter were hoping for YHWH to return, to dwell once again in the Temple in Jerusalem as he had done in the time of the old monarchy". In this, Wright asserts, "we are on firm ground"[36].

Less firm and more speculative (Wright admits) is the parallel tradition within some sections of contemporary Judaism that when YHWH came to act as savior of the Jews and judge of "the nations" (everyone else) he would do so through an agent, an intermediary, an annointed one or messiah, sometimes identified with the book of Daniel's mysterious "son of man", who would in some sense (never clearly articulated) "share the throne of God". "According to some texts from this period, when YHWH acted in history, the agent through whom he acted would be vindicated, exalted, and honored in a quite unprecedented manner"[37]. Moreover, the messiah-figure was closely related to established symbols or ways of speaking and thinking about divine activity. "He would build, cleanse or rebuild the Temple. He might be a great teacher, or at least a great *enforcer*, of Torah [Hebrew law as laid down in the Pentateuch, the first five books of the Bible]. He might, at a pinch, be identified with Logos[38]. As Solomon's descendant, he would of course be endowed with Wisdom as well as with the divine Spirit". This did not mean, says Wright, that first-century BCE Jews expected their messiah to be "divine": they knew only one god. But he "would be the agent or even the vice-regent of Israel's god, would fight his battles, would restore his people"[39]. He would in some mysterious or mystical way partake in God's divinity without compromising Judaism's fundamental monotheism.

For Wright, the well-attested messianic expectation of the Jewish people, understood as the coming kingdom of god to be inaugurated either by YHWH himself or by his agent, the "son of man", provides one crucial context for understanding Jesus as both proclaimer of the kingdom and the agent by which it would come. The second and parallel context is that of the early church and the New Testament. Jesus' followers, from Paul, writing in the 50s, through the synoptic writers of the 70s to 90s and the church fathers of the second century, believed that Jesus had fulfilled these expectations, not only by announcing the kingdom yet again (as John the Baptist had done) but by *embodying* its reality in his teaching, his healings, his manner of living, and, above all, his manner of dying. He had proved himself YHWH's agent, the mysterious "son of man", "vindicated, exalted and honored in a quite unprecedented manner". If either late-Jewish expectations of the kingdom or early-Christian belief in it stood alone, it might be possible to argue that apocalyptic kingdom-teaching was not central to the ministry of the historical Jesus, whatever might be claimed for the "Jesus of faith". But - and this is the essence of Wright's argument - if the outer limits for understanding Jesus are pre-Christian Judaism and post-Judaic Christianity, "the puzzle involves fitting together the bits in the middle to make a clear historical sequence all the way across"[40]. This is Wright's "double criterion of similarity and dissimilarity", by which he concludes that "the bits in the middle", the kingdom-come sayings as reported in the synoptic gospels, are indeed authentic. They fit into "a clear historical sequence". Those who deny the authenticity of the end-time sayings and interpret them as the inventions or misinterpretations of the disciples have therefore got it wrong - or got the wrong Jesus.

So are we back with a devout, well-meaning, but essentially wrong-headed Jesus who forecast an imminent apocalypse which never arrived, either in the life-time of his disciples, as promised, or in the twenty centuries ahead? Was it Jesus himself who got it wrong? Far from it, claims Wright. The proclamations of apocalypse are authentic: Jesus said them. But they need to be interpreted as Jesus' contemporaries would have interpreted them: symbolically, rather than literally. Jesus *announced* the kingdom *and inaugurated it* in his own person, in the belief that the kingdom was coming in and through his own work. He claimed kingship, but his kingdom was unlike any other kingdom. He *announced* the coming of the "son of man", YHWH's agent, and he *was* the son of man (though a son of man who *ascends* from earth to heaven rather than Daniel's son of man who makes the reverse journey, as a *descent*)[41]. When he pronounced judgment - "a devastating catalogue of threats and warnings", as Wright cheerfully acknowledges - he correctly predicted the calamity that was about to fall on those who rejected his message of peace and his peaceable kingdom. When he used the apocalyptic language of the darkening of the sun and the falling of stars, these were traditional and "symbolic ways of indicating the transforming nature of the event, similar perhaps to what people today mean when they describe something as 'earth-shattering'"[42]. When he promised salvation for those who would follow him into a new kingdom of heaven, a new Israel and a new Jerusalem, he was already bringing into being a new people of God who would both proclaim and embody God's rule. Jesus preached kingdom-come and *made* the kingdom come. He was an apocalyptic prophet - and he was right, because he was, simply, the fulfilment of his own prophecy!

But more than a prophet. "Jesus was hinting, for those with ears to hear, that as he was riding over the Mount of Olives, celebrating the coming kingdom, and warning Jerusalem that it would mean judgment for those who rejected him and his way of peace, so YHWH was returning to his people, his city, and his Temple"[43]. The arrival of Jesus *was* the arrival of YHWH, and the arrival of YHWH *was* the promised kingdom of God.

So was Jesus God? Did he think of himself as God? Here the objective academic historian and the orthodox bishop have to resolve what might appear to be uncomfortable differences. This is how he does it. Jesus believed himself to be the promised Messiah, say both Wrights, but "the word Messiah, within Jesus' world, does not refer, in itself, to a divine or quasi-divine figure. There are puzzling and opaque texts in the Hebrew scriptures which speak of the king as one speaks of Israel's god. There are passages where the roles of YHWH and of the king seem to be intertwined. But there is no evidence to suggest that the various messianic and quasi-messianic figures who flit through the pages of first-century history thought of themselves, or were thought of by others, in this fashion"[44]. One point up, then, for Wright the historian.

But if Jesus the monotheistic Jew did not see himself as, or claim to be, God Almighty, the very incarnation of Israel's god or the second person of the Holy Trinity, he nevertheless "believed he had to do and be, for Israel and the world, that which according to scripture only YHWH himself could do or be". That is how Wright the historian puts it in *Jesus and the Victory of God*[45]. In a slightly earlier book, *Who was Jesus?*, Wright the theologian expresses it a little differently. If Jesus really did believe that he was doing what God alone could do, then why should he not "also come to hold the strange and risky belief that the one true God, the God of Israel, was somehow present and active in him and even *as* him?"[46]. A point here for Wright the priest: a one-all draw. But the game isn't over yet. Will Wright the historian proclaim Jesus as Wright the bishop must do, according to the historic creeds and formularies of his church? That will depend on how Wright the historian answers "the Question of God" in the remaining volumes of his series on *Christian Origins and the Question of God.*

Meanwhile, he makes it clear that he sees no conflict between history and theology. For him, the point of studying the historical Jesus is to gain insight into his significance not only for his own time but for ours. For Wright, God does not exist outside and beyond history: his actions and interventions are historical events. More than any human actions, they *make* history. The historical Jesus was God's greatest intervention in human history, and the secular project of separating the Jesus of history from the Christ of faith is born of a simple misunderstanding of both history and theology.

For Wright's admirers - a growing number, particularly in the churches - he is the Jesus-historian who has put other Jesus-historians in their place. He has pronounced judgment on the "First Quest", the "Second Quest" and the "New Quest", proclaiming and embodying the coming kingdom of the "Third Quest". His message is "Jesus saved". He has grabbed the historical Jesus from those who had set him against the church, and restored him to the faithful. For his critics, on the other hand, he has performed a nifty illusion of squaring circles. By sticking to the synoptic gospels as virtually the only sources of value, refusing to evaluate the authenticity of the parts and swallowing the lot as gospel truth, he has produced an historical Jesus with a close resemblance to the Jesus of his church: a Jesus who did God's work "*as* God", who proclaimed the apocalypse in his own time, and can be seen to be *right* if one correctly understands that the kingdom he promised did become a

Cameo: Wright on Jesus as embodiment of the kingdom

*"Jesus' beliefs... remained those of a first-century Jew, committed to the coming kingdom of Israel's god. He did not waver in his loyalty to Jewish doctrine. But his beliefs were those of a first century Jew **who believed that the kingdom was coming in and through his own work**. His loyalty to Israel's cherished beliefs therefore took the form of critique and renovation from within; of challenge to traditions and institutions whose true purpose, he believed (like prophets long before, and radicals in his own day), had been grievously corrupted and distorted; and of new proposals which, though without precedent, were never mere innovation. They always claimed the high ground: fulfilment, completion, consummation.*

"We can summarize Jesus' beliefs in terms of the three most fundamental Jewish beliefs: monotheism, election, and eschatology.

"Jesus believed that there was one God who had made the world, and who had called Israel to be his people; that this one God had promised to be with his people, and guide them to their destiny, their new exodus; that his presence, guidance and ultimately salvation were symbolized, brought into reality, in and through Temple, Torah, Wisdom, Word and Spirit. He was a first-century Jewish monotheist.

"He believed that Israel was the true people of the one creator God, called to be the light of the world, called to accomplish her vocation through suffering. He cherished this belief in Israel's special vocation, even as he challenged current interpretations of it.

"He believed in the coming kingdom of Israel's god, which

would bring about the real return from exile, the final defeat of evil, and the return of YHWH to Zion. He embraced this Jewish hope, making it thematic for his own work.

"The difference between the beliefs of Jesus and those of thousands of other Jews of his day amounted simply to this: he believed, also, that all these things were coming true in and through himself. His particular task was to offer a symbolic encoding (or decoding?) of this entire theology and expectation in terms of his own life and work. The words he spoke as Messiah, on the night he was betrayed, would resonate out prophetically as words of Israel's god, spoken about Jesus himself. 'This is my son, my beloved, in whom I am well pleased'; 'This is my son, my beloved, listen to him'; and now 'This is my body, given for you'.

"Speaking of Jesus' vocation brings us to quite a different place from some traditional statements of gospel christology... Jesus did not, in other words, 'know that he was God' in the same way that one knows one is male or female, hungry or thirsty, or that one ate an orange an hour ago. His 'knowledge' was of a more risky, but perhaps more significant, sort: like knowing one is loved. One cannot 'prove' it except by living it. Jesus' prophetic vocation thus included within it the vocation to enact, symbolically, the return of YHWH to Zion. His messianic vocation included within it the vocation to attempt certain tasks which, according to scripture, YHWH had reserved for himself. He would take upon himself the role of messianic shepherd, knowing that YHWH had claimed this role as his own. He would perform the saving task which YHWH had said he alone could achieve. He would do what no messenger, no angel, but only the "arm of YHWH", the presence of Israel's god, could accomplish. As part of his human vocation, grasped in faith, sustained in prayer, tested in

confrontation, agonized over in further prayer and doubt, and implemented in action, he believed he had to do and be, for Israel and the world, that which according to scripture only YHWH himself could do and be. He was Israel's Messiah; but there would, in the end, be 'no king but God'...

"Forget the 'titles' of Jesus, at least for a moment; forget the pseudo-orthodox attempts to make Jesus of Nazareth conscious of being the second person of the Trinity; forget the arid reductionism that is the mirror-image of that unthinking would-be orthodoxy. Focus, instead, on a young Jewish prophet telling a story about YHWH returning to Zion as judge and redeemer, and then embodying it by riding into the city in tears, symbolizing the Temple's destruction and celebrating the final exodus. I propose, as a matter of history, that Jesus of Nazareth was conscious of a vocation: a vocation, given him by the one he knew as 'father', to enact in himself what, in Israel's scriptures, God had promised to accomplish all by himself. He would be the pillar of cloud and fire for the people of the new exodus. He would embody in himself the returning and redeeming action of the covenant of God." - **"The Aims and Beliefs of Jesus" in Part III of Jesus and the Victory of God, pp 652-3.**

reality in his own life and that of his followers.

But the critics make another charge. Wright's Jesus believed himself to be the agent of Israel's god, proclaiming a kingdom for those who chose to be faithful to their god, and destruction for those who resisted or defied his way of peace. And who proved faithful? Those Jews and God-fearing gentiles who became Christians. And who resisted and thereby deserved the destruction threatened in Jesus' "devastating catalogue of threats and warnings"? The Jews who failed to recognize the man from Galilee as "the Christ". So we are wrenched back to the old charge: the

Jews killed God's son, his blood is on them and on their children, as Matthew put it (27:25). They deserved what they got, which is what Jesus promised. And this way lie the pogroms of the ensuing centuries, culminating in the holocaust. Is this an historical Jesus we can live with, or want to live with? Or is this the nascent anti-semitism of the early church, increasingly separated and alienated from its Jewish roots - and, if they only knew it, from the way, truth and life preached and lived by the teacher they professed to follow?

But this much may be agreed by both Wright's admirers and critics: *Jesus and the Victory of God* is a landmark work. Along with Dunn's trilogy, it squares up to the humanist revolution in Jesus scholarship and breathes an invigorating new life into the conservatives' counter-revolution. Its challenge to the school of the Jesus Seminar in particular opens a new chapter in historical Jesus studies, reopening old debates and introducing brand new ones. If Wright is right, all two hundred scholars of the Seminar are wrong. But if the Seminar's Jesus of Galilee turns out to be the Jesus of the future, the more credible Jesus for the twenty-first century, Wright's "son of god" will look like an ingenious but doomed attempt to rehabilitate the Jesus of Nicea, the Jesus of a church that claimed for itself as the "new Israel" the blessings and privileges of the promised kingdom, coupled with the power to persecute those of the "old Israel" who had turned their back on the king foretold in the Hebrew scriptures.

4. Joseph Ratzinger: a Pope's Jesus

If Tom Wright and James Dunn have kicked off a "post-postmodern" backlash against recent critical-historical scholarship, Joseph Ratzinger has picked up their ball and run with it. In *Jesus of Nazareth*, published in 2007 and billed as "my personal search for the face of the Lord", the Pope himself seeks to re-unite the Jesus of history with the Christ of faith. "What can faith in Jesus as the Christ possibly mean", he asks, "if the *man* Jesus was so completely different from the picture that the

Evangelists painted of him and that the Church, on the evidence of the Gospels, takes as the basis of her preaching?"[47]

What indeed? This begs a host of questions. But Ratzinger's book has a place in this survey because, priest and theologian as he is, he professes to take history seriously. The historical-critical method, he agrees, is and remains "indispensable... for it is the very essence of biblical faith to be about real historical events. It does not tell stories symbolizing supra-historical truths, but is based on history, history that took place here on this earth". Historical fact is "the foundation on which it [biblical faith] stands", so "faith must expose itself to the historical method - indeed, faith itself demands this"[48]. Warming to this theme, he continues: "I hope it is clear to the reader... that my intention in writing this book is not to counter modern exegesis [interpretation of scripture]; rather, I write with profound gratitude for all that it has given and continues to give to us. It has opened up to us a wealth of material and an abundance of findings that enable the figure of Jesus to become present to us with a vitality and depth that we could not have imagined even just a few decades ago"[49].

Such an apparently generous endorsement of historically-based Jesus scholarship would have been greeted with rueful bemusement by the many scholars who, in the not-too-distant past, were denounced or disowned by the Vatican for tasting the forbidden fruit of higher criticism. Until the middle of the twentieth century "modernist" scholarship that questioned or departed from the papal party line was treated as the work of the devil. This began to change when the encyclical *Divino Afflante Spiritus* in 1943 cautiously acknowledged that historical method might have value in supporting rather than subverting faith, and subsequent Vatican pronouncements have opened the door an inch or two wider. But Ratzinger's "profound gratitude" for independent scholarship seems too good to be true.

And so it is. Critical historical scholarship, it turns out, is fine, so far as it goes. The trouble is that it doesn't go very far. Because it lacks the vital ingredient of faith, says Ratzinger, critical scholarship has only succeeded in "obscuring and blurring" the figure of Jesus. Reconstructions of a Jesus "who could only be discovered by going behind the traditions and sources used by the Evangelists became more and more incompatible with one another: at one end of the spectrum, Jesus was the anti-Roman revolutionary working - though finally failing - to overthrow the ruling powers; at the other end, he was the meek moral teacher who approves everything and unaccountably comes to grief". This has led to growing skepticism, with the result that the figure of Jesus himself has "receded even further into the distance".

"All these attempts have produced a common result: the impression that we have very little certain knowledge of Jesus and that only at a later stage did faith in his divinity shape the image we have of him. This impression has by now penetrated deeply into the minds of the Christian people at large. This is a dramatic situation for faith, because its point of reference is being placed in doubt: Intimate friendship with Jesus, on which everything depends, is in danger of clutching at thin air."[50]

The remedy is *scholarship-plus*, scholarship "transcended... to arrive at a genuinely theological interpretation of the scriptural texts"[51]. Historical enquiry will yield up the real Jesus only if it is grounded in faith: faith in the scriptures, faith in the Church's interpretation of the scriptures, and faith that the Jesus we are seeking is already known to us as God made flesh. By "the scriptures" Ratzinger makes it crystal clear that he means the four biblical gospels in their completed form: not the layered texts underlying them, and not the many other gospels accorded scriptural authority by early churches that came to be denounced by Rome as heretical.

"I trust the Gospels. Of course, I take for granted everything that the Council [the Vatican Council's Constitution on Divine Revelation] and modern exegesis tell us about literary genres, about authorial intention, and about the fact that the Gospels were written in the context, and speak within the living milieu, of communities. I have tried, to the best of my ability, to incorporate all of this, and yet I wanted to try to portray the

Jesus of the Gospels as the real 'historical' Jesus in the strict sense of the word. I am convinced, and I hope the reader will be, too, that this figure is much more logical and, historically speaking, much more intelligible than the reconstructions we have been presented with in the last decades."[52]

The logic of Ratzinger's trust in the biblical Evangelists is that the fourth gospel, no less than the three synoptics, is to be taken as historically reliable. He does not shrink from this conclusion, which flies in the face of most independent historical opinion. No matter that John's Jesus is so very different from the Jesus of Mark, Matthew and Luke, not least in his habit of delivering lengthy orations in a high-literary Greek rather than speaking in earthy parables and aphorisms bearing unmistakable witness to peasant-Aramaic origins. Ratzinger has an elaborate explanation for this. John's Greek is not "literary", he argues, but a mannered version spoken by the thoroughly Hellenized Jerusalem upper classes. John 18:15 speaks of an unnamed "other disciple" who was "known unto the high priest", demonstrating that "the circle of the disciples... extended as far as the high-priestly aristocracy, in whose language the Gospel is largely written". Who is this "other disciple"? Following (or swallowing) a somewhat tortuous argument elaborated by Martin Hengel in *The Johannine Question* (SCM Press, London, 1989), Ratzinger suggests the evidence points to John, the son of Zebedee, who, as it happens, "since the time of Irenaeus of Lyon (d.ca.202), Church tradition has unanimously regarded" as the author of the fourth gospel.

He concedes that modern scholars have voiced "strong doubts" about such an identification. "Can the fisherman from the Lake of Genasareth have written this sublime Gospel full of visions that peer into the deepest depths of God's mystery? Can he, the Galilean fisherman, have been as closely connected with the priestly aristocracy of Jerusalem, its language, and its mentality as the Evangelist evidently is? Can he have been related to the family of the high priest, as the text hints?" Ratzinger's answer is a bold "Yes!" *Pace* Hengel's novel but under-evidenced speculations,

John's father, Zebedee, was not necessarily a simple fisherman but "quite possibly" a priest with a fishing business in Galilee and "a kind of pied-a-terre in or near Jerusalem", where he performed his priestly duties and conversed with his peers in upper-class Greek, which became the home language of his son John. So, Ratzinger concludes, "in the light of current scholarship... it is quite possible to see Zebedee's son John as the bystander who solemnly asserts his claim to be an eyewitness (cf. Jn 19:35) and thereby identifies himself as the true author of the Gospel".

But isn't John's gospel far too late to be the work of an eyewitness? Not necessarily, says Ratzinger. "Radically late datings" have had to be abandoned "because papyri from Egypt dating back to the beginning of the second century have been discovered; this made it clear that the Gospel must have been written in the first century, if only during the closing years"[53]. In fact, the earliest papyri fragments of John have been carbon-dated (a valuable but inexact science), not to "the beginning of the second century" but to some time between 125 and 150, so that while the date of composition *could* be as early as the end of the first century it could equally be as late as the fourth or fifth decade of the second. Even if the earliest possible date is preferred, the author, as we noted Geza Vermes commenting earlier, would have to have been "a centenarian give or take a few years" if he was indeed an eyewitness and the self-described "beloved disciple" of Jesus. Moreover, as even Hengel recognized, the "upper-class Greek" words the gospel author puts into Jesus' mouth, are on his own argument the author's words and not those of Jesus himself, which would seem to undercut the entire argument for their historical authenticity.

Where does Ratzinger stand on the interpretation of Jesus' kingdom-sayings? Is he with Vermes and Sanders in seeing Jesus as apocalyptic but wrong, with Wright in understanding him as apocalyptic and right, or with the Jesus Seminar in regarding him as not apocalyptic at all? As we have seen, reliance on scriptural texts is no sure guide here, since all three positions can be argued from Luke alone, let alone the New Testament as a whole. Ratzinger's "personal search", it turns out, leads him to a conclusion where these apparent alternatives are neatly sidestepped.

Jesus' teaching that "the Kingdom of God is at hand" is, he writes, "the core content of the Gospel", the "actual core of Jesus' words and works". This assertion has statistical support. "The phrase 'Kingdom of God' occurs 122 times in the New Testament as a whole; 99 of these passages are found in the three Synoptic Gospels, and 90 of these 99 texts report words of Jesus"[54]. What does it mean? What is this "kingdom"? Ratzinger returns to a solution proposed by Origen in the third century. "Origen, basing himself on a reading of Jesus' words, called Jesus *autobasileia*, that is, the Kingdom in person. Jesus himself is the Kingdom; the Kingdom is not a thing, it is not a geographical dominion like worldly kingdoms. It is a person; it is he... By the way in which he speaks of the Kingdom of God, Jesus leads men to realize the overwhelming fact that in him God himself is present among them, that he is God's presence"[55].

"We can put it even more simply: When Jesus speaks of the Kingdom of God, he is quite simply proclaiming God, and proclaiming him to be the living God, who is able to act concretely in the world and in history and is even now so acting. He is telling us: 'God exists' and 'God really is God', which means that he holds in his hands the threads of the world... 'Kingdom of God' is therefore an inadequate translation. It would be better to speak of God's being-Lord, of his lordship...We see, then, that the divine lordship, God's dominion over the world and over history, transcends the moment, indeed transcends and reaches beyond the whole of history."[56]

Ratzinger summarily rejects any interpretation of the kingdom sayings as a proclamation of the possibility of a better world - which he calls "the secular-utopian idea of the Kingdom". It is rejected precisely because "it pushes God off the stage. He is no longer needed, or else he is a downright nuisance"[57]. The kingdom sayings cannot be called in aid of the notion that human beings are capable of mending a broken world by either gradualist or revolutionary politics (a passing crack at liberation theology). But he also rejects coarse apocalypticism. When Jesus says "the Kingdom of God is at hand" (Mark 1:15), or "has already come upon you" (Matthew 12:28), or "is in the midst of you" (Luke 17:21), he is not proclaiming an "imminent expectation", but "a process of coming that has already begun". Taken together with "the entire corpus of Jesus' sayings", the apocalyptic Jesus "can actually be decisively ruled out. This is evident from the fact that the exponents of the apocalyptic interpretation... are simply forced, on the basis of their hypothesis, to ignore a large number of Jesus' sayings on this matter, and to bend others violently in order to make them fit". This is "methodologically illegitimate... The reality that Jesus names the 'Kingdom of God, lordship of God' is extremely complex, and only by accepting it in its entirety can we gain access to, and let ourselves be guided by, his message"[58].

Why, then, bracket Ratzinger in this chapter with scholars who do see Jesus as, in one sense or another, a prophet of apocalypse? It is perhaps a poor fit, but what he has in common with Sanders, and far more so with Wright, is the conviction that the historical Jesus understood his mission as proclaiming the kingdom as, above all, an act of God, a transcendent, metaphysical, supernatural happening. Jesus Seminar scholars and their ilk, Ratzinger implies, may fancy an interpretation of the sayings that "pushes God off the stage" as "a downright nuisance", but Jesus and his Pope inhabit a different world of understanding.

Given Ratzinger's starting point - that the New Testament scriptures and only the New Testament scriptures, understood as divinely inspired, can tell us anything reliable about the historical Jesus - it is not surprising that his "personal search for the face of the Lord" results in him finding the face portrayed by the scriptures and exalted by the church. As Pope, he begins with the conviction that the Jesus of history and the Christ of faith are one, and as scholar he ends his quest with the same conviction squared. But perhaps the happiest and least expected phrase comes in his Foreword, where, after telling us that the book "is in no way an exercise of the magisterium", he concludes: "Everyone is free, then, to contradict me"[59]. You don't hear that very often from the episcopal see of Rome.

Notes for Chapter 9

1 e.g. *Paul and Palestinian Judaism* (1977); *Paul, the Law and the Jewish People* (1983).

2 Sanders, *Historical Figure* 15-23

3 as above, 22, but see also 282-90

4 as above, 106

5 as above, 101-4

6 as above, 36-7

7 as above, 37-8

8 as above, 34

9 as above, 39

10 as above, 32

11 as above, 48

12 as above, 64

13 as above, 54

14 Powell, *Debate* 126

15 Sanders, *Historical Figure* 58-73

16 as above, 74-7

17 Sanders, *J & Judaism* 321

18 Sanders, *Historical Figure* 291

19 Sanders, *J & Judaism* 319-20

20 Sanders, *Historical Figure* 171-5

21 as above,176

22 as above,178

23 as above,183-4

24 as above,180

25 Powell, *Debate* 142

26 as above,142

27 Meier, *Marginal* Vol 2 4

28 Powell, *Debate* 147

29 Meier, *Marginal* Vol 2 451

30 as above, 453

31 as above, 3

32 Wright, *Origins* Vol 2 xiv-xv

33 as above, 40

34 as above, 615ff, where it is more fully discussed. When Wright is referring specifically to "the god of Israel" he sometimes writes "god" with a lower-case g or prefers the ancient Jewish "YHWH", which was used much as newspapers today (or until recently) use **** to indicate a word that convention decrees should not be spelt out. Originally an encoded alternative to naming a god beyond names, YHWH came to be used as a name in its own right. In the King James Bible it is usually translated as Jehovah, or "the Lord".

35 Bishop Wright appears to think that scholars have neglected this passage. Maybe. But for the rest of us it is impossible to read these words, even in an unfamiliar translation, without finding oneself humming Handel!

36 Wright, *Origins* 621, 625

37 as above, 624

38 John Bowker in *The Oxford Dictionary of World Religions* (p 584) writes that the Christian use of the Greek *logos* has two derivations: "(i) the popular Stoic idea (going back to Heraclitus, c.500 BCE) of a universal reason governing and permeating the world; and (ii) the Hebrew conception of God's word (as of his wisdom) as having an almost independent existence. In pre-Christian Judaism, Philo to some extent already combined both concepts, speaking of the logos both as the divine pattern in the world and the intermediary between God and the people. The prologue to the gospel of John identifies the Logos as incarnate in Jesus. To the apologists of the 2nd cent. the duality of the term was a welcome means of making Christology compatible with popular philosophy".

39 Wright, *Origins* 630

40 as above, 5

41 Against the Daniel derivation of the term "Son of Man", with its fiery apoca-lypticism, some scholars have proposed that Jesus was drawing on Ezekiel's use of the term, where it does not appear to have the same apocalyptic meaning. It is argued that Jesus often quotes Ezekiel but never directly from Daniel. The case for a non-apocalyptic reading of "Son of Man" is summarized by the Quaker writer Philip Oakeshott, with citations, in "A Watchman for the House of Israel: Son of Adam, Son of Man", *Faith and Freedom* No. 163, Autumn/Winter 2006.

42 Powell, *Debate* 168

43 Wright, *Origins* Vol 2 639

44 as above, 478

45 as above, 653

46 Wright, *Who* 103

47 Ratzinger, *Jesus* xi

48 as above, xv

49 as above, xxiii

50 as above, xii

51 as above, 365

52 as above, xxi-xxii

53 as above, 219

54 as above, 47

55 as above, 49

56 as above, 57

57 as above, 55

58 as above, 57-9

59 as above, xxiv

10

A VERY JEWISH JESUS

Our survey of what specialist historians have made of the historical Jesus has so far taken us through two major schools. One, centered on the Jesus Seminar, finds a Jesus more typically Mediterranean than Jewish, more sage than miracle-maker, more concerned with a kingdom of heaven as alternative reality now than a kingdom-to-come by apocalyptic act of God. The other, more conservative in its resistance to Californian innovation, finds a Galilean prophet firmly rooted in a tradition of apocalyptic expectation - a Jesus who believed himself to be the divinely appointed agent of imminent earth-shattering change. In due course we shall look at another school, where Jesus is understood as more mythical than historical - or, if historical, a history now lost and virtually irrecoverable. But before we get there we must pause to examine a strand of scholarship that sees Jesus as one in a long line of distinctively Jewish prophets who had no intention of stepping outside his own tradition, let alone founding a new religion: a very Jewish Jesus.

It is true, of course, that Christian, humanist and Jewish scholars alike agree that whatever else he was (historical, mythical, sage, prophet, son of God, son of man), Jesus was a Jew by birth, location, culture and religion. So what can we expect to find that is distinctive in the work of Jewish historians? We have seen that scholars as radically different as Crossan, Borg, Sanders and Wright have all made the context of early-first-century Jewish Galilee a crucial component of their reconstruction of Jesus. Is there anything more that Jewish scholars can bring to the table?

We can begin to answer that with a reminder of something we noted at the start, when we surveyed the beginnings of the quest for the Jesus of history. We quoted the account by Geza Vermes of what happened in the late Middle Ages when Christian scholars in Catholic Spain turned to the *converso* (the newly and often forcibly converted Jews) to help them understand the Jewish roots of the Jesus movement and the New Testament. Jewish scholars were encouraged to research their own religious history, and while this led to "text wars" between Jews and Christians it also paved the way for what Vermes calls "a quasi-'scientific' use of post-biblical Judaica in New Testament interpretation", not only in medieval Spain but also in 17th century England. If Jewish scholarship was in at the beginnings of the historical Jesus quest, it has also played an important role in our own time. We shall look at three radically different but wholly Jewish reconstructions of Jesus: Hyam Maccoby's Jesus the Pharisee, Robert Eisenman's Jesus the brother of James, and, to begin with, the *hasidic* Jesus of Geza Vermes.

1. Geza Vermes: Jesus as charismatic holy man

Born in Hungary in 1924 to a family that hid its Jewish identity in response to virulent anti-semitism, Geza Vermes was baptized into the Roman Catholic church at the age of seven, along with his parents. The conversion of his parents did not save them from death in the holocaust, but Vermes remained unaware that he was Jewish throughout his childhood and adolescence. It was as a Catholic priest and expert in oriental languages that he first took an interest in the Dead Sea Scrolls which began to come to light in 1947, and in 1962 he was the first scholar to publish an English translation of some of the principal texts then available. By this time he had left the church, resumed his Jewish faith, and moved to Britain to take up teaching posts which led to his appointment as the first professor of Jewish studies at Oxford. Soon he was vigorously campaigning for more open access to the scrolls, which were tightly controlled by a "closed shop" of rarely more than half a dozen scholars approved by the Israeli government. In a lecture delivered in 1977 he famously denounced the slow pace of translation and publication as "the academic scandal *par excellence* of the twentieth century". Even so, it was not until 1991 that he himself was invited to join the expanded team of sixty international scholars, and his revised and expanded translations were eventually reissued in 2004 as *The Complete Dead Sea Scrolls in English.*

The first of his several books on Jesus was *Jesus the Jew: A Historian's Reading of the Gospels*, published in 1973. Strange as it seems today, *Jesus the Jew* was at the time an unsettling title to Christian readers accustomed to thinking of Jesus as founder of a *new* religion, *their* religion, and as one who had both rejected and been rejected by the Jews of his day. That Jesus was Jew*ish* was undeniable, but to call him *a Jew* seemed tasteless, even a little shocking. In Christian America and Britain in the late twentieth century Jesus Christ was understood in much the same way as he was in the Roman world of the late first century, when he was characterized by the writers of the New Testament as scourge of the "scribes and Pharisees", killed at the behest of "the Jews". But in *Jesus the Jew* Vermes distinguishes between the Christian Jesus created by a church that had been ejected from Judaism and the all-Jewish Jesus of the 20s CE who had preached as a Jewish rabbi to Jews, taught Jews from the Jewish scriptures, upheld the Jewish law, worshipped the Jewish god YHWH, promised the imminent restoration of the kingdom foretold by Jewish prophets, and had likened the preaching of the gospel to gentiles as putting pearls before swine.

Vermes has refined this portrait over several books, and the substance of his argument is nowhere better expressed than in a key chapter of *The Changing Face of Jesus* (2001) titled "Beneath the Gospels". The Jesus of the biblical gospels, says Vermes, is a thoroughly theologized Jesus, a Jesus well on the way to his ultimate "elevation... to the rank of the second person of the triune Godhead, the Holy Trinity". Late-first-century documents conceal rather than reveal the Jesus of half a century earlier. "In other words, it is to be feared that not even a highly critical treatment of the New Testament evidence can enable the most adroit historian to re-convert the Christ of the Gospels - even the Jesus of Mark, who is the least concealed - into the real, tangible, flesh-and-blood person who once used to walk on the rocky and dusty paths of first-century rural Galilee"[1]. If only Jesus had written his own gospel, or left us a synopsis of his message! If only the so-called "Jesus Papers" or the letter once claimed to have been written by him to Abgar, king of Edessa, were not patently spurious! If only...

So is a full recovery of the personality of Jesus of Nazareth now beyond anyone's reach? Is the quest for "the real Jesus" a fool's game? The above quotation seems to imply exactly that. But Vermes evidently believes the almost-impossible is worth attempting. He boldly sub-titles this chapter "The real Jesus", a Jesus we can now only hope to find in the real conditions, the total reality, of the Jewish world of his day. "By recreating the milieu of his time, we may be able to catch a glimpse" - compare once again Funk's "glimpse of a glimpse" - "of what he really was. So we must try to retrieve the atmosphere he breathed, together with the ideas and ideals which animated his small world of people living in first-century Palestine, and especially in the backwaters of Galilee: their religious dreams and petty jealousies, and - particularly in Galilee - their love of (relative) independence springing from a freedom from immediate Roman rule and the direct influence of the distant Judaean priestly authority, and from the doctrinal domination of the urban intellectual classes represented by the Pharisees"[2].

As we have seen, "context" was also a key component of the quest for Crossan, Borg, Sanders, Meier, and many of their predecessors. But for Vermes it was, and remains, the *only* component, the master-key that alone can unlock the door we must open if we are to penetrate "beneath the Gospels" and their muddled metaphysics and glimpse "the real, tangible, flesh-and-blood" son of Mary and Joseph.

So Vermes begins, not with Jesus' reported sayings, nor his reported deeds, nor with a side-quest for "early Christianities" in Q, M, L, early-Mark, early-Thomas, early-Peter, but with a broader base of evidence for assessing "the age of Jesus", before turning to see how Jesus himself might fit into what we can discover about his world and his time. First he looks at Galilee, then at popular religion, then at "models of charismatic holy men", all "in the age of Jesus" - and what he comes up with is distinctly different in emphasis from both Crossan's Hellenized context and the world of the Jewish-but-universalist Jesus of Borg and Wright.

(i) Galilee in the age of Jesus

Since the conquest of the eastern Mediterranean by Alexander the Great in 332 BCE, Jerusalem and the Jewish lands had been thrown open to Greek cultural influences, a process summarized as Hellenization. Hellenistic cities were built along the coast: Gaza, Ascalon, Joppa (Jaffa). Inland, the ancient town of Beth Shean was transformed into the Hellenized city of Scythopolis, Samaria into Sebaste, Amman into Philadelphia. Greeks, Macedonians, Hellenized Phoenicians and Egyptians took up residence alongside the Jewish population. After a further conquest by the Seleucids or Syrian Greeks in 200 BCE the process of creeping Hellenization quickened, reaching a climax when the ruler Antiochus IV looted the temple in 169 and installed a statue of the Greek god Zeus in the sanctuary of Israel's god. Although the Jewish revolt that followed, led by the Maccabees, drove the Seleucids out of Judea, re-established an independent Jewish state and restored the worship of Yahweh, Hellenism had become the dominant culture of the known world and continued unabated in Israel. When Pompey transformed the Jewish state into a Roman province in 63 BCE, positions of power, both religious and political, passed into safe and collaborative Greco-Roman hands. In 37 BCE Rome installed Herod the Great as king of all the Jewish lands, but after his death in 4 BCE and the deposition in 6 CE of his successor Herod Archelaus for misgovernment, the kingdom was divided. It was at this time that Judea was placed under direct Roman rule, while Galilee was granted considerable autonomy under Herod the Great's son, the "ethnarch" or under-king Antipas.

Like Sanders, Geza Vermes emphasizes this semi-independence enjoyed by Galilee throughout Jesus' lifetime. "As long as the tributes were paid the Roman overlords did not interfere with [Antipas's] running of the country, which continued to enjoy comparative freedom and autonomy". This political independence was matched by an independence of spirit. Galilee was surrounded by unfriendly territory. To the west lay the coastal strip; to the north Phoenicia (Lebanon), and to the east the confederation of ten Greek city-states known as the Decapolis. All were thoroughly Hellenized: gentiles of all nationalities, but generally lumped together and referred to by Jews as "Greeks", mixed with Jews in the towns and cities, and Jews were by now to be found throughout the eastern Mediterranean. To the south of Galilee was Samaria, ethnically Jewish but intermarried with gentiles and considered hostile and dangerous: a good Samaritan was a dead Samaritan to all but the story-teller Jesus.

"Inhabiting a Jewish island in the midst of a Gentile sea," says Vermes, "the Galileans were renowned for their fighting spirit and chauvinism... Its remoteness from the center and the rugged mountains of Upper Galilee seem to have made of the area an ideal home for revolutionaries". Josephus, who had been commander-in-chief of the revolutionary Galilean forces against Rome in the 60s CE before turning his coat, taking a pension from the emperor and reinventing himself as an historian, praised the bravery of the inhabitants who, he said, were trained to war from childhood. An uprising shortly before Jesus' birth was put down and (again according to Josephus) no fewer than 2000 leading rebels were crucified. Another uprising in 6 CE, at the time of the tax registration wrongly connected by Luke with the census he ingeniously used to get Mary and Joseph from Nazareth to Bethlehem (in order to square his account with an obscure scriptural prophecy that the messiah would be born in "David's city"), led to the launching of the Zealots' movement, which forbade Jews to pay taxes to Caesar.

So, says Vermes, "It is easy to understand... that the Galilean origin and messianic reputation of Jesus, as well as the fact that one of his apostles was nicknamed 'the Zealot', had sinister connotations in the eyes of those [the collaborationist rulers] whose principal aim was to secure the goodwill of the Romans towards the Jewish people in Palestine"[3].

If Galilee was something of a nation of free spirits, it was also reputed to be a green and pleasant land, at least in the southern half (Lower Galilee), where agriculture flourished. Vermes again cites Josephus: "The land is everywhere so rich in soil and pasturage and produces such variety of trees, that even the most indolent are tempted by these facilities to devote themselves to agriculture. In fact, every inch of the soil has been cultivated... there is not a parcel of waste land". Josephus waxed even more lyrical about the low-lying coastal plain around the shores of Galilee and the little fishing village of Capernaum: "There is not a plant which its fertile soil refuses to produce... The air is so well-tempered that it suits the most opposite varieties. The walnut, a tree which delights in the most wintry climate, here grows luxuriantly, besides palm-trees, which thrive on heat, and figs and olives, which require a milder atmosphere. One might say that nature had taken pride in thus assembling, by a *tour de force*, the most discordant species in a single spot, and that, by a happy rivalry, each of the seasons wished to claim this region for her own... For ten months without intermission it supplies those kings of fruits, the grape and the fig; the rest mature on the trees the whole year round. Beside being favored by its genial air, the country is watered by a highly fertilizing spring, called by the inhabitants Capharnaum"[4].

Capharnaum or Capernaum was, of course, Jesus' "own city" (in reality a village), according to Mark (2:1) and Matthew (9:1). And the grapes, figs and corn were the raw materials of his parables, drawn from everyday life. Galilee had its own distinctive culture. Contrary to the views of scholars who stress the penetration of Greek and Roman culture, Vermes insists that outside the few urban areas little or no Greek was spoken. "The idea that the Galileans were bilingual... is not based on any factual evidence... [and] as for Jesus himself being a Greek speaker, this is a wild flight of fancy". As late as the third century, Christian congregations in the Galilean city of Scythopolis required an interpreter to translate Greek sermons into their own Aramaic. Moreover, "the dialect of Aramaic used in Galilee seems to have been a permanent topic of amusement or sarcasm in Jerusalem circles" (as "provincial" dialects and accents continue to be to this day, almost anywhere in the world). This makes sense of the story of Peter's denial of Jesus in Jerusalem, where he is "betrayed by his speech" as a "foreigner" from Galilee, speaking in the same provincial accent as the condemned man from Nazareth[5].

The religious culture of Galilee, too, was different from that of Judea and Jerusalem: less strict in some observances, less sophisticated, and necessarily less temple-centered. It was noted of other religious leaders, as well as of Jesus, that they did not always pay much attention to conventional religious etiquette. Vermes plays down the conflicts with Pharisees, scribes and legalistic rabbis which loom large in the gospel accounts. There were no rabbinic schools in Galilee in the early first century, he says, and, with few exceptions, "there is no evidence that in the age of Jesus Pharisee luminaries settled in Galilee". Some may have visited from Jerusalem, but "it is highly unlikely that Jesus came across Galilean Pharisees of note during his activity in the province". If he had "mini-conflicts with small-minded local scribes", these were of "negligible importance". This points to an important conclusion for Vermes: "The downfall of Jesus was not religiously but politically motivated"[6].

(ii) Popular religion in the age of Jesus

Under the second of his three sub-heads, Vermes argues that from early biblical times the Jewish religion was practised on two distinct levels, official and popular. The official, institutional form was in the hands of priests, who performed the ritual ceremonies and also acted as judges and teachers. "But parallel to it, and often away from the centers [Galilee, for instance], a popular version of Judaism existed", presided over by "persons believed to be directly chosen by heaven". It was through the medium of the "man of God" (*ish ha-elohim* in the Bible) that the ordinary Israelite could come into more intimate contact with God[7].

According to an illuminating essay by J B Segal, cited by Vermes, these "men of God" were believed to be endowed with a mystic/divine gift enabling them to speak and act on behalf of the deity. Although prophets and seers were seen as chosen by heaven, the performance of miracles was regarded as the best evidence that a man was truly "of God" - and the more spectacular the miracle, the stronger the proof. The ancient prophets Elijah and Elisha were especially venerated as "men of God". They could summon fire from heaven (2 Kings 1:9-10), make a mere handful of grain feed a starving crowd (2 Kings 4:42-4), heal the leper (2 Kings 5:8-14), and even raise the dead (2 Kings 4:32-7). It was when Elijah had brought her dead son back to life that the widow Zarephat knew that he was indeed a true "man of God"[8].

Vermes cites Segal again when it comes to fitting Jesus into this category: "It should be remarked that, like Elijah and Elisha, the 'man of God' *par excellence*, Jesus came from northern Palestine... We have miracles - of the food that is not exhausted, and especially the healing of the sick... Jesus, like the 'men of God', was not deterred by fear of ritual uncleanness from contact with the dead and the sick... Like the 'men of God' of the Old Testament, Jesus stood outside the established order"[9]. We might recall that, in what became the concluding sentence of the Old Testament, Elijah's "second coming" is prophesied by Malachi (4:5-6); that both John the Baptist and Jesus himself were identified by some as the returned and reincarnated Elijah; and that Luke's account (24:51) of Jesus being "carried up into heaven" mirrors the chronicler's story of Elijah hitch-hiking through the galaxy to heaven in a fiery chariot, propelled by a whirlwind (2 Kings 2:11).

Citing further stories from the Apocrypha and Josephus, Vermes shows that the "man of God" remained a vital feature of popular Jewish religion right through the Old Testament period, into the inter-testamental years, and throughout Jesus' lifetime. One obvious reason for this was that the "man of God", along with the priest, provided the only health service available. What we might now call secular medicine existed in the

Middle East, but only for the very rich. Vermes points out that the profession of physician is hardly mentioned in biblical Israel. Sickness, of body or mind, was closely connected with sin and the devil, and it took what we would label supernatural power to heal the body or cast out devils. Apart from sorcerers in league with the devil, the proper agents of healing were, at one level, the priests, who demanded sacrifice, penance and prayer as the price for divine healing, and at the popular level, lay "men of God" who cured illness and cast out devils in God's name. Jesus was clearly one such, says Vermes. Faith in God's power was what was demanded of the patient, and faith, then as now, sometimes proved a spectacular healer.

(iii) Models of charismatic holy men in the age of Jesus

Jesus is best understood then, according to Vermes, as a man of early-first-century Galilee, standing four-square in the tradition of Galilean "men of God", chosen by heaven and validated by miracles. The type is well attested in the Old Testament and the Apocrypha, and these "biblical and post-biblical antecedents are highly illuminating in the attempt to understand Jesus". But, Vermes acknowledges, they would be "somewhat theoretical without the support of more or less contemporary figures with whom Jesus can be compared"[10]. He finds just such near-contemporary charismatic holy men in the rabbinic literature (see Cameo, *The Mishnah and the Talmud*), particularly in the persons of Honi the Circle-Drawer and Hanina ben Dosa. Such men "were treated as the willing or unsophisticated heirs to an ancient prophetic tradition. Their supernatural powers were attributed to their immediate relation to God. They were venerated as a link between heaven and earth independent of any institutional mediation"[11].

Honi was a first-century BCE *hasid* or holy man "so close to God that his prayer exhibited miraculous efficacy. Therefore people in need came to solicit his help, especially in periods of drought when it was feared that all the crops might fail and a disastrous famine threatened". The Mishnah records one such miracle. Josephus adds another anecdote, reporting how Honi's piety and courage led to a martyr's death when he refused to take sides in a vicious civil war between the followers of the high priest Aristobulus II and his brother Hyrcanus in 65 BCE. Honi (or Onias, as Josephus calls him, using the Hellenized form) was captured by Hyrcanus, who hoped to utilize his powers as a miracle-worker by having him curse Aristobulus in the name of the God of Israel. Instead, Honi prayed aloud, beseeching God as Lord of both parties to remain neutral - whereupon, says Josephus, "the villains... who stood around him stoned him to death"[12].

Honi is presented in rabbinic literature as if he were the founder of a dynasty of wonder-workers. His grandsons also had a reputation as charismatic rain-makers, and one of them, Abba Hilkiah, is linked in one story to "a Hasid from Kefar Imi", a village which figures in a Galilean context in the Talmud. Vermes acknowledges that nothing is said directly about the geographical origin of Honi and his family, but the implication is that they too, like Jesus, may have been Galileans[13].

The second of Vermes's *hasidim* is Hanina ben Dosa, "probably a younger contemporary of Jesus, from the town of Araba or Gabara, about a dozen miles north of Nazareth... The earliest layers of the rabbinic tradition depict him not only as a holy man who, like Honi and his grandchildren, could miraculously bring rain and stop it again, but as a person of outstanding devotion who was a famous healer and a master over the demonic powers. He was, in short, rabbinic Judaism's most prominent wonder-worker". It was said that Hanina was once bitten by a poisonous snake while praying. He continued his prayers unharmed - and the snake was found dead at the entrance of its hole. Another story has him changing vinegar into oil. In another, he controls the activities of Agrat, queen of the demons, by forbidding her to prowl the streets at night - except on the Sabbath and Wednesdays!

Of several healings, the most renowned was that of the son of Gamaliel (probably, says Vermes, the great teacher mentioned in Acts

5:34 and claimed by Paul as his mentor). Gamaliel sent two pupils to beg Hanina to pray for the boy and he told them to return home, "for the fever has left him". On arrival they found the boy alive and well. Gamaliel asked at what hour Hanina had prayed for his recovery and they told him the precise time, which, conveniently, they had written down. "By Heaven," cried Gamaliel, "it was at that very hour the fever left him and he asked us for water to drink". As Vermes points out, the story is strikingly similar to that in John 4:46-53 and Luke 7:1-10 where Jesus heals the son of a centurion (says Luke) or nobleman (says John) at Capernaum, again at a distance, again by prayer, and again with the result that the child is found to have recovered at the precise hour of supernatural intervention[14]. Finally, some texts in the Talmud describe a heavenly voice calling Hanina "my son", and, like Jesus, both Honi and Hanina are regularly likened to Elijah.

Vermes offers a general sketch of all such charismatic Jewish wonder-workers and "men of God": "In addition to the proverbial humility and unworldliness, poverty was one of their hallmarks. They lived frugally and had scarcely enough to eat... Hanina's weekly food ration was one *kab* (the equivalent in volume of two pints or 1.2 litres) of carob beans, the poor man's diet... and it was rumoured that he was unable to afford bread even for the Sabbath... The Hasidim lived in a state of total detachment from earthly possessions and were ready to share with others the little they had. They professed as their philosophy, 'What is mine is yours, and what is yours is yours...' They rated piety higher than mere ritual... [some] extolled sexual abstinence among the Hasidic virtues... But above all the Hasid was famous for his prayer, which was believed to be all-powerful, capable of performing miracles and revealing his closeness to God, the heavenly Father". It is into this complex model that Vermes fits Jesus. "Many of these traits reflect the Synoptic portrait of Jesus, in particular the absence of anxiety for daily needs, the divesting oneself of riches, even the lack of a home where he could lay his head and the conviction that faith can perform miracles"[15]. Jesus was a Jewish

Cameo: The Mishnah and the Talmud

Some time after the disastrous revolts against Rome and the destruction of Jerusalem and the temple in 70CE, Judaism faced the need for radical readjustment in a world where, in the absence of a single center of religious authority, there was a danger of religious anarchy. During what became known as the rabbinic period, efforts were made to focus Jewish religious identity on agreed teachings and law. While the Hebrew scriptures provided a stable source of teaching, the law was at first transmitted orally and tended to differ from place to place. During the second century CE the first attempts were made to collect and reconcile these different versions. Early in the third century Judah ha-Nasi edited what became the basis of an "authorized version" known as "Our Mishnah" (Hebrew "teaching"), embodying many earlier collections. The text contains several different styles from different periods and locations, and a range of opinions and viewpoints. Although it seems likely that Judah ha-Nasi's version was committed to writing, some commentators believe it was taught orally and only written down centuries later, after many amendments and variations. A "stable" version had to await its first printing in 1492. The result is that there is a wide range of scholarly opinion as to how much of the Mishnah of the third and subsequent centuries was known and applied as early as the first and second centuries.

*Between around 200 and 500 CE the scholars and teachers who interpreted the Mishnah were known as **amoraim** (Aramaic for "spokesmen"). Their discussions, debates and interpretations were recorded in what became known as the "Talmud" (Hebrew "learning"). Two versions of the Talmud developed, one in Jerusalem and Palestine around 500, the other in Babylon*

*(Baghdad) around 600. The Babylonian version achieved supremacy by the eleventh century. It consists of some two and a half million words and is described in **The Oxford Dictionary of World Religions** as "an extraordinary historical source, including folklore, manners, customs, popular proverbs, prayers, ceremonial, and medical remedies". The **amoraim** ordained by the Sanhedrin in Palestine were given the title "Rabbi", and those in Babylonia "Rav".*

As with the Mishnah, the problems of dating events, stories, individuals or particular teachings in the Talmud have long exercised modern scholars. How accurate and authentic is a sixth-century account of a first-century event likely to be? The critical problems involved are of the same, or even greater order, than those facing biblical scholars seeking early-first-century authenticity in late-first-century and second-century writings about Jesus.

"man of God", a *hasim*, a charismatic holy man: one in a long tradition.

Vermes' thesis did not convince all scholars when it was first set out in *Jesus the Jew*. Critics pointed out that while ben Dosa lived in the first century, the Talmudic writings about him date from the third century at the earliest. If the gospels' accounts of Jesus are questionable, as written after a gap of twenty to forty years or more, how much more historically contentious are stories of ben Dosa and Honi written not decades but hundreds of years later? As Mark Allan Powell comments, "The suspicion of many historians, then, is that legends about these men grew over time, possibly in response to the stories Christians told about Jesus. The late traditions regarding Honi and Hanina contain accounts similar to those in the Gospels precisely because Jewish writers wanted to create Galilean holy men of their own who would be on a par with Jesus. John Meier is one scholar who has considered Vermes' thesis carefully only to dismiss it: 'Ultimately, Vermes' acritical use of the sources undermines his whole argument'"[16].

Vermes fights back in *The Changing Face of Jesus*. "By using the descriptions of the two men given in the Mishnah and the Talmud, I am, need I say, perfectly aware of the time factor: most of the written sources postdate them by several centuries. Therefore I will not argue on the basis of details, but from typology which is verifiable in all the periods from the age of the prophets down to that of the rabbis"[17]. In other words, Vermes is not assuming or arguing that the stories of Honi's and Hanina's miracles are historically authentic, any more than he would argue that the stories of Jesus are factually true. The story of Hanina's night encounter with the queen of the demons, for instance, "has the form of a folk legend"[18]. Nor does Vermes expressly dismiss the possibility that the rabbis "borrowed" from the Jesus stories to elevate men like Hanina to a similar status as a "man of God". He is well aware that we know both the Honi/Hanina and the Jesus stories only through later elaborations, accretions, likely inventions - and folk legends. But the stories, as stories, testify to the existence in Jewish tradition of a *type* of miracle-worker, *hasid*, "man of God". Acknowledging and understanding this typology, Vermes maintains, is crucial to understanding where and how the historical Jesus fits into his place, time and religious culture. Vermes is not alone in this. Marcus Borg and John Dominic Crossan both make use of the Honi and Hanina parallels and Borg makes Vermes' category of "charismatic holy man" a major component of his own complex reconstruction of Jesus.

Another criticism of Vermes' thesis, more theological than historical, is that it tends to deny Jesus' uniqueness, reducing him to just one of a kind, "a pale Galilean charismatic, nothing more". Vermes had preemptively rebutted this in *Jesus the Jew*, where he describes Jesus as "second to none in profundity of insight and grandeur of character" and as "an unsurpassed master of the art of laying bare the inmost core of spiritual truth and of bringing back to the essence of religion, the existential relationship of man and man, and man and God"[19]. He repeats this in *The Changing Face of Jesus*, and adds several pages pointing out the *differences* between other *hasidim* and Jesus. This culminates in the eloquent "final distinguishing touch to the portrait of Jesus" in the Cameo: *Vermes' Jesus as Highest and Holiest*, on page 317.

It needs to be said that Vermes' portrait of the historical Jesus, as elaborated over a series of books, is substantially more multifaceted than may appear from this chapter alone. I have emphasized his characterization of Jesus as a charismatic Jewish "man of God" - healer, wonder-worker and teacher - because that is recognized by fellow-scholars as the most distinctive of Vermes' contributions to Jesus scholarship. But in another substantial volume, *The Authentic Gospel of Jesus* (2003), Vermes invades Jesus Seminar territory by subjecting every recorded word of Jesus to detailed scrutiny in order to produce his own "Classification of the Sayings of Jesus"[20]. If his classification is literally less colorful than that of the Seminar, it has its similarities. Sayings considered "authentic or possibly authentic" (the Seminar's red and pink) are marked with an asterisk (*). Others are described as "editorial" - the work of a later editor - of which some are "possibly genuine but heavily reworked", and others "almost certainly inauthentic" (the Seminar's gray or black), reflecting not the point of view of Jesus but that of the early church.

Vermes precedes his classification with a caution. "Any attempt to reconstruct a word-for-word version of the sayings of Jesus is, I believe, a waste of time. The aim is unattainable because the original source, a written Aramaic collection of the sayings, if it ever existed, is no longer available. All we have is a secondary Greek reconstruction. In a domain such as this, at a distance of two thousand years, certainties are beyond the scholar's reach. The least unrealistic task is to weigh up and rank probabilities"[21].

Where Vermes and the Jesus Seminar are furthest apart is, as one might expect, in their different classification of the kingdom sayings.

Cameo: Vermes' Jesus as "highest and holiest"

"Jesus stood head and shoulders above them [Honi and Hanina]. Indeed, let it be understood at the outset that he was not the meek and mild figure of popular Christian imagination. As we have seen, he could be determined, impatient and angry. He inherited the strength, the iron character and fearlessness of his predecessors, the prophets. Like Amos facing up to the priest of Bethel (Amos 7:10-17) and Jeremiah prophesying doom in the face of King Jehoiakim (Jer. 36), Jesus was not afraid to stand up to the powerful. He showed love to children whom he proposed as models for those who sought to enter the Kingdom of God. He welcomed women and felt pity for the sick and the miserable. He surpassed the prophets. They embraced the weak, the poor, the widow, the fatherless; Jesus went further and bravely extended a hand of friendship to the social outcasts, the unclean prostitutes and the despised publicans who were kept at arm's length by his hidebound, pious contemporaries. He is depicted as capable of demonstrating extreme emotions. He could be moved by pity and by anger; he let his fury fly and strike opponents and critics. Slowness in comprehension, let alone lack of understanding, especially on the part of his chosen disciples, often made him indignant. He is on one occasion depicted as being quite unreasonable. When hungry, he apparently cursed a fig tree for being without fruit, although it was not the season for figs (Mark 11:12-14). Or maybe as a Galilean, used to the availability of figs ten months out of twelve, he forgot that Jerusalem at 800 metres above sea-level had a harsher climate than the lakeside! Jesus was a man of steel and warmth at the same time, and a total devotee of God whose perfection and mercy he set out to imitate...

To add the final distinguishing touch to the portrait of the real

Jesus, emphasis should be placed on the eschatological vision and stimulus of his message which, together with the tragic finale on the cross, invest it with a unique urgency and actuality. Proclaiming not just the nearness, but the virtual and more than once the actual presence of the Kingdom of God, he showed himself an incomparable charismatic and religious teacher. His magnetic appeal became more powerful after his death than it could ever have been during his transient ministry in the late twenties of the first century in the Galilee of Herod Antipas and the Jerusalem of Joseph Caiaphas, the high priest, and Pontius Pilate, the imperial legate of Judea.

The face of this Jesus, truly human, wholly theocentric, passionately faith-inspired and under the imperative impulse of the here and now, impressed itself so deeply on the minds of his disciples that not even the shattering blow of the cross could arrest its continued real presence. It compelled them to carry on in his name with their mission as healers, exorcists and preachers of the Kingdom of God. It was only a generation or two later, with the increasing delay of the Parousia [the second coming], that the image of the Jesus familiar from experience began to fade, covered over first by the theological and mystical dreamings of Paul and John, and afterwards by the dogmatic speculations of church-centred Gentile Christianity." -

The Changing Face of Jesus, pp 253-4, 257-8

Vermes sees most of the apocalyptic sayings as "authentic or possibly authentic", where the Seminar marks them black or gray. Vermes lists 60 such sayings, 33 of which get the asterisk of likely authenticity; only four of these muster a Seminar pink (including the key text Luke 17:20-21 - "the kingdom is among you"). The remaining 27 kingdom sayings are considered inauthentic by both parties. Of 40 parable stories and sayings,

18 get a Vermes asterisk and 13 of these a Seminar pink or red. Of 36 "wisdom sayings", 26 are asterisked, of which 18 are Seminar red/pinked. Both camps interpret nearly all Jesus' scripture quotations as editorial. But many of these authentic/inauthentic classifications are qualified or nuanced, and the devil is always in the detail.

2. Hyam Maccoby: Jesus the Pharisee

To most lay students, Geza Vermes' Jewish Jesus is *the* Jewish Jesus. But his portrait is far from universally accepted among Jewish Jesus-scholars. We shall look at the conclusions of two who take a very different view from Vermes, and from each other. Hyman Maccoby is a research professor at the Center for Jewish Studies, Leeds, and author of several books on rabbinic literature, Jewish-Christian relations, early Christianity, and the origins of anti-semitism. His argument that Jesus was not only a Jewish teacher but a practising Pharisee is spelt out in the title of his book, *Jesus the Pharisee*. He acknowledges that in writing it he has built on the life-work of Paul Winter, whom he describes as the first major scholar to assert that "in historical fact, Jesus was a Pharisee"[22].

Maccoby recognizes that this "historical fact" flies in the face of a host of highly critical references to the Pharisees in the New Testament gospels, many of them reported sayings of Jesus himself. Indeed, the long history of Christian anti-semitism "derives very substantially from the Gospel picture of the Pharisees. The very word 'Pharisee' exists in the English language, and other languages, as a synonym for everything contemptible, especially hypocrisy... so that it is impossible for any English-speaking child to grow up without absorbing a strongly pejorative sense of the word"[23]. But Maccoby draws attention to some telling New Testament references which seem to contradict the familiar condemnations and woes, and by interpreting these in the context of later rabbinic writings builds his distinctive thesis. One example on which he relies heavily is the story in Acts 5: 34-40 where Peter and other apostles are brought before the high priest and council (the Sanhedrin) and accused of disobeying the high priest's explicit ban on preaching the doctrines of Jesus. Peter replies that God has decreed otherwise, and "We ought to obey God rather than men". The inference that Peter and the apostles regard the high priest and his council as speaking against God's commandments so enrages the Sanhedrin that it debates a proposal to put the prisoners to death. Then (in the New English Bible translation used here by Maccoby) "a member of the Council rose to his feet, a Pharisee called Gamaliel, a teacher of the law held in high regard by all the people". Gamaliel reminds the Sanhedrin that others before Peter had claimed to be from God, citing rebellions by Thaddeus[24] and Judas of Galilee, both of which had come to nothing. Best, then, he argues, to wait and see in the case of Peter and the apostles. "For if this idea of theirs or its execution is of human origin, it will collapse; but if it is from God, you will never be able to put them down, and you risk finding yourselves at war with God". Gamaliel's plea for mercy (or play for time) prevails and the prisoners are released - after having a warning beaten into them not to preach the doctrines of Jesus again.

Maccoby notes that while the author of Acts describes Gamaliel as merely "a member of the Council" and "a Pharisee", rabbinic literature has him as leader of the whole Pharisee movement. Maccoby suggests that Luke deliberately played down Gamaliel's status, in line with the anti-Pharisee polemic of the rest of his book, but was unable to omit the story altogether because it was so well attested. Whatever Luke's intention, Maccoby argues, Gamaliel's plea on Peter's behalf reveals a hidden truth: (i) Gamaliel was in sympathy with Peter, (ii) since Gamaliel was the leader of the Pharisee party, the Pharisees as a whole were in sympathy with Peter, and (iii) if they were in sympathy with Peter they must have been in sympathy with the Jesus movement, and so with Jesus himself. Therefore the gospels' portrait of Jesus as a bitter critic of the Pharisees is a lie, as is the calumny that the Pharisees hated him and were out to get him. "If Jesus had indeed been the person depicted in the

Gospels as a blasphemer and Sabbath-breaker who so aroused the hatred and anger of the Pharisees that they constantly sought his death, why did the leader of the Pharisees defend Jesus' chief disciple and even state that Peter's advocacy might be 'from God'?" The answer: "Gamaliel is asserting his approval of the Jesus movement as showing no trace of heresy, and therefore as sharing the main tenets of the Pharasaic movement itself"[25].

Maccoby draws far-reaching conclusions from this one incident. First, "it means that Peter was not advocating Jesus as a divine Messiah, but merely as a human messiah whose aim was to liberate the Jews from the Roman yoke... Jesus' movement... had no aim of abolishing the Jewish religion". Second, "another implication... is that the trial of Jesus himself never happened". The reasoning is that "if Peter, Jesus's chief disciple, was defended by the leader of the Pharisees at a meeting of the Sanhedrin on a charge of being a follower of Jesus, where were the Pharisees, and particularly Gamaliel, at the trial of Jesus himself? If Gamaliel saw no harm in the Jesus movement, how could he have seen any harm in the founder of the movement, Jesus? If such a trial had taken place, would [Gamaliel] not have given the same reasons for acquitting Jesus, and declared that his messianic claim should be judged by its results and that it might turn out to be 'from God'?... Does not this show that no such charge was ever made against Jesus?... This incident alone, if taken seriously, is sufficient to invalidate the majority of the Gospel story: the alleged conflict between Jesus and the chief Jewish religious authorities, that is, the Pharisees, the alleged trial of Jesus as a blasphemer, the concept of Jesus' mission as a divine visitant intent on suffering crucifixion in order to bring salvation, and the alleged responsibility of the Jews, rather than the Romans, as the betrayers and killers of Jesus, a charge that gave rise to the demonization of the Jews"[26].

This is revisionism on a sweeping scale; but Maccoby is not content to argue that there were affinities between the Pharisees and the Jesus movement which the gospels hide. He asserts that Jesus himself was an obedient member of the dominant tendency within Judaism, a proper card-carrying member of the Pharisees' party. He cites Jesus' insistence, difficult to reconcile with the view that he was fundamentally at odds with Judaism, that the Jewish law was to be followed to the letter - exactly as the Pharisees insisted: "Till heaven and earth pass, one jot or one tittle shall in no wise pass from the law, till all be fulfilled". Only those whose righteousness exceeded that of the Pharisees had any chance of entering the kingdom of heaven (Matt. 5:18-20). This, says Maccoby, is an endorsement of both Pharisee law-observance and Pharisee right-eousness, since there would be no point in Jesus telling his hearers they must be more righteous than those he was denouncing as hypocrites. So, "Since Jesus is... recommending his listeners to follow the teaching of the Pharisees in every detail, we can safely conclude that he did this himself and that he was therefore a practising member of the Pharisee movement"[27]. QED.

Maccoby offers several more examples. There is Mark's story (12:28-34) of a lawyer who questions Jesus on what he would regard as the greatest commandment. Jesus answers that it is to "love the Lord your God with all your heart, with all your soul, and with all your strength", and adds a second commandment: "Love your neighbor as yourself". The lawyer replies "Well said, Master... that is far more than any burnt offerings or sacrifices", and "when Jesus saw how sensibly he answered, he said to him, 'You are not far from the kingdom of God'". As Mark has it, the exchange is mutually supportive - a friendly chat, Maccoby suggests, between two Pharisees. Maccoby takes "lawyer" as "a term used as an alternative to Pharisee both in the Gospels and in later Christian literature", and points out that in the later version of the story in Matthew 22: 34-40 Jesus' questioner is explicitly described as "one of the Pharisees". Matthew's version, however, omits the friendly exchange. Instead, the Pharisee is depicted as craftily testing Jesus, trying to catch him out. Maccoby draws two conclusions from the two versions: first, "there was no disagreement between Jesus and the Pharisees", and second, "there is a process of editing going on in the Gospels to make it appear that there was"[28]. It is this process of editing, he argues, reflecting the bitter rivalry between "Christians" and Pharisees at the *end* of the first century, that is responsible for all the anti-Pharisee stories scattered throughout the gospels and Acts.

But Maccoby's trump card is not the few apparently pro-Pharisee references that somehow survived the handiwork of late-first-century editors. His speciality is the rabbinic literature - the Mishnah and the Talmud - and it is here that he finds what he regards as clinching evidence of agreement between Jesus and Pharisaic Judaism. Like Geza Vermes, he takes issue with the view of many scholars that these writings, because they were collected and edited centuries after the events they describe and comment on, are unreliable when it comes to reconstructing first-century Judaism. Maccoby goes further than Vermes, arguing that the late written collections are of early orally-transmitted stories and laws, and that there is no reason to suppose they suffered significant change or revision. On the contrary, he sees second-century and subsequent rabbinic Judaism as a direct continuity of first-century Judaism, which he argues was predominantly Pharisaic. (Josephus was misleading, he thinks, to describe the Pharisees as merely one of three sects, alongside the Sadducees and the Essenes. Rather, in Maccoby's view, already in the early-first-century they were the dominant mainstream). Their doctrine and practice carried over not only into rabbinic Judaism but into the Jewish Christianity of the Jerusalem church, before it was overwhelmed by the gentile Christianity of Paul and John.

The rabbinic literature includes parables, aphorisms, language about the kingdom of God, stories of miracle-working, resistance to Roman rule, promises of a coming deliverance - everything that Christian scholars have tended to see as peculiarly or primarily characteristic of Jesus and the early Jesus movement. "It is an extraordinary fact that while Jesus is portrayed in the Gospels as a strong opponent of the Pharisees, he himself is the most recognizable Pharisee in the whole of first-century

Jewish literature... His style of preaching (with parables) and even his modes of expression are so consonant with the style of the rabbinic literature that they alone constitute evidence that rabbinic modes of thought did not begin in the second century (as many would like to think) but already existed in the first century, and that therefore the constant claim of the rabbis that their spiritual roots lay with the Pharisees of the first century has much to recommend it"[29].

Geza Vermes, as we have seen, draws heavily on the rabbinic literature to picture Jesus as a *hasid* (or *chasid*), like Elijah and Elisha before him and Honi and Hanina in his own time. But Maccoby parts company with him, suggesting he makes the "mistake" of assuming that the *hasidim* were separate from, and opposed to, the Pharisee movement, thereby taking Jesus out of Pharisaism. Maccoby charges that "The many admiring stories about the Chasidim in Pharisee literature were discounted by Vermes as disguising the irreconcilable conflict that actually existed between the Pharisees and the Chasidim. The admiration expressed in these stories was interpreted as interpolations; the later rabbis wished to take advantage of the high reputation of the Chasidim by pretending that they too were Pharisees, and therefore they 'rabbinized' these figures and played down the tension and conflict that historically existed between them and the Pharisees. This approach had the advantage, too, of explaining why the Gospels are so anti-Pharisee, and portray Jesus as in serious conflict with the Pharisees". This mistake of Vermes, says Maccoby, led to "a whole new school of New Testament scholars" who have "sought to recover the Chasidim as highly idiosyncratic individuals who had little or nothing in common with the Pharisees" - a school that includes such very different interpreters from Vermes as Marcus Borg and other prominent members of the Jesus Seminar. On the contrary, says Maccoby, the positive accounts of the *hasidim* in the rabbinic literature should be taken at face value as proving that the holy charismatics were part of the rabbinic/Pharisee movement.[30]

This points to the conclusion that Jesus himself was a Pharisee, "but

Cameo: Jesus, the prostitute's fee and the High Priest's privy: a dirty joke

Hyam Maccoby suggests that early rabbinic literature probably contained a considerable body of Jesus stories and Jesus sayings, but when the Jesus movement was declared heretical Jesus lost his status as a rabbi of authority and most of his sayings never made it into the edited Mishnah and Talmud. But he finds one that did: a story of Jesus's witty response to a query about dirty money.

*The story ("which may have been imperfectly preserved", says Maccoby, but "in its kernel [is] very historically reliable") is told and discussed in **Jesus the Pharisee** pp. 144-152 and attributed to Avodah Zarah 16b in the Babylonian Talmud, about 500 CE. (A less earthy version appears in Midrash Qohelet Rabbah, 1: 8).*

Around 100 CE an eminent rabbi, Eliezer ben Hyrcanus, was arrested by the Romans on suspicion of being a Christian. Although found innocent, he concluded that he must have committed some sin to deserve such an experience, which he interpreted as a punishment from God. His pupil, Rabbi Akiva, suggested that perhaps someone had quoted a saying of some heretic to him, and he had received it with pleasure instead of repudiating it. Eliezer then remembered that he had met a disciple of Jesus called Jacob of Kefar Sakhnaya in a street in Sepphoris, near Nazareth. They had a conversation about whether it was lawful for the temple authorities to accept tainted money, such as fees earned by a prostitute. Jacob reported that Jesus had given an answer by quoting the prophet Malachi: "For she gathered it of the hire of a harlot, and they shall return to the hire of a harlot" (1:7). Jacob said Jesus had interpreted this somewhat obscure text to mean that if dirty money was offered to the temple it should not be entirely rejected as unworthy but should be used in a manner

> *consistent with its vulgar origin, such as building a privy for the high priest. Eliezer had enjoyed the joke - until he understood that by giving the teaching of a heretic a sympathetic hearing (presumably with much laughter) he had brought punishment on himself.*
>
> *Evidently the editors who censored most Jesus stories from the Talmud and Midrash found this one too good to lose. Perhaps they calculated that its picture of Jesus as a vulgar joker rather than a holy hasid condemned him out of his own mouth.*

an unusual one in that he belonged to a minority group of Pharisees known as Chasidim". Maccoby concedes that he was also unusual in that he had "active messianic hopes in which he himself played a central role". Nevertheless, Maccoby insists, Jesus was a prominent Pharisee, a major figure in the dominant mainstream Judaism of his day, and not, like Vermes' Jesus, a charismatic rebel against religious authority, or like Crossan's Jesus, "a kind of Diogenes figure, a wandering hippy or self-elected outcast, who despised all norms and authorities, and saw himself in the role of a peasant philosopher similar to the Greek Cynics"[31].

Maccoby's Jesus-as-holy-Pharisee has evoked some interest, but most scholars appear to be unconvinced. If Vermes is criticized for "acritical" use of second- to sixth-century rabbinic literature to illuminate early-first-century Judaism, Maccoby seems even more open to the accusation. His interpretations of the Gamaliel incident and the "friendly" conversation with the Pharisee/lawyer seem somewhat strained. His argument for a direct line of continuity between the Pharisees and the rabbinic teachers remains controversial among Jewish scholars, and that for a parallel continuity between Pharisees and the early Jerusalem church equally contentious among New Testament historians. Finally, his identification of the *hasidim* as good Pharisees, necessary as it is to his thesis, seems to rely on conjecture rather than evidence. But Jesus the Pharisee has joined Jesus the sage, Jesus the prophet of end-time, and Jesus the stand-up comic as one more candidate for the title of the real historical Jesus.

3. Robert Eisenman: Jesus the brother of James

If Hyam Maccoby's Jesus challenges both old and new historical scholarship, let alone old and new theology, Robert Eisenman's Jesus - if you can catch sight of him - is even more problematic and perplexing.

Eisenman, like Geza Vermes (with whom he otherwise has little in common[32]) came to prominence in Jesus and New Testament studies by way of his pioneer work on the Dead Sea Scrolls. He too took a leading role in exposing the restrictive practices of the small team of scholars who claimed exclusive access to the scrolls and were accused of using their privileged position to maintain control of interpretation, translation and publication. Eisenman, then director of the Institute for the Study of Judeo-Christian Origins at California State University, Long Beach, and subsequently a Fellow of the Albright Institute of Archaeological Research in Jerusalem, was one of the first to obtain facsimiles of key scrolls and was in prime position to study the texts and develop his own interpretation of them in relation to other contemporaneous documents, including the New Testament and a wide range of non-biblical material. And his interpretation was certainly distinctive.

After much fierce controversy, a broad consensus had emerged among scholars that most of the scrolls had been written in the first century BCE or earlier. Eisenman, however, controversially proposed a late date for many scrolls (including the important *Habakkuk Commentary*), which would make them contemporary with the beginnings of the Jesus movement. From this he argued that they contained clues not only to the complex nature of early-first-century Judaism in Palestine but also to the origins of Christianity - and, indeed, to the enigmatic person of Jesus himself.

The full fruits of his investigations were published in 1997 in a huge, sprawling, 1074-page blockbuster of a book, *James the Brother of Jesus*. As the title indicates, Eisenman's focus is on James, for whom he argues there are more extensive sources than for any comparable character, including Jesus; but his claim is that once we have unearthed the historical James we find ourselves face to face with his historical brother. Indeed, only *as* James's brother is the historical Jesus visible at all.

Eisenman constructs his historical James by matching the James depicted in the New Testament - mainly Acts - with a host of references he takes to refer to the same James in the Dead Sea Scrolls, the works of Josephus, and non-biblical writings such as the Clementine Recognitions and Homilies, the Apostolic Constitutions, Eusebius, the two James Apocalypses from Nag Hammadi, and even a late version of Acts known as Western Acts. The figure that emerges is very different from, and much more important than, the James who plays a bit-part in Luke's Acts. Indeed, it is Eisenman's thesis that the New Testament writers and the communities to which they belonged deliberately marginalized James, the leader of the Jewish Jesus movement in Jerusalem, in the interests of advancing their own rival gentile Jesus movement led by Paul that had spread throughout the Mediterranean world. He calls this marginalization "one of the most successful rewrite - or overwrite - enterprises ever accomplished"[33] in that it secured the future of Christianity for Paul and his followers, whose faith in a *risen* and *divinized* Jesus eclipsed that of James in his very human and very Jewish brother.

Eisenman sees the James-Paul rivalry not so much as Jewish Christianity versus gentile Christianity but more as a conflict between the "heirs of Jesus" (James and other members of Jesus' family who claimed a kind of hereditary or dynastic leadership of the Jesus movement in Jerusalem) and the "companions of Jesus", the disciples who claimed to be their master's true interpreters. In this he sees a parallel in Islam after Muhammad's death, when his relatives set up a dynastic Caliphate which led to Shi'ite Islam, while "the companions of the Prophet" led what became the Sunni variant. The Jesus movement led by James was the infant church's Shi'ite wing, that led by Paul its Sunni faction.

Eisenman takes the Dead Sea scrolls to be a library of documents representing not just the teachings of one small monastic community at Qumran but the views of a range of sectarian Jewish movements - an "opposition alliance" - loosely grouped together under the umbrella of Essenes. He identifies James as the leader of these groups, either a "parallel" to the mysterious and unnamed "Teacher of Righteousness" in the scrolls or even, he suggests, the Teacher himself[34]. But James is also head of the Jerusalem *ecclesia*, the word originally meaning "community" but later translated as "church". It follows that the Jerusalem *ecclesia* must have been part of the "opposition alliance", or even that *ecclesia* and alliance were one and the same. This would mean that the Jerusalem "church", the Jewish Jesus movement, was essentially Essene - like James himself, "zealous for the Law, xenophobic, rejecting of foreigners and polluted persons generally, and apocalyptic"[35]. It would be closer to the Zealot insurrectionists and the wider liberation movement against Rome than to the non-violent, anti-resistance character of Paul's Hellenized Christianity; closer in style to *The War Scroll* - a key Dead Sea document akin to the Christian book of Revelation, describing with relish the final apocalyptic war against Evil, led by the Messiah and his Heavenly Hosts - than to the gentle Jesus' sermon on the mount, with its blessings on the meek and lowly.

But if this was James's "Christianity", what does that tell us about the brother whose teaching James's community inherited and whose mantle as leader James assumed on the founder's martyrdom? Eisenman answers:

"The proposition would run something like this: let us assume that a Messianic leader known as 'Jesus' did exist in the early part of the first century in Palestine. Furthermore, let us assume that he had brothers, one of whom was called James. Who would have known the character of Jesus better? His closest living relatives, who according to tradition were his legitimate successors in Palestine, and those companions accompanying him in all his activities? Or someone who admits that he never saw Jesus in his lifetime, as Paul does, and that, on the contrary, he was an *Enemy* of and persecuted the early Christian community, and came to know him only through visionary experiences that allowed him to be in touch with a figure he designates as 'Christ Jesus' in Heaven? The answer of any reasonable observer to this question should be obvious: James and Jesus' Palestinian companions".[36]

If James is the Jewish resistance hero, true interpreter and mirror of Jesus, Paul is the arch-villain of the piece. Eisenman suggests that he is the same Saulus who, according to Josephus, was active during the siege of Jerusalem (which would contradict the legend that he had been martyred under Nero some years earlier). He doubts that Paul was really Jewish, and adduces evidence that he was not only thoroughly Romanized but was actually a kinsman of the Herodians, the fake-Jewish quisling royal family, whose interests he secretly served. For good measure, as we have noted, Eisenman's Paul is identified as the "Wicked Priest" and "Lying Spouter" of the scrolls, who repudiated the Law, betrayed the Essene covenant and set himself up as the enemy of the Teacher of Righteousness. One wonders why Eisenman stops short of repeating the calumny put about by Paul's enemies (the Jewish Ebionite Christians) that he only pretended to convert to Judaism because he fancied the high priest's daughter.

James's religion, then, was the religion of his brother Jesus. Since James's religion was one of salvation by works rather than faith alone, a wholly and exclusively Jewish religion, nationalistic, apocalyptic, warning of imminent war in heaven and on earth, that must have been the religion of Jesus, says Eisenman. And that was how "Christianity" was developing within Judaism until the Hellenized pagan Paul came along, saw the potential for creating a new pro-Roman (or at least politically neutered) mystery religion, posed as a Jew, stole the human Jesus and turned him into a divine figure in heaven, to whom he had unique access through visions. The rivalries and conflicts between Paul and James merely hinted at in the New Testament were, on Eisenman's analysis, far more violent and bitter than church apologists, from Luke onwards, have ever allowed us to understand. And it was Paul who came out on top. His letters became new scripture (marginalizing the one letter written in James's name), the narrative gospels were written and edited by his followers, and the church of Rome triumphed over the church of Jerusalem. A "gentilized" Jesus, son of God, replaced the Jewish Jesus, son of Mary and brother of James.

If, indeed, James really had this brother... Eisenman is good at suggesting, hinting, kite-flying, without irrevocably committing himself. Note, for example, the "let us assume that a Messianic leader known as 'Jesus' did exist in the early part of the first century in Palestine", quoted above from his Introduction. "Let us assume" plants the possibility that he *didn't* exist, that he was perhaps an amalgam of Jesuses, even a skilfully contrived fictional family member. Eisenman toys with the admittedly bewildering play of names in the literature; not only the various Marys (including Mary the sister of Mary) and Judases (Judas Iscariot, whom Eisenman thinks did not exist, Judas not-Iscariot, Judas the Galilean, Judas the Twin, etc.), but also the several Jesuses: Jesus the brother of James, Jesus Barabbas, Jesus ben Ananias, Jesus ben Gamala, the sorcerer Elymas bar-Jesus, and so on. Could our Jesus be a conflation of many Jesuses? How secure, in any case, is the generally accepted Jesus chronology?

Without actually committing himself to any of the alternative dates, Eisenman mentions that, according to Josephus, the execution of John the Baptist might have been as late as 35 or 36 CE, which would take Jesus' post-John ministry into the late 30s or even 40s. According to Epiphanius, James's leadership of the Jerusalem church lasted 24 years, which would put Jesus's death in 38 CE if Josephus is right in placing James's execution in 62. Irenaeus reckoned Jesus died at the age of 50 in the reign of Claudius (41-54 CE). But a late work, The Acts of Pilate, puts Jesus' crucifixion as early as 21 CE, while the Talmud has him crucified under Alexander Jannaeus, the great-grandfather of Herod the Great's wife Mariamme, who died in 76 *BCE*! We are left wondering, and it may be Eisenman's intention to leave us wondering (perhaps because *he* is wondering) whether Jesus wasn't the invention of his brother and the Jerusalem church, and the re-invention of Paul.

Eisenman presents his thesis in more than a thousand pages, and develops it further in a follow-up volume, *The New Testament Code: Uncovering the Truth About James the Brother of Jesus and the Dead Sea Scrolls*, published in the United States in 2006 (but still awaiting a British publisher as I write this). As Robert M Price, a sympathetic critic and fellow-scholar, puts it, "*James the Brother of Jesus* often seems too circuitous and redundant, but this is the result of [Eisenman's] having to keep a number of balls in the air at once. He has to begin explaining something here, put it on hold, go to something else that you'll need to plug into the first explanation, then return to it, go on to another, and another, then come back to the earlier items, remind you of them, and then finally assemble the whole complex device. Eisenman is like the Renaissance scientists who had to hand-craft all the intricate parts of a planned invention".

This is a generous way of saying what other scholars have said more astringently: that the arguments are often convoluted, the judgments imaginative, and the conclusions unconvincing. But Price, a Fellow of the Westar Institute and Jesus Seminar, which as a group stands far removed from Eisenman's methodology, ends his review with a positive appraisal: "The book is an ocean of instructive insight and theory, a massive and profound achievement that should open up new lines of New Testament research"[37].

Jesus the Brother of James certainly opened up new lines of specu-lation, if not always research. In his acknowledgments at the start of the book Eisenman thanks one Michael Baigent "for long hours of work labouring over difficult passages and proofs". The same Michael Baigent subsequently co-authored *The Holy Blood and the Holy Grail*, which Dan Brown was accused of plagiarising in *The Da Vinci Code*, and went on to publish *The Jesus Papers*, modestly sub-titled *Exposing the Greatest Cover-up in History*. According to these "papers", what the church (and, it seems, virtually all scholars pre-Baigent) have covered up for two thousand years is the "fact" that Jesus was a political figure trained by anti-Roman freedom-fighters at a secret location in Egypt, that he got religion and started preaching a mystical here-and-now kingdom of heaven somehow related to some tunnels Baigent has explored, that the crucifixion was a trick event staged with the connivance of Pontius Pilate, and that the uncrucified Jesus made it back to Egypt to settle in happy domesticity with Mary Magdalene before finally emigrating to start a new life as an ex-pat in the south of France. That he was not the son of God is proven by two letters written by Jesus himself in Aramaic, explaining that it was all a terrible mistake. Baigent has seen these letters, which were shown to him by an unidentified dealer, but since he couldn't read Aramaic he was unable to verify what would surely have been the scoop to end all scoops, in this world and the next. The anonymous dealer is presumably still looking for a buyer - preferably, I suspect, another scholar who hasn't mastered Aramaic. (Probably a television producer?)

Eisenman's thesis is at least based on real documents, however creatively interpreted, rather than on "now you see it, now you don't" texts plucked from a conjuror's fez. Whether it offers a credible glimpse of Jesus or merely feeds an insatiable appetite for conspiracy theories remains a matter of scholarly judgment and intelligent lay discernment.

Notes to Chapter 10

1 Vermes, *Changing Face* 222

2 as above, 222-3

3 as above, 224-6

4 as above, 224-5

5 as above, 226-8

6 as above, 228-9

7 as above, 230

8 as above, 230

9 as above, 231 citing J B Segal's essay "Popular Religion in Ancient Israel", *Journal of Jewish Studies* 27 (1967), 8-9

10 as above, 237

11 Vermes, *J the Jew* 79

12 Vermes, *Changing Face* 237-9, citing Josephus, *Jewish Antiquities* xiv, 22-4

13 as above, 240

14 as above, 241-6, 13n

15 as above, 240-1

16 Powell, *Debate* 63-4, citing Meier, *A Marginal Jew* vol. 2, 587

17 Vermes, *Changing Face* 228

18 as above, 245

19 Vermes, *J the Jew* 224

20 Vermes, *Authentic* 419ff

21 as above, 419

22 Paul Winter, *On the Trial of Jesus*, Walter de Gruyter, Berlin, 1961

23 Maccoby, *J the Pharisee* 74-5

24 Maccoby's argument has been questioned on the ground that, according to Josephus, the Thaddeus rebellion happened *after* this incident. But Maccoby responds (p 7) that "Luke [the author of Acts] may very well have got a detail wrong in his attempt to reconstruct Gamaliel's words, while correctly reporting Gamaliel's overall attitude".

25 as above, 6-8

26 as above, 8-11

27 as above, 151-3

28 as above, 120-3

29 as above, 141

30 as above, 31-2

31 as above, 39

32 Eisenman says "the best translation [of the scrolls] in English is that of G Vermes", before warning that it "should be used with caution where key formulations are concerned", since "his translations sometimes fall short in key passages,... are inconsistent and sometimes misleading" - *James the Brother of Jesus* p xxxv. The two scholars have famously clashed over some crucial datings. Eisenman understands the Habakkuk Commentary, a chief source of the history of the Qumran sect, as a first-century CE text. But Vermes cites carbon-dating by the University of Arizona that "definitely puts it in the pre-Christian era between 120 and 5 BCE". He comments drily, evidently with Eisenman in mind: "In consequence, fringe scholars who see in this writing allusions to events described in the New Testament will find they have a problem on their hands" - *The Complete Scrolls in English* pp 13-14.

33 Eisenman, *James* xviii

34 Eisenman was not the first to propose an identity for the Teacher. Jacob Teicher, in a series of articles for the Journal of Jewish Studies from 1951 to 1955 had suggested that Jesus was the Teacher and Paul the scrolls' Wicked Priest. In 1992 Barbara Thiering attracted excited attention with her thesis that the Teacher was John the Baptist, and Jesus, who had married, divorced, remarried and fathered four children, was the defector designated the Wicked Priest. For these speculations, see Vermes, *The Complete Dead Sea Scrolls in English*, p 21. Vermes comments: "In my opinion all these theories [including Eisenman's] fail the basic credibility test: they do not spring from, but are foisted on, the texts". And again, they are "to say the least, improbable speculations".

35 Eisenman, *James* xxxii

36 as above, xxix

37 Robert Price, "Robert Eisenman's *James the Brother of Jesus*: a Higher-Critical Evaluation", Institute for Higher Critical Studies, Drew University, Madison NJ, 1997, web version 1998 at depts.drew.edu/jhc/RPeisenman.html

11

HISTORY, MYSTERY AND MYTH:
AN IRRETRIEVABLE JESUS

No-one goes looking for buried treasure unless they have reason to believe the treasure exists and there is at least an outside chance of locating it. But it sometimes happens that the search becomes so complex, so fraught with difficulties, so crossed with red herrings and so overlain with false trails, that the searcher is driven to the conclusion that perhaps there never was any treasure in the first place; or if there was, its hiding place is now beyond discovery.

So too with the quest for an historically verifiable Jesus. Some historians have concluded that whatever a living flesh-and-blood son of Mary may have said and done two thousand years ago in an obscure corner of the eastern Mediterranean has been so smothered, distorted and corrupted by mythology and theology that it is now irretrievable. The history has gone and we have to make do with the mystery - or content ourselves with the claim that the mystery *is* the history.

Such skeptical scholarship is nothing new. In the second century a Jewish scholar named Trypho is quoted by Justin Martyr in *Dialogue With the Jew Trypho*. Justin's opponent charges that "Christ, if he has indeed been born and exists anywhere, is unknown... You invent a Christ for yourself". The same argument was put by the pagan scholar Celsus who published a treatise called *The True Word*, now known only in fragments quoted by Origen in a book called *Contra Celsum*. Celsus' main target was Christianity itself - its exclusiveness in insisting that it was the only true religion, its antagonism towards the rich diversity of ancient cultural and religious tradition, its missionary zeal, and the unneighborly refusal of Christians to perform their social duty by serving in the army and generally contributing to public life. But Celsus also aimed some sharp barbs at Jesus himself. Had he really existed or was he a Christian invention, concocted from vague prophecies and scraps of memory? Did educated Christians really believe all those miracle stories? Why should they be seen as any different from the tales of magical healings and raisings from the dead told about mythical heroes of the past? Was it not clear that the virgin-birth story must have been invented to cover up some embarrassing hanky-panky? (It wouldn't be the first time, or the last). Could the resurrection story be believed when it hung on the word of an hysterical woman? Was not this new religion no less mythologized and fanciful than the older, richer, more tolerant ones it sought to displace? And if some of the words attributed to Jesus were commendably good and wise, were they not derived from the Greek sages and the wisdom of the ancients?

Origen thundered against Celsus's blasphemous skepticism, and Rome soon put a stop to it when it adopted Christianity as the official religion of the empire. But as the power of the church eventually waned in the wake of the European Enlightenment, the questions Trypho and Celsus had posed resurfaced. They naturally came easily to avowedly atheist commentators, and were well known to classical scholars familiar with ancient Greek, Latin and Egyptian accounts of miraculous births, deeds and resurrections[1]. In the late nineteenth century new schools of skeptical scholarship emerged, not least among New Testament scholars working within the Christian tradition but with tools of critical analysis which were now applied where they had never been applied before: to the sacred books of the biblical canon.

1. William Wrede's Jesus as Mark's own creation

One such scholar, whose work was to have a lasting effect, was William Wrede, a professor at the University of Breslau in Silesia (now Poland). Wrede died in 1906 and is now remembered, if at all, only as the last of the old Jesus questers reviewed by Albert Schweitzer in *The Quest of the*

Historical Jesus (subtitled: "From Reimarus to Wrede"). But his most important book, *The Messianic Secret* (1901), continues to hold a contentious place in historical Jesus studies more than a century after its publication, and it does so for two reasons. First, Wrede was emphatic that the Jesus quest demanded the skills and disciplines of the objective historian and a renunciation of the supernaturalism assumed by classical theology. Theological imperatives would always put dogma before historical truth: the serious seeker must be free of dogmatic or doctrinal assumptions and distortions, which could only "obscure things". Naturally, theologians were not slow to point out that Wrede's own ideological assumptions - those of nineteenth-century Enlightenment humanism - were just as likely to "obscure things" and shape *his* interpretations. That debate is alive and well in the academy today, and no doubt shall for ever be so.

More important and far-reaching, though, was Wrede's proposed solution to a puzzle that had troubled Bible students for generations. The problem, signaled in the title of his book, was "the Messianic secret" in Mark's gospel. As we noted when we first focused on Mark, the earliest of all the narrative gospels has a strange feature not found anywhere else. Jesus continually tells his followers to keep his work, his teachings, and above all his status as the Messiah, secret. The leper he heals in Mark 1:40-45 is "strictly charged" to "see thou say nothing to any man". Again, after raising the daughter of Jairus from the dead "he charged them strictly that no man should know it" (5:43). The same command of secrecy is given in 7:36 and 8:26.

When Jesus meets a man with an "unclean spirit", the demon possessing him cries out "I know thee who thou art, the Holy One of God". Jesus tells him to keep his mouth shut: "Hold thy peace" (1: 23-25). But the news gets out and soon Jesus is having to "cast out many devils". Each time, he "suffered not the devils to speak, because they knew him" (1:34). He insists on their silence, not because the devils don't know the truth about him, but because they do! And the devils, we are told, are cowed into obedience.

When Peter himself eventually catches on to what the demons have long understood and blurts out that Jesus is "the Christ", he too, along with the other disciples, is commanded to "tell no man" (8:29-30). When Peter, James and John see Jesus walking on the mountain, "transfigured" in shining white raiment, and hear a voice in the clouds saying "This is my beloved Son: hear him", they are again told to keep secret what they had seen and heard "till the Son of man were risen from the dead" - a command which naturally puzzles them, for they are soon "questioning one with another what the rising from the dead should mean" (9:2-10). Unlike us (and Mark), they don't know how the story is going to end. But they obediently keep the secret of what they have seen, heard and come to understand.

Even more puzzling, Mark tells us that Jesus hid his message in parables, or riddles, precisely in order that he should *not* be understood! On the shores of Galilee he addresses "a great multitude", telling them the parable of the sower (Mark 4). When he is alone with the disciples, they ask him what on earth it means. He reveals the secret meaning, but only to them. "And he said unto them, Unto you it is given to know the mystery of the kingdom of God: but unto them that are without, all these things are done in parables: that seeing they may see, and not perceive; and hearing they may hear, and not understand: lest at any time they should be converted, and their sins should be forgiven them".

Just as (in Mark's story) Jesus has confined the secret of *who he really is* to Peter, James and John, so he confines the secret of *what he really means* to his trusted disciples. He tells them that the whole point of a parable is that no-one will understand it without special instruction; and he doesn't *want* the crowds out there to understand what he means by the kingdom of God. If he speaks plainly and they get the point, they might be converted and get their sins forgiven! God forbid! Why would that be such a tragedy? Because they would immediately go running around telling everyone, and the Messianic secret would be out before its time.

When is its time? When he has risen from the dead.

Why should Jesus want to keep his identity and his message secret until after his death and resurrection? That is what has puzzled generations of pious believers and critical scholars alike. And the puzzle is all the greater in that this obsessively secretive Jesus is only found in (and throughout) Mark. Matthew, Luke and John repudiate Mark's obsessive insistence on this secrecy by eliminating it entirely from their narratives, presumably because it makes no sense to them. So the real question is: what is Mark's purpose in stressing again and again Jesus' antipathy to publicity and actually being understood by the crowds who flocked to hear him? And Wrede the historian, having freed himself from the constraint of having to come up with a theologically correct answer, offers an atheological explanation.

He dismisses as implausible the traditional explanation that Jesus is playing for time, not wanting to attract attention or provoke opposition prematurely. Why, if this were so, would he tell "multitudes" parables he didn't want them to understand? Wouldn't he just keep away from them and explain his message only to his inner circle of trusted disciples? No, something else is going on. The something else, says Wrede, is that Mark invented the "messianic secret". He made it all up.

Why should he do that? In the forty years between Jesus' death and the completion of Mark's gospel, the Jesus movement had split into its two principal factions, a predominantly Jewish one in Palestine and a largely gentile or Hellenized one in Syria and beyond Palestine's borders. The Jewish faction had maintained the memory of a human and very Jewish Jesus, looking to James and the original disciples for leadership. The Hellenized faction, under the powerful influence of Paul, had divinized Jesus, making him God incarnate. Mark's community was a Pauline community, and Mark wanted to present Jesus in Pauline terms as the messiah and "Son of God", as testified by his miracles and his death and resurrection. The problem, Wrede suggests, was that there were people still living, perhaps even members of his family, who had known

Jesus and might say "Hold on! This is not the Jesus we knew back home in Galilee. He made no such claims, and he certainly didn't go around raising people from the dead! We remember him as God's messenger, not as God incarnate." To which Mark has his answer ready: "I can now reveal that he *did* do these things, and he *was* the messiah, the Son of God, but he wanted it kept secret until it was revealed in his death and resurrection. You thought you knew him, but you obviously weren't in on the secret!"

For Wrede, then, Mark's gospel was not an objective historical narrative, drawn from oral tradition and eye-witness accounts, but a polemical fiction. The Jesus of Mark is not the historical Jesus of the early-first-century but a new-model Jesus made to fit the theological framework of Mark's community nearly half a century later in a changed world. As a source of biographical material it is profoundly suspect. And if there is nothing we can rely on in the first narrative gospel, there is nothing to rely on, period. The train has hit the buffers before it has got out of the siding.

A century after its publication, Mark Allen Powell describes *The Messianic Secret* as "one of the twentieth century's most influential works", casting doubt as it did on the possibility of unraveling a factual Jesus from what look like largely fictionalized records.

2. Alvar Ellegard's Jesus one hundred years before Christ

Alvar Ellegard, former Dean of the Faculty of Arts at the University of Goteborg, Sweden, is not primarily a biblical scholar, and, he insists, not at all a theologian. His field is linguistics and the history of ideas. The cover-blurb on his book *Jesus One Hundred Years Before Christ: a Study in Creative Mythology* (1999) hails it as "the result of a modern scholar's purely historical and non-theological approach to the origin of Christianity". As the title suggests, Ellegard's thesis is that the origins of "the Jesus myth" can be traced back into the first century *BCE*, with the invention of an historical Jesus delayed until the second century CE. Thus

Ellegard challenges both two millennia of the church's understanding of Jesus and two centuries of critical biblical scholarship. Small wonder, then, that while his book has attracted a significant general readership it has been effectively ignored by the established theological faculties, and where it has been noticed by specialists in the field it has almost invariably been dismissed for what are regarded as its eccentric datings of primary texts such as the biblical gospels. Where Eisenman's distinctive account of Christian origins depends on later dates for the Dead Sea Scrolls than the overwhelming majority of his fellow scholars are able to accommodate, Ellegard's thesis hangs on later dates for "*all* the earliest Christian documents" (his emphasis), and an interpretation of them as presenting Jesus as "somebody who had lived and died a long time ago"[2].

Ellegard begins with the Essenes, but not the Essenes as known only through the Dead Sea Scrolls. By the first century CE, he argues, the sect founded more than a hundred years earlier by its unnamed "Teacher of Righteousness" had spread throughout the diaspora, shedding much of its early exclusiveness in the process. "The descriptions of the Essenes given by Philo of Alexandria *c.* AD 20, and by the Jewish historian Josephus in *c.* AD 80, portray a much more open community than that of the Qumran documents. Philo's Therapeutae, a branch of the Essenes, had a philosophical, universalistic outlook... The Palestinian Essenes directed their attention more and more to the Diaspora, which in itself would be likely to soften their originally hostile attitudes towards strangers and increase their understanding of non-Jewish, Gentile customs and ways of thinking"[3].

Ellegard lists some of the ways in which Essenes described their own movement: "the Church of God, the Saints, the Elect, the Poor, those of the Way... Their world-view was profoundly messianic and apocalyptic, they believed in immortality, and they interpreted texts in the Hebrew scriptures as prophecies about the coming messiah"[4]. By the early decades of the first century CE, some Essenes or Jewish visionaries influenced by Essene teachings began to develop a spiritualized vision of their

Teacher of Righteousness. He was a divinely appointed prophet and martyr who had been harrassed and put to death by the Jewish priestly hierarchy. But God had raised him from the dead and placed him at his own right hand in heaven. "His resurrection proved what their Church already believed: that immortality was possible for humans." Further, his exalted place in heaven was taken as "a sign that the Last Judgment was near, at which... the Messiah would save those who belonged to the Church he had founded, the [Essene] Church of God"[5].

Among these visionaries were the men we have come to know as Paul, Peter, James, and their fellow apostles. They gave the Teacher of Righteousness a name: Jesus (meaning "God's salvation"). For them, Jesus was not someone they had ever met in the flesh. Like Paul, "They encountered him only in visions and revelations: as a 'spiritual' being. Jesus of Nazareth, born of Mary at the end of Augustus' reign, is a fiction"[6]. Thus the emergent Christian church, traditionally dated to what Paul calls "the beginning of the evangelization" in the 30s, is best under-stood as a development of the Essene "Church of God". Paul and the apostles did not found it; still less did a first-century flesh-and-blood Jesus. The "church" had been going for a couple of centuries before the Teacher of Righteousness began to be worshipped as a divine spirit in heaven, given the name of Jesus, and interpreted as the messiah, the Christ. The communities that worshipped the spirit-Jesus continued to use the language of the Essene church: "the saints", "the elect", "the Way". "*All* Christian writings", asserts Ellegard, "which can be plausibly dated to the first century AD present this 'spiritual' picture of Jesus, Jesus raised to Heaven. The earthly Jesus is clearly of little interest to the earliest apostles"[7].

So what about Matthew, Mark, Luke and John? Did they not show interest in the earthly Jesus? Yes, says Ellegard, but they are not first-century gospels: they were all written, he argues, some time after 100 CE. By this time there was growing confusion and factionalism in the Jesus movement. Churches that emphasized Jesus' resurrection from the dead as proof of immortality came under fire from churches influenced by the Gnostic tradition, which found it hard to accept that a spirit from God could really suffer and die. Perhaps Jesus had only *seemingly* suffered and died - a theory called "docetism", from the Greek *dokein*, "seem". But, as Ellegard puts it, "if Jesus Christ was only *seemingly* a man, and only seemingly suffered and died, how were ordinary men to identify with him, and how could Jesus' resurrection count as a promise of immortality for such ordinary men?... Thus we have at this juncture, around 100 AD, two diverging tendencies in the Christian movement. One was 'physical', giving more and more weight to the earthly Jesus, and the other was 'spiritual', attracted chiefly to the heavenly Jesus"[8].

Step forward Ignatius, bishop of Antioch in the early years of the second century. "He decided that Gnosticism, and particularly the docetic Gnostics, had to be firmly resisted. The spiritual Jesus should not be allowed to overshadow the human one. Instead, the two should be united. Ignatius reached his goal by... asserting, in no uncertain terms, that Jesus was indeed born of a woman, the virgin Mary, that he had been baptized by the well-known John the Baptist, had been crucified under Pontius Pilate and resurrected and raised to Heaven by God"[9]. Ignatius was not an historian. He did not claim to have unearthed evidence to back his assertions. He simply used his authority as bishop in the third largest city of the Roman empire after Rome and Alexandria to assert that the earthly Jesus had been born a century ago and had died when Pontius Pilate was governor of Judea (26-36 CE). "His choice of Pilate as a reference point in time may well be due to his knowledge that Paul had experienced his decisive vision of the risen Christ at that time. Thus at one stroke Ignatius made Jesus a contemporary of Paul and his colleagues among the apostles"[10] - and the Teacher of Righteousness was effectively abandoned to rest undisturbed for a couple of millennia in the sandy recesses of Qumran's caves.

Ignatius' authority as a living bishop was great, but as nothing compared with his authority as a dead saint. During fierce persecution of the Antioch church Ignatius was captured, taken to Rome and thrown to the wild animals. Under escort on his journey to Rome he wrote a series of letters to other churches urging the metaphysical union of the human and the divine in Christ. In his letter to the Christians in Rome he specifically asked that nothing be done to prevent his martyrdom, which he clearly saw as inaugurating his own immortality. His holy heroism guaranteed his authority. All that remained to be done was the compilation of a plausible narrative - and four writers stepped in to fill the gap. In Ellegard's words, "It is to a large extent in accordance with Ignatius' assertions about Jesus' birth by Mary, his baptism by John the Baptist and his execution under Pilate, that all the second-century Gospel writers - Matthew, Mark, Luke and John - built their story of the life of Jesus. In their accounts Jesus was a man who was at the same time divine, the Son of God, and also human, an early first-century Palestinian wonderworker, preacher and prophet. To flesh out Ignatius' bare historical data, the Gospel writers added the considerable number of Old Testament prophecies that first-century Christian writers [including the authors of the epistles of the New Testament] had brought to light in order to show that God had preordained Jesus' life on earth and that Jesus was indeed the Messiah. None of the first-century Christian writers, however, had tried to weave these episodes into a dramatic life story. Nor had Ignatius. The Gospel writers were the first to do so"[11]. Written, in Ellegard's view, not decades but centuries after the events they purport to describe, they have no historical credibility. "They are certainly not eyewitness accounts. Nor are they secondary reports of such accounts. Bluntly: their story is fiction"[12] - as is their Jesus.

Ellegard's interpretation rests on two novel assertions. One is the continuity, indeed the essential identity, of the Essene and the Christian "Church of God". Here his critics reply that so little is known about the Essenes, even about whatever association they had with the Qumran community, let alone their influence on Philo and the Jewish diaspora, that any theory of Essene-Christian identity is at best highly speculative and at worst ungrounded. To rewrite the origins of Christianity and the nature of the historical Jesus on the basis of such insecure data is hazardous.

The second novel assertion on which Ellegard's "study in creative mythology" depends is the late dates, all second century, for the biblical gospels. Here Ellegard claims particular expertise as the author of a book on *A Statistical Method for Determining Authorship*[13]. He cites the linguistic and statistical evidence, commonly accepted by most recent New Testament scholars, that all four gospels must have been written after the destruction of the temple in 70 CE and before 180 when they are mentioned by Irenaeus, and pushes back the later date to 140 for Mark and Matthew, based on mentions by Papias as quoted by Eusebius. In this time span between 70 and the mid-second-century, then, Ellegard admits that "most theological writers prefer the first thirty years, whereas a minority, and I myself, prefer the last thirty years"[14].

Why does Ellegard discount what he accepts is the majority judgment? Because he sees it as the view of "theologians", not objective historians like himself. "It seems obvious to me that the reluctance of almost all theologians to admit that the Gospels and Acts should be placed late rather than early in the interval between AD 70 and 140 is due to their common assumption that the Gospel stories depend on traditions based on memories of Jesus (whether oral or written) which go back to a Jesus presumed to have lived in Palestine in the first three decades of the first century... It is quite clear that scholars' firm adherence to the assumption of a first-century Jesus has prevented them from exploring avenues of research which appear as obviously promising, if that constraint is removed"[15]. The response of critical scholars such as Koester, Crossan, Vermes and Mack, is not, so far as I am aware, on record, but I guess that it could be roundly expressed in a single word - and one not often found in a theological vocabulary. Perhaps it is enough to say here that Ellegard's late dates are not impossible, but the weight of opinion among those whose speciality is the study of these particular texts is so far decisively against him[16].

Alvar Ellegard, then, stands in the Wrede tradition, where the Jesus we think we know is presented not as history but mythology, not as fact but fiction. The quest, then, is not for an ever-elusive and ultimately irrecoverable historical Jesus but for the origins and meanings of the Jesus myth. Ellegard pleads for an "interplay of belief and knowledge", urging that if it is to succeed, "we must realise that neither belief nor knowledge is something absolute, something that we have finally and definitely got hold of. Both are *provisional* means of reaching insights that are hopefully deeper. Though there is no ultimate truth, we must try to reach higher and higher on the way towards it"[17]. Even, it seems, at the risk of over-reaching and falling off the ladder.

3. G.A.Wells: Jesus as myth and legend

As Emeritus Professor of German at the University of London, George Wells is happy to flaunt his status as an "outsider" among specialist New Testament scholars, especially professional theologians. He reminds us that it was Reimarus who initiated the debate about the historical Jesus, and he was no theologian. Voltaire contributed more than any of his theological contemporaries. The Jesus debate is concerned with "a historical problem, to be examined by those who are prepared to use the ordinary tools of historical enquiry. It is not to be settled by enthusiastic believers or disbelievers, whose approach is sentimental rather than scientific, nor by people who allow their profession to influence the conclusion they reach"[18].

The thesis for which Wells is famous is simply stated. Jesus never existed: he was made up. The case is first put in *The Jesus of the Early Christians* (1971, revised as *Did Jesus Exist?* in 1975 and updated 1986) and developed in a series of books culminating in *The Jesus Myth* (1999), where it was given a radical twist. The thesis was progressively nuanced and elaborated as Wells absorbed the new scholarship of the 1980s and 90s. His critics could hardly complain that he did not read widely enough or that he failed to take account of the studies that posed problems for his own skeptical standpoint. R Joseph Hoffman, senior fellow and chair for research development at the School of Theology, Westminster College, Oxford, acknowledging that "Wells is known to swim against the stream in the contemporary debate", describes him as "the most articulate defender of the non-historicity thesis", and J E Barnhart, professor of philosophy and religious studies at the University of North Texas, writes that Wells' work "exemplifies first-rate historical investigation and excellent biblical scholarship. I know of no other author who has shed more light on the question of how Christianity came into being"[19].

Wells's original arguments were novel when first advanced in the 70s, and he has not always been accorded the recognition he deserves for both the originality and the coherence of his early thesis. It owed little to theories of comparative mythology (from Frazer's *Golden Bough* to Joseph Campbell's *Myths to Live By*) that have fed the imagination of many Jesus skeptics. Instead, it was firmly grounded in biblical textual criticism. Ironically, some of his most baffled critics were not the convinced believers but his fellow-humanists who complained that "whether Jesus exists is a trivial matter, not worth writing a book about", let alone half a lifetime's study. Wells replied tartly that "the manner and origin of one of the world's major religions is no triviality"[20].

In *Did Jesus Exist?* (1986 edition) Wells offered an explanation for the invention of an historical Jesus. Jesus had first been conceived as a spirit rather than a mortal man. The gospels were written in response to a perceived need, by the end of the first century, to ground the developing Christ cult in time, place and a flesh-and-blood personality. In this he anticipates Ellegard. Wells stresses that he is "not imputing fraud to the Christians of the early second century" or suggesting that the Jesus myth was "maliciously invented by cynics who knew the facts to be otherwise". On the contrary, "The train of reasoning that I am envisaging... can be summarized as follows: If Jesus is the god of the 'last times' who is soon to bring the world to an end, then his first coming, as well as his second, is surely to be allocated to the 'last times', i.e. is of recent occurrence." The question for these second-century Christians was "how recent?". It could not be within living memory, for self-evident reasons; nor could it be in the distant past, before the beginning of the end-time. So it must be just before living memory. They hit on the period of Pilate's administration in the 20s and 30s. Given his fearsome reputation, attested by Josephus, "he was just the type of person to have murdered Jesus"[21]. Scriptural prophecies were adduced to support the developing story, and teachings drawn from both Jewish and Greek wisdom traditions were attributed to this newly-coined Jesus. It did not take a lot of imagination: "about as much... as was needed by the authors of the Arabian Nights". Nor did the project require a fully-rounded biography. "A man who can raise the dead, walk on water and turn it into wine, and be resurrected after three days of death is obviously not describable in terms of human character, any more than Samson, Hercules or Venus".[22]

This Jesus, then, was not a Galilean teacher-preacher who founded a new religion and a church to preach it. Rather, the leaders of a Christ cult "founded" the human Jesus by turning their heavenly god-spirit into an imaginary, fictional man, born of a woman, killed by an alliance of Roman and Jewish opponents, and, in a thrilling climax to the story, brought back from the dead to ascend to his heavenly home.

This was the thesis Wells elaborated in his four principal books written in the 1970s and 80s. But the 1990s saw a significant shift in his position. Wells caught up with recent Q scholarship, particularly the summary of it by Christopher Tuckett (*Q and the History of Early Christianity*, Clark, Edinburgh, 1996). In his latest book, *The Jesus Myth* (1998), Wells concedes that, unlike Paul and the gospels, Q may after all point to a real historical Jesus. In discussing the theology of Q and the wisdom tradition underlying it, he writes:

"In sum, the religious community responsible for Q cultivated the memory of a Jesus as their founder figure, an authoritative teacher who should be obeyed. They urged their fellow Jews who had earlier rejected his message to change their ways and accept it as a last chance to avoid the doom that would otherwise overtake them. Although there is a good deal of Wisdom-inspired legend in this portrait of Jesus, the specific references to the places and to the relatively recent times of his activities, and the theological orientation which fits the scene of Judaism, make it *reasonable to accept that the whole is based on the life of an actual itinerant Galilean preacher of the 20s or 30s"* (my emphasis)[23]. Wells acknowledges this as "a departure from my earlier position that the Jesus of the gospels resulted purely from attempts to make the vaguely conceived earthly figure of the Pauline Jesus into something more definitely historical"[24]. Noting that "Wells has now abandoned the pure Christ Myth theory for which he is famous", Robert M Price, editor of the *Journal of Higher Criticism*, comments that "his refreshing intellectual honesty is witnessed by the fact that his own views are amenable to evolution and revision"[25].

However, historical Jesus scholars inclined to rejoice over the sinner that repenteth need reminding of Wells's caveat, which completed the sentence italicised above. Accepting that Q might after all point to a real Jesus, Wells adds: "although it is surely hazardous to try and decide which details are really authentic". The shift he makes in a book he still chooses to title *The Jesus Myth* is not a leap that propels him into the arms of the Jesus Seminar. It arguably brings him within shouting distance of the views of Burton Mack, whose hugely influential contribution is about to bring this survey to a close; but Wells's Jesus, even if he is finally recognized as a Jesus of Galilee rather than an imagined holy ghost, is still so smothered in mythological accretion that we cannot be sure we know anything about him, other than that the man who somehow gave rise to the myth (a) lived and (b) died.

4. The gospel according to Mack

Burton Mack, professor of New Testament studies at Claremont, California, was an early member of the Jesus Seminar but dropped out when he found that his colleagues' inability to persuade him of the likely historical authenticity of virtually any of Jesus' sayings obliged him to vote "black" every time. Mack concluded that mythology and theology had obliterated all traces of the historical Jesus. Accordingly, the only Jesus we can now know is the Jesus created as the centerpiece of a "myth of origins" for the post-70 CE Christian community. And the primary myth-maker, says Mack, harking back to Wrede, was Mark.

In the first of his major books on Jesus, *The Myth of Innocence: Mark and Christian Origins* (1988), Mack pictures Mark as an intellectual scribe sitting in his library (Mark as Mack?), surrounded by manuscripts, letters, and snippets of memorabilia, all of which he draws on to invent a Jesus Christ fit for purpose, the purpose being the consolidation of the rival wings and factions of the Jesus movement and a vindication of its divine mission as understood within Mark's late-first-century community. As Mack puts it:

"Mark was a scholar. A reader of texts and a writer of texts... Mark's Gospel was not the product of divine revelation. It was not a pious trans-mission of revered tradition. It was composed at a desk in a scholar's study lined with texts and open to discourse with other intellectuals. In Mark's study were chains of miracle stories, collections of pronouncement stories in various states of elaboration, some form of Q, memos on parables and proof texts, the scriptures, including the prophets, written materials from the Christ cult [Paul's communities], and other literature representative of Hellenistic Judaism... One 'text' he did not have was a copy of a passion narrative because there was none until he wrote it. One might imagine Mark's study as a workshop where a lively traffic in ideas and literary experimentation was the rule for an extended period of time. Colleagues may well have contributed ideas and experimental drafts for many of the little story units used throughout the gospel in a common effort to think things through on the new storyline. The passion narrative is simply the climax of the new storyline. The story was a new myth of origins. A brilliant appearance of the man of power, destroyed by those in league against God, pointed nonetheless to a final victory when those who knew the secret of his kingdom would finally be vindicated for accepting his authority"[26].

Mark, on this account, is not an objective historian, if indeed he can be said to be an historian at all. He is not concerned to sift historically accurate and authentic from innaccurate and inauthentic material. He is not writing a biography, nor is he interested in "the historical Jesus" - a concept that would mean nothing to him. Either alone or with scholarly colleagues from within his own community, Mark is picking and choosing from a range of materials drawn from various sources to present the Jesus his community needs and earnestly desires to present to the world. Later gospel writers do exactly the same, selecting events and sayings that advance their own point of view in the hope of persuading others to share it. John, for instance, is quite open about his objectives, telling his readers that "These [signs] are written so that you may come to believe that Jesus is the Messiah, the Son of God, and that through believing you may have life in his name" (20:30-1). But Mark was the first, the inventor of the genre. And critically, according to Mack, he not only selected material from available sources. Where he couldn't find what he needed, he used his imagination.

Mack proposes southern Syria as the most likely place of composition, and accepts some time in the mid to late 70s as the likely date. "The Jewish War [of 66-74] was in very recent memory and rather vividly so. It had, moreover, created confusion about what it could mean for Judea, for Palestine, for Jews, and for the Jesus people." The mid-century (according to Josephus) had been a period of famine, social unrest, religious conflict, class warfare, banditry, insurrection, intrigue and bloodshed, culminating in the siege of 66-70 and the fall of Jerusalem. These catastrophic events coming together had raised apocalyptic expectations among all Jewish factions: the end-time was surely nigh.

It was in this feverish atmosphere that by the mid-70s a struggle for Jewish hearts and minds both in Judea and in the diaspora was shaping up between emergent rabbinical Judaism led by the now-dominant Pharisees and the Jews of the Jesus movement. Followers of the Jesus movement, who had confidently expected to win over their fellow Jews and lead them into the promised kingdom, instead found themselves being shut out of the synaogogues. "Having thought of themselves as sons and daughters of Israel, failure to find an acceptable arrangement with the diaspora synagogue meant that the kingdom they talked about hardly represented the sect they had become. The Jesus people to whom Mark belonged were in need of figuring things out some other way."

In the first place, that meant figuring out a Jesus who would be recognizable to, and could therefore command the allegiance of, both the Jewish and the more rapidly growing gentile/Pauline strands of the Jesus movement. This was a delicate business, given the diverging christologies of the two wings. Mack argues that Mark assays this by creating a Jesus who is both a good, traditional Jew - pro-law and commandments, pro-marriage, pro-fasting, four-square within the Jewish prophetic tradition - and also one who by his deeds demonstrates that he is the Son of God. So miraculous healings and exorcisms are invented to appeal to a cosmopolitan gentile constituency that would expect this kind of thing of its mythical heroes, and the shameful death of a petty criminal is worked up into a climactic but wholly fictional passion story. This Jesus is carefully calculated to have something for both traditional Jews who revere Jesus as God's messenger and for Hellenized Jews and gentile God-fearers who are busy creating the new Christ cult.

Mark's synthesized Jesus will now figure as the champion of the consolidated Jesus movement against its contemporary rivals for the hearts and minds of Judaism, the movement emerging as rabbinic orthodoxy. This Jesus is portrayed as continually defeating the Pharisees in debate - never mind the fact that (according to Mack) there were few Pharisees in rural Galilee in the 20s and 30s, and the historical Jesus probably had no significant contact with them. Mark needs an authoritative Jesus who speaks with the voice of God, so he creates a Jesus who can now be revealed *as* the Son of God - something Jesus himself had tried to keep secret in his own lifetime, Mark explains, to all but a select group of initiates. Mark needs a Jesus who will make sense of recent trials, tribulations and apocalyptic catastrophes to deliver to all who follow him the promised kingdom, so he creates the apocalyptic Son of Man who not only announces the kingdom but himself inaugurates it. And Mark needs a Jesus whose death was not just a demeaning anticlimax, the snuffing out of yet another Jewish martyr, but the crowning cosmic event by which an Innocent Redeemer wipes away the sins of all who believe in him (that is, all sincere members of the Jesus movement); so he invents a story that fits his purpose, beginning with a fictional cleansing of the temple and gathering pace with the equally fictional betrayal by a fictional Judas, arrest at Gethsemane, denials by Peter, trials before Caiaphas and Pilate, crowning with thorns, darkness at noon, rending of the temple veil... all the product of Mark's creative imagination, driven by an impassioned theological imperative.

And, says Mack, it did the trick. Mark's masterpiece became the foundation document for the whole of the Jesus movement - and for the Christian church the movement was becoming and creating. "It is now possible to emphasize that Mark's accomplishment was an authorial, intellectual achievement. In modern critical parlance, Mark's Gospel is a very richly textured story. Its most distinctive feature is the complexity of what critics call intertextuality, the domestication and integration of diverse texts, genres, and patterns of perception in the formation of a novel literary performance. Mark's Gospel stands at the intersection of many streams of cultural, literary, and social history. It was created by effort, intellectual effort, and it is marked by conscious authorial intention. Mark was a scholar"[27].

Moreover, says Mack, it set the pattern for the narrative gospels that followed. Matthew, Luke-Acts and John are no more factual histories than Mark. Each is the work of an author or community of authors bent, not on *telling it as it was*, but *telling it as the perceived requirements of their own time and circumstances dictated*, with a view to winning converts. "The rule in general was not the 'transmission' of 'received' (sacred) tradition, but creative reworking and creative borrowing, that is, intellectual labor best understood on the model of intertextuality"[28]. There is no more point in searching here for the historical Jesus than there would be in searching for the historical Hamlet in Shakespeare's play or the historical Arthur in Tennyson's *Idylls of the King*. Where Wrede and Schweitzer cast doubt on the validity of the old quest, Burton Mack deposits the new questers in an even deeper cul de sac.

Mark's Jesus (or Mack's Mark's Jesus) does not belong in the early-first-century, in the fertile, fruitful and semi-autonomous Galilee of Herod Antipas. That Jesus had already been mythologized out of mind and memory by the time Mark wrote his novel masterwork. In his place we have a new-model Jesus, the product of the utterly changed post-war, post-holocaust world described in such devastating terms by Josephus. The holy city of Jerusalem has been ravaged, the temple destroyed, the Jewish nation defeated, humiliated, and dispersed. All the signs of the end-times are there for those with eyes to see and minds prepared to draw the right conclusions. The factionalized Jesus movement needs a new Jesus figure, one who combines the humanity of the distantly remembered sage and the divine authority of a Christ, a Son of God. He alone can snatch victory from the jaws of defeat, free the captives, wreak a terrible justice on those who have persecuted the righteous, seize the apocalyptic moment and lead his faithful followers into the promised kingdom. It is just such a Jesus Mark invents in his Syrian study and launches on an eagerly receptive Jesus movement.

So says the Mack of *A Myth of Innocence* in the1980s. But as he was writing it the ground of New Testament scholarship was shifting under his feet, and Q studies were the culprit. Q has a relatively minor role in Mack's first book: it is one of the sources he imagines Mark pulling down from his study shelves from time to time, though the first scholar-evangelist seemingly finds more to suit his purpose in the Christ-cult literature circulating in Paul's communities. But in his next major work Mack was to shift his focus from Mark to Q in *The Lost Gospel: the Book of Q and Christian Origins* (1993), and Q is accorded "enormous importance" in his later book, *Who Wrote the New Testament?: The Making of the Christian Myth* (1995).

In his mature work, then, Mack is persuaded that a proto-gospel we now call Q circulated in written form among some communities of the Jesus movement from about 50 CE till it was absorbed into Matthew and Luke in the 80s, after which it ceased to be copied as an independent text and therefore died out. But where many scholars - particularly the Jesus Seminar - see Q as the key to getting as close as we can ever hope to get to the historical Jesus, Mack interprets Q as doing for the Jesus movement of the 50s and 60s what Mark did in the 70s: combining scraps of memory and imaginative invention to *construct* a Jesus fitting the immediate needs and developing theology of a particular Jesus community, tailored to its own place and time. Q, particularly its earliest texts, may provide clues on which we can base intelligent guesses about the flesh-and-blood Jesus, but Mack insists that, like the narrative gospels that first embraced and then replaced it, Q tells us more about the people who produced it than about the man to whom its sayings are attributed. Even the earliest Q preserves a mythical rather than an historical Jesus.

"For a period of about fifty years, from the time of Jesus in the 20s until after the Roman-Jewish war in the 70s... [a single group of Jesus people] developed into a tightly knit community and produced a grandly sweeping mythology merely by attributing more and more teachings to Jesus. They did not need to imagine Jesus in the role of a god or tell stories about his resurrection from the dead in order to honor him as a teacher... Q brings the early Jesus people [rather than Jesus himself] into focus, and it is a picture so different from that which anyone ever imagined to be startling. Instead of people meeting to worship a risen Christ, as in the Pauline congregations, or worrying about what it is to be a follower of a martyr, as in the Markan community, the people of Q were fully preoccupied with questions about the kingdom of God in the present and the behavior required if one took it seriously... The people of Q were taking it on the bounce, intrigued with what happened when one chose to deviate from the usual norms of behavior and live by the rule(s) of the kingdom of God"[29].

Mack follows the radical Q scholarship of the 1990s in identifying three layers of material, each corresponding to a stage in the history of the Q community. Q1, perhaps dating from around 50 CE, consists of sayings which, although attributed to Jesus, are best understood as expressing "the wisdom of being a true follower of Jesus". In their first twenty years or so, the Jesus people "had been deeply involved in defining exactly what it meant to belong to the school of Jesus. And they had spent a great deal of thought and intellectual effort in finding arguments for a certain set of attitudes and actions as definitive for the kingdom of God"[30]. Mack lists some of these imperatives, familiar to us in their Luke and Matthew embedments: love your enemies; if struck on one cheek offer the other; give to everyone who begs; go out as lambs among wolves; carry no money, bag, or sandals; say "The kingdom of God has come near to you". What comes through is a risky program offering a thorough-going critique of conventional culture:

"Riches, misuse of authority and power, hypocrisies and pretensions, social and economic inequities, injustices, and even the normal reasons for family loyalties are all under suspicion. The kingdom ideal is being set over against traditional mores by directing that the followers of Jesus should practice voluntary poverty, severance of family ties, renunciation of needs, fearlessness in speaking out, nonretaliation, and, in general, living as children of the God revealed in the natural order of the world who 'makes his sun to rise on the evil and on the good'. Quite a program"[31].

The Jesus people of Galilee and the Jewish homelands who compiled and circulated Q1 just as Paul was writing and circulating his first letters to the more Hellenized Jesus communities around the Mediterranean rim were, suggests Mack, advocating a lifestyle remarkably similar to that of the Greek Cynics - "gadflies whose social critique had a point, and who made it with strikingly humorous twists of memorable gestures and sayings". What was different about the Q people, however, was the seriousness with which they took the new social vision of the kingdom of God. "This reflects the influence of a Jewish concern for a real, working society as the necessary context for any individual well-being. It was this interest in exploring an alternative social vision that set the Jesus movement apart from a merely Cynic-like call for an authentic lifestyle only in the interest of individual virtue or integrity"[32].

The material now assigned by some scholars to Q2 is radically different. This, Mack suggests, is marked by the deteriorating situation leading up to the Roman-Jewish war of 66 CE. "The process of social formation had taken its toll. Familes had been torn apart, a Jewish code of strict behavior had been held up by others to chide or ostracize the Jesus people, certain towns had told them to bug off, and some erstwhile members had decided that the stress was too much. Loyalty was now the issue... Thus, instead of a playful, aphoristic style of social critique characteristic of the earliest period of social experimentation, or even the more serious tone of instruction that defined the later development at the Q1 level, these Jesus people had taken up a decidedly judgmental stance toward the world. Threatening apocalyptic pronouncements of doom were being directed against those who refused the kingdom program. And the time for the kingdom's full realization had been postponed until the *eschaton* (last thing, end of history)"[33]. The Jesus movement scribes found themselves having to revise their handbook, retaining the earlier blocks of wise ethical instruction but adding prophetic and judgmental material to match the new mood. This meant re-inventing Jesus. He could no longer be a wisdom teacher alone, showing how the kingdom of heaven could be lived in the present, but must be repackaged as an apocalyptic prophet, the bringer of bad news to the wicked, namely all who rejected his message.

Mack proposes that this was accomplished by another "stroke of ingenious mythmaking". The writers of the revised version, the amalgamated Q1 and Q2, introduced the figure of John the Baptist. (Mack does not suggest they *invented* John, whose historicity is attested by Josephus. But he was evidently known to them, and seen as fitting their purpose). "As these scribes imagined it, Jesus recognized John as the last of the prophets of Israel and thus 'the one to come', and John predicted an even 'greater' one to come, who, of course, was Jesus. Jesus was 'greater', according to the scribes, because he was both a sage *and* a prophet. He was a sage by virtue of his Q1 teachings. He was a prophet by virtue of the apocalyptic judgments that soon would be heard from his lips [in Q2]". The important thing, says Mack, is that John "entered the picture of the Q community's imagination of Jesus' own role... With such a Jesus as one's teacher, how could the Community of Q go wrong? They already knew the standard God would use at the end of time to judge between them and the rest of the world"[34].

The third and final stratum of Q, presumed to have been added after the Jewish war, and classified by Kloppenborg and Robinson as Q3, "upgrade[d] the mythology of Jesus [says Mack] to the level of a divine being who could be imagined talking to God as his Father and debating with Satan as his tempter" (as in the story of Jesus' temptation in the wilderness). Mack suggests that, despite this "upgrade", which would seem to bring the Q community's Jesus closer to the divine savior of Paul and his following, the late additions "dulled the radical edge of the earlier material and made a kind of peace with more traditional ways of being the people of God while waiting for the kingdom"[35]. But Q was already on the way out by the time it was given its final revision. The future was Mark and the new genre of narrative gospels. Q continued to circulate until it was incorporated into the gospels of Matthew and Luke, but thereafter it ceased to be copied and disappeared from view - until modern scholars reconstructed it, finding in it either the earliest and most authentic historical-Jesus material (the Jesus Seminar), or a sequence of stages in the construction of a stable Jesus myth (Mack)[36].

Mack's monumental work on Mark and Q, then, by his own admission, tells us more about the Markan Jesus community and the earlier Q Jesus community than it does about the historical Jesus. As early as the 50s, Jesus is already a fully mythologized figure, and mythologized in different ways for different communities (Paul's and Q1's). Mack tells us we cannot penetrate the mythologies to reach any significant historical certainties. At best, we may look in on Jesus communities of the middle and late first century "when memory and imagination worked only with sayings, teachings, and anecdotes to develop the voice and character of the founder of their schools"[37]. But even this most skeptical of Jesus scholars pays tribute of sorts to the Jesus who lurks somewhere behind the veil of mythology and mystification. This is how he puts it in *Who Wrote the New Testament?*:

"This book does not require a chapter on the historical Jesus. It will contribute to the modern scholars' quest for the historical Jesus in only one respect, and that will be to show that one social role for Jesus is more plausible than several others that have been suggested. That role is a kind of teacher, a conclusion that can be drawn from the nature of the earliest layers of his teachings as his followers remembered them. Knowing Jesus was a teacher is all we need to get started, for the story to be told is not about Jesus and the influence of his unique personality, life and achievements. That would be to continue to think mythically, as if reimagining the historical Jesus could put us in touch with the sources of Christian faith and enlightenment a bit better than keeping the gospel picture of Jesus in mind. No. The story to be told is about the ways in which his followers honored him as the founder of their movements. It is about mythmaking and the investment his followers made in social experiments that resulted from Jesus' teachings.

"The most one can say about the importance of the historical Jesus is that, in light of... the intellectual challenge characteristic for the times, he can be ranked among the creative minds of the Greco-Roman age. But he would have been more the poet or the visionary, less the systematic thinker, for his teachings turned on insights and suggestions... not on strategies for promoting a long-range plan. His importance as a thinker and teacher can certainly be granted and even greatly enhanced once we allow the thought that Jesus was not a god incarnate but a real historical person"[38].

Notes to Chapter 11

1 A comprehensive and eminently readable account of this literature and its relation to the Jesus stories is Robert J Miller's *Born Divine: the Births of Jesus and Other Sons of God*, Polebridge, Santa Rosa, 2003.

2 Ellegard, *J 100 Years BC* 4

3 as above, 259

4 as above, 259

5 as above, 258

6 as above, 257

7 as above, 258

8 as above, 262-3

9 as above, 264

10 as above, 258

11 as above, 264

12 as above, 257

13 as above, 306, note 2

14 as above, 183

15 as above, 184

16 It should be made clear that Ellegard accepts that many individual sayings attributed to Jesus in what he believes to be second-century gospels were written down earlier, particularly those recorded in Q. But his interpretation of Q is similar to that of Burton Mack. The sayings-collections, in his view, are not compiled from memories of what an historical Jesus really said, but reflect what the later Q community understood to be the revealed wisdom of Jesus-in-heaven. It is the *narrative* element of the biblical gospels that Ellegard sees as belonging to the second century.

17 Ellegard, *J 100 Years BC* 269

18 Wells, *Did J Exist?* 2-3

19 Hoffman in Forward to Wells, *J Legend* xii. Barnhart on back cover.

20 Wells, *Did J Exist?* 216

21 as above, 60

22 as above, 1

23 Wells, *J Myth* 102-3

24 as above, 273, note 40

25 as above, quoted on back cover

26 Mack, *Myth of Innocence* 321-323. In a lengthy footnote to this passage, Mack qualifies his picture of Mark as sole author, accepting that the gospel may be "more than a single author's facility in research and creative composition. The kind of vigorous activity in which Mark engaged can be imagined for many others like him. This period of activity was localized loosely in Syria and marked by the authors' awareness of each others' labors, if not the exchange of ideas and materials... 'Markan' authorship has been emphasized nonetheless in order to exhibit both the intentional fabrication (or recasting) of the many stories as well as the coherence of that intentionality when assessed in relation to function within the overall plan for the gospel. One might well imagine, however, many hands at work on the common project, in the course of working out together the new rationale. A lively intellectual atmosphere can easily be imagined" (pp 323-4).

Mack appears to imagine an early Jesus Seminar at work here, with Mark not so much a first-century solitary Mack as a preincarnation of Robert Funk!

27 as above, 321

28 as above, 324

29 Mack, *Who Wrote NT?* 47-8

30 as above, 49

31 as above, 50

32 as above, 50-1

33 as above, 51-2

34 as above, 52-3

35 as above, 53

36 Mack's own English translation of Q is given in *The Lost Gospel*, based on the Greek texts of Matthew and Luke from John Kloppenborg's *Q Parallels*. He presents two versions: an "original Q" (Q1) and a "complete Q" incorporating all three layers as adduced by reference to Kloppenborg and the International Q Project, Claremont. In Mack's "complete Q" the three layers are printed in different typefaces.

37 Mack, *Who Wrote NT* 47

38 as above, 47

PART III

CONSEQUENCES

12

REDS AND BLACKS

We have looked at the sources for hard information on Jesus of Galilee, man and message, and at what rival schools of critical scholarship have made of it all. What conclusions may we now draw? Where does historical Jesus scholarship stand today, a hundred years after Schweitzer? Are we any nearer to answering the question, Who on Earth was Jesus? Or are we in the same position as Fitzgerald's Omar Khayyam, who

> *...did eagerly frequent*
> *Doctor and Saint, and heard great Argument*
> *About it and about: but evermore*
> *Came out by the same Door as in I went.*

We can at least begin by asking what our doctors and saints agree on. Is there a basic minimum of historical data which most if not all our scholars would color red ("That's Jesus!")? Beyond that basic minimum, what are the principal unresolved issues on which the specialists and experts remain divided?

1. The Red consensus

We have summarized the work of a wide range of critical scholars, some with religious convictions and allegiances, some without. Some claim to discover a wholly human sage, story-teller or wisdom teacher, others an extraordinary visionary who spoke with what his hearers sensed as divine authority. Some meet a Jesus familiar to the churches that have worshipped him as the Christ, others a Jesus woefully misunderstood and misrepresented by those who have claimed to be his followers. Some locate him firmly in Second Temple Jewish religion and culture, others in the wider social context of the Hellenized Mediterranean. Some find the real Jesus in his reported or remembered words, others in whatever can be authenticated of his deeds. Some read him as announcing an imminent apocalyptic event in which the kingdoms of the world are toppled and replaced by God's direct rule, others as teaching and enacting a new vision of compassionate living, an alternative life-style brilliantly branded as the kingdom of heaven to distinguish it from the kingdoms of the world. Where, then, can we perceive broad agreement? Is there a "scholars' Jesus", an historians' Jesus, the academy's lowest-common-denominator Jesus?

While every Jesus historian would no doubt wish to qualify each of the following statements - that is what scholars do - I shall venture an inventory of conclusions which could probably muster a red or pink vote across most of the spectrum of opinion we have covered.

• The Jesus story (and therefore the Christian religion) has its origin in a flesh-and-blood Jew named Jesus. Like Alexander the Great and unlike Adam, Jesus lived in history.

• He was probably born in Nazareth to a mother named Mary shortly before the death of Herod the Great in 4 BCE. A virgin birth in Bethlehem, guiding star, shepherds, magi, and mass slaying of Jewish first-born are all legendary, not historical.

• Jesus lived in Galilee and was with John the Baptist in the Jordan wilderness before beginning his own teaching and healing mission in the villages of his home province, probably in the late 20s CE.

• He preached the "kingdom of God" or "kingdom of heaven" with a powerful and inspirational blend of memorable sayings and unique parables. Healings, exorcisms and miracles were widely attributed to him as a prophet or holy man.

• He attracted followers and made disciples.

• About the year 30 CE he took his message to Jerusalem, where he was summarily executed as a trouble-maker.

• His followers came to believe he had been raised from the dead and that his spirit would be with them in spreading his "good news".

This broadly accords with Sanders' "almost indisputable facts", Vermes' "authentic or probably authentic" certainties, and the Jesus Seminar's red inventory. Even Mack and Wells would probably sign up to it. Wright and Dunn would add much more, Ellegard and Eisenman insist on even less. But it seems we can say with confidence that critical scholarship affirms that this extraordinary story does have a factual basis in time, place and history. Most mainstream scholars would probably sign up to the following negatives and positives.

• None of the accounts of Jesus' words and deeds are contemporary eye-witness reports.

• All the written sources available to us date from several years after Jesus' death, by which time the communities of the Jesus movement were already engaged in a complex process of refining and elaborating their ideas of who and what Jesus was, said and did.

• In general, the earliest sources are likely to provide the more historically reliable glimpses of Jesus and his teaching.

• The earliest record of what was remembered as Jesus' teaching, or teaching attributed to him by his disciples, is probably found in whatever we can now recover of the sources used by the authors or editors of the synoptic gospels. Hypothetical Q is probably the nearest we can get to such sources.

• Q may have originated as an orally-transmitted cluster of Jesus' reported or remembered sayings before being added to by the communities using the collection, and eventually written down and embedded in the later narrative gospels.

There are lots of "likelys" and "probablys" here, and every item would no doubt be further qualified in one way or another by each of the scholars whose work we have focused on. But this seems to be as close as we can get to a broad summary of where mainstream historical Jesus scholarship stands today. Bare bones: a skeleton gospel. But they are real bones. Jesus *lived*. And if the quest for the truth about him remains a living scholarly discipline, even a clear obsession, there is a lively sense in which it can still be said two thousand years after his death that Jesus *lives*.

2. Mixed colors

But where does consensus give way to controversy? What are the big unresolved issues still dividing scholar from scholar, historian from historian?

After more than two hundred years of critical scholarship there remain stark differences in the evaluation of the social, political and economic context of early-first-century Galilee; differences in the way source materials are dated and interpreted for authenticity and reliability; differences over the value of Paul's letters as pointers to Jesus' own understanding of his message and mission; differences on whether Jesus is best understood as belonging to the tradition of Jewish prophets and charismatics or as a wisdom teacher in a broader Hellenized middle east; and differences over the manner and meaning of his death..

But the sharpest differences are to be found in the two most funda-mental questions about Jesus, relating to his status and his message. Was he man or god? And did he preach the possibility of *kingdom now*, defined by commitment to a radically transformed way of living, or apocalyptic *kingdom to come*, an imminent day of reckoning when the trumpets would sound and time would be no more?

Historical enquiry cannot provide an empirical answer to the theological question whether Jesus was God incarnate, any more than scientific enquiry can establish whether love and marriage go together like a horse and carriage. Poetry is not amenable to such treatment. But historical scholarship can investigate the process by which Jesus of Galilee came to be called Jesus Christ, God the Son, the incarnate Word. Since Jesus is "the Lord Jesus Christ" in Paul's letters, it is clear that to the writer and to the churches he established as early as the 40s and 50s Jesus was in some sense divine, the Son of God. The biblical gospels a generation later all present Jesus as the Christ or messiah, though they do so in different ways and with different emphases. Mark 8:27-30 has Jesus asking his disciples who they think he is, to which Peter replies "You are the Christ". Jesus tells his disciples to keep this secret until the time comes for him to suffer, die and rise again. When this time does come, and the High Priest asks (14:61) "Are you the Christ", Jesus answers "I am". Matthew 16:13-20 follows Mark in having Peter making the same affirmation, but adding that Jesus is "the son of the living God", to which Jesus replies that Peter will be the rock on which the church will be built. Luke 9:18-21 again follows Mark on Peter's recognition of who Jesus is, but in 22:66-67 it is "the chief priests and scribes" who ask "Are you the Christ?", which Jesus answers more evasively than in Mark, "You say that I am" (or "You tell me!"). In John 1:41 it is Andrew, not Peter, who first realizes that Jesus is the messiah, and Jesus himself affirms this when he meets the woman at the well (4:25) and tells her yes, he is the messiah, in the first of a series of breathtakingly audacious "I am" sayings. They all do it differently, but each of the four evangelists joins with Paul in preaching some kind of divine status for the teacher they call "the Lord". That Jesus speaks with the authority of God himself is the message of all four biblical gospels. Historians may argue about what the ancients meant by these titles, and theologians may discuss what meaning they could possibly have for us today. But that is how the New Testament writers had come to understand Jesus by the last quarter of the first century.

Q, on the other hand, closer to Jesus' own time, has no developed christology. Jesus is a teacher who preaches in aphorisms and parables, including those brought together as the "sermon on the mount". Each saying is simply prefaced by the words "Jesus said". Where disciples or the crowd are mentioned they address him in human terms as "Master" or "Teacher". Thomas too knows no Jesus Christ. Its editors put together a series of "secret sayings that the living Jesus spoke", and "the living Jesus" evidently means the Jesus who lived on Earth, as distinct from Paul's spirit-Jesus in heaven. Given these differences, it is hardly surprising that there is no scholarly consensus on whether the high chris-tology of Paul and the biblical evangelists reflects the way Jesus was understood by his followers during his lifetime or was a mid- and late-first-century development. To put it bluntly, did the historical Peter really acknowledge the historical Jesus to be "the Christ, the Son of the living God", and did this Jesus reply "I am" when asked by "the High Priest" if he was the messiah? Or were these stories introduced by Mark forty years later? Did an historical but anonymous Roman centurion standing in the shadow of the cross really say "Truly this man was the Son of God", or was that another of Mark's inventions to drive home his own under-standing of the gospel message? Did an historical angel Gabriel tell Mary that her child would be called "son of the Most High" whose "dominion would have no end", or does this originate in Matthew's creative imagi-nation 80 or 90 years after Jesus' birth? Did the historical Jesus tell an historical but unnamed woman at the well that he was "the messiah who is coming, who is called Christ", or did John make it up? Did Jesus and his immediate followers in Galilee understand him to be "the Word made flesh" who for all eternity "was with God and was God", or does John's awesome prologue simply tell us how he and his community had come to see Jesus by the end of the first century?

Vermes and Sanders do not dispute that Jesus was said by some to be the messiah in his own lifetime. But they argue that "messiah" (or "Christ" in Greek) simply meant "anointed one", God's messenger. God spoke through him, but that did not make him God. God had spoken through the prophets. He had even spoken through Balaam's ass. The long-awaited messiah who would liberate Israel was understood to be God's servant, not God in person. Similarly, the title "son of God" indicated not an incarnate deity but simply God's approval ("This is my beloved son in whom I am well pleased").

Scholars who see in Q the earliest available record or memory of what Jesus said go further. They conclude that the notion of a divine Jesus developed gradually through the first and second centuries within what would eventually emerge as the dominant faction of the Jesus movement. To begin with, Jesus was understood as God's messenger. After the traumatic shock of his humiliating execution the disciples came to believe that he had risen from the dead - but even this in itself did not make him God: there were precedents in Elijah and Enoch, both of whom who had cheated death and ascended to heaven according to the Jewish scriptures. Within twenty years, however, Paul was investing Jesus' titles with a higher theological significance and Jesus was being worshipped as a divine figure. Mark, Matthew and Luke elaborate this theology in different ways, and John crowns it by making Jesus the eternal Word. The process ends with the creeds, where Jesus as teacher gets no attention at all, entirely replaced by a Jesus who is God the Son, miraculously human and divine, living and reigning in heaven.

These scholars see this process of the divinization of Jesus as telling us more about the history of the early church than about the historical Jesus himself. Jesus was a man: the church turned him into a god. We can speculate how and why. Paul, struggling to convert gentiles, could draw on a long and attractive tradition of semi-divine Greek heroes and Romans celebrated as divine "sons of god". A new and living mystery god - indeed, the very one already celebrated in Athens as "the unknown god" - would have more appeal to gentiles than a dead Jewish rabbi. A similar process was under way in the Jewish Jesus movement. After the destruction of the temple and the sacking of Jerusalem in 70 CE, when the structures of Jewish religion were effectively dismantled, the two principal parties competing for dominance in the recovery, renewal and reformation of Judaism were the rabbinical movement, heirs to the Pharisees, and the Jesus movement. The Jesus movement played what it believed was its trump card: their Jesus was the *divine* messiah, the God of Israel who had descended from heaven to earth, died as an atonement for sin, rose from the dead, triumphantly ascended to heaven, and offered to those who believed in him the promise of a life after death, in paradise. For them, the test of authentic Judaism was acceptance of Jesus as the promised divine messiah. So the divinization of Jesus was a political as well as a theological process, and one that began long before Constantine knocked heads together and tidied up all the confusion in the interests of creating a united religion for a united empire - the very empire that had killed Jesus, though Christians, as their estrangement from Judaism moved towards a final divorce, were happy to rewrite the plot and pin the blame on "the Jews".

Theologians such as Wright and Dunn accuse the Jesus Seminar and liberal scholars in general of pursuing an agenda designed to accommodate the historical Jesus to modern liberal humanism: a Jesus for a secular age and a skeptical sensibility. (The counter-charge, of course, is that the agenda of conservative scholars is to accommodate the historical Jesus to church orthodoxy). But even Wright does not insist that Jesus in his own time was perceived in the same christological terms as those of the later evangelists; rather, in his view, far from turning history into mystery, Paul and the gospel writers came to understand Jesus for what he was (for them, and for Wright): wholly human but uniquely expressing in his life and death, his ministry and his miracles, the embodiment of divine grace, which made him the turning point of human history. On this view, the divinization of Jesus was not a lapse into superstitious misunderstanding but a dawning of truth that had been there all along. In Wright, at least, historian and theologian reconcile their differences. Elsewhere, the arguments continue.

3.The problem of Apocalypse (again)

On no single issue is there greater and more entrenched division than the kingdom question. According to the gospels, Jesus repeatedly proclaimed the kingdom of God, or kingdom of heaven. Questions of sin, salvation, right, wrong, are all wrapped up in his kingdom teaching. What did he mean? Was this kingdom already present in some sense, to be accessed and entered by those who took his message to heart? Or was he forecasting (promise or warning?) a kingdom to come? And if it was to come, would it burst upon the world as an imminent apocalyptic act of God, a cataclysmic supernatural intervention, or manifest itself as a process of transformation and revival that would open the way to an earthly paradise, the prophets' peaceable kingdom? Or should we be looking not for an either/or but a both/and?

Throughout the previous chapters we have seen how scholars have debated these questions without much sign of any emerging consensus. Albert Schweitzer's version of an apocalyptic Jesus held much of the high ground for more than half a century. It came to be challenged by the view that the kingdom Jesus preached might be understood as both present and future, both already at hand and yet only to be consummated in the near future. This opened up new divisions in the world of biblical scholarship. When the Jesus Seminar came up with its own interpretation - that the promised kingdom had an eschatological or future dimension but was not apocalyptic in the manner of the blood-soaked imagery of Daniel, the War Scroll and Revelation - this in its turn failed to convince many outside its own numbers. Sanders, Vermes, Dale Allison, Bart Ehrman and N T

Wright, among many internationally renowned scholars, have not shifted from their conviction that the sheer weight of apocalyptic sayings in the early literature points to Jesus himself having stood four-square in this tradition. We have followed the argument throughout this book. Here it is in summary.

Pro-apocalyptic: waiting for God to act

The strongest case for an apocalyptic Jesus is the argument from continuity. It is the main plank in the case made out by N T Wright and Dale Allison. Allison is credited by Marcus Borg, one of his opponents in this debate, as having made "the strongest contemporary scholarly case for an apocalyptic Jesus", so I shall cite him here as champion of the pro-party. In his contribution to *The Apocalyptic Jesus: a Debate*, Allison makes five linked arguments for his contention that "Jesus was an eschatological prophet with what one may call an apocalyptic scenario", and that this "should remain the matrix within which to establish and interpret authentic traditions"[1].

First, a wide range of New Testament writers apart from the four evangelists indicate that "many early followers of Jesus thought the eschatological climax to be near". Allison cites Acts 3:19-21, Romans 13:11, 1 Corinthians 16:22, Hebrews 10:37, James 5:8, 1 Peter 4:17 and Revelation 22:20, all of which express an eager anticipation of the imminent "coming of the Lord". The same expectation is expressed in the "pre-Easter" period, when "Jesus himself was closely associated with John the Baptist, whose public speech, if the synoptics are any guide at all, featured frequent allusion to the eschatological judgment, conceived as imminent (see Luke 3:7-17, which preserves material from the Q source)." (Allison is keen to make the point that even Q contains sayings supporting the apocalyptic interpretation). He points up the obvious inference: "To reconstruct a Jesus who did not have a strong eschatological or apocalyptic orientation entails discontinuity not only between him and people who took themselves to be furthering his cause, but also between him and the Baptist - that is, discontinuity with the movement out of which he came as well as with the movement that came out of him. Isn't presumption against this?"

Secondly, Allison asks why the canonical gospels, Acts, and Paul's letters all testify to a belief that "at least several pre-Easter followers of Jesus" were declaring soon after his crucifixion that "God raised Jesus from the dead" (Mark 16:6, Acts 2:24, Romans 10:9, 1 Thessalonians 1:10). "The best explanation", he suggests, "is that several influential individuals came to their post-Easter experiences, whatever they were, with certain categories and expectations antecedently fixed: that they already, *because of Jesus' teaching* [my emphasis], envisaged the general resurrection to be imminent". The "general resurrection" of believers was itself, of course, an essential (and most attractive) part of the apocalyptic scenario.

Thirdly, Allison draws attention to the way Mark and Matthew in particular link the death of Jesus to prophecies in the Hebrew scriptures of "signs and portents". Mark 15:33 tells of a strange darkness when Jesus died, taking his cue from Amos 8:9-10. Matthew 27:51-53 adds a mighty earthquake, the tearing apart of the temple veil, and a resurrection of "many bodies of the saints" coming out of their graves and wandering around Jerusalem, reminiscent of passages in Zechariah and Ezekiel. John's gospel interprets Jesus' death as "the judgment of the world" (12:31) and the end of Satan's reign (16:11). Paul understands Jesus as "the first fruits of those who have died" (1 Corinthians 15:20) - "a metaphor," says Allison, "which assumes that the eschatological harvest is underway, that the resurrection of Jesus is only the beginning of the general resurrection". Given this multiple attestation in the synoptics, John and Paul", he argues, "the habit of associating the end of Jesus with eschatological motifs must go back to very early times". Why would they do this? The best answer again, he says, is because Jesus himself had warned them of "apocalyptic suffering followed by eschatological vindication, tribulation followed by resurrection. So when Jesus was, in the event, crucified and seen alive again, his followers, instead of abandoning their apocalyptic hopes, did what one would expect them to do: they sought to correlate expectations with circumstances. That is why they believed that in Jesus' end the eschaton [end-time] had begun to unfold, and why early Christian texts associate the death and resurrection of Jesus with what appear to be eschatological events".

Fourthly, Jesus lived at a time when the expectation of an approaching end-time was widespread, not only in first-century Judaism but throughout the Roman world. Isaiah, Daniel and Ezekiel contain apocalyptic material, and there is more in other writings that were circulating in Jesus' day: the Jewish Sybylline Oracles, the Testament of Moses, and not least the Dead Sea Scrolls. In the decades after Jesus there is more in 4 Ezra, 2 Baruch and the Apocalypse of Abraham. "The point for us is this: to propose that Jesus thought the end to be near is just to say that he believed what many others in his time and place believed".

Finally, Allison finds support for an apocalyptic Jesus in the way New Testament texts compare him with his contemporaries. In Luke 7:33-34 Jesus compares his own ministry with that of John the Baptist. In Mark 6:14 Herod Antipas sees Jesus as the Baptist risen from the dead. Mark 8:28 reports that "the people" are circulating the same rumor. In Acts 5:35-39 Rabbi Gamaliel compares Jesus with Theudas and with Judas the Galilean, both of whom, like the Baptist, "were moved by eschatological expectation or hope for Jewish restoration". These comparisons "would be natural if Jesus was remembered as an apocalyptic prophet who proclaimed that God's kingdom would replace the Roman kingdom. They are not so easily explained if he was not so remembered".

In his summing up Allison asserts: "That Jesus was baptized by an eschatological prophet and had among his followers people who proclaimed a near end, that certain followers of Jesus proclaimed his resurrection soon after the crucifixion, that his passion and vindication were associated with eschatological motifs, that many first-century Jews expected an apocalyptic scenario to unfold in the near future, and that our sources compare Jesus with others who believed in such a scenario or at least expected God soon to rule Palestine - these indisputable facts together tell us that Jesus held hopes close to those attributed to him by Weiss and Schweitzer"[2].

On this argument it follows that "The elimination of millenarian eschatology from the earliest Jesus tradition is not plausible. Jesus' thought focused on the culmination of Israel's story and so his speech was dominated by the hope of salvation and the threat of judgment. His moral imperatives were an urgent plea for the spiritual reformation that was widely expected to herald the advent of the Day of the Lord. Jesus, in sum, was a Jewish visionary who demanded change in the face of the eschatological crisis and interpreted his own person and ministry in terms of scriptural fulfilment. And his chief goal, as the last prophet in the cosmic drama, was to prepare his people for the eschatological finale"[3].

In promising the disaffected and less fortunate a reversal of fortune and a righting of wrongs, understanding the present and near future as a time of suffering and catastrophe, promoting a coming egalitarianism, dividing the world into two camps, the just and the unjust; in breaking hallowed religious taboos, replacing traditional family bonds with ties to a charismatic leader, understanding his teaching to be the product of a special revelation; in looking to a divinely-wrought deliverance rather than political liberation, expecting a miraculously restored paradise - in all this, says Allison, but especially in the warning/promise of the end of the world as we know it, Jesus and his followers prefigured movements familiar in our own day and time: "Pacific cargo cults, Jewish messianic groups, Amerindian prophetic movements, and Christian sects looking for the end of the world"[4].

If other apocalyptic movements through the ages have been mistaken, was Jesus also mistaken? Yes, says Allison, as Schweitzer had dared to say before him. Allison closes his book *Jesus of Nazareth: Millenarian Prophet* (1998) with the assertion that "Jesus is the millenarian prophet of consolation and hope who comforts those who mourn. He sees the poor, the hungry and the reviled, and he proclaims that the last will be first... He declares, against all the evidence, that the oppressed and the destitute are not miserable but blessed. They will have treasure in heaven. They will be rewarded at the resurrection of the just." But the poor remained poor, the hungry hungry, the oppressed oppressed, and as the years went by there was no second coming signaling the general resurrection that would bring the poor their promised blessing. "Jesus the millenarian prophet, like all millenarian prophets, was wrong: reality has taken no notice of his imagination. Was it not all a dream, an unfounded fantasy?" Maybe, says Allison, but "his dream is *the only dream worth dreaming*. If our wounds never heal, if the outrageous spectacle of a history filled with catastrophic sadness is never undone, if there is nothing more for those who were slaughtered in the death camps or for six year olds devoured by cancer, then let us eat and drink, for tomorrow we die. If in the end there is no good God to calm this sea of troubles, to raise the dead, and to give good news to the poor, then this is indeed a tale told by an idiot, signifying nothing"[5].

Apocalypse as miraculous second coming, miraculous resurrection of the just, miraculous punishment of the unjust, miraculous righting of wrongs in a life after death, is justified for the comfort and consolation it brings to those who cannot bear the bleakness of a story without a happy ending. But what can this mean in modernity? As Marcus Borg comments, "I have difficulty imagining post-mortem justice... I cannot imagine what it means to say, 'All the victims will live again in a state of blessedness' (presumably with the corollary that the perpetrators will not share in the blessedness)"[6]. And can this dream, "the only dream worth dreaming", bring comfort and consolation if we acknowledge, as Allison himself does, that it *is* just "a dream, an unfounded fantasy, a myth in the derogatory sense of the word"?[7]

Anti-apocalyptic: waiting for us to act

The debate between historians who conclude that Jesus shared the apocalyptic world-view of his times and those who think he transcended that tradition is not simply a matter of text wars, pitting the few kingdom-among-you sayings against the many kingdom-come sayings. The non-apocalyptic school does not dispute the considerable volume of documentary evidence supporting the contention that Jesus was both preceded by an apocalyptic Baptist and followed by an apocalyptic Paul whose expectations find echoes in all four canonical gospels, non-Pauline letters and Revelation (or the Apocalypse). What it does dispute is that this tradition necessarily takes in Jesus himself, and its doubts on this score derive from the importance it places on recent Q and Thomas scholarship. Thus, Allison, Sanders and the modern apocalypticists are criticized for reading the New Testament uncritically, having failed to keep up with trends in scholarship that have moved away from the assumption of Weiss, Schweitzer and the "Old Quest" that the synoptics in their late-first-century forms represent a mainstream of tradition about Jesus that is both early and essentially reliable.

Borg, Crossan and Stephen Patterson all make a major plank of their anti-apocalyptic case the recent studies of Q and Thomas. As we have seen, in *The Formation of Q* John Kloppenborg proposed that Q is best understood as not one but a series of collections of sayings attributed to Jesus, made at different times between the 40s or 50s and the 70s, each layer reflecting the developing theologies of its editors. Thomas too was seen as a sayings collection built up over two or more generations, and in both "gospels" the different layers may plausibly be separated out by literary analysis. What Kloppenborg and the majority of Jesus Seminar scholars concluded was that the earliest layer of Q (Q1) was made up, for the most part, of wisdom sayings in various forms - aphorisms, beatitudes and parables - with Thomas showing similar editorial development.

As Patterson puts it, "All of this suggests that Jesus' sayings were originally collected by followers who were interested in him as a wisdom teacher, or perhaps as Lady Wisdom's prophet, a figure common in Jewish Wisdom theology. Later, people associated with the development of the synoptic tradition began to interpret Jesus' message in light of Jewish apocalyptic theology"[8]. This explains the many apocalyptic sayings *attributed* to Jesus by the synoptic evangelists. "It appears that the apocalypticism of the synoptic tradition was built upon an earlier wisdom foundation, much of which can still be recovered through critical analysis. As the followers of Jesus reflected on his significance in the years following his death, at least two streams of thought quickly developed: one that came to understand him in terms of Jewish apocalypticism [reflected in Q3], and another that saw him rather in terms of the more esoteric forms of Jewish wisdom theology [Q1] and eventually Gnosticism [the later layers of Thomas]. The most logical inference from this", Patterson concludes, "is that Jesus presented himself neither as an apocalyptic prophet, nor as a Gnostic revealer sent from God. He was seen, rather, as a teacher of wisdom, or perhaps one of Wisdom's prophets"[9].

Where apocalyptic-Jesus scholars assume a mainstream orthodox tradition in the first-century texts, from which other less authentic or "heretical" traditions (like gnosticism) parted company in the second century, Q/Thomas scholars suggest a less homogeneous picture. Patterson again: "Christianity was a diverse phenomenon from the very beginning; there is no mainstream. The synoptic tradition stands alongside others: Johannine Christianity, Thomasine Christianity, pre-Pauline Hellenistic Jewish Christianity, Palestine Jewish Christianity, etc., each of which may be glimpsed from the sources. But embracing this view means approaching the quest for the historical Jesus in a different way. The decisive issue is not who preserves the voice of Jesus most reliably, but what sort of message and ministry we can posit at the beginning of this diversity that will plausibly account for it"[10].

Borg and Crossan take a slightly different tack from Patterson. They share his confidence in the Q/Thomas revolution and the diverse Christianities it reveals from the very beginning - even in the "pre-Easter" Jesus movement. But both seem more prepared than Patterson to see eschatological, even apocalyptic elements, in the earliest Jesus tradition. Borg is willing to go along with what he calls a "secondary apocalyptic" paradigm, where Jesus is understood *primarily* as a wisdom teacher and charismatic healer who *also* believed that God would soon intervene to vindicate or complete what he, Jesus, had begun. "But apocalyptic conviction was not the primary energy driving his mission or shaping his teaching. Rather, it is one element in a fuller understanding of Jesus"[11].

Crossan, too, reaches for an understanding of apocalyptics that rejects the falling stars, melting elements, Armageddon and "rapture" but acknowledges a sense of the beginning of the end of the old world and the dawning of a new. He envisages "an eschatological but non-apocalyptic Jesus": that is, a Jesus driven by a sense of the end-time, the end of the world as it was known, but proclaiming a kingdom "where the emphasis is on transformative, social, secondary, positive, active, and durative apocalyptic rather than on destructive, material, primary, negative, passive, and instantive apocalyptic... close to what I have termed ethical eschatology or the radicality of divine ethics... But what makes *such* an 'apocalyptic' Jesus persuasive is not that it agrees with me but that it explains what actually happened to the Kingdom movement across its first hundred years"[12].

Borg contributes a simpler explanation of why the early Jesus movement so quickly developed Jesus' kingdom teaching into a primary, cataclysmic-apocalyptic scenario. "In the early 40s, the Roman emperor Caligula issued an order to erect a statue of himself in the temple. Caligula's plan generated massive Jewish protest demonstrations and threatened to result in war. His death before the order could be carried out ended the crisis. But the crisis called to mind a time two centuries earlier when another pagan emperor had erected a statue of Zeus in the temple, an event called 'the desolating sacrilege' or 'abomination of desolation' in the apocalyptic scenario in the second half of the book of Daniel. "A generation later, in the year 70, the Jewish people experienced their single greatest catastrophe in ancient times: the devastating Roman response to the Jewish revolt of 66. Roman legions reconquered the Jewish homeland and Jerusalem, with enormous loss of Jewish life, and then destroyed both Jerusalem and the temple."

Both these events, Borg suggests, "are likely to have intensified apocalyptic expectation among Jews, including Christian Jews. In particular, the Jewish apocalyptic books of Baruch and 4 Ezra both respond to the events of 70. Mark, our earliest canonical gospel, reflects the circumstances of the year 70, most clearly in the 'little apocalypse' of Mark 13. Indeed, all of the canonical gospels were written after the 'apocalyptic event' of the Jewish war against Rome and its aftermath. Thus I think there is strong evidence for heightened apocalyptic expectation of early Christianity during the decades [in] which the traditions about Jesus took shape". And Borg speaks for the Jesus Seminar consensus when he concluded: "I locate the apocalyptic expectation of early Christianity in the post-Easter community" - that is, with Jesus' followers rather than with Jesus himself.[13]

Both/and: God and humanity act together

There is finally the position advanced by N T Wright: Jesus preached apocalypse, and *he was right*. The point was not to wait for God to act, nor was it to suppose that God sat idly by, waiting for us to act. God and man acted together, because God and man were one in Jesus. Jesus preached a kingdom that was already coming into being, already evident, already trailed by his miraculous healings, exorcisms and "signs and wonders". He *performed* the way of the kingdom, and lo! the kingdom dawned. Since this was the turning point of history, only the heightened language of apocalyptics could begin to do it justice. The falling stars, mighty earthquakes, glorious appearance in the skies, melting elements and the dreadful Day of Judgment were not to be understood literally but metaphorically; poetically, not prosaically.

This argument evinces from Crossan the comment that "A metaphor must be a metaphor for something. So we would still have to ask what the something is"[15]. Why paint the turning-point of history in such violent colors? Can cataclysmic destruction be a metaphor for peaceful transformation? In any case, Wright soon abandons metaphor and retreats to a naked literalism when it comes to the single event that precipitates the apocalypse: the raising of Jesus from the dead. For Wright this is non-negotiable: it happened in history and it changed history. This will not do for historians who see Jesus within a long, tragic history of mistaken apocalyptic expectation, nor, of course, for those who find no apocalypse and no risen Christ in what they take to be the earliest Jesus collections. The both/and position only makes sense, they would say, when history is forced to play second fiddle to theologically motivated compromise.

Where will this debate go? Apocalypticists and non-apocalypticists will no doubt continue to slug it out in the hope that their own side can deliver a winning punch, an apocalyptic or sapiential sockdolager. It seems likely that if anything turns up to decisively shift the consensus one way or the other it will be somewhere in the still developing field of Q scholarship. As Q continues to be interrogated critically, tested by the full range of academic disciplines from literary analysis through form criticism to comparative and contextual scrutiny, it could either win over the doubters or collapse under the assault of rival interpretations. But if Q stands the test, Jesus was primarily a wisdom teacher, not a prophet of imminent apocalypse. And if Q falls, especially if it drags early-Thomas with it, in the absence of anything that can be reliably dated earlier than Paul and the canonical gospels, we are back with uncertainty. Lacking any final resolution we are forced to choose between uncertainties. And how we choose is not without consequences.

Notes to Chapter 12

1 Allison in *Apocalyptic J* 20ff

2 as above, 24

3 as above, 29

4 as above, 28. "Cargo cults" is the name given by anthropologists (Peter

Worsley, G Cochrane and others) to South Sea island millennial movements where local prophets predict an imminent golden age when dead heroes or ancestors will return carrying a "cargo" of goods or cultural benefits as gifts of distant white civilisation. The movements have taken many forms, some of which have been assimilated into local pentecostal churches. See the entry in *The Oxford Dictionary of World Religions* p 196.

5 Allison, *Millenarian Prophet* 217-9

6 Borg in *Apocalyptic J* 117

7 Allison, *Millenarian Prophet* 217

8 Patterson in *Apocalyptic J* 73

9 as above, 74

10 as above, 80

11 Borg in *Apocalyptic J* 44

12 Crossan in *Apocalyptic J* 69

14 Borg in *Apocalyptic J* 39-40

15 Crossan in *Apocalyptic J* 55

13

WHICH JESUS?

If Jesus is approached as a figure of historical interest but no contemporary relevance, like Alexander the Great or Nebuchadnezzar, it would hardly matter whether he was seen as a teacher like Socrates, a social activist like Gandhi, or an end-time doomster like David Koresh. But Jesus is accorded contemporary relevance by millions around the world, either because he is believed to be God incarnate, or God's messenger, or because he is acknowledged as an enlightened teacher who by virtue of the unique place he is accorded in our culture continues to influence our lives two millennia after his death. If historical enquiry cannot establish something as theologically formulated, subjective and emotionally charged as his "divinity", nor cast much light on what that might mean, it can and does sift the evidence on where he stood in relation to the long tradition of apocalyptic scenarios. Since that tradition has come to dominate much of the religion and politics of the twentyfirst century, the question of where we position the historical Jesus on this single issue is highly relevant - and fraught with consequences.

Let us, as we reach the beginning of the end of this book, take one step further our investigation of the apocalyptic tradition. That will entail attention to a broader range of scholarship. It will also test - I fear to breaking point - my resolution to maintain a respectable neutrality in the face of scholarly dissension.

The "Making Wonderful Time"

Ancient religious cultures understood time as circular rather than linear. Vedic Indians, forerunners of the Hindus, saw the world as a recurring cycle of wars, plagues, floods, droughts, all the products of supernatural forces, and all without either beginning or end. The ancient Babylonian religion as revealed in the *Epic of Gilgamesh* likewise envisaged a perpetual recurrence of events in a world without end. But around 1200 BCE a prophet arose in the far-east provinces of what is now Iran. Zarathustra, or Zoroaster in Greek, taught that the cosmic struggle between good and evil forces was not destined to last through all eternity but would come to an end. After a final cataclysmic battle, during which the sky would crack open, rivers would be contaminated by salt, plants, animals and humans would die, and even the purest element, fire, would be engulfed in smoke and darkness, the good god Ahura Mazda would prevail over the evil one, Angra Mainyu. The wicked, men and spirits, would be crushed and Ahura Mazda would usher in the "Making Wonderful" time. The souls of the dead would be led to the Bridge of Judgment where those who had lived good lives would be allowed to cross into Paradise, while the wicked would fall from the bridge into the House of Lies, a place of poisoned food, terrible smells, pain, torment and woe. Zarathustra preached his apocalyptic message as an itinerant teacher, rejected by his family and neighbors, refusing hospitality and befriending the poor. In later tradition he was honored as Sosyant, the expected savior, and miracles were attributed to him (including the healing of the king's favorite but mortally sick horse).

Why this great change in religious understanding? Why was cyclical time suddenly rejected in favor of linear time which had beginning and end? Historians speculate that Zarathustra's people were suffering from violent raids by nomadic warriors which were devastating their lands and decimating the people. Zarathustra associated Mazda with peace and Angra Mainyu with violence. A ravaged people needed reasurance that there would ultimately be justice, wrongs would be righted, the wicked would get what they deserved. Their savior-prophet, Mazda's "annointed" (messiah), told them the end-time would come and good would triumph. The apocalyptic sign was the appearance of great fireballs that would turn rivers into torrents of molten metal. Men and women would be engulfed, but "for him who is righteous it will seem as if he is walking through warm milk; and for him who is wicked it will seem as if he is walking... through molten metal". Angra Mainyu himself would be banished to the realm of darkness, entered by a cave, and the molten metal would seal the mouth of the cave for ever[1].

"Showers of blessing"

By the late sixth century BCE Zarathustra's new apocalyptics had spread through the whole of ancient Persia (modern Iran). But Persia's rival, Babylon (modern Iraq), was also in conquering mode under its king, Nebuchadnezzar, who had invaded Israel in 586, destroyed the temple and exiled thousands of Jews. This national catastrophe gave rise to a new and essentially Jewish eschatology in the writings of the prophets. Ezekiel promised that the exile would not last for ever: there would be "showers of blessing" in "the latter days" (35:26). Isaiah comforted the exiles with Yahweh's promise that he would create "new heavens and a new earth" where "the voice of weeping shall be no more heard... nor the voice of crying". Infant mortality would end, everyone would live to a ripe old age in their own house, tending their own vineyard. "The wolf and the lamb shall feed together, and the lion shall eat straw like the bullock: and dust shall be the serpent's meat. They shall not hurt nor destroy in all my holy mountain" (65:17-25).

Fifty years after the Babylonian captivity, in the year 539, Persia's Cyrus the Great conquered Babylon in a series of campaigns that extended his empire to Northern India, Egypt, Greece and ancient Palestine. Zoroastrianism was now proclaimed the official state religion, but Cyrus permitted his conquered territories to retain or renew their own religious practices. Jews returned from exile in Babylon and were encouraged by Cyrus to rebuild their temple. Chapter 45 of the book of Isaiah actually hails the Zoroastrian king as "the Lord's annointed" or messiah, charged to "subdue nations before him"[2]. In this happy coexistence, the dominant state religion inevitably influenced the less powerful culture of what was still a conquered people. The Jewish prophetic tradition with its "covenant of peace", shaped in Babylonian exile, began to be subtly transformed as it borrowed from the Zoroastrian ascendancy sterner notions of the end-time, resurrection, eternal reward and punishment, and messianic imagery.

"The vision of the Time of the End"

But empires come, empires go. Greece revolted, and in the fourth century Alexander the Great ("the Accursed" in Zoroastrian texts) conquered Persia and all its territories. Tolerance and coexistence was no longer the name of the game: the new empire would be made to cohere through a process of Hellenization - the spread of Greek culture. After Alexander's death his vast realm was divided into dynasties, with ancient Palestine coming under the Seleucid dynasty, based in Syria. Under Antiochus Epiphanes IV, who assumed the Greek-Seleucid throne in 175 BCE, the Jews suffered their worst repression since the days of Nebuchadnezzar. In 169 Jerusalem was sacked, all Jewish religious practices were banned, and Antiochus ordered the erection of a statue to Zeus in the temple. This provoked a guerilla resistance, and in 164 a force led by Judas Maccabee retook the temple, repurified it, and restored Jewish religion in the Jewish homeland.

This cycle of war and peace, coexistence and extermination, produced a new literature. Probably not one but several authors contributed to what would eventually be edited together as the book of Daniel. Here the tangled tale of Jewish history over the previous five centuries is allegorized in a dream. Four beasts arise from the sea. A lion with eagle's wings is Nebuchadnezzar's Babylonian empire, a bear with three ribs in its mouth is the Persians, a four-headed winged leopard is the Greeks. But the fourth beast is more "dreadful and terrible", with "a look more stout than his fellows". It has iron nails for teeth and brass knives for claws, with which it proceeds to "devour the whole earth, and tread it down, and break it in pieces". This beast is crowned with ten horns, but three disappear, to be replaced by a new one with eyes and a mouth. This horn speaks "great words against the most High", such words as will "wear out the saints" (Daniel 7:19-25). The ten-horned beast is the succession of Seleucid kings, and the seeing-talking horn is Antiochus himself.

But all is not lost. In Daniel's dream, the God of Israel will surely come to rescue his people and give them justice:

"I beheld till the thrones were cast down, and the Ancient of Days did sit, whose garment was white as snow, and the hair of his head like the pure wool: his throne was like the fiery flame, and his wheels as burning fire. A fiery stream issued and came forth from before him: thousand thousands ministered unto him, and ten thousand times ten thousand stood before him: the judgment was set... I beheld even till the beast was slain, and his body destroyed, and given to the burning flame... And, behold, one like the Son of man came with the clouds of heaven, and came to the Ancient of Days, and they brought him near before him. And there was given him dominion, and glory, and a kingdom, that all people, nations, and languages, should serve him: his dominion is an everlasting dominion, which shall not pass away, and his kingdom that which shall not be destroyed... Hitherto is the end of the matter" (Daniel 7:9-14, 28).

As Simon Pearson comments in a racy re-telling of the story, "The prophecies which predate the Book of Daniel contain apocalyptic elements but are not in themselves apocalypses. What distinguishes Daniel's prophecy from previous ones [in the Jewish tradition] is the emphasis it places on a total and utter transformation of the created order: corrupt earthly empires are destroyed and replaced, once and for all, by a totally new order of things. Rather than it being a narrowly nationalistic celebration of Israel's future glory, Daniel's vision has cosmic dimensions to it, raising it to an apocalyptic level. Biblical scholars are generally agreed that it is the first true apocalypse in the Hebrew Bible. The imminence of salvation for the righteous and destruction for the ungodly is a two-fold process that has become the paradigm in apocalyptic religious literature. What further distinguishes Daniel from the earlier prophecies is 'The Vision of the Time of the End' which appears in the tenth chapter. It is an extraordinary climax to an extraordinary book, a step-by-step account of what will actually happen at the end of the world. Troop movements, the clash of arms, dynastic struggle and the fall of great empires: all are depicted in astonishing and unforgettable detail. These are the 'signs' of the end-times"[3].

Seleucid rule was indeed replaced by a new kingdom, but not the one Daniel dreamed of. In 63 BCE Judaea was invaded once again, this time by the Roman general Pompey, and the Jews remained a conquered, client people under a new set of masters, their deliverance deferred. But an odd fact about apocalyptic scenarios is that every time the prophecy fails to materialize it seems to gather strength rather than fall into oblivion. Daniel's Zoroastrian-influenced apocalypticism, with its blessed assurance of victory for the righteous and just deserts for the wicked, inspired more such writing, such as the five so-called Books of Enoch, and the Dead Sea Scrolls attributed to the sect of the Essenes. In *The War of the Sons of Light against the Sons of Darkness*, also known as the *War Scroll*, the last great battle sees an alliance of God's angels and righteous Jews against an axis of evil - Belial's devils and wicked gentiles. The outcome is never in doubt. After "the great hand of God [is] lifted up against Belial... for an eternal slaughter", a new Jerusalem, paradise, kingdom of God, "Making Wonderful Time", is established for all eternity.

The *War Scroll* was probably written just about the time of Jesus' birth. Whether or not the adult Jesus bought into this dream of reward and revenge by divine violence, the contemporary sense of impending apocalypse followed him from his time with John the Baptist to his death on the cross, and the movement he started found in the apocalyptic paradigm an explanation of the catastrophe of his death, the miracle of his resurrection, and the certain victory of his kingdom. To them, Jesus was the one who had come before Daniel's Ancient of Days "in the likeness of the Son of man", to whom would be given the kingdom, the power and the glory.

The dream of "the Day of the Lord"

As we have repeatedly seen, there are apocalyptic passages scattered throughout the canonical gospels and the epistles. But specifically Christian apocalypticism reaches its climax in the Book of Revelation - *the* Apocalypse. Again, a specific wave of oppression and persecution is behind this bizarre but immensely influential work. Nero's persecution of the Jesus movement in the 60s, followed by the destruction of Jerusalem and the temple (again) in 70, drove many Jews, including Jewish Christians, out of Palestine and into Asia Minor and Greece. But persecution followed them under the emperor Domitian (81-96). The "John" who wrote this book, probably in the 90s (and few scholars believe it was authored by whoever wrote John's gospel[4]) appears to have led a community of Jewish Christian exiles on the remote island of Patmos, only to find they had no safe haven from Rome's seek-and-destroy mission. The Roman emperor was addressed as *dominus et deus*, "*the* Lord and God", and John defiantly contrasts this imperial god with "*our* Lord and God". The conflict between "the saints" and Rome assumes cosmic proportions as John dreams that he is transported to the future "Day of the Lord" for a preview of the end-time, which revelation he is commanded to report back to the churches.

His theme is the conflict between the power of the world, in Satan's grip, and the people of God. The war is waged by "the Lamb", a symbol of Christ slaughtered and sacrificed, and his adversary, the "whore of Babylon... drunk with the blood of saints" (17:6). Clearly following Daniel's language and imagery, John sees in his vision "one like unto the Son of Man, clothed with a garment down to the foot, and girt about the paps with a golden girdle. His head and his hairs were white like wool, as white as snow; and his eyes were as a flame of fire". He lays his right hand on John and tells him, "Fear not; I am the first and the last: I am he that liveth, and was dead; and, behold, I am alive for evermore... and have the keys of hell and of death" (1:10-18).

Payback time

In Daniel, God had hidden the final mysteries and the full end-time scenario in a great book sealed by seven seals. In Revelation, this same book is brought to the Lamb by an enthroned figure surrounded by twentyfour crowned elders and four beasts with six wings and multiple eyes. It is time for the seals to be broken and the book to be opened. The first four seals reveal in turn the fearful "four horses of the apocalypse": one white for conquest, the second red for civil war, the third black for famine, and the fourth ghostly-pale for death. These are to be the Lamb's secret weapons against his enemies. When the fifth seal is opened John sees "the souls of them that were slain for the word of God" cowering under the altar and pleading for vengeance. They are told to be patient. More martyrs must be killed before things take a turn for the better.

Let Simon Pearson describe what happens next (though you need to turn to your Bible to get the full flavor of it): "The opening of the sixth seal unleashes a vortex that sucks up the whole created order. There's an earthquake. Then the sun turns nightmarishly black, the moon into a lurid shade of blood red. Stars fall to earth. The firmament is rolled up like a scroll and the mountains and islands move. Such disturbances engender extreme perturbation in the rich and powerful; they attempt to hide themselves from God's wrath in caves and dens. John regards such pathetic scenes with undisguised relish. This is payback for the underdog"[5].

But first God must mount an emergency rescue operation to pluck the faithful from this mounting chaos. Four angels controlling the winds from each corner of the earth are instructed to hold back the final storms. First 144,000 Jews, 12,000 from each of the twelve tribes of Israel, are branded on the forehead to mark them out for deliverance. (This John is evidently a faithful Jew as well as a Christian). Next, he sees "a great multitude, which no man could number, of all nations, and kindreds, and people, and tongues". They are clothed in white robes and they join with the angels in singing (to Handel?) blessings and honor, power and glory to "him which sitteth upon the throne, and unto the Lamb". These, John is told, are those who "came out of great tribulation, and have washed their robes, and made them white in the blood of the Lamb" (7:1-14).

With a first batch of the saved now out of harm's way, God's onslaught against his enemies can begin in earnest. The seventh seal is opened, followed by half an hour of Quakerly silence. Then trumpets sound. Hail falls, mixed with fire; the seas turn red with blood; wells and rivers are poisoned. There is an invasion of giant locusts with human faces, horses' heads and scorpions' tails. In the massacre that follows, a third of humankind is wiped out. Then Satan himself appears in the form of a fearsome dragon and is met in battle by Michael and his hosts, who drive him from the heavens to earth. Here, in the form of a seven-headed and ten-horned Beast, part leopard, part bear, part lion, he rules the world for forty-two months, during which time those who serve him, rich and poor, slave and free, are branded on the hand or forehead with the mysterious figure 666. An angel, with harp accompaniment, announces what will happen to those who carry the mark of the Beast: "The same shall drink of the wine of the wrath of God, which is poured out without mixture into the cup of his indignation; and he shall be tormented with fire and brimstone in the presence of the holy angels, and in the presence of the Lamb. And the smoke of their torment ascendeth up for ever and ever: and they have no rest, day nor night" (14:10-11). To soften them up for this eternal horror, they first suffer a plague of gaping sores, gigantic hailstones, and the destruction of their homes in earthquakes, before they are brought face to face with God's hosts "at a place called in the Hebrew tongue Armageddon", scene of "the battle of that great day of God Almighty" (16:14-16).

But John is on a roll, seemingly unwilling to bring his end-time orgy to an end. He introduces another tableau before this ultimate confrontation when the forces of evil are finally crushed. We are introduced to "a woman sitting upon a scarlet colored beast, full of names of blasphemy". Her steed has the familiar seven heads and ten horns, and its rider is arrayed in purple and scarlet, tarted up with gold, precious stones and pearls. She carries a golden cup "full of abominations and filthiness of her fornication". And she is drunk, not on wine but "with the blood of the saints, and with the blood of the martyrs of Jesus". Across her forehead are the words "MYSTERY, BABYLON THE GREAT, THE MOTHER OF HARLOTS AND ABOMINATIONS OF THE EARTH". John learns that the woman is "that great city, which reigneth over the kings of the earth" - a barely-coded image of Rome and its empire. The seven heads are the imperial city's seven hills, the horns are the kings who have served her. But the whore of Babylon is about to be destroyed. The ten horns will turn on her, for "God hath put it in their hearts to fulfil his will... These shall hate the whore, and shall make her desolate and naked, and shall eat her flesh, and burn her with fire" (17:3-18). God is not above using evil means - the four fearsome horsemen, and now the whore's own servants - to achieve his ends.

Sure enough, another angel enters and cries "mightily and with a loud voice, saying, Babylon the great is fallen, is fallen, and is become the inhabitation of devils, and the hold of every foul spirit, and a cage of every unclean and hateful bird". There is rejoicing in heaven, but John describes at greater length and with more relish the anguish of the whore's lovers and minions. "The kings... who have committed fornication and lived deliciously with her" now bewail and lament for her. The rich merchants of goods, foodstuffs, slaves, and souls of men now "weep and mourn over her: for no man buyeth their merchandise any more" (18:1-13). Blessed are the poor, for their revenge is sweet!

Now John sees heaven open, "and behold a white horse; and he that sat upon him was called Faithful and True, and in righteousness he doth judge and make war. His eyes were as a flame of fire, and on his head were many crowns... and he was clothed in a vesture dipped in blood: and his name is called The Word of God... And he hath on his vesture and on his thigh a name written, KING OF KINGS, AND LORD OF LORDS" (19:11-16). In his train ride the armies of heaven, angels on white horses, all clothed in white linen. An angel standing in the sun calls on birds of prey to gather in readiness for "the supper of the great God", when they shall "eat the flesh of kings, and the flesh of captains, and the flesh of mighty men, and the flesh of horses, and of them that sit on them, and the flesh of all men, both free and bond, both small and great". The battle is short and swift. The beast and its worshippers are captured and "cast alive into a lake burning with brimstone". Then Jesus himself slays the remnant with his own sword and the vultures get their supper, being "filled with flesh".

By now, not altogether surprisingly, John's chronology has become somewhat confusing. The confusion has kept prophets of the end of the world guessing for two thousand years. We have had Armageddon and the destruction of the Beast in chapter 16, and a *coup de grace* by Jesus himself in chapter 19. But it seems that all is not yet done. In the following chapter an angel enters, carrying the keys of the bottomless pit and a great chain. The angel lays hold of the dragon, "that old serpent, which is the Devil, and Satan", and chains it up for a thousand years. This is the millennium, during which time of peace those who have not worshipped the Beast are resurrected to live and reign with Christ. But when the millennium is up, Satan is unchained and set loose to wreak more havoc before God engulfs him in fire from heaven. Satan's hosts are devoured, and Satan himself is (again) cast into a lake of fire and brimstone, this time "for ever and ever".

And so to the great denoument. John witnesses the day of judgment, when "the dead, small and great, stand before God" and the book of life is opened to reveal their works, by which they are judged. "And whosoever was not found written in the book of life was cast into the lake of fire". The end time has come to an end. "And I saw a new heaven and a new earth, for the first heaven and the first earth were passed away... And I John saw the holy city, new Jerusalem, coming down from God out of heaven, prepared as a bride adorned for her husband." The celestial city had walls and foundations of precious stones, streets paved with gold, and each of the twelve gates was a giant pearl. There was no sun, no moon, no night, no candle, for the Lamb was all the light this city required. As Isaiah had prophesied centuries earlier, and Zarathustra centuries before him, there would be an eternal "Making Wonderful" time when "God shall wipe away all tears from their eyes; and there shall be no more death, neither sorrow nor crying, neither shall there be any more pain: for the former things are passed away. And he that sat upon the throne said, Behold I make all things new" (20:11-15, 21:1-5).

What a story! Small wonder that this late-first-century masterpiece of imagination, with its grotesque menagerie of multi-headed, multi-horned dragons and beasts, trumpeting angels, fountains of blood, fearsome tortures, lakes of fire and brimstone, and a whore to end all whores, has maintained such a grip on successive generations. The imagery of apocalypse has penetrated deep into our language, literature, art - and religion. Victory for the just is assured and is all the sweeter in contemplation of the perpetual agonies of those we have demonized as God's enemies. Simon Pearson sums it up:

"After all the terror and the darkness... we are left with a vision of dazzling light - the New Jerusalem coming out of the skies. For the faithful the End of the World is not a terminus but a radically new beginning, the start of a journey above and beyond to a realm of eternal peace, beauty and harmony. Such a vision held a special appeal in the last centuries of the Roman era, as the empire tottered, fragmented and finally disintegrated. The twelve pearly gates are always open to those of pure heart, closed to those 'unclean'. Christ assures John that he will come 'quickly', a word which recurs repeatedly, suffusing the whole narrative with a sense of crisis and feverish expectancy. As time speeds up to its final consummation, locality after locality passes before our eyes in phantasmagoric blur. This time-space compression induces a sense of delirium which is finally resolved in the vision of the celestial city descending from the clouds. Static, unchanging and tightly bounded, such a place reveals the Jewish-Christian desire to have a place called home in a world rent with conflict and persecution, injustice and suffering"[6].

The apocalyptic drama which had gathered strength for twelve centuries, from Zarathustra through Daniel, the *War Scroll*, the works of the Essene prophets and the Apocalypse of John, had a long run ahead of it. "Chiliastic" expectation - the Greek term for millenarian apocalypticism - was rife in the early churches. Towards the end of the second century Montanus and his two prophetesses, Priscilla and Maximilia, announced precisely when and where the New Jerusalem would make its descent: not in the former Jewish capital but in a tiny Turkish town called Pepuza. Thousands of Christians gathered at the appointed place on the appointed date. Nothing happened. The date was hastily rearranged and the Montanist movement continued to grow in strength, spreading across Asia Minor, Africa, Rome and Gaul. Only when Augustine persuaded the Council of Ephesus in 431 that Revelation was to be read allegorically - the promised kingdom was none other than the Roman church - did Montanism become a heresy, and even so it survived for another four hundred years, its influence detectable in the early writings of a new apocalyptic religion, Islam, in the sixth and seventh centuries. In the 12th century Joachim of Fiore interpreted the victory of Saladin over Christians in the east as the tribulation preceding Christ's victory over the seven-headed dragon. The Black Death, which killed a third of Europe's population in 1348-9, was read back into Revelation, as were the horrors of the "hundred years war" (1337-1453) and the English civil war (1642-51).

As the great historian of "the ancient roots of apocalyptic faith" Norman Cohn has put it, history bears witness to "the urge to purify the world through the annihilation of some category of human beings imagined as agents of corruption and incarnations of evil". There have always been times when "this underworld emerges from the depths and suddenly fascinates, captures and dominates multitudes of usually sane and responsible people who thereupon take leave of sanity and responsibility. And it occasionally happens that this underworld becomes a political power and changes the course of history". To understand Jesus as a prophet of God's own apocalypse is to place him at the center of this recurring nightmare. Recurring, because this is not just ancient history. Christian, Jewish and Islamic apocalypticism is alive and well in the 21st century.

When the trumpet of the Lord shall sound and time shall be no more,
When the morning breaks, eternal, bright and fair,
When the saints of God are gathered over on the other shore,
When the roll is called up yonder - I'll be there!

Apocalyptic liberation is proclaimed by a host of competing Christian fundamentalist sects - Plymouth Brethren, Jehovah's Witnesses, Latter-Day Saints, Seventh Day Adventists - and in the heartlands of American evangelicalism, reaching into the White House and George W Bush's born-again administration, where the decisive victory of the Zionist state of Israel is interpreted as a necessary preliminary to, and sign of, the impending Rapture. The term "Zionist" is itself indicative of Jewish apocalypticism: Zion is the new Jerusalem. And radical Islam too sees in the decadence of the West and the occupation of Palestine by Israel signs of an approaching Armageddon when Allah will lead the faithful to a new Islamic heaven on earth, cleansed and scoured of infidel Christians and Jews. Such is the strength of human need for assurance of a happy ending, an ultimate justice, and the sweet satisfaction of seeing the wicked come to a sticky end at pay-back time.

Common to all forms of religious apocalypticism over three thousand years is the foundational conviction that the promised good times will come, not by human endeavor, but by act of God. Furthermore, this magic intervention will be intensely violent, cruel, bloody, full of cosmic horrors: devouring beasts, ravenous demons, plagues of monsters, lakes of fire. (Even if these are understood as metaphors and allegories, what can they signify other than inexpressible terrors, amounting to cosmic intimidation?). No short sharp shock for the wicked, no remedial justice, but eternal torment. God had form in this: according to the scriptures he had wiped out all but Noah and his family by water. Next time he would consume all but a remnant of his own human creation by fire. His sacrificial Lamb, the Word of God, would mow down his enemies with a sharpened sickle and tread them underfoot. That is God's plan. That is how he wins his victory and delivers to the faithful few a promised peace that passes all understanding. His celestial city is hauntingly beautiful - until we see that it floats in a sea of blood. This is what God *is*, what God *does*. Who are we, his humble creation, to question his ways? When a human ruler resorts to apocalyptic tyranny - Hitler's holocaust, Stalin's mass elimination of "enemies of the people", Pol Pot's massacre of an entire class (all in the interest of creating a secular paradise) - we cannot find adequate words to express the depth of our condemnation. But when God unleashes his cosmic weaponry on men, women and children whose misfortune is that they are not among the chosen whose names are written in the Lamb's Book of Life, he requires us to glorify and magnify his holy name, pronouncing him just, merciful, compassionate. *What kind of God is this?*

And that leads to a crunch question for those in search of the historical Jesus. What does it mean to see Jesus within this apocalyptic tradition? *What kind of Jesus is this*?

"The Biggest Evil around"

If the Jesus of history endorsed a violent God, albeit in the cause of some kind of ultimate justice and salvation, what would it mean to follow him? As Crossan puts it, "If... God's final solution to the problem of evil is the slaughter of the evildoers, why can we not do the same here and now in preparation, participation, or even initiation of apocalyptic consummation? Do we not have the right or even the obligation to be the killer children of a Killer God?"[7]

Here, says Crossan, is where the contemporary question presses most heavily. "I take it for granted that we have just finished the most violent century in the history of the world... Against that background, apocalyptic consummation by final extermination of evildoers puts transcendence squarely within the ambience of evil. It is simply the Biggest Evil around. And, as such, it justifies all the lesser evils done in its name"[8]. What kind of sense can it make, then, to interpret Jesus as the annointed messenger of transcendent evil, "the Biggest Evil around"? But that is the Jesus we seem to be stuck with if we conclude that the apocalyptic sayings attributed to him by the evangelists came from his own lips and expressed his own convictions. Either that or a deluded Jesus prone to violent fantasies expressed as the word of his violent God.

In his summary contribution to Robert Miller's *The Apocalyptic Jesus* Stephen Patterson concludes that the quest for the historical Jesus leaves us facing two Jesuses.

There is the Jesus of Mark 13:14-27, who quotes Daniel's warning of the "abomination of desolation" near at hand, when there will be "affliction such as was not from the beginning of the creation", a "tribulation" following which "the sun shall be darkened, and the moon shall not give her light. And the stars of heaven shall fall, and the powers that are in heaven shall be shaken. And then shall they see the Son of Man coming in the clouds with great power and glory. And then shall he send his angels, and shall gather together his elect from the four winds, from the uttermost parts of the earth to the uttermost part of heaven".

And there is the Jesus of Luke 17: 20-21 who tells the Pharisees, who are demanding to know just when this kingdom of his is going to arrive, that it will not come with signs to be observed, so that people can say "Lo here! or Lo there!". It just isn't that kind of kingdom. The kingdom of God is right here under your noses, *among* you. By the grace of God, however you understand the term, you may enter it, live it, and *make* it.

"Between these two texts," writes Patterson, "a choice must be made. They are not compatible, even though Luke the evangelist does his best to braid them into a single strand (see 17:22ff). Luke was not confused. He was just eager to write Christian history into a single, unified story - a well-known tendency of this writer. But if Jesus had said both of these things, we would have to assume that he was confused, and that his preaching was not coherent. Is the kingdom already present or does it lie beyond a future, cataclysmic horizon? Are there to be signs of its coming or not? When one thinks about these two different approaches to the presence of God in human life, one soon discovers that beneath these surface contradictions there lie two very different ways of being religious, perhaps even two different religions."

In one, God is revealed through esoteric interpretation of scripture and encoded revelation, a God whose arrival is marked by violent upheaval and destruction, a God whose commandments are observed in fear and trembling, a God who achieves justice through terror, a God whose Christian soldiers are forever marching as to war. "Forward into battle see his banner go!"

In the other, God is "revealed through contemplation of the human situation". He is "present in insight and wisdom, and is made known through acts of wisdom, justice and mercy". (William Blake would say he *is* wisdom, justice and mercy).Where apocalyptic ethics require obedience, wisdom ethics require discernment, a human "seeking after the good, the right thing to do in the midst of life's complexities". Wisdom and justice must be learned by experience, not experienced by force.

So, Patterson continues, "The apocalyptic Jesus and the sapiential [wisdom] Jesus are two quite different figures, and they inspire different religions. This is what is at stake for modern Christianity. If Jesus and his preaching still matter to Christian faith today, then the debate we are having is really about what sort of religion Christianity is. What is its claim about God? Is the Christian God the fearsome God of apocalyptic, who brings about justice through violent intervention? Or is the Christian God the one who beckons in the voice of Wisdom, standing on the street corner calling the world passing by to a new commitment to love and justice? Or, as Dom Crossan has so succinctly put it: should we be waiting for God to act, or is God waiting for us to act?"[9]

History is more than the accumulation of factual evidence. It is also about interpretation of that evidence. To interpret the historical Jesus as one whose wisdom teaching *contradicted* rather than *reinforced* the conventional apocalypticism of his time does not mean that he must be divorced from Jewish tradition. There is the pre-apocalyptic tradition of the prophets who preceded the writers of Daniel, Enoch and the scribes of Qumran, the tradition voiced by first-Isaiah. There is no blood and no dragon in Isaiah's utopian vision of a kingdom in which the poor get justice and the meek equality. If the wicked are to be smitten, it is with words, not seven-headed ten-horned monsters. In this imagined paradise, "The wolf also shall dwell with the lamb, and the leopard shall lie down with the kid; and the calf and the young lion and the fatling together; and a little child shall lead them... And the lion shall eat straw like the ox. And the sucking child shall play on the hole of the asp, and the weaned child shall put his hand on the cockatrice' den. They shall not hurt or destroy in all my holy mountain" (Isaiah 11:1-9). This is no less metaphorical than Daniel and Revelation, but Isaiah's images are metaphors for peace, justice, reconciliation, concord, where those that have their roots in Persian apocalyptics are metaphors for violence, terror, misery and suffering without end.

Today's post-religious consciousness may complain that Isaiah's peaceable kingdom, no less than violent apocalypse, is accomplished by miraculous act of God. But how else would an early Iron Age prophet writing for an Iron Age people express his vision? How else convey the mystery and magic of imagined perfection? It is not difficult to situate the historical (later Iron Age) Jesus in this tradition. He inherits apocalyptic, only to subvert it. The kingdom will come, on earth as in heaven, not by violent cataclysm but by stealth. Live justly, wisely, compassionately, equitably and the kingdom is among you. It has a present, and its present could flower into a future.

"The utopia that sets history in motion"

As the apocalyptic tradition both preceded and succeeded Jesus, so too has the dream of utopia. The Bible itself begins with a tale of Paradise (a word apparently coined by Xenophon in the fifth century to describe the perfection of a Persian garden). If this Paradise was lost, the utopian tradition affirms that it can yet be regained. If only in our dreams, there is a land flowing with milk and honey, a world where swords are beaten into ploughshares and spears into pruning hooks. The liberation theologian Gustavo Gutierrez, in *The God of Life*, sees Jesus as envisaging "the utopia that sets history in motion"[10], and once in motion it branches out in many directions, religious and secular: Thomas More's *Utopia*, Gerrard Winstanley's Christian-communist republic of heaven, William Blake's new Jerusalem, William Morris's *News from Nowhere* and *The Earthly Paradise*, Martin Luther King's dream of an America where all may enjoy the inalienable rights of "life, liberty and the pursuit of happiness".

These are dreams - but they need not be pipe-dreams. They jolt the imagination, alert us to new possibilities, show us alternative ways of living, of being human. They are *enabling dreams*, at the opposite pole to the *disabling nightmares* of bloody apocalypse. They do not rely on a naive assumption that "all will be well and all manner of things will be well", that ultimate justice is guaranteed, that perfection is attainable; indeed, all our human experience tells us otherwise. But they energize that in the human spirit which inspires us to reach for the impossible, promising that paradise lies in the attempted journey rather than a guarantee of safe arrival. As Fiona MacCarthy writes of Morris's *Earthly Paradise*, "Love usually fails. Heartfelt hopes are shattered. The consolation rests in the intelligent attempt".

To search for the Jesus of history is to search for the Jesus who lived in a late Iron Age village in a remote corner of the Roman empire. The framework within which he taught was the framework of his own time and place. That he could and did stretch that framework is evidenced by his unique and lasting influence, but no historical human being can step outside his specific historical circumstance. We are creatures of our time and place, our culture, our little stories and grand narratives. The historical Jesus was a first-century Jew in a Hellenized Roman empire, immersed in a monotheistic Judaism which had absorbed Persian, Babylonian, Greek and Roman influences but triumphantly retained its own distinctiveness. The kingdom he preached and promised was a kingdom conceived within that particular, distinctive religious and social culture, expressed (and subtly modified) in the language of that culture. His glimpse of an alternative reality, his envisioned paradise regained, was a *kingdom*; the *king* was *God*. There was no other language available to a Galilean peasant-artisan unaquainted with Philo and Plato, let alone Hume's reason and Blake's imagination.

Two thousand years later we live in a different world. His Iron Age has given way to successive ages, and our specific historical situation is that of the Space Age. Our secular age, scientific age, age of reason and age of reaction against reason, is not tied to localized first-century concepts of transcendence and supernaturalism. Concepts of *kingdom* and *God* have become optional extras; even if we choose to retain that language we invest it with new meaning appropriate to our times. If *God* is not dead, he, she or it is de-anthropomorphized, de-personalized, re-envisioned as the imagined embodiment of those human values we have chosen to treat as having an "ultimate" claim upon us. And *kingdom* too is an archaism in the modern world, where crowned heads have either rolled or been downgraded to mere figure-heads. In a democracy, we the people are sovereign.

So for the kingdom of God read the republic of heaven. This is not the language of Jesus, because his language is not ours. But the *enabling dream* transcends the language in which it was first expressed in those uniquely expressive parables and aphorisms, mangled as they were by zealous evangelists and their editors, spirit-filled prophets and power-conscious priests bent on creating new hierarchies. After two thousand years of white noise, those who have ears to hear may still pick up the authentic voice of a man of his own age who somehow contrives to speak to ours. And what is the alternative to seeking the republic of heaven on earth? We should know, because the world seems hell-bent on a new apocalyptic. Accelerating human-made climate change threatens to engulf us within a century; a continuing nuclear arms race looks like giving us the opportunity to end the world as it began, with another Big Bang; and apocalyptic Christianity squares up to apocalyptic Islam. John's most terrible Jesus, his eyes aflame, his sword proceeding from his mouth, rides in on a white charger and scatters his enemies on the hill of Meggido. That was John's dream. But the historical Jesus had a different experience: "My God, my God! Why hast thou forsaken me?" Perhaps in his death he experienced the truth of his life: that in the dreamed-of coming kingdom, the kingdom already in the making, it was the poor, the oppressed and persecuted, the merciful, the peacemakers, *the God-forsaken*, who would lay the foundations of his visionary kingdom, our republic of heaven, "where the voice of weeping shall be no more heard, nor the voice of crying".

Notes to Chapter 13

1 *A History of Zoroastrianism: The Early Period,* Vol 1 p 242, by Mary Boyce, as cited (p 24) by Simon Pearson in *The End of the World: From Revelation to Eco-Disaster.* For much of what follows in my summary of the apocalyptic tradition I am indebted to Simon Pearson's work, which itself follows Norman Cohn's pioneering books *The Pursuit of the Millennium* (1957, expanded ed. 1961) and *Cosmos, Chaos and the World to Come* (1993, rev. 2001).

2 The prophet Isaiah lived two centuries before Cyrus, but chapters 40-56 of the book that bears his name were compiled later by an unknown author or editor

and are referred to by scholars as "Deutero-Isaiah".

3 Pearson, *End* 42-3

4 Gerd Theissen writes in *The New Testament* 164: "In the Gospel of John and in the Apocalypse of John we... find ourselves in different worlds. If they were written by the same author, he would have to have experienced a complete break in his thought and language. So even in the early church there were doubts about his identity."

5 Pearson, *End* 69-70

6 as above, 74-5

7 Crossan in *Apocalyptic J* 158-9

8 as above, 159

9 Patterson in *Apocalyptic J* 161-3

SELECTED BIBLIOGRAPHY

Allison, Dale: *Jesus of Nazareth: Millenarian Prophet*, Fortress, Minneapolis, 1998

Altizer, Thomas J J: *The Contemporary Jesus*, SCM Press, 1997

Borg, Marcus: *Meeting Jesus Again for the First Time*, HarperSanFrancisco, 1994

- - (with N T Wright): *The Meaning of Jesus*, SPCK, 1999
- - *Jesus: Uncovering the Life, Teachings and Relevance of a Religious Revolutionary,* HarperSanFrancisco, 2006

Bornkamm, Gunther: *Jesus of Nazareth*, Harper & Row, New York, 1960

Bowker, John: *The Oxford Dictionary of World Religions*, OUP, 1997

Boyce, Mary: *A History of Zoroastrianism: The Early Period,* Vol 1, E J Brill, Leiden, 1975

Cameron, Ron: *Sayings Traditions in the Apocryphon of James*, Harvard Theological Studies 34, 1984

Campbell, Joseph: *Myths to Live By*, Viking / Penguin, 1972

Chilton, Bruce, and **Neusner**, Jacob: *Judaism in the New Testament*, Routledge, London and New York, 1995

Corley, Kathleen E: *Women and the Historical Jesus: Feminist Myths of Christian Origins*, Polebridge, Santa Rosa 2002

Crossan, John Dominic: *Jesus: A Revolutionary Biography*, HarperSanFrancisco, 1994

- - *The Birth of Christianity*, HarperSanFrancisco, 1998
- - *The Historical Jesus: The Life of a Mediterranean Jewish Peasant*, HarperSanFrancisco, 1991

Dungan, David L: *Constantine's Bible*, SCM Press, London

Dunn, James D G: *Jesus Remembered*, Vol 1 of *Christianity in the Making*, Eerdmans, Grand Rapids, 2003

- - *A New Perspective on Jesus: What the Quest for the Historical Jesus Missed*, Baker, Grand Rapids, USA, and SPCK, London, UK, 2005

Ehrman, Bart D: *Lost Christianities*, OUP, Oxford, 2003

- - *Lost Scriptures*, OUP, Oxford, 2003

- - *Misquoting Jesus*, HarperSanFrancisco, 2005

Eisenman, Robert: *James the Brother of Jesus*, Faber, London / Viking Penguin, New York, 1997

Ellegard, Alvar: *Jesus One Hundred Years Before Christ: a Study in Creative Mythology*, Century, London, 1999

Funk, Robert W: *Jesus as Precurser*, Fortress, Philadelphia, 1975. New edition Polebridge, Sonoma, 1994

- - (and others): *The Five Gospels: The Search for the Authentic Words of Jesus,* Polebridge/Scribner, 1993

- - (and others): *The Acts of Jesus: What Did Jesus Really Do?*, Polebridge/HarperSanFrancisco, 1998

- - *Honest to Jesus*, Polebridge/HarperSanFrancisco, 1996

Hill, Christopher: *The World Turned Upside Down*, Temple Smith, London, 1972

Hoover, Roy W (ed.): *Profiles of Jesus*, Polebridge, Santa Rosa, 2002

King, Karen L: *The Gospel of Mary of Magdala*, Polebridge, Sonoma, 2003

Kloppenborg Verbin, John S: *The Formation of Q: Trajectories in Ancient Wisdom Collections*, Fortress, Philadelphia,1987

- - *Q Parallels: Synopsis, Critical Notes and Concordance*, Polebridge, Sonoma, 1998

- - (with Marvin Meyer, Stephen J Patterson, Michael G Steinhauser, Preface by Robert W Funk, Foreword by James M Robinson): *Q/Thomas Reader*, Polebridge, Sonoma, 1990

- - *Excavating Q*, Fortress, 2000

Koester, Helmut: *Ancient Christian Gospels*, Trinity Press International, Harrisburg, Pennsylvania / SCM Press, London, 1990

- - *Introduction to the New Testament* Vol 1, *History, Culture and Religion of the Hellenistic Age*, Fortress, Philadelphia, 1980

Lüdemann, Gerd: *The Great Deception*, Prometheus, NY, 1999

- - (trans. John Bowden): *Jesus After Two Thousand Years: What he Really Said and Did*, SCM Press, London, 2000

Maccoby, Hyam: *Jesus the Pharisee*, SCM Press, London, 2003

Mack, Burton L: *The Myth of Innocence: Mark and Christian Origins*, Fortress, Philadelphia, 1988

- - *The Lost Gospel: The Book of Q and Christian Origins*, HarperCollins USA, Element (UK), 1993

- - *Who Wrote the New Testament?: The Making of the Christian Myth*, HarperSanFrancisco, 1995

- - *The Christian Myth: Origins, Logic, and Legacy*, Continuum, 2003

Marsh, Clive, and **Moyise**, Steve: *Jesus and the Gospels* (2nd ed.), Clark, London and New York, 2006

Meier, John: *A Marginal Jew: Rethinking the Historical Jesus*, Vols. 1-3, Doubleday, New York, 1991, 1994

Metzger, Bruce M: *The Canon of the New Testament: Its Origin, Development and Significance*, Clarendon Press, Oxford, 1987

Milavec, Aaron: *The Didache: Faith, Hope, and Life of the Earliest Christian Communities 50-70 CE*, Paulist, New York

- - *The Didache: Text, Translation, Analysis, and Commentary*, Glazier (Liturgical Press), Minnesota, 2003

Miller, Robert J [ed]: *The Complete Gospels*, Polebridge / HarperSanFrancisco, 1994

- - (ed.): *The Apocalyptic Jesus: a Debate*, Polebridge, Santa Rosa, 2001

- - *Born Divine: The Births of Jesus and Other Sons of God*, Polebridge, Santa Rosa, 2003

Pagels, Elaine: *The Gnostic Gospels*, Vintage, New York, 1989

Pearson, Simon: *The End of the World: From Revelation to Eco-Disaster*, Robinson, London, 2006

Perrin, Norman: *The Kingdom of God in the Teaching of Jesus*, Fortress, Philadelphia,1963

- - *Rediscovering the Teaching of Jesus*, Harper & Row, New York, 1967

- - *Jesus and the Language of the Kingdom*, Fortress, 1976

Powell, Mark Allan: *The Jesus Debate*, Lion, Oxford, 1998

Ratzinger, Joseph (Pope Benedict XVI): *Jesus of Nazareth*, Bloomsbury, London and New York, 2007

Sanders, E P: *Jesus and Judaism*, Fortress, Philadelphia, 1985

- - *The Historical Figure of Jesus*, Penguin, London, 1993

Schweitzer, Albert: *The Quest of the Historical Jesus: A Critical Study of the Progress from Reimarus to Wrede*, Macmillan, 1968 (original ed. 1906)

Scott, Bernard Brandon: *Hear Then the Parables*, Fortress, Minneapolis, 1989

- - *Re-imagine the World: an Introduction to the Parables of Jesus*, Polebridge, Santa Rosa, 2001

Shanks, Hershel (ed.): *The Search for Jesus*, Washington DC, Biblical Archaeology Society, Washington DC, 1994

Theissen, Gerd, and **Merz**, Annette, translated by John Bowden: *The Historical Jesus*, SCM Press, London, 1998

Theissen, Gerd, trans. John Bowden: *The New Testament*, T&T Clark, London, 2003

Tuckett, Christopher: *Q and the History of Early Christianity*, Clark, Edinburgh, 1996

Vermes, Geza: *Jesus the Jew: A Historian's Reading of the Gospels*, Collins, London / Fortress, Minneapolis, 1973

- - *The Changing Face of Jesus*, Penguin, 2001

- - *Jesus in his Jewish Context*, SCM Press, London, 2003

- - *The Authentic Gospel of Jesus*, Allen Lane (Penguin), 2003

- - *The Complete Dead Sea Scrolls in English*, Penguin, revised ed. 2004

- - *Who's Who in the Age of Jesus*, Penguin, 2005

- - *The Nativity: History and Legend*, Penguin, 2006

Walter, Nicolas: *Blasphemy Ancient and Modern*, Rational Press Association, London, 1990

Wells, G A: *Did Jesus Exist?*, Pemberton, London, 1975 (revised ed. 1978)

-- *The Historical Evidence for Jesus*, Prometheus, New York, 1988

-- *The Jesus Legend*, Open Court, Chicago, 1996

-- *The Jesus Myth*, Open Court, Chicago, 1999

White, L Michael: *From Jesus to Christianity*, HarperSanFrancisco, 2004

Wink, Walter: *Naming the Powers: The Language of Power in the New Testament*, Fortress, Philadelphia, 1984

-- *Unmasking the Powers: The Invisible Forces that Determine Human Existence*, Fortress, 1986

-- *Engaging the Powers: Discernment and Resistance in a World of Dominion*, Fortress, 1992

-- *The Powers That Be: Theology for a New Millennium*, Doubleday, 1998

Wrede, William: *The Messianic Secret*, James Clarke, 1971 (original ed. 1901)

Wright, N T: *Who Was Jesus?*, Eerdmans, Grand Rapids, 1992

-- *Christian Origins and the Question of God. Vol 1: The New Testament and the People of God*, SPCK, London / Fortress, Minneapolis, 1992

-- do. Vol 2, *Jesus and the Victory of God*, SPCK, 1996

-- (with Marcus Borg): *The Meaning of Jesus*, SPCK, 1999

INDEX OF NAMES

Principal entries in bold

ALSO BY DAVID BOULTON...

'Affectionate, sane, learned'... 'A great gift of being funny and serious at once'... 'Entertainment, scholarship and provocation'...

The Trouble with God: Building the Republic of Heaven
O Books, £11.99 (US$24.95), ISBN 1-905047-06-1
A thoroughly modern, intellectually defensible faith, unashamedly religious in commitment, and frankly secular in its concentration on this world and this age.
'A wonderful repository of religious understanding and a liberal theologian's delight'.

Gerrard Winstanley and the Republic of Heaven
DHM, £9, ISBN 0-9511578-4-1
The life and works of the 'True Leveller' leader in the revolutionary 1640s, when the church lost its power, the king lost his head, and God was re-envisioned as 'the creator, Reason'.
'David Boulton demonstrates that Winstanley's enabling dream is not fixed and confined to a romantic past but remains relevant today' - **Michael Foot**

Real Like the Daisies, or Real Like I Love You?: Essays in Radical Quakerism
DHM/ Quaker Universalist Group, £7.50, ISBN 0 9511578-5-X
Is God 'real' like daisies and diamonds, or 'real' like love and beauty? 15 essays exploring radical Quaker and religious humanist ideas.
'Not for the theologically faint-hearted' - **'The Friend'**

In Fox's Footsteps

by David and Anthea Boulton

DHM, £11.50, ISBN 0-9511578-2-5

George Fox's journey from Pendle Hill to Swarthmoor in 1652 gave Quakerism 'lift-off'. The Boultons retrace his steps - but they also map the journey from the religious world of the 1650s to 21st century postmodernity.

'It is precisely this mixture which makes the book so engrossing... packed with erudition, but all carried effortlessly by the narrative... Extremely lucid and satisfying as it tracks from Fox to the present' -
Anne Ashworth, 'Universalist'

Godless for God's Sake: Nontheism in Contemporary Quakerism

by 27 Quaker Nontheists, edited by David Boulton

DHM, £9.50, ISBN 0-9511578-6-8

27 Friends from 13 Yearly Meetings in four countries explain how they combine committed Quaker membership with rejection of traditional belief in a transcendent, personal and supernatural God.

'Thoughtful, articulate, and challenging religious thought...The most exciting book of theology I've read in years' -
Chuck Fager, Editor, 'Quaker Theology Journal'

TO OBTAIN THESE BOOKS, PLEASE NOTE...

ONLY *THE TROUBLE WITH GOD* is published by O Books and distributed by Orca.
ALL OTHER TITLES ARE AVAILABLE FROM YOUR LOCAL BOOKSHOP (QUOTING ISBN NUMBERS) OR DIRECT FROM DHM, HOBSONS FARM, DENT, CUMBRIA LA10 5RF, UK -
telephone **01539 625321**. When ordering direct from DHM, add £1 per book for postage in UK, £2 overseas. Cheques payable to DHM in GB pounds.

BOOKS

O books
O is a symbol of the world, of oneness and unity. In
different cultures it also means the "eye", symbolizing
knowledge and insight, and in Old English it means "place
of love or home". O books explores the many paths of
understanding which different traditions have developed
down the ages, particularly those today that express
respect for the planet and all of life.

For more information on the full list of over 300 titles
please visit our website
www.O-books.net

Censored Messiah
The truth about Jesus Christ
Peter Cresswell

This revolutionary theory about the life of Jesus and the origins of Christianity describes his role in the Nazorean movement, linked to the Essenes and other contemporary groups opposed to Roman rule- one that reflected the tensions between active revolt and the expectation for divine deliverance. The gospels do provide narrative and an explanation for something that really happened, but were censored and edited by later followers after the destruction of Jerusalem to disguise Jesus' Jewish roots and protect sources.
190381667X 248pp **£9.99 $14.95**

The Gay Disciple
Jesus' friend tells it his own way
John Henson

John offers the reflective reader a perspective on incidents and characters which at the very least make one think and which often help sharpen ones perception of what was, or might have been, going on. He manages to combine the strengths of the Sunday papers columnist approach with the radical evangelical message delivery of one who invites you to think! **Meic Phillips** ONE co-ordinator
184694001X 128pp **£9.99 $19.95**

The Laughing Jesus
Religious lies and Gnostic wisdom
Timothy Freke and Peter Gandy

The Laughing Jesus is a manifesto for Gnostic mysticism. Freke and Gandy's exposition of Gnostic enlightenment is lucid and accessible; their critique of Literalist religion is damningly severe. **Robert M. Price**, Professor of scriptural studies, editor of *The Journal of Higher Criticism*
1905047819 272pp **£9.99**
UK and Commonwealth rights only

The Creative Christian
God and us; Partners in Creation
Adrian B. Smith

Enlivening and stimulating, the author presents a new approach to Jesus and the Kingdom he spoke of, in the context of the evolution of our Universe. He reveals its meaning for us of the 21st century.
Hans Schrenk, Lecturer in Holy Scripture and Biblical Languages, Middlesex University.
1905047754 144pp **£11.99 $24.95**

The Gospel of Falling
Mark Townsend

Humble, searching, faith-filled, and yet risky and creative at the same time. **Richard Rohr** OFM
This little book is tackling one of the biggest and deepest questions which, unexpectedly, brings us to the foundation of the Christian faith. Mark has discovered this through his own experience of falling down, or failure. **Bishop Stephen Verney**
1846940095 144pp **£9.99 $16.95**

I Still Haven't Found What I'm Looking For

Paul Walker

Traditional understandings of Christianity may not be credible but they can still speak to us in a different way. They point to something which we can still sense. Something we need in our lives. Something not just to make us decent, or responsible, but happy and fulfilled. Paul Walker, former *Times* Preacher of the Year, rejoices in the search.

1905047762 144pp **£9.99 $16.95**

An Introduction to Radical Theology
The death and resurrection of God

Trevor Greenfield

This is a clearly written and scholarly introduction to radical theology that, at the same time, provides a contextualised and much needed survey of the movement. At times and in turns Greenfield is passionate, ironical, polemical and acerbic. A significant and valuable addition to the literature. **Journal of Beliefs and Values**

1905047606 208pp **£12.99 $29.95**

Tomorrow's Christian
A new framework for Christian living

Adrian B. Smith

This is a vision of a radically new kind of Christianity. While many of the ideas here have been accepted by radical Christians and liberal theologians for some time, this presents them as an accessible, coherent package: a faith you can imagine living out with integrity in the real world. And even if you already see yourself as a "progressive Christian"

or whatever label you choose to adopt, you'll find ideas in both books that challenge and surprise you. Highly recommended. **Movement**
1903816971 176pp **£9.99 $15.95**

Tomorrow's Faith
A new framework of Christian belief
Adrian B. Smith

2nd printing
This is the most significant book for Christian thinking so far this millennium. If this does not become a standard textbook for theological and ministerial education, then shame on the institutions! **Revd Dr Meic Phillips**, Presbyterian
1905047177 128pp **£9.99 $19.95**

The Anglican Quilt
Resolving the Anglican crisis over homosexuality
Robert van de Weyer

2nd printing
It should be read by everybody who cares about the future of the Anglican Church…an alternative strategy to schism that could prevent the Anglican Church from committing suicide. **Nicholas Stacey**, clergyman and former deputy director of Oxfam
1903816890 240pp **£9.99 $14.95**

Gays and the Future of Anglicanism
Responses to the Windsor report
Andrew Linzey and Richard Kirker

These essays by an extraordinary gathering of Anglican theologians from around the world add up to a crushing analysis of the Windsor Report.

This important book should be read with care by those who are concerned for the future of Anglicanism, both third-world Anglican cultures and the Anglican provinces in the West. **Covenant**
190504738X 384pp 230/153mm **£17.99 $29.95**

The Windsor Report
A liberal response
David Taylor and Jonathan Clatworthy

You need to read this book to understand the battles going on within the Anglican Church, as well as other churches.

Jesus challenged the conservatives of his day; we must challenge those of today and recover the Church for Jesus. Read it and make up your own mind. **David Storey**, CANA
1905047290 128pp **£7.99 $11.95**

The Thinker's Guide to Evil
Peter Vardy and Julie Arliss

2nd printing
As a philosopher of religion Peter Vardy is unsurpassed. **Dialogue**
Peter Vardy is the best populariser of Philosophy of Religion in Britain today. **Theology**
A challenging and wide-ranging discussion, clearly and engagingly written and thoroughly illustrated, it is an excellent book for anyone concerned to think seriously about these important issues. **Dr Jeremy Hall**, University of Glasgow
1903816335 196pp full colour throughout **£9.99 $15.95**

The Thinker's Guide to God

Peter Vardy and Julie Arliss

2nd printing

What a magnum opus! From Pluto's feet to Dawkin's Selfish Gene, this provides a magisterial survey of Western thought about God. **Rev Henry Kirk**, Principal Examiner

An excellent modern introduction to the various theories. **Bishop William Kenney**

Vardy and Arliss have their finger on the pulse of today's world. **Dr Beverly Zimmerman**, Catholic Schools Office

190381622X 264pp full colour throughout **£9.99 $15.95**

The Thoughtful Guide to the Bible

Roy Robinson

A liberating experience. There is a great deal of factual information. The difficult questions are not avoided. Roy Robinson does not pretend that the Bible is always historically accurate or morally admirable. He has no time for a simplistic fundamentalism that trivialises the concept of inspiration. But from a critical position he offers a strong defence of the Bible as the church's main source of authority. **Reform**

1903816750 360pp **£14.99 $19.95**

The Thoughtful Guide to Christianity

Graham Hellier

A rough guide to the Christian faith for anyone within or without the Church, and a resource for teachers, preachers and discussion groups. Designed to give material for reflection, the guide is drawn from over

700 sources, including some of which are deeply critical of Christianity and the Christian Church. **Reform**
1903816343 360pp **£11.99 $17.95**

The Thoughtful Guide to Faith
Trevor Windross

2nd printing
This is a splendid book! Its author is ambitious for Christianity and his aim is the development of a voice coming from the Church that is truly radical and can be heard alongside those of traditionalists and funda- mentalists, without trying to un-Church people from those backgrounds. Hasten to your bookshop. **SoF**
1903816688 224pp **£9.99 $14.95**

The Thoughtful Guide to God
Making sense of the world's biggest idea
Howard Jones

The wide scope of this fusion of theology, philosophy and science makes this an important contribution to a study of the divine that is easily readable by the non-specialist. **Dr Verena Tschudin**, author of *Seeing the Invisible*
1905047703 400pp **£19.99 $39.95**

The Thoughtful Guide to Religion
Why it began, how it works, and where it's going
Ivor Morrish

This is a comprehensive and sympathetic approach to all religions of the world, including the lesser-known ones, sects, cults and ideologies. Broader than "comparative religion", it uses philosophy, psychology, anthropology and other disciplines to answer the key questions, and provides a holistic approach for anyone interested in religious or philosophical ideas.

190504769X 384pp £24.99 $24.95

The Bhagavad Gita

Alan Jacobs

Alan Jacobs has succeeded in revitalising the ancient text of the Bhagavad Gita into a form which reveals the full majesty of this magnificent Hindu scripture, as well as its practical message for today's seekers. His incisive philosophic commentary dusts off all the archaism of 1500 years and restores the text as a transforming instrument pointing the way to Self Realization. **Cygnus Review**

1903816513 320pp **£12.99 $19.95**

Everyday Buddha

A contemporary rendering of the Buddhist classic, the Dhammapada

Karma Yonten Senge (Lawrence Ellyard)

Foreword by His Holiness the 14th Dalai Lama

Excellent. Whether you already have a copy of the Dhammapada or not, I recommend you get this. I congratulate all involved in this project and have put the book on my recommended list. **Jeremy Ball** Nova Magazine

1905047304 144pp **£9.99 $19.95**